Justus A. Griffin

Ontario history

vol. 15-17

Justus A. Griffin

Ontario history
vol. 15-17

ISBN/EAN: 9783741135330

Manufactured in Europe, USA, Canada, Australia, Japa

Cover: Foto ©ninafisch / pixelio.de

Manufactured and distributed by brebook publishing software (www.brebook.com)

Justus A. Griffin

Ontario history

Ontario Historical Society

PAPERS AND RECORDS

VOL. XV.

TORONTO
PUBLISHED BY THE SOCIETY
1917

CONTENTS

I. Canadian History as a Subject of Research. CLARANCE M. WARNER - 5

II. The Ridgeway Semi-Centennial. JUSTUS A. GRIFFIN - - - 18

III. Robert (Fleming) Gourlay ; Reminiscenses of his last days in Canada. MRS. SIDNEY FARMER - - - - - - - - 28

IV. Military Register of Baptisms for the Station of Fort George, Upper Canada, 1821 to 1827 - - - - - - - - 35

V. The Last of the La Guayarians (Wellington County, Ont.) The late C. C. JAMES, C.M.G., LL.D. - - - - - - - 40

VI. President's Address, June 6th, 1917. PROF. JOHN SQUAIR - - - 44

I.

CANADIAN HISTORY AS A SUBJECT OF RESEARCH.

By Clarance M. Warner, President, Ont. Hist. Society (1914-1916).

The President's Address, June 7, 1916.

"And I, too, must frankly confess that I have great pleasure in pondering over and musing upon the scenes of bygone days, and in thinking over again the hardships and struggles of pioneer life.... The man of seventy, who has either lived in Canada or the United States all his lifetime, will have witnessed greater changes and more material improvement than has probably taken place in Europe for a thousand years anterior to his time." This quotation taken from the introduction in a book written by Joseph Gould, which gives a most entertaining story of his life and times, expresses a feeling which it has been my privilege to hear expressed by a great many men in Ontario, men who have lived the allotted three score years and ten and men who have been proud of the advancement which this fair land has made during their comparatively short lives. Perhaps this fact more than any other made me decide to attempt to write an address which may, in some small way, express the pleasure which a student of, and a worker in, Canadian History has for his reward. Perchance these remarks may fall upon fertile ground and be the means of interesting some of the younger men and women of the Province in the work, thereby wonderfully increasing their pleasures and at the same time adding materially to the collection and preservation of our records.

One of the most difficult things is to convince the general public that history, particularly the history of America, is anything but a dry subject. The greatest cause of this misapprehension is that very, very few of the people understand that they are really making history themselves and that the history of their period in this world is but a record of what they do. One of our modern writers has put much common-sense in this sentence: "History is not to be written as a Sunday School tale for children of larger growth." Perhaps Wordsworth in his "Convention of Cintra" has given us the most concise and easily understood definition of what should go to make a history of any country: "The history of all ages; tumults after tumults, wars, foreign and civil, with short or no breathing spaces, from generation to generation; wars—why and wherefore? yet with courage, with perseverence, with self-sacrifice, with enthusiasm.... The visible and familiar occurrence of daily life in every town and village; the patient curiosity and contagious acclamations of the multitude in the streets of the city and within the walls of the theatre; a procession, or a rural dance; a hunting, or a horse race; a flood, or a fire; rejoicing and ringing of bells for an unexpected gift of good fortune, or the coming of a foolish heir to his estate.''

Of course the methods adopted in writing history have much to do with the interest excited in the general public. We in Canada have been fortunate in having many writers who have recorded the facts as they found them or thought they found them, for there are unquestionable examples where myths have been manufactured to order, but these usually add to the interest of the tale and are not to be altogether condemned. Some of our more serious historians may frown upon this theory, but it is my opinion that the historical pioneer has done more to preserve our records than those who have written with a truer sense of literary proportion; for the pioneer has used imagination, and thereby considerably enriched our field—particularly on its controversial side.

II.

In the field of historical research here in Ontario, the investigator has opportunities which make it almost a study of our own times. The Travels of Champlain have been minutely recorded by that great explorer and the French traders left many records of their flights through the Province. The records of the Indian tribes who first inhabited the country are not so perfect, but a fair idea of these strange peoples may be obtained from many sources. The fact that these records are incomplete and that the investigator cannot secure a complete history only adds to the pleasure in pursuing the subject. Rev. John Maclean, in his entertaining volume, "Canadian Savage Folk," expresses this feeling in the preface in these words: "Hidden in the memories of the Red Men of Canada, there lie weird legends and strange stories of bygone years. Pictures and poems wrought by the fancy of the native historians and medicine men, bring home to us the primitive civilization which still lingers at our doors. The customs of our savage folk and the wealth of their language and literature are interesting to us, as belonging to a people who were the pioneers of our land, and they open a new world of myth, religion and native culture." Some writers appear to think that the books which have been published concerning the Red Race are of doubtful scientific value, but this does not make them of less interest to the historian, and in addition to the Indian material there is usually to be found in them stories which give us vivid pictures of the men and women who had to win the country for the white race. Many of these make us ashamed of the treatment the aborigines received, but this in itself is an important page in our history.

After we leave the Indian and French periods in Ontario History we come to the settlement of the Province by the English, and it is here that we who have worked in the Local and Provincial Societies have found the greatest pleasure. The fact that the present generation and the one immediately preceding it have been privileged to hear stories told by the first settlers has contributed materially to the keen interest which has developed in the study of the life and times of the pioneers of Ontario. These stories, supplemented by hundreds of volumes which were written in the early days by men and women who had first-hand knowledge have made us feel that we were indeed fortunate. Some of these books furnish amusing instances of prophecy, others show great imagination on the part of the authors, still others confuse us by their direct contradictions of facts which we have proven by original documents, though not a few show calm, clear judgment and undoubtedly record what actually happened.

The War of 1812 provided a great field for the partizan writer. Probably no single event in our history has been so profusely written about, and certainly a stranger reading the early accounts of that war written by English, Scotch, Americans and Canadians would never dream that the same events were being described. Two examples will suffice to illustrate. A certain John Lewis Thomson wrote a history of the war published in Philadelphia which does not admit that there were many British or Canadian successes of note, yet he says in his preface, "The author cannot conclude this preface without assuring his readers, that no efforts have been neglected to ascertain the principal facts connected with the events of the war. Persevering as he has been, however, he fears that some omissions have been made, or that some mis-statements may have crept into the work...." Another Thompson, this time David T., wrote a history of the same war, but he was giving the Canadian viewpoint. Of course we think that he told the truth, and nothing but the truth. However, an American might quite properly take exception to many of his statements. In his preface he says, "As regards talent in the execution of this work, the writer would beg leave to say, that to such he disclaims all pretensions. The humble sphere in which he has moved did not probably afford any of those bright and flowery avenues to the temple of literature to which many more fortunate individuals have had access; his primary aim, through the whole, has been the acquisition of truth to lay before his readers...." Thus we see that each of these men thought he was giving the world an impartial history. There are numerous similar examples, while the work done by many of the Americans leaves much to the imagination. True, they were not united in the conflict and, when reading a book like "The Adventures of Uncle Sam in Search After His Lost Honor," one appreciates the bitterness which the New Englander felt for Madison and his following. Perhaps no single volume displays such a strong American bias in recording the events of this war as "The Pride of Britannia Humbled; or, the Queen of the Ocean Unqueened, 'by the American Cock Boats'", which was written by one William Cobbett.

English travellers through Canada have handed down many interesting works telling of their adventures and what they saw of the country. The early geographers add something to our information, but it is surprising that more is not told by them. I have come to the conclusion that few of them thought Ontario worthy of attention. George Alexander Cook, in his rather pretentious work published in 1807, did say that "The great river St Lawrence is that only upon which the French (now subjects of Great Britain) have settled of any note; but if we look forward into futurity, it is not improbable that Canada, and those vast regions to the west, will be enabled of themselves to carry on a considerable trade upon the great lakes of fresh water which these countries environ." And the same gentleman, an Englishman, gave us a map which shows that the boundary dispute as settled by the Ashburton treaty was, after all, a victory for Canada.

Between the war of 1812 and the next event which claims special attention in our history—the struggle for Responsible Government in Ontario—there were many years of important development. Stories of the first settlements of the various Counties, the surveys of most of the country that is now occupied, the starting of the villages, towns and cities, building of roads and the stories of the backwoodsmen make most interesting reading, and in this field we are usually able to prove our statements by the actual documents of the period. There is much recorded about men like Col. Talbot, who were leaders in their respective districts, and in almost every locality we find one or more outstanding figures who seemed to be looked up to by the rest of the people. A great opportunity is open for some writer to give us a book on the Country Squire. There was one in almost every village in the Province.

After 1833, our history becomes controversial. Many of the events of these years, when clear, calm judgment was absent on the part of the people in control of the affairs of State and of those in Opposition, are today given us in books, pamphlets, newspapers and other documents, and some day the unbiased story will probably be told. The man who can find the happy medium and eliminate his personal feelings on the subject has yet to appear. But that is one special reason why our Societies should continue in their work. Some have said that all of the material is already preserved. That is a great mistake. In my own work I have quite recently discovered two important letters written by Marshall Spring Bidwell. In one he declines to return to Ontario to accept a nomination from his old constituents for the Ontario House—and in the other, written 1838, he says, "I have left Upper Canada forever, at the request of Sir Francis Head, to whom I have given a written pledge not to return. I was not implicated in the recent revolutionary movement; but was an object of suspicion on account of my political opinions and supposed influence." By such new discoveries we see that all the material is not safely deposited, and we should make efforts to have every existing record secured for future generations. Those were stormy days, but in the end matters seemed to adjust themselves as the people wished, and before very long the question of Confederation occupied the scene. We can usually trust the people in important matters. As one of our early newspaper men expressed it in an able address delivered in 1844, "The people send their Representative to Parliament, and, met on that stormy arena, all soon find their level; the man of talent, the orator, and the man of energy rise in the scale of public estimation, and having gained the confidence of his fellow Representatives, he is selected for the high honor of being Advisor of the Crown."

Much more might be said of the pleasures in store for the one who is doing research work in our history. It is a wonderful chapter, the rush of energy which has found a country, settled it, and built up a structure on an economic basis in a little over a hundred years. We should be proud of the privilege of helping to preserve this record. Some one has said that "History is past politics and Politics are present History." In work of this kind it is not always necessary to give the viewpoint of the trained historian to make the results valuable. The dabbler in history, the one who writes an historical monograph, may be the means of digging up material that would otherwise be lost.

III.

In the collection of Canadiana one finds another most delightful hobby associated with the study of his Country's history; and while this particular branch of the work may prove to be somewhat expensive at times, there is always the satisfaction of knowing that after you have finished with the books, they will be of invaluable aid to others. It is somewhat of a shock to the uninitiated to discover what a tremendous number of books there are in existence which relate to affairs in Canada. One starts out with a very small beginning, and before many years have passed he finds that more room is required in the house to store the books he has collected. What pleasure is experienced with each new "find" can safely be left to the imagination, and when some particularly rare volume is picked up at a bargain it provides a pleasure which has to be experienced to be appreciated. The whole subject grows on you so rapidly that you soon find yourself consulting Phileas Gagnon or some other reliable authority to discover how near you are to having a real library.

For the collector of pamphlets the field in Ontario is particularly rich. In this the local worker has a great advantage, for he can frequently secure a pamphlet printed in his home town which has been missed by others employed in a similar search. True, it is difficult to find anything that has escaped the eyes of our present Dominion Archivist or his predecessor, but there are many rare works which even those indefatigable workers have missed. And what a pleasure it is to read some of these strange essays. Those dealing with the troubles over the Family Compact and Responsible Government have for me the greatest interest. The statements of one side followed by equally strong opinions on the other must have caused much bitterness when they appeared, but they afford an insight into the conditions at that period as nothing else could. Some one has said that "the great historian of the future will have easy access to innumerable facts patiently gathered by tens of thousands of investigators." Surely he will have difficulty in separating the wheat from the chaff as found in our Ontario pamphlets.

At the present time the collection of magazine articles has added materially to the work. In these, one is apt to find a more even literary standard because an historical article which has been accepted by an editor must have some merit besides its story of an historical event. One of the ex-presidents of the American Historical Association has said that "the historical work which does possess literary quality may be a permanent contribution to the sum of man's wisdom, enjoyment and inspiration." Perhaps that is the reason for the ever increasing demand for material which has passed the Editor's censor, for historical Reviews which aim at and reach a very high plane in literary finish, and for a specially high standard in reviewers of works on history.

I should overlook an important detail in the matter of collecting were I to fail to mention the second-hand bookdealer. Could one imagine a more interesting character than this man who hates to part with his wares yet wants you to have them because he knows that they will help to complete your collection and that you appreciate their value. He usually saves a few particularly valuable items until such time as you should drop into his store. And his prices—well, be it to his credit that you can seldom beat him down. He knows that you like him, partly for his personality, sometimes for the treasures with which he is surrounded, but mostly because he is catering to your favorite hobby— the hobby which gives you your greatest pleasure. Even though you have never been in his shop or met him, the receipt and perusal of his periodical catalogues give a pleasant feeling of congeniality. The man to be successful in this business must combine other qualifications with shrewd business instinct. We shall agree that Toronto has been favored in her men who have and are upholding the traditions of "The Little Old Book-Shop."

IV.

Reading what others have written on a subject in which one is particularly interested is a great source of joy to the historical worker. When Thomas Conant wrote the closing sentence for his "Upper Canada Sketches," he saw fit to use these words: "May I also indulge the hope that they have given some pleasure and profit in the reading, and add that it is my earnest desire—may it also be yours—that our Country, which we all love, may be guarded and led by the great Omniscient in the future as it has been in the past." The idea that pleasure as well as profit may be obtained from reading our books on Ontario's history should be borne in mind.

Possibly Champlain did not look so far ahead when he gave the world his story, yet one cannot but feel that he realized how some day, when the great new country was settled by the white race, its people would appreciate his efforts. We know that Francis Parkman wrote with a fixed idea, and we also know that he wrote under great difficulties. His health and failing sight precluded steady application to his work for long at a time, and often he was unable to read or write for more than five minutes continuously. Notwithstanding these almost insurmountable barriers, his works were usually written from personal knowledge. One authority has said that Parkman's works are "devoid of proportion" and that he "left behind a succession of historical monographs," but he also adds that they are the "most individual, tasting most racily of the soil." A quotation from his autobiographical notes gives us an insight into his feeling for his subject. He says, in speaking of the Old French War, "that is, the war that ended in the conquest of Canada—for here, as it seemed to me, the forest drama was more stirring and the forest stage more thronged with appropriate actors than at any other passage in our history. My theme fascinated me, and I was haunted with wilderness images day and night." It is my opinion that no other single writer has done more to make our history an interesting study than Francis Parkman. Were his works placed in every school of this Province and made easy of access —particularly should they be read to the primary school children—I believe it would make hundreds of our boys and girls search for further information on these subjects. They would soon appreciate the romance in the history of their own country.

Contemporaneous with Parkman, and even before his day, there were a great many who wrote of our Province in an interesting but narrow way. "The historian is exposed to the danger of dealing with the complex and interacting social forces of a period or of a country, from some single point of view to which his special training or interest inclines him," says one writer, and we have many such examples to study. Properly to understand this author's meaning one should read a number of books which deal with special topics. "The Scot in British North America," by Rattray, "Irishmen in Canada," by Davin, "History of Methodism in Canada," by Playter and "History of the Presbyterian Church in Canada," by Gregg, are random suggestions. Still other books give amusement by many of their interesting observations. Mrs Susanna Moodie, who published a volume of poems in 1831, wrote her "Roughing it in the Bush" feeling none too kindly toward her adopted country. Still that work has very recently been republished in a new form and the Canadian reviewers, almost without exception have treated it favorably. Two of her comments will suffice to show the general character of the book: "They talked of log houses to be raised in a single day, by the generous exertions of friends and neighbors, but they never ventured upon a picture of the disgusting scenes of riot and low debauching exhibited during the raising, or upon a description of the dwelling when raised—dens of dirt and misery, which would, in many instances, be shamed by an English pig-sty." Again she says, "Excellent cider and ale are made in both provinces; and whiskey, generally of the most abominably deleterious kind, is distilled in great quantities in Upper Canada, often from rye, pumpkins, potatoes, turnips, and even rotten apples." Mrs. Jameson, in "Sketches of Canada," gives the following interesting description of our Capital when she spent some time there during the period of the Rebellion of 1837. "What Toronto may be in summer, I cannot tell; they say it is a pretty place. At present its appearance to me, a stranger, is most strangely mean and melancholy. A little ill-built town, on low land, at the bottom of a frozen bay, with one very ugly church, without tower or steeple; some government offices, built of staring red brick, in the most tasteless vulgar style imaginable; three feet of snow all around; and the grey sullen wintry lake, and the dark gloom of the pine forest bounding the prospect; such seems Toronto to me now. I did not expect much; but for this I was not prepared." Those who think that Mrs. Jameson should have been less brutally frank will feel more kindly toward her when they read of her visit to Colonel Talbot. Her description of the old Colonel, his home and his country should be read by every boy and girl in Canada.

These books by outside writers form a distinct and valuable division of our descriptive literature. Every tourist who could write anything has left us a description of the Falls of Niagara. A collection of these pictures of the great cataract in one volume would be interesting to read.

Many books have appeared which give us great delight. The first is far too long to attempt to mention any of them, but we should be very thankful that men like Canniff, Dent, Kingsford, Stone, Ryerson, LeMoine and a host of others devoted much time to writing. Then there are the men and women who are writing at the present day. "The Chronicles of Canada" will serve to show to what high standard we have been elevated and that "Company of One Hundred Associates" with a few others make a most formidable array. Is it too much to say that the Ontario Historical and its affiliated Societies have done much to encourage many of these men in the pursuit of their hobby? The first sentence in the introduction to the first volume of "Papers and Records" published by our Society, and printed in 1899, reads as follows: "The Ontario Historical Society presents to its members the first volume of what it is hoped will be a long list of valuable papers and records." Since that time much has been written and the series of books which we started in 1899 now numbers thirteen. Most of our writers are represented in these books by one or more articles.

V.

In criticism, favorable and unfavorable, there is much to delight the historical worker. When he feels competent to enter the field, whether or not he gives his opinions to the public, he has the keen satisfaction of knowing whether his views are entertained by others, for there have always been many who enjoy commenting upon the work of others. In the olden times the historian was subject to many attacks which, although possibly merited, would hardly be made at the present time. Horace Walpole said a century and a half ago, "So incompetent has the generality of historians been for the province they have undertaken, that it is almost a question, whether, if the dead of past ages could revive, they would be able to reconnoitre the events of their own times, as transmitted to us by ignorance and misrepresentation." Another more recent critic says that "Writers have been known to inject modern ethical theories into the judgment of men and things of bygone times."

Our present day critics have eliminated the bitterness which was frequently displayed in former times. Many of my hearers will remember a pamphlet written by Nicholas Flood Davin in 1882 with the object of showing that the Royal Society, so far as it was to act as an encouragement to literature, was a misplaced institution. Speaking of the appointment of Bourinot as Secretary of the Society, he says, "I can conceive no greater insult to the intelligence of Canada than for one knowing the literary imbecility of Mr Bourinot, to appoint him Honorary Secretary to a Society which is meant to lead the van of literary progress."

Even the men who have worked for years in this department have changed their views upon the manner in which historical writing should be treated. One who has been privileged to go carefully through the various issues of "The Review of Historical Publications Relating to Canada" will note a decided change in the attitude of the reviewers. In some of the more recent issues the tendency has been to treat weak efforts by new workers with great consideration. Thereby many have been encouraged and the popularization of history has been fostered. Dr. Wrong told us when reviewing Kingsford's "History of Canada" in 1896 that "Second-rate writers in all Countries are too blindly patriotic." The same criticism might properly be applied to many who are writing in Ontario to-day, but in some way we have come to accept it; and future generations will know that these men and women were close to the generation which they addressed and that, while the sense of literary proportion and form may be lacking, they have in reality been valuable historical writers.

Of course there are many books written about Canada that are interesting to read, but of little value to the student. These are not as injurious as are books which are filled with mis-statements of facts. No excuse exists for the palpable errors that have been made in some of the recent volumes. An author might be excused for saying that "Worship of wealth and envy of material success have almost no part in Canadian life," but the same writer cannot be excused when she says that " . . . the ultra-English Loyalists trekked in thosands across the boundary to what are now Montreal and Toronto and Cobourg." These remarks which appear in the beginning of a new book on Canada make one look with suspicion upon what follows.

Adverse criticism has undoubtedly done much to correct errors in our work, to make writers more keen on their facts, to stimulate research before publishing, to encourage the younger writers and to eliminate much that might otherwise have crept into our books, as a result of distorted imaginations.

VI.

Association with those who have the same line of work probably gives as much pleasure as any of the many ways in which one is rewarded. Albert Bushnell Hart tells us that "The basis of history is human nature, and the expression of human nature is through history, whether scientific or literary or judicial or imaginative; and therefore history must include the study of persons." While our distinguished authority probably did not mean that remark to be taken to apply to the study of a gathering of people assembled as are we, or to the study of the reasons for one's interest in those who are in kindred lines of work, yet it seems to me to be very apt at this stage of my subject. The benefit derived from the association of such people as the members of the Ontario Historical Society is easily perceived. They are gathered together because, while their viewpoints may be different, their aims are similar. The Women's Canadian Historical Society of Ottawa, in the preface to its first volume of "Transactions" published in 1901, used this paragraph to tell its aims: "This Society has for its object the encouragement of study of Canadian history and literature, the collection and preservation of Canadian historical records and relics, the cultivation of a national spirit, and the building up of a Canadian loyalty and patriotism." If any of those who have followed the fortunes of our Society through the years which it has existed should be asked what has given them the greatest pleasure in these meetings, they would say the meeting of old friends and the making of new ones. The very fact that few if any of the members who have once begun to attend the meetings ever absent themselves unnecessarily is proof sufficient of their power to hold as well as to attract. Associations thus formed often ripen into strong personal friendships—not only pleasant but profitable because of the interchange of ideas along the line of individual work.

How much these personal friendships have influenced our workers is impossible to estimate. Emerson says that, "You shall make me feel what periods you have lived." Certainly whatever effect has been produced has been for good. Frederick J. Turner, one of the past-presidents of the American Historical Association, has said, "Unquestionably each investigator and writer is influenced by the time in which he lives, and while this fact exposes the historian to a bias, at the same time it affords him new instruments and new insight for dealing with his subject." To know and associate with those who have been workers in this and other like Societies has for me been one of the greatest pleasures.

It is not necessary to have the same view-point to feel the spell of meeting and mingling with men and women who receive pleasure in working at history. The Literary and Historical Society of Quebec, the oldest Society of the kind in Canada, in its first volume, published in 1829, started with these sentiments: "When the members of this young Society reflect upon the successful efforts made by similar Institutions in the Old World in the pursuit of knowledge, they feel, in regard to their own humble exertions, that there are different gradations in the scale of merit. They have, however, this gratifying recollection, that all additions to the sources of literary and scientific information are valuable and meritorious."

VII.

What can exceed the gratification of writing history? To see one's productions increasing year by year surely gives the keenest pleasure. My knowledge of the author's feelings when doing this line of work has been gained from association with many men who have given us good historical work.

When a subject has been chosen, sometimes because the writer thinks he has discovered new material to give to the public, sometimes because he thinks what has already been written does not treat the question fairly and sometimes because it is an entirely new one, think of the pleasures that are in store for the author. He starts out, remembering that the public will demand the truth, and that told entertainingly, and searches every source he can discover for information. Documents, letters, newspapers and books are carefully scanned, and in this work he is frequently thrown in contact with many who delight to give aid. One writer tells us that "In the field of historical research an immense amount can be done by men who have no literary power whatever." Should the writer we are following be new in the work, he will probably have occasion to thank this authority for his kindness in giving the sentiment to the public. Another authority tells us that "the greater portion of the history of any country has little value being but a record of small accomplishments, and that as among nations in history as among men the commonplace is the rule—but that whether ordinary or exceptional—each has its place." This makes the local writer feel that his work may be of some value.

Possibly our writer has chosen to prepare a biography and has had long and happy acquaintance with his subject. He delights to give expression to his thoughts and opinions; and perhaps by a little well placed imagination kindles the interest of the reader in his subject. We have in Ontario examples of biographies in which the writer sympathized far too much and thereby spoiled his work; and we have examples in which the other extreme was followed. A striking example of the last mentioned class is the pamphlet on Dr Ryerson which was published in 1852. This sentence quoted from it will give a fair idea of its flavor: "Those who have read the various productions of his (Ryerson's) pen, will bear me out in the remark that they evince rather the tact of one who is adroit at intrigue and wily in dispute, than the sentiments of an ingenious mind." Fortunately most of our biographers have been fair in their treatment of our great men, with the result that we have to our credit in this field a remarkable collection of books for so young a country.

Macaulay said it was easy "to write history respectfully." Our Canadian writers have as a rule followed that method. When they have their material at hand they have usually revised it with care and had it published only when they thought it right. And whether produced by a man of letters with a due sense of literary proportion and form or by the historical pioneer who may have lacked a vigorous and elegant style it has generally been of value because it gave facts.

After the book is published and is in the hands of the public the writer has new situations to face, some pleasing, others less so. If he feels as Dr. Hart thinks, he may be disappointed in the reception of his work. That distinguished teacher says that "Every historical student likes to look on his own work as a road-book which not only describes the bridges and the turns and the hills but tells you where you can put up for the night and how far it is to Rome." However this may be, certain it is that for Ontario historical writers the congratulatory messages, both from reviewers and others, always outnumber the unfavorable comments, and the writer is thereby spurred to further effort. To those who should not have been so kindly treated, if such there are, this old Proverb may be of some slight consolation: "He that is first in his own cause seemeth just; but his neighbor cometh and searcheth him."

Even though our writer's treatment by his publisher may not be encouraging and his pleasure somewhat dampened by the lack of financial reward for his labors, his joy in the finished production is so great that the money consideration is forgotten.

VIII.

In conclusion, I would say that the various routes to pleasure that are open for the worker in our local historical field are broad and have infinite possibilities, whether through research, collecting, reading what others have written, criticism, association with those who have the same hobby or through writing. He should reflect diligently upon the words of our old friend Nicholas Flood Davin who says in his book on "Irishmen in Canada": "When the future historian of Canada sits down to write a story which, we may hope, will be illustrious with great achievements and happy discoveries, triumphs in literature and art, in his library, side by side with lore it has not entered into the heart of man as yet to conceive, will be found records such as the historian of Greece, or Rome, or Ireland, or Scotland, or England, looks for in vain." And he should read carefully the last paragraph from the Introduction in the first volume published by our Society: "A large portion of this Province is now beyond the mere bread and butter conditions; and, with an admirable school system, the time has come when our people may, with dignified leisure, recall the days of old, while it is a duty, as well as a privilege, of the younger generations to study by-gone events in the light of the present day, and to lay the foundations of the future aided by the experiences of the past."

CANADIAN HISTORY AS A SUBJECT OF RESEARCH. 17

This subject, of the pleasures we owe to the historical hobby, has been interesting to think of and study. Sometimes in looking for material the volumes consulted have been so fascinating that an evening has passed while the usable material has been but a single quotation. Many times I have felt like echoing the sentiments of our fellow member, Mr. H. F. Gardner, when he says in his preface to "Nothing But Names": "Should any reader of this book feel disposed to demand his money back, his outraged feelings may be mollified by the assurance that the book was not written with malice aforethought. Like Mrs. Stowe's Topsy, it never was born—it grew."

When we look into the future we understand what every new recruit for the work means. We must aim to make the beginner's lot entertaining, and in a very short time he or she will be as enthusiastic as those of us who already delight in the work. When John M'Gregor wrote his book on British America in 1833, he must have had visions of this country's greatness in the twentieth century, so it will not be inappropriate for me to close this paper of many quotations with one from his pen. At the present time it seems particularly fitting. "Men who can, with the minds of great statesmen, appreciate the present value of the British North American Colonies, will clearly anticipate, and justly estimate, not only their future grandeur, but their importance in maintaining the influence of England over the whole of the western world, and their consequence in preserving British power in Europe."

June, 1916.

II.

THE RIDGEWAY SEMI-CENTENNIAL.

By Justus A. Griffin.

At this time, during the progress of the greatest war this world has ever known, it appears at first glance inappropriate to speak or write of a small engagement like that which was fought near Ridgeway.

But things are not always what they seem. Trivial actions frequently lead to important events, or prevent great evils. History has many an account telling how a small number has performed deeds that have had a deciding influence upon the course of events.

In telling of the fiftieth anniversary of the battle of Ridgeway it appears fitting to say something of the antecedent circumstances which resulted in that fight.

One result of the collapse of the Confederate States of America in April, 1865, and the discharge from military service of many hundreds of thousands of veteran soldiers, was a great addition to the membership of the Fenian societies then existing in the United States. The adoption of a militant policy by these societies accelerated their growth. And when they organized companies and regiments throughout the country many veterans joined who cared nothing about Ireland. These, with a multitude of Irish and Irish-Americans, were rapidly armed with rifles which the government was offering for sale at a low price, and which the Fenians converted into breech-loaders.

The number of men enrolled in this organization and armed is not known, but it is certain that there was a very large number.

A personal experience may help to prove this statement: In February, 1866, while a private in the 1st Provisional battalion of volunteer militia, and quartered in barracks at Windsor, a forty-eight hour leave of absence was given me, with permission to visit friends in the United States; but with the proviso that civilian clothes must be worn. It was not safe to cross the border in a red coat. The friends to be visited resided in the town of Wyandotte, and while there a visit was paid to the great iron works which were the pride of the town. Introductions were given to some of the foremen and to expert workmen. Later, when out of the hearing of these men, came the information that these men were all members of a Fenian regiment of 600 men which was drilling two nights a week. My informant was a Canadian who had been resident there some time and become very friendly with all classes.

Our Government was not ignorant of this movement; but had information that a raid would be made when the rivers were frozen and a crossing could easily be made. In November, 1865, three battalions of volunteers were placed on the frontier. The 1st battalion was sent to guard the Detroit and St. Clair border, with headquarters at Windsor; the 2nd had its headquarters at Niagara-on-the-Lake, and the 3rd battalion was posted along the St. Lawrence River and on the Quebec border.

Early in March, 1866, alarming reports reached the authorities through the secret service, and on the 10th of March ten thousand more volunteers were called out and strong re-inforcements sent to the border. This show of force caused the Fenians to change their plans and no raid took place at that time. In April nearly all the volunteers were returned to civil life, and in May the Government evidently thought the danger over for they dismissed the few remaining guards.

The Fenians thought this was their opportunity and at the end of May they began to gather on the border. Many thousands met in Buffalo, Detroit and other cities. On June 1, 1866, about 1200 crossed at Fort Erie, cut the lines of communication and proceeded toward the Welland Canal. They may have intended to use the Buffalo and Lake Huron Railway as a means of transport, for among them were many skilled mechanics, including trained railway men. If that was their intention their plans were frustrated by the superintendent of the railroad. On the arrival of the enemy in Fort Erie he removed all his locomotives and all or nearly all the rolling stock to Port Colborne and rendered the bridges in the vicinity of Fort Erie useless for the time being.* This body of Fenians considered themselves as the advance guard of a large invading army and they knew that many thousands were already in Buffalo and more on the way.

In the meanwhile, however, the Government of Canada had not been idle. Early in the morning of June 1st the alarm was sounded by bugle and gun in every village, town or city where there was a volunteer corps. These men were fairly well trained citizen soldiers, armed with Enfield muzzle-loading rifles and comfortably clothed, but otherwise without equipment for a campaign. They had but a small supply of ammunition, no camp equipage, no reserve ammunition, no commissariat, no ambulances and no transport except railways. At that time there were a few Imperial troops garrisoned in Canada and these co-operated with the militia, though none of them were at Ridgeway.

On the evening of June 1st a force of about 800 men had been gathered at Port Colborne, being composed of the 2nd Queen's Own Rifles of Toronto, the 13th Infantry of Hamilton and two independent rifle companies from the villages of York and Caledonia. They spent the night crowded in railway cars, having scarcely any provisions and getting little or no sleep. At an early hour in the morning of June 2, Lieut.-Col.

*This information is derived from an article about the raid written by the then superintendent of the Buffalo and Lake Huron Railway, and published in the Hamilton Spectator several years after the raid.

Booker, the senior officer and acting brigadier of this small brigade, received orders to proceed by train to the village of Ridgeway and thence to march by the nearest route to Stevensville, where they were to join the 16th regulars and a battery of Royal Artillery. These troops were then at Chippawa, commanded by Colonel Peacock of the 16th, under whose orders the volunteer force was acting. Lieut.-Col. Booker and his men set out to obey this order, soon reached Ridgeway and proceeded by the Ridge Road toward the rendezvous. They had only marched about two miles when they came in view of the Fenians who had established themselves in a good position directly in the way which our men must take to reach Stevensville. The action which ensued resulted in the retreat of the Fenians; but the false report of cavalry, shortage of ammunition and apparently conflicting orders* prevented our force from obtaining the full success they had earned. When Lieut.-Col. Booker ordered the skirmishers to retire and form on the reserve, the Fenians, who had been forced back a considerable distance, rallied a little, but soon resumed their retreat to Fort Erie. Here another small force of volunteer militia, less than 100 men, met them with an active resistance. By this time another large body of Fenians had embarked at Black Rock and were about to cross to Canada, but were speedily disembarked and the transports used to convey back the crestfallen invaders, except those that had been killed, wounded or made prisoners.

So ended the Fenian Raid of 1866, and what promised to be and might have been a very serious invasion was promptly met and turned away by volunteer militia. Many students of the history of that time believe that had the Fenians been unmolested for a couple of days longer they would not only have seriously damaged the Welland Canal, but would have established themselves in such force as to have made it very difficult to eject them. Perhaps the confederation of the provinces would have been prevented.

Now fifty years have passed, the men who promptly rallied to arms in 1866 planned a great demonstration in commemoration of the Battle of Ridgeway, and their friends gave much assistance. The Militia Department also gave its aid by sending a battalion of the Overseas Expeditionary Force and detachments from the Queen's Own Rifles, the 10th Royal Grenadiers, and the 12th York Rangers of Toronto, the 13th Royal Regiment of Hamilton, the 19th Regiment of St. Catharines and the 44th Lincoln and Welland Regiment.

One feature of the celebration decided upon was the dedication of Memorial Park, on the ridge overlooking the battle-field, a beautiful site. This historic spot is the generous gift of five veterans who were engaged in the battle, viz.: Major-General Sir Wm. D. Otter, C. V. O., K. C. B., of Ottawa; Brig.-General Sir John M. Gibson, K. C. M. G., of Hamilton; Lieut.-Col. J. E. Farewell, R. O., of Whitby; Sergt. E. Wheeler, of Tor-

---

*These messages and other information regarding the raid were published in a pamphlet written and published in 1866 by Alexander Somerville, "The Whistler at the Plow."

onto, and Henry Swan, Esq., of Toronto. All were expected to be present to make formal presentation of the Park to the permanent Board of Trustees.

The Weather Bureau predicted showers for the day, yet the early morning of June the 2nd, 1916, opened bright and pleasant, and the veterans cheerfully gathered at their various headquarters, hoping that the predicted showers might be brief and light. But these hopes were doomed to be extinguished by floods of water.

Rain began to fall before noon, just when the various groups were about to prepare for their luncheon, and it soon increased to such a downpour that all, soldiers, veterans and civilians were glad to seek shelter under the nearest roof. Schoolhouses, churches and halls were thrown open and crowded, while verandahs of dwellings and hotels were all occupied. But even in these adverse conditions all managed to have their luncheon, and enjoyed meeting old comrades and discussing old times.

It had been arranged that the parade should be organized on the school grounds and streets adjacent thereto at 1:20 and move off at 1:30, proceeding through the village of Ridgeway by the Ridge Road to Garrison Road, and thence to the Flag Staff on Memorial Park site. Following is the previously arranged Order of Exercises at Memorial Park:

Arrival of His Honour, Colonel Sir John Strathearn Hendrie, K. C. M. G., C. V. O., Lieutenant-Governor of Ontario.

1.—The National Anthem .... Massed Bands
2.—Invocation. .By Rev. Nathaniel Burwash, S.T.D., (a veteran of 1866)
3.—Presentation of addresses to His Honour, the Lieutenant-Governor and His Honour's reply. Presentation of flowers to Lady Hendrie
4.—Presentation of Memorial Park to the Trustees, on behalf of the donors of the site, by Lieut.-Col. Farewell, R. O.
5.—Song—"O Canada" .... Church Choirs and School Children
6.—Dedication of Memorial Park ...... By His Lordship the Bishop of Niagara and clergy.
7.—Music .... Regimental Bands
8.—Raising the Flag—By Major-General Sir W. D. Otter, K.C.B., C.V.O.
9.—Song—"We'll Never Let the Old Flag Fall" ....
Bands, Choirs and School Children
10.—Formal Laying of Foundation for proposed Monument....
By His Honour the Lieutenant-Governor of Ontario.
11.—March Past and Review of the Surviving Veterans of 1866.
Band Music: "The Boys of the Old Brigade."
12.—Song—"The Maple Leaf Forever" ..... Choirs and School Children

13.—Address............By Brig.-General Sir John M. Gibson, K.C.M.G.
14.—Song—"The Red, White and Blue"....Choirs and School Children
15.—Short Addresses by Distinguished Visitors.
16.—Demonstration on the Battlefield: .
   Attack: By 176th Battalion, C. E. F. Lieut.-Col. Sharpe.
   Defence: Composite Battalion. Lieut.-Col. Robertson.
      Major-General Otter in Command.
17.—Inspection and Review of Troops by His Honour, the Lieutenant-Governor of Ontario.
18.—Song—"God be with you till we meet again".............
   Choirs and School Children.
      GOD SAVE THE KING.

A very comprehensive programme indeed, and one that would doubtless have been very interesting had it been carried out. But the exceedingly heavy showers, never ceasing entirely, though slackening a little occasionally, drenched those who ventured out without raincoats or umbrellas. The arrangements were therefore altered, as it was considered impossible to take the choirs and children in such weather to the Park for the open air programme. About 2:30 there was a lull in the storm, when the parade was organized and passed in review before His Honour the Lieutenant-Governor, who took his stand in front of the town school and there received the salute.

The formation of the parade was as follows:
Marshall, William G. Athol, with six assistant marshalls; standard bearers; band of the 123rd Battalion, C. E. F.; surviving veterans of 1866, brigaded under Lieut.-Colonel J. E. Farewell, R. O., in the following order: Veterans' Association of Toronto, Capt. John A. Macdonald, president; Hamilton Veterans' Association of 1866, 50 men, Lieut. James Hooper, president; Veterans' Association of London, E. T. Essery, president; Veterans' Association of St. Catharines and Niagara District, R. J. Black, president; Veterans of 1866 from other points; Queen's Own Rifles Bugle Band, in command of Bugle-Major Charles Swift (a veteran of 1866); Composite Battalion, commanded by Lieut.-Col. R. A. Robertson, consisting of 168 officers and men from the Queen's Own Rifles, 109 men from the 10th Royal Grenadiers, 110 men from the 12th York Rangers, of Toronto, and 174 officers and men from the 13th Royal regiment, from Hamilton; a company from the 19th and 44th Lincoln and Welland regiments; the 176th Battalion, C. E. F. (Niagara Rangers); officers and committee of the Ridgeway Battlefield Association; members of Parliament; clergy and invited guests; reeves and councillors of Bertie and adjoining municipalities.

The oldest man in the parade was John Marshall, of Lockport, who was in the Governor-General's Body Guard at the time of the raid and who is now 94 years of age.

The programme was continued in the Methodist church. Here occurred one of the many meetings after many years of men who had been together on the fateful day of fifty years ago. Col. John Stoneman, who was quarter-master's sergeant in 1866, met for the first time in fifty years Rev. Nathaniel Burwash, S. T. D., and recalled the day of the battle when he drove the carriage which conveyed the chaplains, Rev. Mr. Burwash, Methodist, and the late Rev. Dr. Inglis, Presbyterian, to the battlefield, where they were of great service in the care of the wounded.

Rev. Dr. Burwash pronounced the invocation. This was followed by the presentation of addresses to Lieut.-Governor Sir John Hendrie by Reeve Wilson, of Bertie, and Capt. John A. Macdonald, president of the Toronto Veterans' Association. The latter address was signed by the presidents of the other Veterans' Associations.

His Honour replied in suitable terms, thanking the tenderers of the addresses for their kind sentiments and the warm reception given to himself and Lady Hendrie, and then referred to the significance of the Battle of Ridgeway. He said: "The veterans and the country are to be heartily congratulated upon the fact that the movement to erect a monument has reached its present definite form and on having secured the park site. No men in the province could feel prouder than the donors, who by their liberality have been the means of preserving that part of the battlefield for all time. The enlightened intelligence of the people now unchallengeably upholds historic memorials of past deeds, and it is indeed well that this should be so. For people who do not reverence their past, who do not cherish and preserve their history and value their historical sources neglect a potent influence for good. While the community which has undertaken the work is not large, it has undertaken a task that bears on the history of the country as a whole. It is well that posterity should keep green and honour the memory of the men whose blood was shed in the defence of home and country. I am proud to know that the spirit which animated those whose memory we are honouring still animates Canadians of the present generation."

For the dedication of the park, the flag raising and the laying of the corner stone, participants in the ceremonies proceeded to the battlefield. They were preceded there by many of the veterans and others who, not being able to get into the crowded church, braved the mud and the rain and went to see the battlefield, some on foot and many in hired automobiles. Others followed later and the automobiles were kept busy.

On the historic spot Lieut.-Col. Farewell, R. O., formally presented the Memorial Park site, where the battle was fought, to the citizens of Ontario. The land was dedicated by the Bishop of Niagara, who said:

"Dearly beloved,

"We are gathered here in the sight of God to settle upon this plot, consisting of five acres of land, being a portion of the old Ridgeway battlefield, and to dedicate it as a memorial unto the people of this land forever of the victory won under God by our brave troops, on this property 50 years ago, and of the deliverance of our people from the hands of their enemies, and of the preservation of our country as a part of the British dominions.

"Acting under the warrant of the holy scriptures, after the example of God's people in all ages, and in agreement to the Divine commands, let us humbly ask God's blessing upon what we are about to do."

After a brief prayer he continued:

"In the faith of Jesus Christ we dedicate this plot of ground to the glory of God, and as a memorial unto the people of this land forever, of the victory won here 50 years ago by our brave troops in defense of homes and empire, in the name of Father, Son and Holy Ghost."

He then prayed as follows:

"Blessed be Thy Name, O Lord, that it has pleased Thee to put into our hearts, Thy servants, to offer this gift to Thy honour and glory, and as a memorial of Thy mercy and love and kindness in delivering them and the people of this country from their enemies. Be pleased to accept the same and let Thy blessing be upon the donors, their families and their substance and accept their gifts. And we further devoutly ask Thee to bless all who may in any way help forward its completion, and bestow Thy blessing upon their efforts, through Jesus Christ, our Lord."

Major-General Sir W. D. Otter, K. C. B., C. V. O., was to have raised the flag on the 100-foot pole on the grounds, but was unable to be present. Lieut.-Governor Hendrie handed the flag to Sir John M. Gibson, who completed the ceremony.

This was followed by the laying of the corner stone for the proposed monument to mark the spot of the engagement, the corner stone being laid by His Honor the Lieut.-Governor.

Brigadier-General Sir John M. Gibson then gave the address of the afternoon. He said:

"Fellow veterans, after fifty years, here we are again, what are left of us. I had often determined, with some of my friends, to revisit the battlefield and go over the ground, but had never found the convenient season, and you all know as you grow older, how rapidly the time slips by. It is not my intention to go into details of the attacks by the Queen's Own and the Thirteenth on that memorable morning of June 2, 1866; but it is a misrepresentation to say that the affair terminated unfavourably for the Canadian forces. They had driven the Fenians back from a line of barricades they held at the beginning of the action, and well I remember my own—the leading company—and other companies of the Thirteenth, after an admirable advance in extended order, occupying the barricaded position which the Fenians had held and from which the Canadians were peppering the enemy very effectively with no thought of retiring. There is no doubt that the Fenians had retreated and that the bulk of their forces were on the run to Fort Erie before the unfortunate cry of cavalry produced the confusion which deprived our forces of the full glory which practically had already been achieved. The Fenians had been driven back, and were all but completely routed or the result to our forces would have been very much more serious. In effect and virtually it was a victory for our forces.

"The alacrity displayed by the Queen's Own and the Thirteenth and the independent companies in mustering and proceeding to the front as they did is undoubted evidence of the loyalty and martial spirit animating the young Canadians who filled the ranks of these battalions. There is no room for even suspicion of want of bravery. The Fenians were heading for the Welland Canal; they were met, and as the result of the action they scampered back to Fort Erie, and many of them were taken prisoners before they could recross the Niagara. The object for which our volunteers had left their homes with most remarkable celerity and with no preparation of equipment, had been achieved—the enemy escaping from the country as rapidly as they had entered it. Without, however, fighting the battle over again, we are here on this occasion to commemorate the valour and patriotic spirit of those who lost their lives in a noble fight. While a goodly number of the veterans of '66 are still to the fore, the great majority of them have passed away. All honour to the memory of our departed comrades, including the late Lieut.-Col. Booker, who commanded the Canadians; Lieut.-Col. Gilmore, a most enthusiastic officer, who as major commanded the Queen's Own; Lieut.-Col. Skinner, that stubbornly brave old officer who, as major, led the Thirteenth, and who was afterwards for so many years its commanding officer. One must not individualize; but we had expected to welcome the presence of a most distinguished officer, Major-General Otter, K. C. B., honorary patron of the Veterans of 1866, who was with us at Ridgeway, and whose life has ever since been devoted to the service of his country in his military capacity, who prominently distinguished himself in the northwest campaign and in the South African war. Of him it may truly be said that no one has ever rendered more valuable and prolonged military service to Canada.

"I had been attending law lectures in Toronto on the day the battalions were suddenly sent to the front, and it was only by travelling all night that I was able to reach the train, in the early morning, at Port Colborne, on which the Queen's Own and the Thirteenth were enjoying their red herring breakfast just before moving on to Ridgeway. My fellow travellers that night, in a box car, had been some linemen sent down to repair telegraph lines which had been cut by the Fenians near Fort Erie; Major Askin, here to-day full of the enthusiasm of fifty years ago; Col.-Sergt. McCracken of the Thirteenth, and the two chaplains appointed by the Ministerial Association of Hamilton, Rev. Dr. Burwash and Rev. Dr. Inglis. All are pleased to see on the present occasion the first-named of these two chaplains, the other having been called to his reward many years ago. Both had shown conspicuous bravery throughout the engagement, exposing their lives to imminent danger in discharging their sacred duties. Not having been regularly enrolled, Dr. Burwash was too modest to apply, or at all events had not applied for the 1866 medal; but I, on my own motion, made the application which was readily granted, and no one to-day has a better right to wear, or more worthily wears, the same than our venerable and affectionately esteemed chaplain, Dr. Burwash.

"While to-day our attention is directed to the important operations in which we are more immediately concerned, it is fitting that we should commemorate the spirited manner in which the whole volunteer force rose to arms in readiness to join in the defense of their country, and the general population everywhere organized into home guards. It was a convincing proof that Canadians were the reverse of lukewarm as to what might be the future destiny of their country."

The General continued in eloquent terms to speak of the progress of Canada politically, materially and nationally during the past fifty years. In closing his remarks in reference to the part that is being taken by Canada in the great world war now in progress, he said:

"Canada has stepped out into the world's arena, and amid the applause of nations, has joined in the struggle against Prussian ambition for universal domination, in the struggle for democratic liberty and freedom, for the rights of smaller nationalities and for the establishment of a perpetual peace.

"Fellow veterans who are still answering the roll call, soon we shall join the ranks of those who have already gone. May it always be said by those following us that in a critical time in the history of our country, the memory of which we are to-day reviving, we to our utmost strove to do our duty."

As the grounds were a sea of mud and the rain descending in torrents, the demonstration on the battlefield was eliminated, and the programme was closed with the singing of "God Be With You Till We Meet Again," and "God Save the King."

Notwithstanding the unfavourable weather, quite a large crowd had gathered on the battlefield and during the ceremonies their umbrellas formed a roof which made quite a display to the occupants of the many automobiles standing near. The veterans present found that some changes had taken place in half a century; but they easily recognized the place and found most of the buildings and other landmarks standing as of yore, the marks of the bullets still being plain in some places. "There stands the barn where most of the wounded were carried," "This is the tree where two of us tried to get shelter at the same time, while we fired at the Fenians," "Here is where our company extended in skirmish line," "There is where the square was formed," and such like remarks were exchanged as the men viewed the grounds.

The generally expressed opinion was that while it was a disappointment to have the programme so interfered with, and opportunities for sight seeing so curtailed, yet there had been much pleasure in the occasion, and all or nearly all were glad to have been present. Old friendships were renewed and there was a determination soon to visit the place again. The visitors to Ridgeway were much pleased with the welcome they received from the citizens and the officials of the town and the preparations which had been made for their comfort. Finally, it is gratifying to note that not an accident occurred to sadden the occasion, and the pleasant recollections outweigh the disappointments.

III.

ROBERT (FLEMING) GOURLAY.

Reminiscences of his Last Days in Canada.

By Mrs. Sidney Farmer.

Following Mr. Justice Riddell's paper on Robt. F. Gourlay in the last number of the Ontario Historical Society's "Papers and Records", these notes may be interesting concerning Mr. Gourlay's life and family both at Mount Elgin, Canada, and in Edinburgh, Scotland.

My father, John McLellan Smith, of Sunnyside, Toronto, acted as Mr. Gourlay's agent and confidential adviser for many years, and was also an intimate friend of the family. Mr. Smith lived at that time seven miles away from Mt. Elgin, in the village of Campbellton, of which he was sole owner. It contained three large houses and about a dozen small ones for the use of his men; also a supply store, a blacksmith shop, and a saw-mill. And to this tiny village Mr. Gourlay fled from his persecutors many times. Mr. Smith was Warden of the County in 1861, and Reeve for 13 years in succession, and a Justice of the Peace for many years. He was a native of the Island of Islay, Scotland, and came to Canada when very young, settling first in Dereham, afterwards removing to Toronto, and dying in 1883. His wife was a daughter of Col. Charles S. Perley, of Burford, who was a prominent military man in Western Ontario, and descended from U. E. Loyalists on three sides of the family. Smith is the Anglicized form of McGowan, the name his ancestors were known by.

Mr. Smith had a high opinion of Mr. Gourlay, and said his ideas were good, and that he was persecuted unjustly, but the great trouble was that he was ahead of his time, and Mr. Smith lived to see fulfilled later many of the principles for which Mr. Gourlay lived and suffered. He was instrumental in securing pensions for life for the daughters after Mr. Gourlay's death from the Government, which had found that Mr. Gourlay was really a benefactor rather than a busybody.

He had an enormous number of lawsuits to contest, some from his own ideas of justice, and others seemingly from scheming tenants and neighbours (for he owned over 1000 acres of farming land in Ontario), and his second marriage proved most unfortunate. He had an extremely good housekeeper who proved so efficient in cooking, nursing, and making his life comfortable, that Mr. Gourlay married her—when she became just the opposite. As a wife, she refused to continue to work, and demanded so much, and acted so disagreeably, burning many of Mr. Gourlay's very valuable papers, taking his property, etc., that Mr. Gourlay was obliged to leave her, and make a settlement with her. Indeed at this time (1858) Mr. Gourlay fled several times in the night to Mr. Smith's house to get away from Mary.

ROBERT. F. GOURLAY
1863
AGED 85.
"TO BE SHEWN TO FRIENDS IN CANADA."

JOHN McLELLAN SMITH
Mr. Gourlay's Agent and Confidential Adviser in Dereham.

MISS HELEN GOURLAY
(About 1858)

MISS JANE GOURLAY
1870

Mr. Smith employed a great many men in his mills, of which he had several (some working for him for 35 years), and he was considered an adept in smoothing out difficulties, and it is said the only person he could not manage was this same Mary Reenan—Mr. Gourlay's second wife. She would go on sueing for this and that, thinking Mr. Gourlay was enormously wealthy, whereas he was getting poorer all the time. And after he returned to Edinburgh, in 1859, Mr. Smith, as his agent, had all these suits to look after, and then for the daughters after his death. Mr. Gourlay did have a great deal of money at times, but spent it lavishly on printing his books, pamphlets, etc., and also spent a large sum on the city of Edinburgh, of which, justly, he was very proud.

His daughters were highly educated; one—Miss Jane Gourlay—was a noted philanthropist of Edinburgh in her time. She was the originator of the "Settlement Houses for Girls," and had schemes and plans in such good working order, and so much accomplished, that she felt she could leave it to others to carry on, and sought to help elsewhere, going out to South Africa, in the early seventies, where she did good work until called to cease her labours in this world.

Miss Helen Gourlay was a great traveller, having visited many countries, and had a very charming manner. She was extremely religious, and the trouble her father had with Mary Reenan was most distressing to her, and she tried in every way to conciliate her, but without avail; she was quite fond of her before the marriage, of which she quite approved. She was with her father during this return visit of his to Canada. She was a scholar, and translated the Greek Testament into English, and had memorized every Collect in the Church of England Prayer Book, and could tell where to place them for the different seasons. She was a most devoted churchwoman. She visited Mr. Smith again at Sunnyside, Toronto, staying nearly two years—from 1876 to 1878—but during that time paid several visits to friends and relations elsewhere. She spent a short time with the authoress, Miss Agnes Maule Machar, of Kingston, who is a relative, and brought back some charming books written by that lady. She also visited her cousins, the Hamiltons, at Kingston, Princeton and Drumbo, and other places, and spent two months with relatives in Virginia, who lived in a once lovely Colonial mansion situated on the Rappahannock, which had been sadly disfigured during the Civil War. There were so many historical incidents connected with it that Miss Gourlay wrote an article on the subject for the Edinburgh "Scotsman." Her photo appears in Miss Carnochan's article (Niagara Historical Society, No. 18) that was taken at this time, in 1878. She left Mr. Smith's house in 1878 for New York en route to her home in Edinburgh, that being her last visit to Canada; but Mr. Charles Perley Smith, barrister, of Toronto, Mr. Smith's only son, visited her in 1891, and found her very well, and as much interested in Canada, and all her friends and relatives there, as ever. She died about 10 years ago. He also visited Mr. Alexander Duncan, Mr. Gourlay's only grandchild, of whom he was very fond, and whose mother, one of Mr. Gourlay's daughters, died very young. Mr. Duncan's father, John Duncan, was a naval officer in the East India Service. Mr. Alex. Duncan's wife is the daughter of Admiral Sir Wm. Edmonstone, and they have two daughters and three sons, all living. These sons are Mr. Robert F. Gourlay's great-grandsons, and are all at present in responsible positions serving their country:

Commander John Duncan, R. N. C. V., Royal Arsenal, Woolwich.
Capt. Basil Duncan, serving at the front.
Capt. Wm. Duncan, in the Royal Field Artillery, who has recently won the Military Cross.

NOTE.—I wish to thank Mr. Lockhart Gordon for the latest information regarding the great-grandsons of Mr. Gourlay.—Margaret McLellan Farmer.

April, 1917.

[The illustrations from photographs of Robert (Fleming) Gourlay and two of his daughters appear in these pages through the kindness of Mrs. Sidney Farmer, who also sends these reminiscences.]

IV.

MILITARY REGISTER OF BAPTISMS FOR THE STATION OF FORT GEORGE, UPPER CANADA, 1821 TO 1827.

This list was found in the Register of Births, Deaths and Marriages kept by the Rev. Robt. Addison, from 1792 to 1829, in Niagara, or Newark, and in possession of St. Mark's Church. It is arranged in seven columns, neatly ruled, with: Date of baptism, date of birth, Christian name of child, Christian names of parents, surname, quality, etc., of father, by whom the ceremony performed—apparently half sheets of foolscap, and sewn together. There are altogether eighty-five baptisms; the rank of the father varying from full private to K. C. B., Major General and Lieutenant-Governor, the regiments being 68th, 70th, 76th, and Royal Artillery; the officiating clergymen being W. Cokayne Frith, LL. D., and R. W. Turney, both Chaplains to the Forces, also Thomas Handcock, acting Chaplain to the forces at Ft. George, in one case the Rev. R. Addison, of St. Marks, and the last recorded is the baptism of Emily Sophia, daughter of Lady Sarah and Sir Peregrine Maitland, by Charles, Bishop of Quebec.

I have copied exactly the text, omitting the headings and division lines:

Baptized 7th Aug., 1821, born 17th May, Julia Catherine, of George and Sarah McDonald, Capt. 68th Regiment, by W. Cokayne Frith, LL. D.

2nd Sept., born 21st Aug., Wm. Henry, of James and Mary Ann Duff, Sergt.-Major 68th Regt.

10th Sept, born 8th April, James Septimus, of James and Susan Read, Surgeon 68th Regt.

10th Sept., born 9th Sept., James, of Patrick and Mary Feely, Private 68th Regt.

10th Sept., born 9th Sept., Rosanna, of Bryan and Mary Gibbons, Private 68th Regt.

9th Sept., born 24th Aug., Agnes, of William and Jennett Airde, Sergeant 68th Regt. (This baptism was performed by Robert Addison, acting Chaplain.)

21st Oct., born 6th Oct., Margaret, of Christian and Archibald Paterson, Sergeant 68th Regt.

23rd Oct., born 15th Oct., Charles, of John and Mary Lavell, Corporal 68th Regt.

27th Oct., born 13th Oct., Frances Ottley, of Robert Henry and Elizabeth Dee, D. A. Comng. Genrl.

28th Oct., born 22nd Oct., Hugh, of Maxwell and Hannah Crawford, Bugler 68th.
9th Dec., born 30th Nov., John Andrew, of Thomas and Eliza Pope, Private 68th.
15th Dec., born 28th Nov., Mary Ann, of Thomas and Eleanor Tisdell, Private 68th.
1822.
24th Feb., born 29th Jan., Mary Cokayne, of William Cokayne and Mary Frith, Chaplain to the Forces.
3rd March, born 26th Jan., Robert, of Robert and Mary Duncan, Sergeant 68th Regt.
10th March, born 8th Feb., Frances, of Joseph and Jane Jewitt, Private 68th Regt.
11th March, born 19th Nov., 1821, James Alexander, of James and Isabella Mitchell, Lieutenant 68th Regt.
17th Mar., born 24th Feb., Thomas, of William and Elizabeth Crawford, Private 68th.
31st Mar., born 18th Mar., Josephine, of James and Hester Morrow, Private 68th.
14th Apr., born 23rd Feb., Theresa, of James and Catherine Ferrigan, Sergt. 68th.
1st July, born 23rd June, James, of William and Jane Butcher, Private 68th.
1st July, born 22nd June, Agnes, of Samuel and Agnes Fleming, Corporal 68th.
25th Aug., born 9th Aug., Catherine, of Patrick and Jane Walsh, Sergeant 76th.

These twenty-two baptisms were all performed by W. Cokayne Frith, LL. D., except one 9th Sept., 1821, by Rev. Robert Addison, the writing very fine. The 68th Regiment must have left at the end of August and was succeeded by the 76th, the Chaplain of which was R. W. Turney. The notices are continued in the same way, the writing somewhat heavier with very black ink.

Birth 1822.
31st Aug., at Fort George, U. C., baptised Oct. 6th, Edward, of Richard and Mary Hiscott, Sergt. 76th Regt., by R. W. Turney, Chaplain to the Forces.
Sept. 10th born, bapt. Oct. 6th, Benjamin, of James and Margaret Simmons, Private 76th.
Sept. 22nd, bap. Nov. 1st, Elizabeth Bartlett, of Robert and Frances Coles, Major 76th Regt.
Oct. 19th., bap. Nov. 10th, John, of George and Mary Slack, Sergt. 76th.
1823.
Mar. 21st, bap. Apr. 13th, Caroline, of George and Jane Smart, Corporal 76th.

MILITARY REGISTER OF BAPTISMS FOR FORT GEORGE, 1821-1827

Apr. 6th. Apr. 27th, William, of William and Mary Hemmissley, Private 76th.
Apr. 3rd. Apr. 27th, Ann, of Martin and Margaret Godfrey, Private 76th.
Apr. 16th. May 11th, Jane, of John and Mary Cusick, Private 76th.
Nov. 19th, 1822, bap. Apr. 25th, 1823, Lucy Sarah Thillepson Gordon, of Robt. Wm. and Jane Turney, Chaplain to the Forces.
May 7th, 1823, bap. May 21st, Henry Ontario, of Robt. Henry and Elizabeth Dee, Dept. Asst. Comr. Genrl.
Aug. 2nd, bap. Aug. 24th, Ellen, of Martin and Mary Freeman, Private 76th Regt.
Sept. 27th, at Stamford, Sept. 28th, Charles Lennox Brownlow, of Sir Peregrine and Lady Sarah Maitland,* Lt.-Gov. and Maj.-Genl.
Sept. 8th, bap. Sept. 28th, Charlotte, of John and Ann Morris, Sergt. 76th Regt., by Robert Addison, Minister.
Oct. 25th, bap. Nov. 9th, Mary, of Joseph and Mary Hullott, Sergt. 76th, by Robert Addison, Minister.
Nov. 2nd, bap. Nov. 16th, Sidney Ann, of Francis and Sarah Moore, Private 68th Regt.
Dec. 15th, bap. Jan. 25th, 1824, Joseph, of William and Mary Thomas, Private 76th.

1824.
Mar. 7th, 1824, bap. Apr. 11th, Robert, of Robert and Charlotte Bemrose, Sergt. 76th.
May 8th, bap. June 7th, Edward, of Edward and Mary Amelia Hetherington, Captain 76th Regt.
Apr. 29th, bap. Sept. 15th, Margaret Dudley, of Benjamin and Caroline Jane Hedley Routh, Lieut. 76th.
Aug. 28th, bap. Sept. 25th, Charles Fortier Nepean, of John Birlasson and Mary Gates Flanagan, Surgeon 76th Regt.
Sept. 24th, bap. Oct. 10th, Arabella, of James and Catharine Wilson, Gunner.
Oct. 16th, bap. Oct. 17th, Fanny, of William and Mary Stevenson, Gunner.
May 1st, bap. Nov. 1st, Charlotte Dee, of Benjamin Robt. and Ann Ottley, Lieut. 61st Foot.
Aug. 23rd, bap. Sept. 5th, Edward, of William and Mary Ambler, Private 76th Regt.
July 9th, bap. Sept. 12th, John, of Thomas and Mary Small, Sergt. 76th.
Dec. 7th, bap. Jan. 1st, 1825, Mary, daughter of George and Mary Slack, Sergt. 76th.
Dec. 18th, Jan. 1st, 1825, William, son of William and Catharine Paulson, Sergt. 76th Regt.

*Charles Lennox Brownlow Maitland was received into Church May 22nd, 1825. Sponsors: Charles Duke of Rutland, Brownlow Bertie Matthew, Esq., Lady Mary Fitzroy.

Jan. 21st, 1825, bap. Feb. 16th, James, son of Richard and Mary Hiscott, Sergt. 76th Regt.*

1825.

Feb. 9th, bap. Feb. 18th, Lucy Gordon Thillason, daughter of Robt Wm. and Jane Turney, Chaplain to the Forces.

Mar. 7th, bap. Apr. 4th, Henry, son of George and Jane Smart, Corporal 76th.

Mar. 7th, bap. Apr. 4th, John, son of John and Ann Morris, Sergt 76th.

June 25th, 1803, bap. Apr. 8th, 1825, William, son of Susannah Newman, Private, illegite.

Apr. 26th, 1825, bap. June 19th, Jane, of John and Ann Grant, Gunner Royal Artillery.

July 1st, bap. June 28th, Frances, of John and Ann Lundy, Corporal 76th Regt.

June 5th, July 3rd bap., Harriett, of John and Mary Ann Kelly, Gunner R. A.

June 4th, bap. July 3rd, Thomas, of William and Mary Hammesley, Private 76th.

July 12th, bap. July 21st, Charles Edwin, of Hermann and Mary Anne Lott, Paymaster 76th Regt.

July 11th, bap. July 31st, William, son of John and Mary Cusick, Private 76th.

Mar. 1st, bap. Sept. 22nd, John Withers, of John and Jane McGlashen, Storekeeper.

Sept. 24th, bap. Oct. 9th, Mary, of William and Mary Cuddy, Sergt. 76th Regt.

Oct. 7th, bap. Oct. 30th, James, son of Joseph and Mary Cant, Private 76th.

Jan. 9th, 1826, bap. Jan. 15th, David, of Thomas and Honora Bannister, Gunner Royal Artillery.

Jan. 23rd, bap. Feb. 12th, Mary, of Richard and Sarah Brown, Private 76th.

Jan. 27th, bap. Feb. 19th, Thomas, of Richard and Mary Hiscott, Sergt. 76th Regt.

March 8th, bap. Apr. 2nd, Ann, of Wm. and Mary Thomas, Drum Major 76th Regt.

May 3rd, May 13th, John Henry, of John and Sarah Eden, Private 76th.

May 25th, June 2nd, John Berney, of Alexander and Sarah McIntyre, Private 76th Regt.

June 30th, bap. July 23rd, Thomas, son of George and Catharine Patton, Corporal in Major Pilling's Co., Sap. 2 R. Art., by Thos. Handcock, Acting Chaplain to the Forces.

July 1st, bap. July 29th, Alexander Peter, son of John and Jane McGlashan, Commissariat Clerk.

*Major Jas. Hiscott died here June, 1917, ex-M.P.P. for Lincoln.

MILITARY REGISTER OF BAPTISMS FOR FORT GEORGE, 1821-1827

Aug. 15th, bap. 15th, William, of William and Mary Ann Stevenson, Gunner 1st Battln. Royal Artillery.
Dec. 3rd, bap. 7th Jan., William Matthew, of John and Margaret Calent, Pensioner 76th Regt.

1827.
Feb. 16th, bap. Feb. 27th, Vesey Temple, of Thomas and Catherine Handcock, Acting Chaplain to the Forces.
Mar. 26th, bap. Apr. 15th, Alicia, of Neil and Alicia McNeil, Colour-Sergt. 70th Regt.
Apr. 12th, bap. Apr. 16th, Anne, of John and Anne Grant, Gunner in Major Pelleg's Co. R. Arty.
June 6th, bap. June 23rd, John, son of Alexander and Elizabeth McGuigen, Private 70th Regt.
July 10th, bap. July 19th, William, son of Robert and Sarah Chambers, Private 70th Regt.
June 7th, bap. July 20th, Frances Anne, of Robt. Henry and Elizabeth Dee, Dep. Asst. Com'y Gen. H. P.
Dec. 16th, bap. July 25th, William, of Robert and Anne Armour, Private 70th Regt.

1827.
Aug. 6th, ———— Louisa, of Alexander and Amelia Garrett, Lieut. H. P. 49th Regt., Barrack Master.
Mar. 19th, bap. Aug. 22nd, Mary, of Robert and Barbara Brown, Corporal 70th Regt.
June 11th, bap. Aug. 22nd, Hannah, of John and Elizabeth Lavery, Private 70th Regt.
July 14th, bap. Aug. 27th, Francis, of James and Martha Batchelor, Gunner Royal Artillery.
Aug. 22nd, bap. Sept. 11th, Emily Sophia, of Peregrine and Sarah Maitland, K. C. B., Major-General, Lt.-Governor, by Charles Bishop of Quebec.

During the period from 1821 to 1827 there are recorded in St. Mark's Register three baptisms of the 68th or 70th Regt., and many are recorded as performed in St. Marks by R. W. Turney, probably during the absence or illness of Rev. R. Addison.

—Copied by permission of Rev. Canon Garrett,
by Janet Carnochan.

V.

THE LAST OF THE LA GUAYRIANS*.

(Wellington County, Ont.)

By the late C. C. James, C.M.G., LL.D.

The Canada Company had been formed to take over and settle a large area of land in Upper Canada. John Galt, the novelist, had been sent out to act as superintendent. One of his first acts was to lay out a town which has grown into the substantial City of Guelph. He wrote home to a friend an account of the inauguration of this work, dating his letter from Guelph, 2nd of June, 1827. By accident this letter some time later came under the eye of the editor of Fraser's Magazine, and was printed in the issue of November 30th, 1830. As an introduction to this article we reproduce a portion of the letter as follows:

"The site chosen was on a 'nameless stream's untrodden banks', about eighteen miles in the forest from Galt—a great future city founded by a friend of mine, with a handsome bridge over the Grand River, and of which I had never heard until it had a post office. Early on the morning of St. George's Day I proceeded on foot towards the spot, having sent forward a band of woodmen with axes on their shoulders to prepare a shanty for the night—a shed made of boughs and bark, with a great fire at the door. I was accompanied by my friend Dunlop, a large, fat, facetious fellow, of infinite jest and eccentricity, but he forgot his compass, and we lost our way in the forest. After 'wandering up and down' like babes in the woods, without even a blackberry to console us—the rain raining in jubilee—we came to the hut of a Dutch settler, in which no English was to be obtained. However, after much jabber, loud speaking, and looking at one another with mouth, eyes and nostrils, in addition to ears, Mynheer gave tongue that he could speak French, which he did, no doubt, perfectly; as, in telling us that he had cleared a farm in the States which he had exchanged for his present habitation, he expressively said, 'Je Swape'. We hired him for our guide.

"It was almost sunset when we arrived at our rendezous; my companion, being wet to the skin, unclothed and dressed himself in two blankets, one in the Celtic and the other in the Roman fashion—the kilt and the toga; the latter was fastened on the breast with a spar of timber that

*From the Canadian Courier, 28th Nov., 1908.

might have served for the mainmast to 'some great admiral'. I 'kept my state' (as Macbeth says of his wife at the banquet) of dripping drapery. We then, with surveyors and woodmen (Yankice, choppers), proceeded to a superb maple tree, and I had the honour and glory of laying the axe to the root thereof, and soon it fell 'beneath our sturdy strokes' with the noise of an avalanche. It was the genius of the forest unfurling his wings and departing forever. Being the King's name-day, I called the town Guelph—the smaller fry of office having monopolised every other I could think of; and my friend drawing a bottle of whiskey from his bosom, we drank prosperity to the unbuilt metropolis of the new world.''

Accompanying the letter there appeared a sketch of the town showing a clearing, a bridge across the Speed, the stump of the maple tree neatly fenced in, the Priory facing the river, the market building, the school, and a number of houses. For a time, the Priory was Mr. Galt's residence. Later it was used for offices and for the temporary accommodation of new arrivals. Visitors to the Royal City will have noticed the picturesque log station of the C. P. R.—it is the Priory site preserved and welcoming as of old the newcomers to the city of John Galt.

Mr. Galt in his autobiography tells us that soon after the beginning of the town he found it expedient to make his headquarters at some more convenient point, and so he took up his residence at a house on Burlington Bay, thus locating midway between York and Guelph. He says: ''I had not been long settled in this domicile, when one Sunday morning a deputation came to me, from a body, I think, in all, of fifty-seven emigrants, who had come from New York, where they had been landed from La Guayra, South America. . . . . I considered that as the Company had work it would be doing service to Government to employ these people, accordingly directed them to proceed to Mr. Prior at Guelph, till I had time to consider their case.''

This event in the early settlement of Upper Canada is recalled by the death of Mr. David Stirton, of Guelph, who passed away recently in his ninety-third year. Mr. David Stirton was born in Scotland in 1816; came to Upper Canada in 1827; from 1858 to 1874, represented the county of Wellington in the Parliament of Canada; for nearly thirty years, from 1876 to 1904, held the position of postmaster at Guelph; and now, after being a lone survivor of the early pioneers, he has passed away at a fine old age. It is not of his interesting parliamentary career that we propose to write, but we remember that he was "the last of the La Guayrians", and in these days of revived immigration and of pioneering "made easy", it may be of interest to recall the story of the little band of Scottish settlers of which he was the last survivor.

Turn to the map of Venezuela in South America. You will find the city of Caracas in the north, lying a few miles inland from the coast. Its seaport is La Guayra. In 1825 the country, then known as Colombia, was in a state of unrest. The sovereignty of Spain had been thrown off by Bolivar. The old plantation proprietors were uneasy; they were anxious to dispose of their estates. Coffee was the chief crop grown for exportation, the work being done by slaves. These estates were advertised in Europe as most attractive properties, and the suggestion was sent abroad that here was the place for the industrious Scottish emigrant. Scotland was uneasy at the time. Her people were streaming out of the western ports across the Atlantic to the United States and Canada. There was, however, but little shipping from the eastern ports for America. This presented a new field for the promoter. A company was organized, a plantation purchased in Colombia and advertisements of most attractive nature scattered up and down the eastern shires of Scotland.

A London sailing vessel of 600 tons called The Planet was chartered to take out the settlers. The boat left the Thames with a few English emigrants and then picked up the rest of her passengers, 250 in all, in the Bay of Cromarty. This was in 1825. They sailed for La Guayra, calling at Madeira on the way to take on a cargo of wine. Twelve weeks out from Cromarty Bay, the party were landed at La Guayra. Disappointment met them from the first. The country was in disorder, life and property were insecure, the climate was unsuited to the Scotsmen of the north, the estate that had been purchased by the company was composed partly of barren mountains and partly of valleys that required irrigation. Transportation had been provided and land allotted by the company to the settlers who were bound by written contract to locate upon the land and to repay their debt in ten years. The poor, deluded people were thus left in a most pitiable condition. After vain efforts to make a living and to reconcile themselves to their inhospitable surroundings, they were gradually forced to abandon their lots and soon found themselves gathered together in temporary quarters at Caracas.

Here at least they had some chance of defending themselves against bandits and outlaws. They laid their case before the British consul, and with the help of Mr. Lancaster, the Quaker educationist, who happened to be there at the time, they sent home an appeal for help. This did not fail. A British frigate was despatched to their assistance. The captain in charge was a brother of Sir Peregrine Maitland, then Governor of Upper Canada. After consultation, they decided to accept the offer of transportation to Canada. They were taken north and landed at New York, where they were met by Mr. Buchanan, the British consul, who also acted as agent of the Canada Company. It should be noted here that Mr. Stirton's father reached New York by an earlier boat, as he had saved enough of his money to pay for passage for his family. Twenty-two families in all were sent forward from New York consigned to the care of Mr. John Galt who was building up the settlement in the County of Wellington. Mr. Stirton some years ago told the story of his journey. His father and family sailed up the Hudson to Albany, thence by canal boats to Rochester and by schooner to the head of the lake. Half a dozen houses stood on the present site of Hamilton; Dundas was somewhat larger; but Ancaster ("The pretty, breezy town of Ancaster on the hill," Galt called it) was the most promising town of the district. Over the primitive roads they made their way, reaching Guelph on September 8th, 1827, less than five months after the time of the cutting of the first tree. The Stirton family slept on the first night in a loft of the Priory.

Another chapter now opened in the history of the La Guayrians. Mr. Galt gave them welcome and made out a plan for forming with them a model settlement which was to extend four miles in length along the Elora Road. Their locations were laid out on paper, irrespective of the configuration of the country. The Company undertook to assist in the building of the houses. Winter came on before they were ready and the poor immigrants, dependent solely upon the assistance of the Company and unacquainted with Canadian pioneer life in the bush, suffered to the limit the hardships of backwoods life. For a year or more they worked along increasing their clearings and improving their houses, but still dependent upon the Company. A change then suddenly took place. Mr. Galt and the officials at home had a misunderstanding, the result of which was that he resigned and returned home and his place was taken by another. The work provided by the Company upon which they depended for a living was stopped, supplies were shut off, and in a short time the La Guayrians were scattered over adjoining townships and they had to begin once again the battle of life in the deeper recesses of the King's bush.

May the Twentieth Century bring as good citizens as the La Guayrians!

VI.

PRESIDENT'S ADDRESS
Annual Meeting, June 6th, 1917.
By Prof. J. Squair, President

PART I.
AN ELECTION IN 1867.

This is the jubilee year of the Confederation of Canada, and perhaps it will not be inappropriate for me to give some personal reminiscences of a parliamentary election held in 1867 as part of a Presidential Address to this Society. I was then seventeen years of age, and although I remember some previous elections, it was the first in which I took a real interest. Unfortunately I have no written or printed documents to guide me, but some of the events made a deep impression upon me, and so my recollection may be trustworthy enough to justify me in regarding them as real historical material.

The election in question was held in my native locality, the West Riding of Durham, Ontario. West Durham at that time was looked on as a Liberal riding, although at the previous election Mr. John Milne, the Conservative candidate, had almost defeated Mr. Henry Munro, the Liberal. With an untried outsider, Mr. Edward Blake, as Liberal candidate, Mr. Milne at first considered his chances of winning the riding as very good, and every energy was put forth by him, and naturally by his opponents as well, in what was expected to be, but did not turn out to be, a close election.

It was my fortune to be present during the contest at three meetings. The first was on a very warm July evening, in haying time, in the little court-house of the Village of Newcastle. That was the first time I saw, or heard of, Edward Blake. It was a great revelation. About ten o'clock on that sweltering evening, after the audience was weary of local speakers, that impressive figure arose, and with his ringing voice and majestic sentences imposed attentive silence on all. The effect was magical. With no tedious exordium, no funny stories, at once he was into the exposition of his subject, in his clear and dignified manner. The tired backs straightened, the hum of voices at doors and windows, inside and outside the building, ceased, and a hush of admiration fell upon the audience, hitherto so unruly and inattentive. It was a notable example of the power of oratorical genius. I have long since forgotten the arguments of the orator, but the music and rhythm of his speech still ring in my ears.

The second meeting occurred on another sultry evening during the
spring wheat harvest. It was held in the newly erected drill-shed in the
village of Orono. The chief speakers were the Hon. Wm. McDougall and
Mr. Edward Blake. It had become clear to Mr. Milne that, in order to
cope with Mr. Blake on the public platform, the best speakers in the
Conservative party would have to be called on, and a number of these
honored the riding with their presence. On this occasion it was, as I
have said, Mr. McDougall. He spoke well, but was not a match for Mr.
Blake. The meeting was large and noisy, and Blake only was able to
hold it in control. In the middle of the night the proceedings were in-
terrupted by a sharp thunderstorm, accompanied by heavy rain, which
lasted perhaps half an hour. After the storm was over the combatants
resumed their arguments and the meeting continued till day-break. We
went home to build the fire for breakfast and milk the cows. That night
we had no sleep. We took our politics in large doses in those times.

The third meeting was the one that fell on nomination day. It was
held in the drill-shed in the town of Bowmanville in the end of harvest.
Mr. Milne and his committee had determined to have a great rally on
that occasion, and invited the Prime Minister, Sir John A. Macdonald,
to be present and address the electors. Mr. Blake and his friends thought
they could not do better than invite the Hon. George Brown to be present
also and reply to the Premier. Both these eminent gentlemen accepted
the invitations and made speeches. According to the custom of the time
both were nominated as candidates so as to give them the right to speak
from the hustings, and Sir John Macdonald was nominated before Mr.
Brown and had the right to speak first, a right which he did not exercise,
however. When his turn to speak came he was nowhere in sight. The
crowd began to call for Macdonald, but no Macdonald arose. Then there
were cries for Brown, and presently the great meeting became a babel.
A regular hubbub prevailed for what seemed a very long time. Finally,
to quiet the confusion, George Brown, who had been sitting in full view
on the platform, rose to speak. No sooner did he rise than the Premier
suddenly appeared and sat down a few feet from Brown, in front of the
latter, looking up saucily into his face. Here he remained until Mr.
Brown had finished speaking and then he took his turn.

Of the speeches of these two great men on that day I now remember
only certain things, and those in a very general way. Exact expressions
and arguments I cannot recall. Mr. Brown appeared to be angry at what
he called the pusillanimous conduct of the Premier of Canada in hiding
away and declining to speak first. "Why should he be afraid of a private citizen? (Mr. Brown had two or three weeks before this been defeated
in the neighbouring riding of South Ontario by Mr. T. N. Gibbs.) Such
a man," he said, "is unworthy of his high office. He is afraid to tell the
electors what policy he intends to pursue. He is what he always has
been, a mere opportunist. He would, indeed, never have adopted Confederation if it had not been forced upon him. I," said Mr. Brown,
"forced the appointment of a committee of the House upon him and the
committee brought in a report favourable to Confederation." It was a

powerful speech, and, coming as it did after what seemed to be an attitude of fear towards Mr. Brown on the part of Sir John Macdonald, it probably cost Mr. Milne some votes.

But the speech of the Premier in reply was in reality the greater of the two. Delivered to a somewhat hostile audience, which was rendered still more unsympathetic by the irritating delay already mentioned, it was a marvel of frank, reasonable, tactful speaking. He admitted that he would have preferred a legislative to a federal union, but since the latter had been adopted he would be loyal to it. He gave George Brown credit for his help in carrying the scheme of Confederation through and very pertinently asked why his great opponent had not continued in the coalition cabinet for the purpose of completing the good work which had been so auspiciously begun. Why could Mr. Brown not be as reasonable as Mr. Wm. McDougall or Mr. W. P. Howland and others of his old friends? He professes to be opposed to coalition on principle, but if a good measure like Confederation was carried by a coalition, could not other good measures be carried by the same form of political machinery? "How can he tell," exclaimed Sir John, "whether our policy and administration will be worthy of opposition? All we ask for is a fair trial. If we prove worthy of condemnation, condemn us, but give us a chance. Do what nearly all other Canadians are doing, i. e. promising us their support for the present until they see how we turn out. In fact, every man elected up to the present, with the single exception of Mr. Joseph Rymal, has promised us his support." And so he went on, in his good-natured, unpretentious way, chaffing his great opponent about his long face and the "long finger that he often has shaken at us," and looking on all with his jaunty, waggish air as he said those simple, sensible things which generally carried conviction. But he could not redeem West Durham. Shortly after for two days it rode hotly to the polls and gave Mr. Edward Blake his send-off into public life with a majority of several hundred.

PART II.

A LETTER WRITTEN IN 1836.

Allow me now to contribute a second item of historical material in the shape of a letter written by an uncle of mine, Robert Squair, from Whitby, U. C., to a brother-in-law of his, John Grant, at that time living in Forres, Scotland. It is dated August 29th, 1836. In copying the letter I have made corrections in spelling and grammar sufficient to bring it into harmony with accepted standards.

(Copy of letter)

Whitby, 29th August, 1836.

Dear Friend:

I take the opportunity of writing to inform you that we are both well at present and hope that this will find you in the same state. We have enjoyed good health since we left home. Thanks to the Lord for it. I think you have settled in your minds before this time that you are coming to America, and if you come bring all your tools with you because they are all very dear here and not so good as at home. I may mention to you what things to take for the voyage—1 boll[1] oatmeal, ½ hundredweight sea biscuit, 1 firlot[2] oats baked (oat cakes?), 20 lbs. beef, 20. lbs. pork, 16 lbs. butter and a cheese, some sowans[3], 2 pints whiskey, ½ anker[4] beer, 9 lbs. sugar, ¼ lb. tea, 1 lb. coffee, 6 doz. haddocks, some white puddins[5], 1 firlot potatoes, some pepper, some mustard, some eggs and other things which you may think of. I need not mention to you about my voyage as I wrote a letter to my father when I arrived at New York, and one to Lewis when I settled in Whitby. We were 28 days at sea and I was well all the time, but Jane was not well. We had a pleasant voyage and not very rough. We paid £5 each for a two-cabin passage and we paid about £2 each going up to Toronto, but you will require £25 to take with you. And if you ship at Liverpool take no paper notes with you because you will not get them off in England, but try to sail from Cromarty because it is very expensive to go to Liverpool or Greenock.

The carpenter's is a very good business in this country because all the houses are built of wood. You would wonder as much to see a stone house in Canada as to see a wooden house in Forres. The mason's is not a good trade in Canada, but it is good in New York. Masons there get 3 to 4 dollars a day and carpenters 2 to 3 dollars, and pay 3 dollars a week for board, but in Canada you will get a dollar per day and board. You will wonder how large they make their barns. The common size of them is 36 to 40 ft. broad, 60 to 70 ft. long, 20 to 25 ft. high in the walls. They hold all the corn and hay. Men drive in their horses and wagons into the barn and empty in the inside. All the wagons are 8 to 12 ft. long and pulled with 2 horses. There are no coups[6] here as at home. You will get £15 to make a waggon.

Jane and I wish very much that you come out, and Janet is intending to come with you. Sandy is well. I had two letters from him since I came here and he is staying in the same place. He is to have £50 in the year and board. Sandy received a letter from Janet from John Bain, Nairn, and he sent one home.

I could wish you would all come here to a land of liberty and plenty. Donald Munro and I intend to buy some land and we shall not get it cheap here as in some other places. You need not write to me because I do not know where to direct you to write, but you can write to Sandy and he will let us know about you. Sandy Ross lives in the same place as we are in and he and his brother have taken 200 acres of land in Goderich.

[1] Boll—140 lbs.
[2] Firlot—¼ of a boll.
[3] Sowans—"Oat-shells" from which a palatable food is made.
[4] Anker—A cask of 8¼ gallons (imperial).
[5] White puddins—"sausages" made of oat meal, suet and onions.
[6] Coups—"dump-carts."

Dear John, Jane and I are as well pleased to live in Canada as at home and we get a great deal more for our work and better provisions. The whole family eats at one table. Master and servants are all alike, all eat and work together. I lived one month with Mr. Hall but for my own profit I left him and went to Mr. McPherson to take charge of his farm. He lives beside Mr. Hall's farm and Donald Munro and I see each other every day. We have a house to ourselves and the use of the cows and as much potatoes as we need and I have £3 10/ per month. He is going to part with the farm and he wants me to take it on shares—that is to have the half the increase of the land and he affords everything it needs. I am not sure which to do, that or take land of my own in another place or to stay and work as I am doing just now. What do you think?

Jane desires you to take Janet with you to help you on the sea to nurse the children and if Peter comes to take Janet McBeath with him. There is plenty of work here and good pay. You will get as much here in two months as you will get in six months at home. I was told before I left home that this country was very hot, but it is as hot at home as here this season.[1] Donald Munro is well and family and bids you to send word west to her people that they received a letter from them on the 22d Aug. and that they got no letter from John yet. You will not write me till you get another direction from me because Donald and I are thinking of taking land of our own.

We remain, etc., etc.,

ROBERT SQUAIR.

Here the letter closes, but there was still vacant space on the sheet of paper, and since the postage paid was 25 cents, Scottish thrift demanded that all space should be filled. Here follows the filling:

Give my best wishes to Alexr. and Robert and your mother and to William and tell Sandy that I expect he has got married before this time. He better not come here without a wife. Sandy Margach says he would live a bachelor all his days before he would take a Yankee to wife. They are very lazy women and are good for nothing but to sit in their rocking chairs and eat their meat.

Be sure to send west word to the old people that we are all well and quite happy to live in Canada and that we have enjoyed good health since we left home. Give my best respects to all enquiring friends, especially to my parents and sisters and brothers, and let them know that I intend to write to them in October, and let my mother be in no way uneasy about me as I am as well and as contented as at home. Tell them not to write me till I send them a letter as I am not sure what place I shall be settled in.

You can write to Sandy and he will send me word. You were afraid that his direction was not right but the same direction will do as before.

[1] Sir Frederick Stupart, Director of the Meteorological Service, Toronto, kindly informs me that the records show that the summer of 1836 was unusually cool.

A faithful copy of the letter ((verbatim et literatim) made by our obliging Secretary, Mr. A. F. Hunter, is herewith attached. I should be glad to give the original to the Society if it possessed suitable means for the preservation of such documents.

As regards the contents of the letter it is certain that a goodly part of it contains information already well known to all interested in the history of Ontario. What it says regarding the manner of travelling on sailing ships, the wages received by working men, the material employed in building or the like, is matter recorded in other places, although what is here may perhaps serve a useful purpose as a sort of check list. But there is one thing in the letter which rather surprised me when I obtained it some ten years ago, and that is the absence of any reference to political dissatisfaction in the country, and the optimistic insistence with which it dwells upon the fact that Canada is a land of liberty and plenty. If in 1836 in the township of Whitby a man had said "that the administration of justice is in the hands of a party forming among themselves a Family Compact, that, owing to these circumstances, property and liberty are held by a very precarious tenure, and that as a consequence of this state of things there is little immigration," I certainly should not have been surprised.[1] But we have the very opposite. Hence there is a difficulty here. What is the explanation? Did the writer not know what was going on about him? There have been plenty of examples of such men in the most stirring times. We have all heard of the mythical old man who, after Napoleon became Emperor, was found in Paris, and yet had never heard of Louis XVI., Napoleon or the Revolution. But Robert Squair had the reputation with his family of being an alert man, although not a wise one.

Perhaps, however, there was not enough political commotion in Whitby to disturb the material progress of the community, although in 1833 the people of that locality had sent a petition to the Lieutenant-Governor stating that "Loyal as the inhabitants of this country unquestionably are, your petitioners will not disguise from your Excellency that they consider longer endurance under their present oppressions neither a virtue nor a duty."[1] I leave the difficulty with you.

[1] See "Life and Times of Wm. Lyon Mackenzie," by Charles Lindsey (1862), vol. I., p. 353.

[1] See Lindsey's "Life and Times of William Lyon Mackenzie." Vol. I., p. 299.

Ontario Historical Society

PAPERS AND RECORDS

VOL. XVI.

TORONTO
PUBLISHED BY THE SOCIETY
1918

CONTENTS

I. President's Address, June 5th, 1918. PROF. JOHN SQUAIR 5

II. The Books of the Political Prisoners and Exiles of 1838.
J. DAVIS BARNETT, C.E. 10

III. The Latest Milestones in the History of Civilization.
LT.-COL. A. E. BELCHER 19

IV. A Lóyalist of the St. Lawrence. HENRY HARMON NOBLE 29

V. The Rev. John Barclay, M.A. MISS A. BLANCHE BURT, B.A. 37

VI. History of the Windsor and Detroit Ferries.
F. J. HOLTON, D. H. BEDFORD AND FRANCIS CLEARY 40

VII. The Founding of Kirkfield, Ont. A. F. HUNTER 52

I.

PRESIDENT'S ADDRESS, JUNE 5, 1918.

By Prof. John Squair.

Some three weeks ago there came into my possession a set of minute-books and ledgers which had been the property of the Society whose name was "Orono Division, No. 79, of the Sons of Temperance of Ontario." Since the dissolution of the Division these books had been in the custody of Mr. D. T. Allin, of Orono, a former member of the institution, and from him I received them on the understanding that they should be deposited in a place of safety. Such a place, within the precincts of the Education Department, has been promised to me by Dr. A. H. U. Colquhoun, Deputy Minister of Education, and thither I intend to transport them.

Orono is a police village forming part of the Township of Clarke in the County of Durham in this Province, and has never had a separate corporate existence. The Division was organized on February 26th, 1850, but the earliest minute-book has disappeared. Those now in my possession are eight in number and cover the following periods: No. 1, 1853-1854; No. 2, 1854-1859; No. 3, 1863-1864; No. 4, 1866-1870; No. 5, 1870-1877; No. 6, 1877-1881; No. 7, 1881-1891; No. 8, 1891-1896. In addition to these eight volumes there are two treasurer's books in which receipts and expenditures are entered as well as a number of signatures of members and a list of 541 names of persons who belonged to the Division between 1850 and 1871, of whom sixteen were ladies.

These volumes contain a partial record of the activities of a group of people, representative of a large number throughout the Province, who contributed to the formation of a new mentality in regard to the use of alcoholic beverages and they may perhaps prove to be unique. If so, they may be very useful as historical material.

There can be no doubt that, as compared with the majority of the people of Europe, and with himself as he existed a hundred years ago, the Anglo-Saxon of North America has a very special way of regarding the use, moderate or immoderate, of alcoholic liquors. In all times and places drunkenness has been reprobated, but the intense feeling of opposition to even a moderate use of such things as wine, which we in this country know, has not been common amongst men. In France, for instance, the making of wine is one of the important industries, and its daily consumption is looked on by most Frenchmen as natural, proper and wholesome. Neither they nor Italians have adopted the maxim, "touch not, taste not, handle not," as regards alcohol. The proportion of teetotallers in the British Isles is considerably larger than on the continent of Europe, but the intensity of feeling in favour of legal interference with the use of liquor is much below what it is with us. And it has not always stood as high in Canada and the United States as it is at present. How the change has come about is one of the most important historical questions which we can discuss. A good many forces have been at work, some noisy, some silent. Not the least important of these factors has been the influence of the quasi-secret societies like the Sons of Temperance and the Good Templars which arose and came actively into play about the middle of last century.

Not that no anxiety was felt in the community regarding the evils of drinking before the organization of such societies. In fact we see indications of such anxiety as early as 1794, when it was enacted by Parliament that no person was to have a tavern license unless he first obtained from the magistrate a certificate of fitness, and the quarter sessions might limit the number of licenses to be granted in the Province. And the number of licenses could not be increased except on production of a testimonial under the hand of the parson and church or town wardens or of four householders. An innkeeper could be disqualified for allowing gambling in his house or any disorderly conduct. In 1818 it is enacted that innkeepers shall be "sober, honest and diligent persons and good subjects of our Lord the King."

But drunkenness appears to increase. E. A. Talbot, in his "Five Years Residence in the Canadas," published in 1824, makes the remark that "gentlemen in Canada appear to be much addicted to drinking." During the years 1824-1850 many amendments are made in the laws regarding liquor licenses with the evident purpose of decreasing the evils connected with drinking, but small improvement apparently results, for in 1836, for instance, we find the Rev. Robert McDowell of Toronto and thirty-nine others presenting a petition to Parliament to limit the use of ardent spirits.

In 1850 an "Act for the More Effectual Suppression of Intemperance" was passed, the preamble of which: "Whereas experience hath shewn that the laws now in force are insufficient to suppress the great evils arising out of the abuse of spirituous liquors," clearly proves that Parliament was cognizant of the evils of drinking at that time. It is interesting to note what some of the remedies were which Parliament then adopted. One was that tavern-keepers were subject to imprisonment and a fine of from £25 to £100 for fatal accidents to intoxicated persons. The fine was to be paid to the heirs of those hurt. Another was that temperance houses might be established. Another was that parties found intoxicated might be brought before the magistrate. And another was that distillers and wholesale dealers were not to sell liquors in less quantities than one gallon, except wine, which might be sold by the bottle. These were not to be drunk on the premises.

By the Act of 1849, municipal councils (coming into existence in 1850) were to have power to limit the numbers of tavern licenses and to pass by-laws for their regulation. And this right is confirmed by subsequent Acts.

The middle of the nineteenth century is an important point in the history of what is sometimes called Old Ontario. A new municipal law was enacted, a new school law had been adopted, a new and sturdy General Superintendent was beginning to arouse the people to the importance of the primary school, the population of the country was expanding, new lands were being cleared, new villages and towns were being built, new industries were being founded, such as saw-mills, grist-mills, tanneries, distilleries. Wealth was increasing, traffic on the roads was developing and taverns for travellers sprang up fast. There was a spirit of progressive hopefulness prevalent which manifested itself sometimes in generous treating in the barrooms and at those social functions called "bees" convened for such worthy purposes as burning the logs from a clearing of land or raising a barn for garnering the sheaves from the newly-cleared acres. The men were jolly and the climate was rigorous; there was no wine or cider, for vineyards and orchards had not had time to grow. But distilleries were numerous and excise duties were low, and crude whiskey became a common and frequently a harmful beverage.

The popular conscience was touched and men began to band themselves together for the purpose of creating the custom of abstinence from alcoholic beverages. First they formed societies with moderate pledges asking their members to abstain merely from ardent spirits, but finding that too large a loophole was left by the permission to partake of fermented liquors, the "cast-iron" pledge of abstinence from *all* spirituous and fermented liquors, cider (old or new), wine and beer was insisted on.

One of the earliest societies of this class was the Sons of Temperance, which originated in the United States and was introduced into Canada in 1849. The local bodies of this order were called Divisions, and Orono Division No. 79, as I have already said, was organized on February 26th, 1850. Many other Divisions were established in the surrounding region, and indeed in all parts of the Province, and in 1851 the Parliament of Canada passed an Act incorporating the Grand and Subordinate Divisions of Canada West. Many other societies were also formed, such as the "Temperance Reformation Society of the City of Toronto," incorporated by Act of Parliament in the same year, 1851, and the "Good Templars," incorporated at a later date.

All these were genuinely democratic societies arising independently of ecclesiastical influence or political suggestion, solely, as the Act regarding one of them recited, "to suppress by precept, example, and unity of effort, the dangerous and injurious practice of drinking intoxicating liquors," and in the early stages of their history they did not seem to try to influence the making or enforcement of law as much as the correcting of bad drinking habits and the inculcation of the practice of total abstinence. The means employed were lectures, public or semi-public, music, debates, declamations, dramatic representations and the like in which the dangers of moderate drinking and the degradation of drunkenness were the chief topics.

Sometimes the arguments employed were extravagant or fantastic, as for instance when it was urged that even the smallest quantity of alcohol taken into the human system was injurious on account of the fact that some medical men had pronounced alcohol a poison, or again as when it was urged that the Bible could not be construed as approving of the use of wine for the reason that both in Hebrew and in Greek there were words for wine, one set of which were used with approval and the others with disapproval.

But these extreme forms of argument did not militate against the valid, practical reasons urged in favour of teetotalism and strict regulation of the liquor traffic, and in time these made themselves felt and were accepted by a large number of people throughout the community. Gradually the word temperance took on a new meaning, becoming practically for the majority the same as abstinence. The expression "temperance man" came before long to mean one who was committed to the policy of legal prohibition of the manufacture and sale of alcoholic beverages. And soon the voters influenced politicians and many restrictions were placed on the freedom of the persons engaged in making and selling liquors. The number of licenses was reduced, larger fees were imposed, excise and customs duties were increased, the hours in which selling could take place were reduced, the classes of persons to whom liquor might be sold were limited. These forms of restriction did not satisfy the extreme temperance people. They called for total prohibition by means of a law such as had been enacted in the State of Maine in 1851, and Parliament made an attempt to satisfy them by passing, in 1864, an Act called popularly the Dunkin Act, by which municipalities might refuse to allow the sale of alcoholic beverages within their respective limits. Some temperance men received the Act with enthusiasm, although some thought it would be ineffective, and it was voted on and carried in many municipalities. However it did not remain long in force in any but a few places. The vast majority returned to the license system. Still we must not forget that the agitation consequent on the adoption and failure of the measure did influence the public mind in favour of prohibition.

The next important parliamentary enactment was the so-called Crooks Act passed by the Ontario Legislature in 1876. It was a license law, but was supposed to be a much stricter measure than any law which had been adopted hitherto. It took away a good deal of power from the municipalities and placed it in the hands of the Provincial Government. (Appointment of license commissioners, limitation of number of licenses according to population, increase of license fees, etc.)

Then in 1878 the Parliament of Canada passed "The Canada Temperance Act of 1878," popularly known as the Scott Act. It was a prohibitory measure, a sort of improved Dunkin Act, and evoked a good deal of enthusiasm and was adopted by a good many municipalities.

In 1890 the Ontario Legislature passed an "Act to Improve the Liquor License Laws," which is generally known as the "Local Option Act," on account of the fact that it gave unequivocally to the municipalities the right to prohibit all selling of liquor. Under its operation the number of licenses was gradually reduced until by 1916 they had disappeared entirely in many rural municipalities.

Lastly, in 1916, the Ontario Legislature adopted the "Ontario Temperance Act," which is now in force, and by whose provisions we have legal prohibition of the sale of alcoholic beverages.

One may ask how such a measure came to be received with so little protest. One reason was that it was regarded as a war measure, but another more potent reason was that a large part of the Province was already under prohibition by virtue of the provisions of the Local Option Act of 1890, and even in large cities like Toronto where there were licenses these were proportionately so few in number that the persons directly interested could be disregarded by the political parties.

The agitation initiated by the teetotal societies in the middle of the nineteenth century and maintained with such persistence down at least to the last decade of the century had borne its natural fruit. The making, selling and drinking of alcoholic beverages, even of such as wine, beer and cider, were regarded as harmful and disreputable and legal enactments which seemed unlikely or even impossible to eminent publicists say of 1870 were put into force with at least the apparent approval of the vast majority in 1916.

There are some who regret that such a radical measure was the only one which, to the majority of our democratic community, seemed adequate to the suppression of the evils of drinking. Sometime perhaps in the far distant future a population may arise which may be able to sit under their own vines and enjoy all forms of the produce of these vines without abusing them, but for the present the public conscience is too sensitive on this point to tolerate full individual liberty. This sensitiveness is as genuine a feeling as any which we may hope to find in a whole community, and we must not expect it to pass away very quickly. It is likely to be persistent and to influence our laws and customs for long years to come.

II.

THE BOOKS OF THE POLITICAL PRISONERS AND EXILES OF 1838.

By J. Davis Barnett.

Part I—Introduction.

Earl Durham, when he came here in '38 as High Commissioner, thought —and we cannot but feel with him—that the Lower Canadian rebellion prisoners of '37 should have had their punishment settled upon and meted out before he came into his busy, brief lease of undefined colonial power.

However, they were easily persuaded to plead " guilty." He was anxious, for humanitarian and political reasons, to avoid the death penalty; and believing he had the power, he exiled them (temporarily, he hoped) to " pleasant " Bermuda, a country over which he had no jurisdiction, nor even on his order could its governor legally detain them.

When Durham learned, as he did through New York newspapers, that the British Cabinet who had appointed him, giving him large powers and the promise of full support, did not legalize his humane action, they nervously paying too much attention to the pettifogging comments of Brougham and similar opposition party cavillers, he resigns and sails for home before the somewhat similar cases in Upper Canada have to be settled. It is some of the experiences and indignant feeling shown in the now scarce books of these prisoners that this paper attempts to group, the bibliography being its last part.

(1) The first author is Wm. Gates, " one of the Canadian Patriots." As he tells his story, he is an American, 22 years of age, unmarried, and apparently a farmer. Says he actively sympathized with the Patriot Movement " which had for its object the liberation of the Canadas from British misrule and oppression." . . .

Gates joins the " Hunters' Lodge " at Lyne, Cape Vincent (south of Kingston), and in November, 1838, in a schooner, is with other members towed across and down the St. Lawrence to Prescott, and there takes part in a private in the battle of Windmill Point, of which he gives a clear description. The numbers in action are not given in Sir John Colborne's report sent to England, but Gates says: " The 83rd Regiment, numbering one thousand veterans, supported by twelve hundred provincial soldiers, aided by an unknown number of militia, composed the force. We were a small band of about two hundred and fifty souls, with but four days' provisions at the most, and a very scanty supply of ammunition." Though beaten, he is proud of American fighting capacity, and says, " thus ended this brief, unequal struggle, which had resulted in a loss of near six hundred killed and wounded on the part of the British, while on that of the patriot side, if I remember aright, but fourteen were killed and twenty-seven wounded."

In the endeavour to boat across to Ogdensburgh to get the doctor's forgotten instruments and medicines, he is caught by the steamer *Cobourg*, and is eventually imprisoned at Fort Henry, Kingston, and with others is tried by court martial, about which he is sarcastic.

" Our indictment being read, we were severally asked, ' Guilty or not guilty?' 'Not guilty,' was our response. The Queen's witness was asked if he recognized us, to which he replied, ' I do not.' No other questions were asked, and we were remanded back to our prison room, wondering what the sentence of the court would be on such overwhelming testimony! In a similar manner were all our comrades tried, often a dozen or fifteen at a batch, whilst the whole time occupied, from the moment they left the room till their return to it again, would not exceed generally over one hour. All that seemed necessary was to bring the culprit into the presence of the court (?) to hear his indictment, and to give him the opportunity of repeating ' guilty ' or ' not guilty,' either of which repetitions was sufficient to warrant a condemnation."

Different as was the case of these invaders, caught red-handed, from the native rebels of Lower Canada, who, indirectly, so deeply influenced Durham's life and political usefulness, the then British Executive seems worried in deciding what to do with them. After a lapse of ten months—28th September, 1839—they, unsentenced, sail in the *Buffalo* from Quebec for a port not announced to them, which proves to be a convict camp in V. D. L. (Van Dieman's Land, or Tasmania).

Gates' life there is pitiable enough for six years. Pardon comes the 13th September, 1845, but that meant he was turned adrift without means, eventually getting to Australia, and thence home by a whaling ship to New Bedford, Mass., the 31st May, 1848.

(2) The second book is by Ben Wait and his courageous, active wife. Of his offence he talks ambiguously. From Schlosser, N.Y.: "Consequently, twenty-six, all Canadians, daring fellows, ready to be sacrificed in the field or on the scaffold, penetrated, doubly armed, without hope of return, to the heart of the enemy's country, surrounded on every side by the regular infantry, lancers, volunteers, and Indians (where a few Americans came to us) on a secret mission—the object of which I am not yet at liberty to detail—to which, however, let it suffice that I declare there was nothing in the slightest degree dishonourable or disreputable attached, notwithstanding subsequent surmise and evil report.

" After a trifling, successful irruption upon a company of insulting Orange lancers, etc., far outnumbering us, whom we took, detained a short time, then dismissed, our little band retreated and dispersed, when a part were captured and sent, with twenty or more of the innocent inhabitants, to a jail where we were all separately indicted for high treason. . . ."

Judge Jones' sentence, given August 11th, 1838, was, Benjamin Wait, between the hours of 11 and 1, August the 25th, " you shall be drawn on a hurdle to the place of execution, and there hanged by the neck until you are dead, and your body shall be quartered."

The dramatic part of this book gives his wife's exertions to mitigate the death sentence, eventually amended to exile in V. D. L., and his acute suffering there.

" A wife's devotion. A Canadian heroine of sixty years ago," is Maria Wait's (*nee* Smith) story, as told by Janet Carnochan in No. 13 of the issues of the Niagara Historical Society, 1905. Both man and wife were born not far from Niagara, and she was educated by Robert Randall, who was also his early patron and friend. On Randall's tombstone, Lundy's Lane, 'tis recorded he was a "victim of colonial missrule." He probably knew it, for he was fourteen years in the Legislature, and crossed the Atlantic to give voice to the wrongs of Canada.

It is part of the pathos of this story that so many of the appeals she and others made should have been to Durham, who was sickening to death, out of power, and possessing so little influence with the government that H. Martineau indignantly mentions that they would not give him a copy of the Blue Book containing his "Report," which he desired for a friend's use.

(3) Miller's chief note of complaint is that he was treated like a slave. His case was exceptional in that he and eleven others appeared before an English as well as before a Canadian, court. See Book 19 of this list.

(4) As Wright's account is written for him by Caleb Lyon, it does not rank in interest with such personal stories as Gates' description of the battle at the Windmill, Prescott.

(5) Of Marsh I have seen but one copy, the personal property of Dr. F. H. Severance, in the Historical Museum, Delaware Park, Buffalo, Ontario losing a copy in the last fire of the Legislative buildings. For most students the synopsis of this rarity, and of Marsh's life, given in Severance's "Old Trails on the Niagara Frontier," 2nd, 1903, p. 159 to 180, will save time and patience.

(6) Snow, when I commenced this paper, was to me a singleton, and is in the reference collection of the Toronto Public Library, but the Bibliothèque Saint Sulpice, Montreal, has two copies. He says: " I entered the Patriot service with the best of motives, only wishing that our Canadian neighbours might, in the end, enjoy the same civil, religious and political freedom with which the citizens of the U. S. were blest " (3 p.). He had listened to Dr. Duncombe, who said that LIBERTY—the inestimable birthright of man—was unknown on the other side of Lake Erie. Leaving his Ohio home he, on the 4th of December, 1838, with 163 others crossed from Detroit to Windsor, where no Canadians joined them (a common experience, and the commencement of their disillusion), and after some loose fighting and wandering in the woods he was caught when he came to St. Clair River, which he was now anxious safely to recross. He was taken to Chatham, Toronto, Ft. Henry and Quebec, sailing from there in the *Buffalo* to an unknown port. After a four and one-half months' voyage he was landed at V. D. L., the French-Canadian prisoners on board being taken to Sidney, N.S.W.

(7 to 13) Sutherland—a newspaper man—the most voluminous of these otherwise amateur authors, was a prisoner but not exiled, and seems to have kept up through the daily press—as far as its editors would give him space—an agitation for the release of the U. S. exiles, and also a sort of roll-call of them. Under the title of "A Patriot General," a lively account of him is given by Justice W. R. Riddell, in Vol. 44 of the *Canadian Magazine*, Nov., 1914, and Robert B. Ross, in the *Detroit Evening News* of 1890, under the title, "The Patriot War," refers at length to Sutherland, mentioning only two of his books. This communication is reproduced in full in the "Michigan Pioneer and Historical Society collection," Vol. XXI, pp. 509-612, and was

issued as a separate octavo pamphlet, in paper covers, of 101 pages. He makes brief mention of twenty-one men figuring in the rebellion, but it is a '37, not a '38, history. Ross was from New Brunswick, and a voluntary exile from December, 1837, to the spring of 1844.

References to Sutherland may also be found in the " Michigan Collections," Vol. VII, pp. 82-92.

The other numbers in the list, and their authors, have only a secondary interest, but seemed worth recording after turning them up in the search.

This still hunt also revealed interesting rare French books, chiefly dealing with 1837 and the kindlier treated exiles to Bermuda and Australia, and do not naturally list with the records of the harsher treatment of Upper Canada's 1838 prisoners.

It is this contrasting situation that makes this story interesting to the author. Durham, of set purpose, treated the 1837 offenders leniently, hoping to heal the breach, converting the rebels and their friends into good citizens, and this generous treatment of them was the cause of his own loss of power. To get the home view of this situation it would be interesting to see a British Museum item (8154 dd. 22 (2)), " Should Lord Durham be Impeached?" By a Freeholder (?) London, 1839, 8vo.

These 1838 men, independent of nationality, stoutly maintained in court and out, to the end of their days, that their trials and unannounced sentences were illegal, that their treatment as prisoners, and eventually as felons, in the matter of food, dress, and vermin, was foul and inhuman, and their punishment in no way remedial. This is all done without result. No one pays any attention to them or their grievances. No one is impeached, none give help; as if the then public sentiment was that hardship was right, moderation wrong.

Part of the criticism of Durham's leniency by his English political opponents was that he had no legal right to choose the penalty for prisoners of state, or decide how they should be tried. It is not for a layman to say what the suspension of constitutional rights during his brief colonial reign did give or cancel, but gleaning in our statutes of this period we met: " Chapter 7, William IV, passed 4th March, 1837 (p. 31)," an Act that says transportation may be substituted for banishment, and that either may be substituted for death conviction, and defining the penalty for too early a return.

It adds something pathetic to this situation to note that the first four Canadian Acts that Victoria, the girl queen, has to sign are aimed at treason.

How far Fenian feeling influenced the invaders from the States is now difficult to trace, but it was felt to be there, and we must allow for it in estimating the situation. That the American Government could or would do nothing in mitigation of the pains of its citizens held prisoners is explained by a brief comment of O. F. Tiffany, in his Ph.D. Thesis, " The Relations of the U. S. to the Canadian Rebellion of 1837-1838," printed in Vol. No. VIII, Publications of the Buffalo Historical Society, 1905. He says this rebellion taxed the military vigilance and friendly feeling of both governments, led to international complications, and in America furnished new instances of internal conflict between State and Federal authority, contributing somewhat to the defeat of the Van Buren administration, and downfall of the Democratic party.

One of the broad features of these out-of-the-way books is that they reflect the surprise the invaders felt when the local dissatisfied Canadians did not rally to them, and that the militia they faced "shot to kill."

Also, some of them, in view of the sacrifices they had made for others' liberty, freedom and democratic governance, could never see the gravamen of their offence, so that they feel they have made a point when they contrast the harshness of their punishment among Botany Bay felons, with their original mild aspirations.

When release came no provision was made for these emaciated men to get to their homes, a whole hemisphere away, and with most it took from ten to twelve months in a whaler.

One who was wrecked coming home in such fashion left a manuscript account of his V. D. L. experiences, which ultimately reached relatives in Ontario, and is now existent and unprinted. The author failed to persuade the possessor to let him use it, which he much regrets.

Of collateral interest only is a small rare book in the author's collection, one of the earliest outputs of the Tasmanian press, when her total population (bad and good) was 21,125.

"The Van Dieman's Land Anniversary and Hobart-Town Almanack, for the year 1831, with embellishments , . . by J. Ross (price 10s.)."

Chapter 13 on the penal settlements, which "consist of three establishments remote from the main colony, and communicating with it only by water," makes it of interest to us as confirming the harsh conditions of life reflected in the exile books.

"No beasts of burden are allowed . . . and as the whole of the timber" for ship and house building "is obtained by human hands alone, the labour is often of the most excessive kind" (p. 262).

"The manner in which the men are fed during this labour may also be considered some addition to the severity of the discipline. As soon as they are called from rest in the morning they are served with a dish of porridge, composed of flour and water, and a little salt; after which they embark in the boats and row to their several wood-cutting stations, where they continue to work without any other provision until they return at night, when they are supplied with a substantial meal, the main repast of the day. If the weather should happen to be rough or the wind adverse, so as to impede the progress of the boats, this meal is sometimes delayed till late, when of course the cravings of appetite after the exercise of the day must be great" (p. 263).

A frequent complaint was that the only flesh issued for this so-called substantial meal, was mutton, and it was freely stolen by the promoted penal convict officers, through whose distributing and cooking hands it had to pass.

Part II—Book List, Giving Title Pages of the Books.

(1) Recollections of Life in Van Dieman's Land; by William Gates, one of the Canadian Patriots. "A good man commendeth his cause to the one great Patron of innocence, convinced of justice at the last, and sure of good meanwhile." Lockport: P. S. Crandall, Printer; office of the Lockport *Daily Courier*. 1850.

(2) Letters from Van Dieman's Land, written during four years' imprisonment for political offences committed in Upper Canada. By Benjamin

Wait. "It is better to fail in striking for so noble a thing as LIBERTY, than not to strike at all; for reform never dies."—Bacon. Embodying, also, letters descriptive of personal appeals in behalf of her husband, and his fellow prisoners, to the Earl of Durham, Her Majesty, and the United Legislature of the Canadas, by Mrs. B. Wait. Buffalo: A. W. Wilgus. 1843.

(3) Notes of an exile to Van Dieman's Land, comprising incidents of the Canadian rebellion in 1838, trial of the author in Canada and subsequent appearance before Her Majesty's Court in Queen's Bench in London; Imprisonment in England and transportation to Van Dieman's Land. Also an account of the horrid sufferings of six years in that land of British slavery, together with sketches of the Island, its history, productions, inhabitants, &c., &c. Slaves can breathe in England: by Linus W. Miller, Fredonia, N.Y. Printed by W. McKinstry & Co. 1846.

(4) Narrative and recollections of Van Dieman's Land during a three years' captivity of Stephen S. Wright; together with an account of the Battle of Prescott, in which he was taken prisoner; his imprisonment in Canada; trial, condemnation and transportation to Australia; his terrible sufferings in the British penal colony of Van Dieman's Land; and his return to the United States: with a copious appendix, embracing facts and documents relating to the Patriot War, now first given to the public, from the original notes and papers of Mr. Wright, and other sources. [Then follow eight lines of a Byron quotation.] By Caleb Lyon of Lyonsdale, New York. J. Winchester. New World Press. 30 Ann Street. (Entered) 1844.

(5) Seven years of my life, or a narrative of a Patriot Exile who together with eighty-two American citizens were illegally tried for rebellion in Upper Canada in 1838, and transported to Van Dieman's Land. Comprising a true account of our outrageous treatment during ten months' imprisonment in Upper Canada, and four months of horrible suffering in a transport ship on the ocean, with a true but appalling history of our cruel and unmerciful treatment during five years of unmitigated suffering on that detestable Island. Showing also the cruelty and barbarity of the British Government to the prisoners generally in that penal colony, with a concise account of the Island, its inhabitants, productions, &c., &c. By Robert Marsh. Buffalo: Faxon & Stevens. 1847.

(6) The Exile's Return: or, Narrative of Samuel Snow, who was banished to Van Dieman's Land, for participating in the Patriot War in Upper Canada, in 1838. Cleveland. Printed by Smead R. Cowles. Central Building. 1846.

(7) A letter to Her Majesty the British Queen, with letters to Lord Durham, Lord Glenelg, and Sir George Arthur: to which is added an appendix embracing a report of the testimony taken on the trial of the writer by a court martial at Toronto in Upper Canada. By Th. Jefferson Sutherland. Albany. Printed by C. Van Benthuysen. 1841.

(8) Loose Leaves from the Port Folio of a late Patriot prisoner in Canada.

"Not fame I slight—nor for her favours call.
She comes unlooked for, if she comes at all."

New York: William H. Colyer, Printer, No. 5 Hague Street. 1840.

(9) The above is by Thomas Jefferson Sutherland, and bound up with Mr. Severance's copy of it is a small pamphlet of 18 pages—on green paper—without title, dated New York, 1st July, 1841, which is an appeal on behalf of those yet held captive in Van Dieman's Land, viz.: 73 from New York State, 15 from Ohio, 3 from Michigan, and 18 to him unknown, or 109 Americans captured in Upper Canada; and he thinks 50 more captured in Lower Canada. It has copies of letters written to the American newspapers, government officers, and prominent politicians; and he gives the replies he got from Daniel Webster, Secretary of State; Fernando Wood, M.C. for N.Y.; R. C. Davies, M.C. from Dutchess Co.,; J. McKeon, M.C. from N.Y. City; from Major Davizac, who originally was aide to General Jackson at the battle of New Orleans, 1815, and afterwards chargé d' affaires for the U.S. in Holland and Naples; from C. P. Van Ness, once Governor of Vermont and Minister to Spain; from John W. Edmonds, late Senator; from F. A. Tallmadge, recorder of N.Y. City; and last from M. Munroe, a prisoner yet in exile. All are dated 1841, that is, later than the book the pamphlet is bound up with.

The purpose of this, to me, unique green pamphlet was to secure certificates that these captives were American citizens and previously of good character, so that Secretary Webster could legally advise the English Government, through the U. S. Minister at St. James', of the situation, and thus get them release or relief.

The book proper, "Loose Leaves," was written about December, 1838, when, as Sutherland says, "I was detained in the Citadel, Quebec—as a prisoner of state—even after Her Majesty's Government in England, on my appeal, had declared my court martial trial irregular. Issued as it was in a series, in newspaper form, under the title of *Stadacona Gazette*, it advertised my case outside."

To the writer its interleaved rhymes have no merit. It is interesting to note that in the Citadel these prisoners, with much spread-eagleism, celebrated Independence Day on July 4, 1838, with toasts and speeches at a good dinner, which the much-berated British Government cheerfully paid for (except the wines).

(10) In a footnote (p. 19), Sutherland says: "A work bearing title [Navy Island; or, the First Movements of the Revolution in Upper Canada] has been prepared by me, and is now ready for press. But, as I have been indicted in the U. S. court for an alleged violation of the neutrality law, in the establishment of a military force on Navy Island, in December, A.D. 1837, it would be altogether inconsistent with my interest for me to publish any account of those proceedings, for which I am to be tried, until after my trial shall have been gone through with." Probably this book was never printed, at least the author has so far met no trace of it.

(11) "A letter to Lord Brougham, in behalf of the Captive Patriots. To which is annexed a list of their names. New York, 1841." 12mo., pp. 12.

(12) "A canvass of the proceedings on the trial of William Lyon Mackenzie for an alleged violation of the neutrality laws of the United States, with a report of the testimony, etc., and a petition to the President for his

release." By Th. Jefferson Sutherland. New York: Sackett and Sargent. Printers, No. 1 Nassau St., corner of Wall. 1840. pp. 140, small 12mo.
(This is item 1282, p. 176, in the Gagnon Catalogue, No. 2.)

(13) Three Political Letters addressed to Dr. Wolfred Nelson, late of Lower Canada, now Plattsburgh, N.Y., by Th. Jefferson Sutherland. N.Y. 1840. pp. 64., 16mo.
(These refer only occasionally to Canadian troubles, being chiefly aimed at Harrison's candidature for president.)

(14) "The Empress of the Isles; or, The Lake Bravo. A romance of the Canadian struggle in 1837." By Charley Clewline. Cincinnati. Published by V. P. James, No. 167 Walnut Street."
(This is a thin 8vo. of 128 pp., of poor small print, which uses the patriot camps on the islands of the St. Lawrence as scenic backgrounds for its melodrama.)

(15) "An Adventure on a Frozen Lake; a Tale of the Canadian Rebellion of 1837-8, by J. Hunt, Jr. Cincinnati. Printed at the Ben Franklin book and job office [C. Clarke and Co.], Walnut St., above Pearl. 1855. (38 pp.) Travellers' edition, 10,000 copies." Continuously paged with it is another story, "The Massacre at Owego: An Indian Tale."
(This is literally a specimen of yellow back literature, as it has lemon-yellow paper covers, and looks very cheap.)

(16) "The Prisoner of the Border: a tale of 1838. By P. Hamilton Myers. New York. Derby and Jackson, 119 Nassau St., 1857."
(It has one chapter devoted to the battle of Windmill Point, and another to Sir George Arthur, who is the one man in this literature for whom no one has a good word. A careful historian credits him with 1,500 legal deaths.)

(17) Edward Alexander Theller was not exiled, as he, after trial, escaped at Quebec, and his two volumes are easy to get, although it is not a common book. Their title page runs: " Canada in 1837-38, showing by historical facts, the cause of the late attempted revolution, and of its failure: the present condition of the people, and their future prospects, together with the personal adventures of the author, and others who were connected with the revolution. By E. A. Theller, Brigadier-General in the Canadian republican service.

' " Who strikes at sovereign power had need strike home,
For storms that fail to blow the cedar down,
May tear the branches, but they fix the roots.'

In two volumes. Philadelphia: Henry F. Anners. New York: J. and H. G. Langley, 1841."

(18) Under the heading of " Another Patriot General," Justice Riddell, at page 220 of the *Canadian Magazine* for July, 1916, tells Theller's life story in brief, and says he hated and despised Sutherland, who for him had the same measure of contempt.

(19) "Report of the case of the Canadian prisoners, with an introduction on the Writ of Habeas Corpus, by Alfred A. Fry, of Lincoln's Inn (one of the Counsel in the case). A. Maxwell. London, 1839, pp. 106, 8vo."

(20) C. Faxon, Buffalo, in 1839 prints an 8vo. pamphlet of 14 pp., being an "Address delivered at Niagara Falls. on the evening of the 29th December, 1838, the anniversary of the burning of the *Caroline*. By Thomas L. Nichols."

For courtesies received when making this search I wish to thank G. B. Krum and staff of the Burton Historical Collection. Detroit; F. H. Severance and staff of the Buffalo Historical Society, and G. H. Locke and staff of Toronto Reference Library; but chiefly I am grateful for the personal help and interest of Aegidius Faciteux, of the Bibliothèque Saint Sulpice, Montreal.

III.

THE LATEST MILESTONES IN THE HISTORY OF CIVILIZATION.*

"The world moves by the creative power of man."

BY LT.-COL. A. E. BELCHER.

Some years ago in a municipal address I used these words: "The World Moves," to arouse the people to a sense of what was taking place and (predicting to some extent) what was rapidly coming into the work of life and the lives of the people, by the efforts of the great men who were giving their time, their means and their genius to solving problems, to producing marvels of mechanism, diving deep into the unknown depths of the mysterious; unearthing and producing what seems impossible and incredible; and it would seem that we are approaching that period where the Divine in man is becoming more apparent, as he who was created a little lower than the angels, and was given dominion over the earth and air, has commenced to reign. His conquest over material conditions, step by step, one advancement after another, has begun, and the onward march is still in progress. Man has proven himself great: he will go on and prove himself still greater. Even now we raise our heads as we observe the wonders and glories of the present day.

In this mercenary age, in the mad race and rush after the "almighty dollar," few stop to think, or try to do, what in them lieth. Thank God for an Edison, Bell, Marconi, Burbank, and others. What time have we given, or what effort have we individually made, to make the world and the people thereon better, brighter, happier; or to think out some one thing that would add to the comfort, ease the labour, or increase the blessings? Some will answer, "What can I do?" The Creator said, "Let us make man and let him have dominion over all the earth." Perhaps that which is proving us most God-like in our creative power, is the rapid advancement that has been made in, or during, the last century, especially in the last thirty-five years, and it will be interesting and educating to make some comparisons. It is difficult to determine where to commence.

Looking backwards, to me the conditions now seem to be more like a dream than a reality. It appears to me the nineteenth century is the most fascinating story of man's upward progress, or as I would prefer to say, man has exhibited his mastery of mind over matter, and proven that he partakes of some at least of the divine attributes.

There is no parallel to be found in the misty ages of the past. Let us glance at the past and compare it with the present. There is at least one billion nine hundred millions of people in the world; of this immense host there is not more than one in a million who saw the commencement of the last century. At the commencement of the twentieth century, of this innumerable multitude now living not one in a million will see its end.

*A paper read before the York Pioneer and Historical Society, March 2nd, 1915.

The question that has agitated philosophers of the past has been *how to live*. The question most interesting to us is *when to live*. Gladstone, a past thinker among men, said that "of all ages of the world the last fifty years of his life he would select." It would take volumes to picture the changes that have taken place since our forefathers wrote 1800. Centuries have come and centuries have gone, but for unparalleled and matchless achievements to benefit mankind, all the former centuries put together are not equal to the nineteenth. We should be grateful that our lot has been cast in this part of an enlightened and progressive history-making age; this is a priceless privilege; we have a heritage kings never had, and the common people never dreamed of, in the centuries of the past.

They had days of tinder boxes and no stoves, when churches and schools were unheated. Days of human slavery, unscientific diet and short life; days of bad roads and slow travel; the log cabin and the town unlighted; days of superstition and religious intolerance. Those were the days spoken of by our grandfathers as the *good old days*. You and I may be ever so poor, yet we can have more comfort and conveniences in our humble homes than the monarch and the millionaire had a hundred years ago. Many living to-day were born before the postage stamp came into use; the popular pen was the goose-quill; one of America's greatest writers learned to write by tracing the letters on the sand; books were a luxury and found only in the homes of the rich. The public school did not exist, colleges were few, and universities none. When people began writing '18 instead of '17 it was a different world. Steam had not moved a boat or a car, electricity had not begun to talk, no oil wells were giving light to the world; the great achievements of Fulton, Watt, Stephenson, Howe, Morse, Edison and hundreds of others were never heard of. From 1800 to 1912 has been the longest step the human race has ever taken on this planet.

To the amazing progress which has rapidly created a new world, this continent has contributed more than its share. Fulton started steam boats on the Hudson, Morse made wires talk, Field abolished the difference of a week between the old world and the new. Some one has said that necessity is the mother of invention. I think natural genius and God-given talents play a part. In this new world man entered the wilderness as a rude settler and God had made him a child of progress. Man touched the bitter apple and it became the golden pippin; he touched the sour grape and it became the Catawba; he touched the forked stick and it became the steel plow; he touched the rude sickle and it became the reaper; he touched the old wagon, now an iron engine; the hollow log into a steam ship; the iron wire into a steel cable. He touched the raw cotton and it became calico; and the cocoon became silken garments; he touched the sea shell with strings across its mouth and it became a piano; he touched the rude type and it became the printing press. Soon the wilderness was a garden and the solitude became a city. Where once rose the smoke of the Indian wigwam and the sound of the Medicine Man's drum, there rose instead the hum of industry, the halls of science and the temples of religion. Vices became virtues, slaves became citizens, for a man *is* the child of progress because he *is* the child of God. Steam and electricity are the twin powers of the century. To Fulton belongs the fame of the first steam boat in 1807. The birthday of our late Queen Victoria, May 24th, 1819, the first steamer that ever crossed the Atlantic, or any other ocean, started from Savannah to Liverpool and crossed in twenty-six days. That was nearly a hundred years ago. Now the time is often less than six days. Say about a hundred years ago, there was not a mile of railroad in the world. There is now a total of over 670,000 miles. Last year's earnings of all the railroads of the world was $50,000,000,000, an amount beyond human conception. In the year 1800 the revenue of England, Scotland and Ireland and all the colonies of the British Empire was less than the earnings of the New York Central Railway in 1900.

In 1802 coal was rediscovered and sent to Philadelphia, and strange as it may seem it took years before any more was shipped, and then Colonel Shoemaker was arrested for taking money under false pretences, for the people considered the stuff only good to build sidewalks with. To-day this is the universal fuel that creates power for steam on land or sea.

Before 1844, the year of my birth, there was not a foot of telegraph wire anywhere in the world. In that year, 1844, Morse sent the first message, "What God has wrought." Prior to 1858, when Cyrus Field's first Atlantic cable was laid, it took ten days to communicate between the two continents. There are now over thirty cables. In 1875 there was not a telephone in existence; it was estimated that on January 1, 1913, there were 13,570,800 in use throughout the whole world. Our present day judgment would be that the best barometer the world has had in civilization during the century is the postal system. It was in 1837 that Rowland Hill introduced the postage stamp in England. In 1800 there were only a few post offices in all this fair Dominion, and less than a hundred in the United States. To-day there are hundreds of thousands. During the year 1900 the United States alone had 23,000 postal cars, a solid train over seventeen miles long, filled with mail, weighing some 22,000 tons.

We could talk of the arts, the sciences, the press, the pulpit, education, books and hundreds of other things that have done so much for advancement; but what have the nations done during the past hundred years for humanity? As in the first years of the nineteenth century, so in the first of the twentieth—wars and rumours of wars. Then, as now, Europe trembled under marching orders; Napoleon was exiled. Whose turn will come next? In this there is food for thought, remembering the recent wars in China, the Philippines, South Africa, Turkey, the Balkans, and Mexico, and now this world-wide cruel war. We have not reached "Peace on earth and good-will to men," down nineteen bloody "Christian" centuries. Emerson exclaims, "Nothing can bring on peace but the triumph of principles." As is the case with individuals, so it is with nations. The energy and enterprises which freedom brings, count for so much in natural life, that it has revolutionized the world for a wider education, and a truer Christianity. This is the dominant feature of the most progressive race on the face of the globe. Wherever the banner of our nation has been planted it has been in behalf of a better civilization and the advancement of the brotherhood of mankind. A striking example is from the beginning of British rule in India. There came a gradual cessation of the bloody wars between native rulers and by foreign invaders, which had sacrificed so many lives and destroyed cities and homes from the earliest history of that great and densely populated peninsula. No native prince in India ever built a road. When Britain assumed the government there was not a mile of road over which a wagon could pass. There were, in 1917,

210,000 miles of the very best highways maintained by public authorities. In 1854 India had twenty-one miles of railway; in 1916 there were 35,833 miles, connecting province with province, city with city, penetrating the native states, bringing them into close relationship, carrying the native products to the seaboard, and in towns bringing to the natives the products of other parts of the world. In 1856 there were in all India 753 post offices; in 1916 there were 69,012 post offices and letter boxes. There were 86,067 miles of telegraph lines in 1916 that handled 18,129,748 paid messages. There were in 1904 36,000 miles of canals, irrigating 47,193,925 acres; not an acre of this produced before Britain's occupation. In 1866 educating the masses began, and in 1913-14 there were nearly 8,000,000 pupils in the schools of India. The exports from British India have grown from $64,000,000 in 1848 to $620,000,000 in 1914-15, while the imports during the same period grew from $41,000,000 to $555,000,000.

I have referred so much in detail to these as an example to show that all nations do not abuse imperialism nor make unrighteous war for territorial acquisition, but for the uplifting of humanity. The desire of all enlightened nations has been to improve the economic, social and moral conditions of the races. The past century, and so far in the present one, has brought many strange and unparalleled blessings to mankind. Statesmen have recognized the fact that universal education is the keynote to power, and the more we develop this the more do we unfold the divine and creative power in man.

Have the nations made as much moral as material progress? There are certainly more people living in the world than there were a hundred years ago. Are the people better from a religious point of view? The *Outlook* says, " In the beginning of the nineteenth century God was conceived as an embodied Person inhabiting some central place in the universe, the great first cause, the creator of matter and force." The present tendency is to conceive of God, not as a great first cause, but as the one holy, omnipresent, universal cause: the supreme and eternal energy from which all things proceed. These are two conceptions of the human race a hundred years apart. Voltaire, that brilliant Frenchman, predicted that " The nineteenth century would find that the Bible would be remembered only as an historical event and that men would have no more use for it." What do we find? that his name and predictions have almost been forgotten, while the Book of Books has never attracted so much attention, and its influence upon the world has never been so potent as it is to-day; never was it read and circulated so widely. It has a fast anchorage on the hearts of humanity, because we find that in the past century 300,000,000 have been circulated, while at least 500,000,000 more are found in Christian homes. It is estimated that Great Britain and the United States contribute to the churches the stupendous sum of $200,000,000 yearly. Through reading this great Book of Books, we draw inspirations that put us on a higher plane and incite loftier ideals, and what with time, opportunity and ample means we are unfolding day by day the many hidden secrets that have not as yet been revealed to us.

Some few of the marvellous and wonderful things that have always been with us, but only lately become known, I venture to draw attention to. A giant in the land, known by the name of "Hydro," was always with us, but not in evidence until the Provincial Government took him by the hand and appointed the Hon. Adam Beck to introduce him; and although he is still young he has performed great feats. From present appearance he is destined to cut a great figure in the future. Water is the natural mate of electricity. They go together and cannot get along without each other. Electricity, like water, traverses the earth, trees, clouds, etc., and comes to us at our bidding. In 1876 Edison sent a current of electricity through a vacuum and confounded the Solons, who declared that there could be no light without combustion, and no combustion without oxygen. Edison got his light without either of them.

What our forefathers were satisfied with, and what we have been depending upon, is fast disappearing. Anthracite coal will be exhausted in less than 200 years; many oil wells in Pennsylvania that produced abundantly are now dry; a hundred years ago whale oil was the chief illuminant; petroleum is from coal deposits, stored and preserved in nature's laboratory; you empty the pocket and you exhaust the supply. Human mind has now evolved so that man in a degree controls nature. The hidden divine in him is unfolding, and the way he controls nature is by loving her and working with her, never opposing—just as the Creator intended. Man can make pyramids and he can remove mountains. He can crumble the hills to dust, transport them to distant points, and then reconstruct them. The buildings of the future will be concrete; the Egyptians knew the secret and it died with them, but we have now rediscovered this inexhaustible building material. The mountains, rock-ribbed and lasting as the sun, are nothing but natural concrete—God's concrete, mixed, smelted and melted by heat and pressure and time. Man can now supply heat and pressure, and can eliminate the item of time, and can make granite in a day. Concrete is the coming material for constructions; none can dispute its qualities. While other things were becoming dearer, it was becoming cheaper. It is now serving us in many capacities; in future it will become the hand-maiden in our homes.

Take, again, the work of our own Graham Bell, of Brantford, to whom we are indebted for the telephone with all its usefulness, speed, comfort and advantages, linking man to man, home to home, town to town and nation to nation. Let it speak for itself. In October, 1907, at the initial test, telephone communication, *without wires*, was maintained between the United States Navy Yard and the cruiser *Vigilance*, a distance of five miles; the *Tennessee* kept in touch with the Navy Yard a distance of twelve miles, and on one of the Old Dominion steamers, off Cape Charles, music and messages were clearly heard a distance of twenty miles. *Talking without wires* through brick walls has been successfully accomplished. It seems only a short time since Marconi startled the world with his great achievements in wireless communication, but it is now a comparatively old story; yet, nevertheless, new features are presented day by day, until now he can send sounds over oceans, and it will not be long until a sound can be sent and will echo around the world. Man can to-day build a comparatively good dwelling in a day, and a large manufacturing plant in forty days.

Edison gave us the use of all sorts of contrivances for brilliantly lighting our streets and homes, bottling up the human voice which once had an existence and has gone, so that we who are left can recall and reproduce it at our pleasure; and made it possible for the poorest of us to have the best of music, of voice or of instruments, in our homes, besides innumerable other things in other lines, all the outcome of his genius and power over matter and the elements, which are now and always have been round and about us.

What of transportation—one of the chief factors in our business as well as our social life? Look back upon the ox team, and now see the bicycle, the automobile, the trolley, and the airplane, all of which have come to stay. Milton wrote in his day: "In future we will touch a button on the wall and a figure will spring forth to serve us." Surely Milton prophesied. Behold the submarine boats, which run under water at a high speed, with entire crews on board bottled up in their prison without discomfort.

And only a short time since, when 'phone and telegraph systems were all put out of business by a great storm of rain and wind, the Lackawanna Railway operated all their trains within a radius of one hundred miles from New York by the wireless station. Eventually we will be able to communicate one with the other by a wondrous telephone system, lately invented, viz., a pocket edition of wireless by which one is able to communicate at some distance with persons supplied with duplicate instruments.

Dr. Barringer Cox, of Bedford, New York, has an invention of a wireless apparatus which may be strapped about the waist and deftly hidden in the folds of a cloak. A picture I have seen shows Dr. Cox with his cane, or receiver, raised for a message. The apparatus has a range of eighteen miles.

We have air ships which can sail upside down, can steer against adverse currents as nicely in the air as a boat upon the water, and will shortly sail in the air across the ocean. We now know that we can send messages through the air without a wire, but it has just been announced that a man has succeeded in sending *wireless power* to some distance. This means that the new invention will dispense with wires and complete the development of navigation of the air, through **a flying machine**, which will receive its power from the ground without wires, and, avoiding the carrying of fuel and a heavy engine, will be enabled to conquer adverse winds. At present there are new facilities for travelling on land and sea. A Swiss inventor has devised a roller skate with large pneumatic wheels that will go over ordinary roads. Peter Hewitt, in trying to build an aeroplane to sail in the air, discovered a new type of boat that would travel on top of the water. The faster the boat was driven the more it rose to the surface of the water, and skimmed along the top at a tremendous rate.

What of Luther O. Burbank, the wizard in plant life? He has been enabled to grow yellow violets on trees; he has made grain bear two heads on the same stem where one grew before, so that every acre of land will yield double in the future. The wild pea he has reduced in size and made it as tender as the French pea. He has made the cactus of the desert so smooth that one can rub his face along the leaves without suffering irritation, and at the same time made it as delicious a food as the egg plant. The wild cactus of the desert can be grown on millions of acres of waste land and become as valuable as alfalfa land of to-day. Cattle will live for ten months without any water other than that which the cactus furnishes, and they fatten upon it better than on ordinary meadow grass.

Our forestry commission estimates that in twenty years our forests will all be gone; there will be little wood left to build houses with and very little wood left to make paper with. In the future straw, palmetto and cactus will furnish our paper. But in twenty years we may raise new forests, for Burbank has taken the English walnut and crossed it into the California, and in fourteen years these trees stood eighty feet high, their branches seventy-five feet across, and the trunks free from branches ten to fifteen feet in height. The studies of this great man, the products of his thought, the plants growing and developing in his garden, his ideals, purposes and plans, would mark him as a wonderful example of the divine in man.

We are seeing miracles accomplished in these days; a hundred years ago men shook their heads solemnly and said the limit of human invention had been reached. The inventions in the past few years keep us busy speculating on what may come next, for we know little of the real nature of things on earth and can loose ourselves in conjectures. Even now the wireless is used for stopping trains, independently of the engineer. We can now make daylight by artificial means. Sir Oliver Lodge says we can control the weather and supply rain or shine; if rain is wanted we must send up negative electricity. The heat of Sahara deserts can be trapped, packed and sent to all parts of the world. We have wireless telephone from a moving train, and wireless 'phones from house to house. We will be able to see each other when we are telephoning to one another, for seeing by wire is no longer a dream. Our canal boats are now drawn by "electrical mules," in the form of the trolley. Will it startle you to be informed that Professor Delage has artificially produced life? The intervention of the male parent was replaced by a purely chemical process. He obtained real sea urchins furnished with the most characteristic organs, spines, pedicels, etc. Several were able to climb up the glass sides of the vessel in which they were developed. These urchins are high in the animal scale, higher than worms and a little below insects. They have a nervous system, a well developed alimentary canal and framework of bone to which the muscles, which work the teeth, are attached. Delage formed the theory that they could be reproduced; this he did by using tannic acid for the purpose of coagulation and liquefication—just such a process as takes place in the development of an egg after fertilization.

We now see New York's forty-eight-storey building; the thirty thousand ton steamships; the trans-Atlantic wireless telegraphy; the war airships; the wonderful moving pictures; Edison's cement house that can be built in a few hours. Why not quote, "Speak to the earth, and it will teach thee."

You have all heard the expression, "There is nothing new under the sun." That phrase has come down through the ages, but the wealth of ideas men bring forth in a never-ending stream disproves it. A genius has developed an apparatus that ships may telegraph one to the other through the depths of the ocean by Morse code, when thirty miles apart; speech can be heard one-half mile distant.

A new battleship is being constructed which will be driven by electricity; even now, every task aboard ship from peeling potatoes to turning the monster gun turrets is done by electricity.

And now we have an inventor who can supply an aerial, wireless-controlled torpedo, which could be launched from the top of a tower and smash any enemy's ships. The wireless operator directing its flight can keep in touch with it and absolutely control its movements.

Wireless waves sent five miles have started the engine of a motor car.

The experiment was made at the Indiana State fair and has naturally, in the present state of the public mind, suggested new possibilities of destruction. And now they are providing us with a burglar alarm which actually shouts for help. It is called the "watchful voice." The inventor found a man with a well-nigh deafening voice which he has styled the "burglar proof tone." Its "Hello!" can be heard for miles in open country and also when the voice yells "Police! Help! Stop thief!" This voice he harnessed to his phonographic burglar alarm, and it was intensified by a mechanical process. It is the greatest thing since the automatic piano. The "watchful voice" has much to recommend it even in its mildest moods.

Remarkable success has been obtained by a young Italian engineer, who in his latest experiment fired explosives contained in a gutta-percha bag covered with fibre and enclosed in a porcelain box, which again was placed in an asbestos box with a wrought iron casing. These elaborate contrivances were sunk in the River Arno. Ulivi, the inventor, took his ray apparatus ten miles away from his objective. Within thirty minutes of receiving the signal Ulivi's apparatus exploded the sunken mines. To further test the apparatus Admiral Fornieri sank corded bombs at different points and within fifteen minutes Ulivi's apparatus had scoured the river, located the bombs and exploded them. He now intends to perfect a new apparatus capable of firing explosives within eighty miles.

Edison claims that electricity is a cure for the world's ills, but until we know more about ourselves it will be difficult to tell what can be done with electricity as a medical aid. He once asked DuBois-Reymond, the physiologist, "What makes my finger move? It is not heat, light, electricity, magnetism; what is it?" In the future we will have a new supply of electricity direct from coal without steam boilers.

Another achievement in wireless communication has been announced by the American Telephone Company. Just about three weeks after the human voice was heard at Honolulu by wireless from Arlington. Va., observers listening at the Eiffel Tower in Paris heard an engineer of the company greet them at the Arlington Station three thousand miles away. Communication is now an established fact from the Atlantic seaboard to Hawaii, a distance of 4,600 miles.

Jokes often end in truths. Some joker said that some cereals were made from peanut shells, and the man who said candy would grow in the fields proves it by producing some seventy-five different sorts of candy from alfalfa. Presently we shall have alfalfa flour, which is superior to all other flours for baking.

Coal is sunlight locked in profound sleep, and I believe there are secrets in using the power of the sun the key of which is yet to be found. Man will yet discover the ways of controlling and hoarding the sun fire as it pours into the world from the heavens. He can learn the secret of rocking the sun fire to sleep, so that he may awaken it at will. He will learn to use this fire as it comes into the world in its infinite plentitude. It is said man is destined to live in the world for millions of years to come. He must not be afraid to chain and control the heat of the sun. We will, doubtless, be attempting to signal the people of Mars within the next century. Professor Bickerton, President of the London Astronomical Society, in a late lecture on life in Mars, predicted that in the future people of the earth will be in communication with Mars.

Our wildest imagination cannot picture what our descendants will see, hear and enjoy. We do not know but the story of Aladdin's Lamp will be repeated one hundred years hence, and a fairy palace be erected in a night, because the great work of Edison, Marconi, and other inventors has stimulated hundreds of men to renewed efforts, and the thoughts of thousands of bright boys are turned toward scientific pursuits and engineering careers.

Emerson says, " We come to our own and make friends with nations which the ambitious chatter of the schools would persuade us to despise." No man may know the future or even guess what may not look foolish in half a century. The possibilities of talking over water, or sending sound thousands of miles, has always been here, but man has only *now* discovered it. We may be only beginning our conquest, and time may yet solve the problem of utilizing the tremendous power engendered by the rise and fall of the tide. If we only knew how to apply this power, we could run all the machinery used in factories, and light and heat the cities of the world and houses of the people. It was only very lately that we harnessed up the mighty Niagara; the bit is in her mouth and the hand of man controls and guides her.

The Creator has provided for the future supply of energy, as the Victoria Falls, with a volume twice as large as Niagara and twice as high, is estimated to produce thirty-five million horse power.

If nature has placed obstacles in the path of man, one by one they are being overcome. The millions of money and the years that have gone into the struggle through his science, and his brains, aye, his very life—with these nature will be overcome.

This is a new age, a new country and a new people. We are not called to go back but to go forward to higher levels of living. This is our day. We are glad and grateful to greet the unborn future. The past inspires us, the present enthralls us. The future draws us upward and on. We may respect ourselves as creative spirits, each having a special task to do what no one else can do, showing our wonderful individuality. To-day we labour to advance the life and interests of this age. Thousands of us have the habit of thinking in a large and social way. This makes us aspire to attain, and to prove that progress is the law of life. In these moments our thoughts are lofty and our vision clear. Our deeds should be noble. We become aware of our unlimited strength; self-distrust causes cowardice; therefore, we may trust ourselves to think and ponder and consider, that we may know more and more. Through knowledge we gain power. In a reasonable measure man has mastered the elements. He has conquered the earth and subdued it. He has made the air and the water to carry him. All this means an activity which is fitting to man, and proclaims him to be a creative spiritual being. Man must continue to plant new ideas which shall grow, blossom and bear fruit into new and serviceable institutions. We are capable of producing greater things still, each person filled and growing with a sense of our creative ability. Let us make the most of ourselves; the present is the child of the past, and the present can also be a creative parent of the future. For each of us there is access to all the creative power, all the goodness and all the progress which the world contains and of which human nature is capable. Change is a law of life.

This many-sided marvel rules everywhere. We have plucked the heart out of the great mystery and we stand to-day on the eve of great conquests, possessing the great conquering power which has been transmitted to us by the Creator of all things. Naturally, we respect the institutions inherited from former ages, but still more we should respect our capacity to create other institutions which shall more fully express our aspirations, and better serve every high human purpose.

There is money enough in the world to pay men to give their best thoughts in this direction. Most of us remember when a millionaire was a curiosity. Thousands of past inventions and discoveries occasion our gratitude and thanks, and we should not forget the "One Mind" that controls the universe and holds the planets in their places. Have we been but dreaming in the past, and are we thoroughly awake even now? For hath He not said, through St. Paul the Apostle, "Eye hath not seen nor ear heard, neither hath entered into the heart of man, the things which God hath prepared for them that love him." This does not mean, as so many imagine, that all this is to be revealed in the hereafter—but now! But there is a condition, and that is the greatest thing in the world—love. And the greater and truer our love, the more rapidly all will be revealed to us. David said, "Lift up your heads ye gates." So may we exclaim and act, we in our richness of the privileges of life; rich in luxuries; rich in comforts; rich in blessings; rich in companionships and friendships; rich in the gospel of salvation, which has never advanced in price, free to all; rich in the prospects of a better inheritance. Lift up your heads, acquit yourselves like men, measure up to the possibilities of your original creation in the image of your Creator, and only a little lower than the angels, and exclaim:—

> "For all that is, and for all that was,
> And ever more shall be,
> Thank God our Heavenly Father,
> Each day on bended knee."

Now, Mr. Chairman, we live in a great country; we are a great people; we acknowledge no superior; we live under the folds of a great flag, that we should all be proud to follow; that flag represents our nationality and our faith. It is the flag of three crosses, whose attributes are sacrifice, mercy and benevolence. This flag is the hope of the oppressed. It has often been assailed, but has always been carried to a triumphant place.

> "Ever victorious over the world,
> Honour it, stick to it, keep it unfurled.
> It shall not be beaten, round it we'll stand,
> The flag of old Britain, the flag of this land.
>
> For centuries it's floated on high,
> On earth and on sea, against the blue sky,
> True sailors and soldiers it never will lack,
> The flag of old Britain, the old Union Jack."

IV.

A LOYALIST OF THE ST. LAWRENCE.

An Address Delivered July 4, 1913, at Block House Point, North Hero, Vt.

BY HENRY HARMON NOBLE.

Delivered on the occasion of the erection and unveiling by the Vermont Society, Sons of the American Revolution, of a boulder and inscribed tablet in commemoration of the building in July, 1781, on this spot, of Loyal Block House, and of its builder, Captain Justus Sherwood, of the Queen's Loyal Rangers.

Published by the Ontario Historical Society, by permission of the author, Henry Harmon Noble, Essex, N.Y.

Mr. President and members of the S. A. R., Colonel Sherwood, Friends:— I cannot but express the great pleasure that I experience in that I am permitted to be present on this most auspicious and interesting occasion, but I can assure you that my pleasure would be greater, if it had been given me to be present as a spectator, instead of having been given such a prominent place in the ceremonies of the day.

Since I rashly gave my promise to Mr. Clark to deliver what your programme styles an "Historical Address," I am frank to say that I have viewed the matter with considerable trepidation. I have never pretended to any particular literary style, beyond possibly a reasonable knowledge of the correct use of the English language, and while I may have some knowledge of the history of this beautiful valley of ours, my contributions on the subject have been in the nature of monographs, and those of no great length, so that if in this effort I fall short of your expectations, I can but say with the poet of our youthful days:

"Don't view me with the critic's eye,
But pass my imperfections by."

It seems particularly fitting while the survivors of the opposing armies of the most remarkable battle of the most remarkable war in the history of the world, are commemorating together, and in amity, the fiftieth anniversary of that titanic struggle, that the Vermont Society, Sons of the American Revolution, descendants of the men who fought for the Colonies, in the struggle for American Independence, are commemorating here to-day, and on this spot, the erection of this ancient fortification, and the memory of a gallant foe, its builder.

Of the controversy over the New Hampshire Grants, and of the negotiations between Vermont and the British authorities in Canada, conducted on this very spot, it perhaps does not become me, a New Yorker, to speak. As I wrote Mr. Clark, I had hoped that perhaps that phase of this most interesting subject might have been handled by a Vermonter, and more sympathetically, than it could be by me. It has been told, in printed works, by men of Vermont whose ability in the field of history far exceeds mine, and I feel that had I the time, which I have not, I could add nothing to what has been written on the subject.

As I have said before, my historical writings have been almost entirely monographs, and they have been written, I may also say, in most instances as the result of queries that have come to me from far and wide from other seekers for "Historiæ Veritas," the truth of history regarding some matter of which apparently no one has ever before heard. My friends tell me that I am of an enquiring, not to say, inquisitive disposition, so not to belie my reputation, when these queries have come to me, I have gone to work at the matter, and literally dug it up by the roots, and by the sweat of my brow.

It was in this way, that from an enquirer in the Dominion of Canada, came to me, in the summer of 1910, the query regarding this historic spot.

I am free to say that at that time I at first had no recollection of ever having heard of it, but in the dim recesses of my memory, it came to me that in the files of that wondrous store house of lore relating to the history of our valley, the good old Plattsburgh *Republican*, edited by my old and valued friend, the late Dr. George F. Bixby, somewhere—I had seen the names, Loyal Block House—and Dutchman's Farm. And it was there that I found the key.

In the Historical Department of the Plattsburgh *Republican* for May 23, 1896, appeared this query: "British evacuation of Lake Champlain. Date wanted. Some time during the year 1896 there will be celebrated the one hundredth anniversary of the final relinquishment by the British of their Military posts on Lake Champlain after the close of the Revolution, under the Jay treaty of 1794. The ascertainment of the exact time of. this event is an important desideratum. Can any of our readers furnish data which will facilitate this inquiry? When did the British finally relinquish their possession of Lake Champlain to the United States? These military posts were at Point au Fer and Loyal Block House, or Dutchman's Farm."

At the time of the publication of this query in the *Republican*, the Honourable John B. Riley of Plattsburgh was American Consul General at Ottawa, and through him as I have understood, Dr. Bixby was enabled to publish in the next succeeding issue of the *Republican*, May 30, 1896, the following most valuable and enlightened historical document, copied through Judge Riley's kindness from the Dominion Archives at Ottawa.

Dominion Archives, Haldimand Papers. Series B. Vol. 176. Page 142.

Dutchman's Farm, 1st July, 1781.

Sir,—I arrived here yesterday with 23 men including old men, Boys & unincorporated Loyalists. I am building an oven & hutting the men; shall begin to-morrow felling timber for the block house.

Timber is not so plenty here as I expect'd & must draw it a mile at least. I find that I was mistaken in supposing the point I shewed His Excellency on the map to be the Dutchman's Farm. It is about 200 yards east of that point & being separated from it by a narrow channel makes part of the Grand Isle.

However, it is the place that I meant to point out to the General & as it is every way situated (in my opinion) to answer the purpose intended we shall proceed to get the timber & bring it together, after which if I have no orders to the contrary we shall set up the house. I think any ship in the Lake may lie with safety in the channel above mentioned. The spot on which I propose setting the Block House is a rise just at the extremity of the point about five yards higher than the other ground & may be fronted with an Abbatis of about 50 yards in length from water to water. The plain beyond this is Level & entirely clear to a distance of near one hundred yards northward.

From this point we have a southern view of the Lake near four leagues but cannot see above half a league northward on the Lake. The Isle a Motte prevents our seeing what passes to the westward between Pt. o Fare and Rush Point.

I am informed by Mr. Saunders, Ast. Engineer, that this is a bad season to cut oak, hickory & cherry or birch timber as it will be too open & brittle for any fine work, or for duration. I likewise find the rapids so low that a raft cannot be taken down till the fall of the year, but the pine timber can be cut in & formed into a raft. The hickory & oak can be cut in October, & then deliver'd at Quebec in November.

Mr. Saunders wishes to have a party of my men to assist him in getting hay at Misisquoi. I suppose I could place them in such a manner as to serve the purpose of guarding him & at the same time be able to discover any scouts from Vermont by the way of the Onion River, but I mention this only by Mr. Saunders' request. I enclose Levi Warner's report, & beg you will please to let me know His Excellency's pleasure on the different subjects herein mentioned.

I am with much respect & esteem,
Sir, your most obed't hum'l servant.
J. Sherwood.

(To) Captain Mathews.

The report of Levi Warner mentioned in the foregoing letter is as follows:

" Levi Warner arriv'd from Connect River the 28th of June & reports that Joseph Taylor, a Rebel Spy, is in Canada at Belle Isle where he has been some time secreted by the Canadians. Soon after Col. Allen's report was read & the whole Convention except two men voted to accept of Gen'l Haldimand's proposals to Vermont. Judge Jones is made Chief Justice & Cols. Wells & Alcot, Royalists, Ass't Judges for Vermont. The people on the east side almost all in favour of Gov't & intend to join with Canada if they can, but they are very much afraid of the people on the west side of the mountain who are almost all Rebels & begin to threaten Govr. Chitenten & the Allens very much."

From the Dominion Archives, Haldimand Papers, Series B. Vol. 176, at page 184, the following extract from a letter to Captain Mathews from Captain Sherwood is taken. (Capt. Mathews was Secretary to Governor Frederick Haldimand.)

Loyal Block House, July 29th, 1781.

I have built a very good and large block house & on the most advantageous spot of any on the Lake. I wish I knew whether it was to be an establish'd post as in that case it should be picqueted.

It is my humble opinion that there is not so proper a place on the Frontiers as this for the residence & departure of secret scouts & I think when the Block House is Picqueted 50 men may defend it against 300 with small arms as two or three swivels may be placed in it to advantage.

Thus we have the record, my friends, of the building one hundred and thirty-two years, to the day, of this ancient work whose erection, and its builder we here commemorate to-day.

Of detailed history, or narrative, of this work during the time it was garrisoned by British troops, none exists, save the frequent incidental mention, in the reports and correspondence in the Canadian archives.

From that source, we glean these documents of exceedingly human interest, which I trust I may be pardoned, if I take a few moments of our time to read. For these, also, we are indebted to the Historical Department of the Plattsburgh *Republican*, January 29, 1898, a copy of which I hold in my hand and from which I read:

Dominion Archives, Haldimand Papers, B. 162, Page 168.

St. John's, 22nd Jan'y, 1784.
Sir:

I take this liberty of troubling you with an affair, which I hope will not appear disagreeable nor offensive, but will interest Your Kind Interference and Assistance as you shall judge best in the matter.

I had the Honor to Command the Loyal Block House for seven or eight months During which time I was visited by many Passing and Repassing to and from the Colonies, on Acc't of which I was obliged to support the Dignity of an Officer, to be at no small expense, more than my pay was sufficient to support. Not doubting, with your Representation, but the Commander in Chief will take it into consideration. I submit the whole to your discretion, and at the same time refer you to Captain Sherwood for particulars.

I am Sir with much respect.

Your most obt. Servant,

Major Mathews,   J. Dusenbury,
Quebec.   Ens. L. B.

Dominion Archives, Haldimand Papers, B. 162, page 22.

St. John's, 28th March, 1784.

I have sold my farm at Dutchman's Point, to a Dr. Washburn of Vermont, reserving the Block House as King's property. Mr. Washburn seems very anxious to know when the King's Garrison will be withdrawn from there, and particularly requests me to inform him several days before it takes place, but I have assured him that he is not to expect any information from me on that subject without permission and direction from His Excellency the Commander in Chief.

I am with great Respect,

Sir your most obedient and most Humble servant,

J. Sherwood.

Dominion Archives. B. 155, page 116.

Return of Stores, Tools and Materials belonging to the Engineer. Department at Dutchman's Farm, the 7th of September, 1784.

Felling axes	11	Hoes	6
Broad "	1	Iron wedges	2
Augers	1	Planes	2
Chisels	1	Pick axes	6
Drawing knives	1	Saws, cross cut	2
Frowers	1	" hand	2
Grind stones (compleat)	1	" whip	1
Guages	1	Shovels, iron	2
Hay knife	1	Scythes (compleat)	1
Hammers	2	Saw box	1

(Signed) Henry Rudyard,
Com'ing Engineer in Canada.

Dominion Archives, Haldimand Papers, B. 175, page 268.

Arlington, April 15th, 1784.

Sir:—

Since peace has taken place between Great Britain and America and as in consequence thereof the British Post on the Island now called the Hero's in this State, named the Loyal Block House, will probably be evacuated some time this year.

I shall esteem it a mark of your Excellency's favour if you would direct the Commanding Officer of the Post to certify to me the time of its evacuation, that an Officer from this State may take possession thereof.

Such a favour will be gratefully acknowledged by,
Sir, your Excellency's most obedient Humble Servant,
Thos. Chittenden.
(To) His Excell'y
Gen'l Haldimand.

It is positively known that this post was garrisoned by British troops as late as September 20, 1792. This is shown by the affidavit of that date of Ebenezer Marvin, of Alburgh, which is found in Vermont Papers, Volume 30, page 181. In it he states: "The British have another post at Dutchman's Point on North Hero," and "The garrison at Dutchman's Point has never interfered in any way with the inhabitants or done any thing besides keeping their own sentries."

The exact date when this post was given up, or evacuated by the British authorities, is not shown in any records which have been accessible to the writer. The official correspondence in the Canadian Archives simply shows that the posts on Lake Champlain were to be given up by the British, some time during the summer of 1796, exactly when, a careful search of the records does not disclose. The records of the United States at Washington are equally silent on the subject.

The Adjutant-General, United States Army, under date of June 15, 1911, writes as follows: " An exhaustive search of the few records on file in the War Department for the approximate period, has resulted in failure to find any record showing the date upon which the British evacuated the posts on Lake Champlain, referred to within."

" It is possible, however, that some information on that subject may be obtained from the Department of State, Washington, D.C."

In a letter to the writer from the Secretary of State of the United States, under date of August 4, 1911, it is stated " that the archives of this Department have been examined, and that nothing concerning the evacuation by the British of the posts at Pointe au Fer, and Loyal Block House has been found."

And what of the builder?

Justus Sherwood, a native of Connecticut, and of English stock, was an early settler in New Haven, Vermont, whence he came in the year 1774, settling on the farm, on Lanesboro Street, afterwards owned by Judge Elias Bottum, and still known as the Bottum place. It was Lot No. 31 of the town as laid out under its charter from Governor Benning Wentworth of New Hampshire. I am informed by Mr. Clark, who visited the site of Justus Sherwood's old home last fall, that a house erected by Captain Sherwood is still standing there.

He was proprietor's clerk of New Haven from 1774 to 1776, when, as the records have it: " He was a Tory and fled to Canada."

But let us analyze this brief statement a little. To my mind and from the deductions I draw from a more or less close study of the subject of Tories or Loyalists generally, I claim that he whose memory we honour here to-day was a consistent Loyalist, and that by whatever name he was called, be it Loyalist or Tory, it was a badge of honour, and borne by one whose honour and constancy was never questioned, by friend or honest foe.

Holding as he did, his land in New Haven under the New Hampshire title, he was not involved in the bitter controversy between New York and Vermont known to history as the New Hampshire Grants Controversy, and consequently we must believe, and know, that he was not embittered and driven out by this internecine strife, but that from a sense of duty he left his home in Vermont, and giving up his all for him whom he considered his lawful ruler, he went away, sorrowfully as must have been, to make a new home in a new and strange land, but among men whose principles he approved.

I must confess that I have never had that bitter hatred for the English that seems to obsess some of our countrymen, of American birth, even to this day. Coming as my forbears did from old Connecticut, " the land of steady habits," and from a town where a town meeting met to discuss urgent public affairs at the outbreak of the Revolution was opened by these words, " With hearts full of loyalty and duty to our rightful Sovereign King George the Third." This is the expression of men who were subsequently second to none in their devotion to the cause of American Independence, in which, I trust I may be pardoned if I say that my own ancestors bore no inconsiderable part. When an old and highly-esteemed friend of Irish birth tells me that he firmly believes that the salvation of the whole world depends on English law, and the English sense of right and justice, I do not feel that I need make apology or defence, in that I hold to-day a brief for a patriot, for such was Justus Sherwood, a man of Anglo-Saxon blood, of the race from which I am sprung, and in whose destiny I firmly believe.

Justus Sherwood, after leaving New Haven, appears to have taken up his residence, during the war at least, at St. John's, in the neighbouring Province of Quebec, Canada. It was from here we may assume that he was commissioned a Captain, in the Partizan Corps raised from among the American Loyalists, and known as the "Queen's Loyal Rangers." This Corps was commanded by Lieutenant-Colonel John Peters, a native of Hebron, Connecticut, and also, as was Justus Sherwood, a *consistent Loyalist*.

That the Regiment, or a portion of it, was engaged at the Battle of Bennington, history relates, and it is said that in that action Captain Justus Sherwood "behaved with gallantry." Colonel Peters says of him that he was "active," that he was "a man of culture," that he was "forward in every enterprise of danger to the end of the campaign."

Of the service of the Regiment, as a Regiment, and of the services of Captain Sherwood with it, aside from the above, the details given by written history are meagre, but of the detached service of Captain Sherwood, in enterprises similar to the building of the work where we stand to-day, the Canadian Archives are filled. The trusted officer of the representative of his Sovereign in Canada, he was throughout the war, "forward," not only as his Colonel states, "in every service of danger," but in every enterprise of the Crown in Canada, which called for the services of a man of known intelligence, skill, and tried and true loyalty to his King.

The accounts of the labours of Justus Sherwood, in the land to which he "fled," are written large in the history of the Dominion.

Subsequent to the war, Justus Sherwood was granted by the Canadian Government, a tract of 1,000 acres of land near Brockville, Ontario, upon which he settled, and where he died.

My study of the history of the American Loyalists, induced by a desire for information regarding this fortification and its builder, has led me to the sincere belief that they were men imbued with motives of at least equal patriotism, to that which induced our ancestors to engage in the struggle leading to American Independence.

That the term "United Empire Loyalist" was a badge of honour in the country of their adoption, is evinced by the following "Order in Council," passed at Quebec, Monday, 9th November, 1789:—

"His Lordship intimated to the Council, that it was his wish to put a Marke of Honour upon the families who had adhered to the Unity of the Empire, and joined the Royal Standard in America before the Treaty of Separation in the year 1781."

"The Council agreeing with His Lordship, it is accordingly ordered:

"That the several Land Boards take course for preserving a Registry of the names of all persons falling under the description aforementioned to the end that their posterity may be discriminated in the Parish Registers and Rolls of the Militia of their respective District and other public Remembrancers of the Province, as proper objects, by their persevering in the Fidelity and Conduct so honourable to their ancestors, for distinguished benefits and Privileges."

"And it is also ordered that the said Land Boards may in every such case provide not only for the sons of those Loyalists, as they arrive at full age, but for their daughters also, of that age, or on their marriage."

That they were the villains that some of your Vermont writers like

Thompson and Robinson would have us believe, is not borne out by a careful study of the actual facts.

It is stated by as accurate and candid a writer as Dr. Asa Fitch, the historian of Washington County, New York, that a belief in the supposed villainy of the American Loyalists was sedulously cultivated by interested persons, who feared that they, the former owners of their lands, might return and take from the then holders, these lands which had been confiscated. Dr. Fitch mentions particularly the case of Major Philip Skene, settler of Skenesboro, now Whitehall, New York, and owner of large tracts of land in that vicinity which had been confiscated by authority of the State of New York. That children were taught in answer to the question as to which they would rather meet, " old Skene or the devil," to reply the latter.

And what was our loss was Canada's gain. In every subsequent generation have the Sherwood family been distinguished. Justus Sherwood's son, Livius Peters Sherwood, born in St. John's in 1777, was a man learned in the law, Justice of the Court of Queen's Bench, Speaker of Parliament of Upper Canada, and a Colonel in the War of 1812. His son, Edward Sherwood, removing from Brockville, Ontario, to what was subsequently selected as the Capital of the Dominion, also engaged in a distinguished career at the bar. And of his son, your honoured guest to-day, and of his long and honourable career in the public service of Canada, it is my high privilege to speak. For thirty-one years Superintendent of Dominion Police, a Lieutenant of the Governor-General's Foot Guards, Captain, Major, and Lieutenant-Colonel commanding the 43rd Rifles, a member of the Canadian Rifle Team at Wimbledon in 1885 and 1889, President of the Canadian Military Rifle League, and Captain of the Canadian Rifle Team at Bisley in 1903, Honorary Aide de Camp to Lord Minto, Earl Grey, and His Royal Highness the Duke of Connaught, Companion of the Order of St. Michael and St. George, and member Victorian Order—and his son who is here to-day, serving his King, as have his forbears, faithfully and well.

I do not know that I am called upon to point a moral to adorn a tale, but I cannot forbear to give utterance to a thought that has come to me in my study of this most interesting subject.

There is one point that I would make here to-day: That it is right to follow the dictates of one's own conscience, as did these American Loyalists. Let us say in the words of the " immortal poet ": " This above all, Horatio, first to thine own self be true, and it shall follow as the night the day, thou canst not then be false to any man."

And we Americans may well honour, as we do to-day, the memory of the American Loyalist, Justus Sherwood, the builder of Loyal Block House, true to himself and loyal to his King.

V.

THE REV. JOHN BARCLAY, M.A., THE FIRST PRESBYTERIAN MINISTER SETTLED IN KINGSTON.

By Miss A. Blanche Burt, B.A.

Our country is not rich in Church Mural Tablets, especially of the quaint and imaginatively suggestive kind so common in the old land, some of which seem in a few words to suggest the very essence of the person's life. In an old cloister in London is a tablet with the inscription: "Jane Lister, dear childe," which to me is infinitely appealing and perfectly sufficient in its simplicity.

In St. Andrew's Church, Kingston, in a prominent place near the choir, is a white marble slab with the following inscription: Sacred to the memory of The Reverend John Barclay, M.A., First Minister of St. Andrew's Church; ordained by the Presbytery of Edinburgh, Scotland, Sept. 26th, 1821; died Sept. 26th, 1826. "A man greatly beloved."

One feels almost envious as one gazes at the words: envious of the beauty of the God-like character which could inspire such a tribute.

It seems a strange coincidence that the one sermon of the Rev. John Barclay which I have found, dated Kingston, U.C., 1822, has the following text: Ephes. 5: 2. "Walk in love, as Christ also hath loved us, and hath given himself for us an offering and a sacrifice to God for a sweetsmelling savour." The paper on which the sermon is written is yellow with age, but otherwise quite intact; the handwriting small, neat and delicate, but very legible.

The sermon is too long to quote in full, but I shall give two paragraphs which will give some idea of its trend and also of the character of the man who wrote it.

"Let us do justice to the benevolent and kindly nature of the precepts of the Gospel. Let us by an observance of them in their true spirit of kindness and good will to all men shew to those who form their opinion of Christianity from the lives of those who profess it, that its precepts are precepts of love, and that they are far from fostering a harsh, censorious or uncharitable disposition, as is, alas! too often the case in half-Christians or in pretending Christians. Let us by an observance of the precepts of the Gospel in their true spirit of kindness and good will (to all men) shew to these persons who may take notice of us that their observance of them too, far from shutting them out from the innocent and cheerful and enlivened enjoyment of life, would increase their own happiness and the happiness of their associates, and let us thus lead directly to the sweeping assurance that an observance of these precepts by the whole of mankind would increase the happiness of the whole of the world."

"Say not such a one has injured me so much that I cannot walk in love with him. I must be allowed to hate him and to wish to be revengeful of him. Christians, what would have been your case if this had been the rule which had determined Christ's treatment of you? It was when you were enemies to Him that Christ died for you. Walk, therefore, in love as Christ has loved you, and given Himself for you. Cultivate a general spirit of meekness, gentleness and forbearance and charity. Do what is in your power to give occasion to the using again of this beautiful observation and noble testimony of esteem. 'Behold how these Christians love one another.' Finally, walking in love is an essential part of the necessary preparation for acceptably partaking of that solemn ordinance of the Sacrament of the Lord's Supper, which you have so nearly in view. 'If thou bring thy gift to the altar and there rememberest that thy brother hath aught against thee, leave there thy gift before the altar and go thy way; first be reconciled to thy brother and then come and offer thy gift.'"

"Now may the God of Love and of Peace be with you and bless you forever."

That the life of the speaker of these words must have been an example of his own teaching needs no greater testimony than the few words. "A man greatly beloved."

The simple and meagre facts of the life of the Rev. John Barclay are as follows: He was born at the Manse, Kettle, Fife, on July 9th, 1795, the eighth child of the Rev. Peter Barclay, D.D., the minister of the parish. He probably received his early education at the Kettle school, where his older brothers had been taught by Mr. Strachan (late Bishop Strachan). From there he went to Edinburgh College, from which he graduated with the degree of M.A. In 1819, after having been licensed to preach the Gospel, he became assistant to Mr. Walker of Collessie, a neighbouring parish, which post he held till Mr. Walker's death two years later. He was then chosen by the Presbytery of Edinburgh as minister of Kingston, Upper Canada, and ordained by them to that charge on Sept. 26th, 1821. He left Kettle Manse a month later, on Oct. 20th, 1821, to sail from Greenock for New York, en route to Kingston, to begin his ministry there.

The only account of this ministry which I have been able to discover is in the Rev. Mr. Gregg's "History of the Presbyterian Church in Canada," which is as follows:—

"In Kingston the Presbyterians had been divided into two parties known as the Scotch and American. Messrs. Smart and Bell had vainly endeavoured to re-unite them, but two congregations were formed. A handsome stone church, called St. Andrew's Church, was erected by the Scotch congregation on an acre of ground granted by the Government, and an application was made by the elders and trustees to the Presbytery of Edinburgh to appoint a minister for the congregation. They selected Mr. Barclay, who arrived in Kingston in 1822, and officiated as pastor of St. Andrew's Church till his death on the 26th September, 1826, in the thirtieth year of his age, and exactly five years after the date of his ordination. The high esteem in which he was held as a pious and devoted minister is indicated in the following words, which occur in an application made to the Edinburgh Presbytery to appoint his successor: 'The success which attended the ministerial labours of our late lamented pastor induces us to state that the greater number of points in which the gentleman whose name you may determine to insert in the accompanying call resembles him whose early removal from among us we so deeply and so justly deplore, the more acceptable will he be to us, and the more likely to promote the interests of this congregation.' "

There is no one living who remembers Mr. Barclay, and I have not been able to discover any of his writings with the exception of the sermon which I have mentioned, so that there are few facts of a personal kind about him. The following story was told to my great-aunt (a niece of the Rev. John Barclay), some years ago by an old parishioner of his: In a family in Kingston where Mr. Barclay was a frequent guest, were two little twin girls who had been given two dolls dressed as babies. One day they were missed by their nurse, and she finally traced them to the door of the Manse, where they were interviewing the housekeeper, who was telling them that the minister was not at home. When their nurse asked why they had gone to Mr. Barclay's, they replied that they wanted to get their dolls baptized.

At the time of his death Mr. Barclay was engaged to be married to a young Kingston lady—an aunt of the twins, I believe—and my great-aunt remembers seeing years ago an invoice of the household furnishing for which Mr. Barclay, in preparation for his marriage, had sent to the Old Country.

He died a few days after returning to Kingston from London, where he had ridden to hold communion services. In the words of an old newspaper clipping: "He died in the same month (as his ordination), in the fifth year of his ministry, in the flower of his manhood, deeply regretted by his congregation. The monument erected by the people stands in the old Presbyterian burying ground in the north part of the city."

VI.

HISTORY OF THE WINDSOR AND DETROIT FERRIES.

By F. J. HOLTON, D. H. BEDFORD, AND FRANCIS CLEARY.

In the early days of the eighteenth century in the Great Lakes region, transportation was to a great extent carried on by means of birch bark canoes and bateaux. A bateau was a particular kind of boat very generally used upon the large rivers and lakes in Canada. The bottom of it was perfectly flat and each end was built very sharp and exactly alike. The sides were about four feet high, and, for the convenience of the rowers, four or five benches were laid across, according to the length of the bateau. It was a heavy sort of vessel for either rowing or sailing, but preferred for the reason that it drew little water and carried large loads, and was safer on lakes or wide rivers where storms were frequent. The bateau was at times propelled by means of sails, oars, and poles. The early inhabitants brought their furs to market either in canoes or bateaux. The furs were exchanged with the traders in return for supplies, ammunition, trinkets, etc.

In this region, nearly surrounded by water, the question of transportation was a most important one, and in the early days of the nineteenth century one among the modes in vogue between Detroit and the Canadian shore, of which we have definite knowledge, was that of a log canoe owned by a man named Pierre St. Amour, who, during the period of 1820-1830 kept a small tavern about where the north-east corner of Sandwich Street and Ouellette Avenue now is, and ran his ferry from the shore there across to Detroit, and landed his passengers as might best suit them, either at Griswold Street or Woodward Avenue.

The other ferry was log canoe (No. 2), owned by a man named Francois Labalaine, who lived on the Jeanette farm, about where the Canadian Pacific Railway station now stands. He ran his ferry from the shore at that point to the Detroit side of the river. At the door of his home was hung a tin horn, four feet long, which was used by Madame Labalaine to call him from across the river when passengers were waiting to cross over.

In the winter at that period, and for a long time previous to that time when the river was frozen over, the trip was made in sleighs crossing over on the ice. They were guided by brushwood placed at intervals on each side of the course to be followed. Crossing in this way was attended by great risk of danger and even by loss of life at times. As a proof of this the following is taken from the parish records of the Church of the Assumption, Sandwich, under date of January 1st, 1785: "Time, 8 a.m.; Menard, wife of Belair, was drowned with Demer's little girl while crossing the ice on a cutter. Demer's wife, who held her one-year-old child in her arms, was rescued by her husband. Were rescued also Belair and Duroseau, who hung on to Demer's cape."

Friend Palmer, in his book, "Early Days in Detroit," published in 1906, gives the following account of a trip he made from Buffalo, N.Y., to Detroit,

40

Mich, in May, 1827: "We came from Buffalo on the steamer *Henry Clay*, Captain Norton. She was a luxurious boat and the captain was an aristocrat. While walking on the streets of Detroit he was the observed of all observers. The trip covered a period of two days and two nights. After passing by Sandwich, the first sight that greeted us was that of the Windmills—three on the Canadian side and two on the American side. On nearing Detroit a more interesting sight was that of a horse-ferry boat, Captain John Burtis, running between Detroit and the Canadian side. It was propelled by a horse walking around in an enclosure which looked like a large cheese box on a raft."

The ferry business at that time was not a very paying one, as is shown by the following statement, taken from an old record of 1828: "John Burtis filed his statement of income in 1828 of the Ferry between Detroit and the Canadian side. The income was $1,325.66 and expenses $1,704.33, leaving a deficit of $378.67."

It is very well known that Robert Fulton was the first one who successfully developed the idea of the steamboat. In 1807 he brought out the steamer *Clearmont* on the Hudson River at New York City, and for some time she made regular trips between New York and the City of Albany at a speed of five miles an hour. One of the first steam-propelled ferry boats between Detroit and the Canadian side was the *Argo* (No. 1), built by Louis Davenport, of Detroit, in 1830. It was built on the catamaran plan, being composed of two dugouts decked over and propelled by steam power. In 1836 Mr. Davenport built the steamer *United*, and in 1837 and for a number of years after that she ran as a ferry between Detroit and the Canadian side.

Captain John D. Sullivan, at one time superintendent of the Detroit & Windsor Ferry Company, in his account of the Battle of Windsor, which took place on the 4th of December, 1838, makes reference to the steamer *United*, as follows: "The old officers' quarters were occupied by Robert Motherwell and family, the father and son being respectively first and second engineers on the steamer *United* of forty tons, a ferry between Detroit and the Canadian side. This boat was some years afterwards destroyed by an explosion of her boiler, and Engineer Motherwell killed."

The *United* was under command of a Captain Clinton, father of Captain W. R. Clinton, who at a later date was for many years connected with the Detroit & Windsor Ferry Company.

The ferry *United* ran from the lower Ferry Street dock to the Griswold Street dock in Detroit. In connection with the landing on the Canadian side, the location is set forth in the following advertisement of Provett's Hotel, which appeared in 1838: "Windsor Castle Ale and Beer House. S. T. Provett respectfully informs the inhabitants of Windsor and Sandwich that he has opened a small establishment on the old country plan, where he always keeps on hand good schnaps in the Edinboro Ale, Sandwich and Detroit Beer brewed from the London recipe. Soda Water, etc., etc. A good snack in the shape of spiced beef and tongue, boiled eggs, pickled fish and crust of bread and cheese, Tarts, crackers, etc., always on hand. Moreover, a private room where an old countryman or others who prefer it may enjoy the river breeze over a jug of the best beer this country affords and their pipe and tobacco or first rate cigar. The Windsor Castle stands on the Ferry wharf between the two tailor shops."

The small, square, two-storey brick building at present standing on the wharf on the west side of Ferry Street was occupied as a customs house in the days when the first steam ferries ran from that dock to Detroit. Between the years 1845 and 1858 the ferries brought out were the *Alliance*, afterward called the *Undine;* the *Mohawk*, Captain Thomas Chilver; the *Argo* (No. 2), built by Louis Davenport, of Detroit; and the two steamers *Ottawa* and *Windsor*, built by Dr. George B. Russell, of Detroit, who was a son-in-law of Mr. Davenport.

The *Ottawa* and *Windsor* were used as ferries by the Great Western Railway between Windsor and Detroit. The *Ottawa* carried freight, and the *Windsor* carried both passengers and freight. When the late King Edward VII, as Prince of Wales, visited Canada, he arrived in Windsor at the Great

THE WATER FRONT IN THE LATE FIFTIES. (Looking toward Detroit.)
Old Type of Steam Ferry in Central Position.
(By courtesy of the Pere Marquette Railway.)

Western Railway station in September, 1860, and crossed over on the ferry *Windsor* to the Woodward Avenue dock in Detroit.

The *Argo* (No. 2), Captain James Forbes, ran on the regular ferry route until 1872. The steam ferries previous to 1858 ran from the lower Ferry Street dock in Windsor, but after 1858, in which year the town dock was built at Upper Ferry Street (Brock Street), the dock at the Lower Ferry Street was then abandoned, and the boats afterwards ran from the Brock Street dock in Windsor to the Woodward Avenue dock in Detroit. This change was made on account of the building of the old Great Western Railway into Windsor and the locating of the passenger station at the foot of Brock Street. The old passenger station is still standing, having been for a number of years past used as a freight shed.

HISTORY OF WINDSOR AND DETROIT FERRIES

The town dock at Brock Street had the distinction of being the site of the original Windsor water works, viz., the town pump, from which anyone with a horse and wagon and a barrel could fill the barrel with water and sell to anyone desiring to buy the same for the sum of fifteen cents a barrel, a common practice before the establishment of the present fine water works system in 1872.

The old Great Western Railway (now a part of the Grand Trunk system since 1882) was built into Windsor in 1853, and the passenger station built at the foot of Upper Ferry Street (Brock Street). The road was opened for traffic on the 31st of January, 1854. To connect with the railways in Detroit the company operated ferries for passengers and freight. The steamer *Transit* (No. 1) was put on the ferry between Windsor and the Third Street dock of the Michigan Central Railway of Detroit, and the steamer *Windsor*, built by Dr. Geo. B. Russell, of Detroit, was run as a ferry between Windsor and the Brush Street dock of the old Detroit and Milwaukee Railway Company.

In 1856 the Great Western Railway Company had under construction the steamer *Union*, which was built by Henry Jenking at his ship yard, which was then located at Walkerville, on the Canadian side just above Windsor, and the *Union* made her first trip in June, 1857. She was a large side-wheel steamer, with a large cabin and dining room on the upper deck, and had two smoke stacks standing side by side. She was equipped with powerful condensing engines, consisting of two cylinders placed in the hold at an angle inclined upwards to connect direct with the wheel shaft. She was put on the run between Windsor and the Michigan Central Third Street dock, Detroit.

The smaller ferries at that time burned wood for fuel, but the *Union* was one of the few coal-burning boats and had a coaling dock enclosed at the sides and located at the foot of Church Street, where the Cadwell Sand & Gravel Company now is. She was the ice-crusher of that period, and, besides helping to keep the river clear of ice in winter, often went to the assistance of the smaller boats. During the years 1857 to 1870 the *Union* was often resorted to by the residents of Windsor in crossing the river in winter when the smaller ferries were laid up on account of the ice.

After the *Union* was brought out, the *Transit* (No. 1) was used for ferrying cattle across the river until 1867. Captain Charles W. Stone was her captain for a number of years previous to that time. The propeller *Globe* was also used by the Great Western Railway for ferrying cattle across the river until March, 1866, when, at the Michigan Central Third Street dock in Detroit, owing to a rush of cattle on board, she capsized and sank. Of the eighty head on board, a number swam across the river and landed on the Canadian shore.

The steamer *Windsor*, Captain W. R. Clinton, ran until the night of the 29th of April, 1866, when, at the Brush Street dock in Detroit, she was burned. The fire started in the warehouse, and, fed by the oil stored there, burned so rapidly that it spread to the boat, cutting off all means of escape by way of the dock and leaving only one way of escape for those on board, and that was by jumping overboard into the river. Twenty-eight lives were lost by drowning. Others were rescued, a number being saved by the efforts of two sons of John Horn, of Detroit. The son, John Horn, Jr., was for years afterward the champion life-saver of the river front.

From 1854 to 1867 no cars were taken across the river on car ferries, but in 1866 the Great Western Railway Company had under construction the steamer Great Western, the first car ferry which was to take cars over the river in train-loads. She was built of iron, on the Clyde, in Scotland, brought over in sections, and put together in Henry Jenking's shipyard at Walkerville, and made her first trip on the first of January, 1867, from the slip dock at the foot of Glengarry Avenue, in Windsor, under command of Captain John D. Sullivan, who had been transferred to her from the steamer *Union*. The steamer *Great Western* was at the time of building generally spoken of as "the iron boat," being one of the first boats to be built of iron in this locality. When first built she was enclosed the entire length over the tracks, giving her much the appearance of a floating tube. This was later removed on account of the weight, leaving her deck clear. At the time she was launched many in the crowds who witnessed the launching expected to see her sink when she took to the water, but in this they were, of course, disappointed.

The steamer *Union* was continued in service until 1874, when all the trains, both passenger and freight, were taken across the river on car ferries. At that time she was under command of Captain D. Nicholson, who afterwards became superintendent of the Detroit & Windsor Ferry Company.

It was in the latter part of 1874 that Lord Dufferin, then Governor-General of Canada, in making a tour of the West, landed at the Great Western Railway station in Windsor and crossed the river on the *Union* to the Woodward Avenue dock, where he was given a great reception by the citizens of Detroit after he had landed. After being taken off the ferry run the *Union* was laid up at Sarnia, on the St. Clair River, and shortly afterwards burned to the water's edge.

In 1872 the *Transit* (No. 2), a twin-screw wheel steamer, was built at Jenking's shipyard, and in 1873 the large side-wheel steamer *Michigan* was built at the same shipyard, and both vessels added to the fleet of the Great Western Railway car ferries.

In 1858 the small side-wheel steamer *Gem* was brought out by W. P. Campbell, of Detroit, owner, and Thomas Chilver, captain; and about 1863 the side-wheel steamer *Essex*, built by Henry and Shadrach Jenking, of Walkerville. Captain George Jenking was her captain. He was noted for the care and attention he gave to the matter of dress and to his personal appearance. About 1865 the side-wheel steamer *Detroit*, W. P. Campbell, owner, and Thomas Chilver, captain, was put on the ferry between Windsor and Detroit, and ran until 1875. After the death of Captain Thomas Chilver, his son, Captain William Chilver, for a time sailed the *Detroit*.

The years from 1858 to 1870 marked the first period of the ferry development proper, and that during the time of the American Civil War period—1861-1865. After the steamer *Detroit* came on the ferry run, the steamer *Gem* was run as a ferry at Sandwich for one season during the year 1865, and ran from the town dock in Sandwich across to Clark's dry dock opposite on the Detroit side. On the dock at Sandwich at one side of the landing, and opposite the Custom House, there was a saloon kept for the accommodation of the patrons of the ferry. It was owned by a man known only by the name of "The Indiana Banker." He was one among the large colony of both Northerners and Southerners who sought a temporary refuge in Canada during the trying times of the American Civil War. From 1865 to 1870 the three regular ferries running between Detroit and Windsor were the steamers *Argo* (No. 2), Captain James Forbes; *Essex*, Captain George Jenking; and *Detroit*, Captain Thomas Chilver, and they ran from 6 in the morning until 6 at night. The steamer *Gem* then took the night run from 6 o'clock until 11 o'clock at night. The night ferry at that time was not a particularly good paying business, for Captain J. R. Innes, in his application to the Windsor town council for a license for a night ferry, dated 29th June, 1866, asked the council to be as moderate as possible in the fee charged, as the night ferry business was not a very profitable one. Of this period, among the very few remaining veterans of the ferry service is Captain James Carney, retired, of Windsor, who was mate on the steamer *Essex* from 1867 to 1870. During those years the not very powerful regular ferry boats experienced considerable trouble at times in crossing in winter when the ice was heavy.

Owing to a peculiar action of the current in the river at about the foot of

THE STEAMER GEM.
This was the first steam ferry that plied between Sandwich, C.W., and Springwells, Mich., in 1865.

Glengarry Avenue, Windsor, and extending across to the elevator on the Detroit side, there is many times an open space there when the lower river is blocked with ice, so that, in order to keep navigation open as much as possible, the open space above was taken advantage of, and the boats crossed there when possible until the regular crossing was again opened. To reach this landing it was necessary to walk along the Great Western Company's docks as far as Glengarry Avenue, and after landing at the elevator in Detroit, to cross over the tracks of the Detroit and Milwaukee Railway to get to the city proper.

In 1869 the screw-wheel steamer *Favorite* was built by John Horn, of Detroit, and in 1870 put on the ferry run, with W. L. ("Lew") Horn as captain. She was the first regular screw-wheel ferry, and was a greater success as an ice boat than any one of the side-wheel ferries had been up to that time. In 1873 John Horn bought the side-wheel steamer *General Grant*, in Sandusky, Ohio, and, with Captain Lew Horn, she ran as a ferry in the years 1873-4-5. A screw-wheel steamer, the *Clara*, Captain J. R. Innes, and owned by W. P. Campbell, ran as a ferry during the period 1870-1871.

In the spring of 1870 a new and larger side-wheel steamer was brought out by George N. Brady, of Detroit, and Captain W. R. Clinton, of Windsor. She was named the *Hope*. In their application to the Windsor town council for a license, her dimensions were given as: Length, over all, 104 feet; breadth, 25 feet; and depth of hold, 8 feet 2 inches. The *Hope* had a one-cylinder, high-pressure engine, placed in the hold just back of the middle part and inclined at an angle upwards to connect direct with the wheel shaft. Captain W. R. Clinton had always considered a side-wheel boat as the only effective ice-cutting boat, but a later experience with the *Hope* converted him over to the screw-wheel type.

It was in the heavy ice in the following winter that the *Hope* became fast in the ice and was held so for hours. At that time the screw-wheel steamer *Favorite* was making the passage across all right, and Captain Clinton at last called upon Captain Lew Horn of the *Favorite* to come to his assistance, which he did, and released the *Hope*. Captain Clinton then became convinced of the superior ice-cutting powers of the screw-wheel ferry, and in December, 1872, Messrs. Brady and Clinton brought out the screw-wheel steamer *Victoria*, the most successful ice-cutting boat at that time, and one whose model has never been improved upon, and in the main has been followed in the building of all the larger ferries since that time. She is still running regularly on the ferry after forty-three years of service.

The second period of the ferry business development was during the years 1871-1883. The regulation of the ferry service between Detroit and Windsor on the Canadian side had been granted to the town of Windsor for a term of twenty-five years by a lease from the Province of Canada, under letters patent, dated at Quebec, the 1st of October, 1863. The lease provided for boats propelled by steam, of not less than a 60-foot keel, and to have an engine power of at least 20 horses—a power just about equal to the ordinary automobile of the year 1916.

In February, 1873, Mr. Brady applied to the Windsor town council for exclusive rights to the ferry for the unexpired term of the government lease to the town of Windsor, viz., fifteen years, basing his claim on the fact that the screw-wheel steamer *Victoria* had during the previous severe winter kept the ferry service open between Detroit and Windsor. A special ferry committee of the council considered the request, but decided not to comply with it at that time. Competition from then on became keener between the rival ferries. In May, 1874, Messrs. Brady and Clinton again made application to the Windsor town council for exclusive rights to the Detroit & Windsor Ferry Co. (with the steamers *Victoria* and *Hope*), under which name they had organized the company under American letters patent, dated October 13th. 1873. At the same time the rival association, under the name of the Windsor and Detroit International Ferry Co., also made application for exclusive rights. This association was represented by W. P. Campbell, for the steamer *Detroit;* W. L. Horn, for the steamer *General Grant;* and Henry and Shadrach Jenking, for the steamer *Essex*. The steamer *Essex* had, during the period 1872-1873, been rebuilt, and nine feet added to her length.

The ferry committee of the town council, after due consideration of the two petitions, refused both requests. All five boats were now running from the Brock Street dock. They were the steamers *Hope, Victoria, Detroit, Essex* and *General Grant*. Competition was not then working in the best interests of the public, for the rivalry was carried so far in the early part of 1874 that the boat coming into the dock would attempt to crowd out the boat then lying at the dock, and at other times they would land alongside of each other two and three at a time, much to the inconvenience of the travelling public.

To endeavour to straighten out matters the town council appointed one John Foster, a bailiff at that time, to act as a ferry boat starter. For a while he was stationed at the dock and ordered the time of staying and leaving of each boat. A by-law was also passed by the Windsor town council on the 15th June, 1874, providing for the regulation of ferries of a length of not less than 75 feet and breadth not less than 19 feet—30 feet over all—and fixing the rate of fare for single passengers at five cents from April 1st to January 1st, and 10 cents from January 1st to April 1st in each year.

In 1875 the screw-wheel steamer *Fortune* was brought out by Walter E. Campbell and placed on the ferry run, and the steamer *Detroit*, Captain George Beane, was then taken to Sandwich and opened up a ferry route between the town dock in Sandwich and Clark's dry dock on the Detroit side. She ran only during the season of 1875, being destroyed by fire of mysterious origin while lying at the Sandwich dock in September, 1875. In 1876 the screw-wheel steamer *Excelsior* was brought out by John Horn, of Detroit, Lew Horn as captain, and the steamer *General Grant* was then taken off the ferry and laid up.

During the period 1875-1877 Messrs. Brady and Clinton, with the steamers *Hope* and *Victoria*, opened up the ferry route from the lower Ferry Street dock in Windsor and landed on the Detroit side at the west side of Woodward Avenue, thus leaving the Brock Street dock to the rival ferries, the steamers *Essex*, *Fortune* and *Excelsior*. About 1877 the different interests united under the name of the Detroit and Windsor Ferry Association, and on March 28th, 1878, the Windsor town council granted to W. R. Clinton and others the right to erect a gate at the Brock Street dock for the collection of fares before going aboard the boat. The lower Ferry Street dock was then abandoned for a while and all of the boats ran from the Upper Brock Street dock.

The closing of the lower Ferry dock caused considerable dissatisfaction in the western part of the town, and as time went on this increased so that on February 14th, 1881, James Lambie, a merchant at that time, and other business men and residents of the town petitioned the town council "that boats may be caused to run to both docks." As a result of the petition, and to satisfy the public generally, the ferries were again run from the lower dock in connection with the upper dock, all of the boats running alternate weeks from the upper and lower docks during the period 1881-1883. This arrangement caused a great deal of confusion and inconvenience, for many times persons would go to either one of the ferry landings only to find that the boats were running to the other landing during that week. This in time called for a remedy and that remedy was brought about chiefly through the efforts of Francis Cleary, ex-Mayor of Windsor, and Dr. John Coventry, Mayor in 1882.

At that time Mrs. Lucetta Medbury, of Detroit, was the owner of the land on the north side of Sandwich Street, extending from the corner of the Upper Ferry Street and west of the line of Ouellette Avenue. Mr. Cleary and

Dr. Coventry interviewed Mrs. Medbury, and succeeded in convincing her of the gain both to herself and to the town of Windsor by opening up Ouellette Avenue through her property to the river front and there establishing a central and permanent ferry landing. Mrs. Medbury consented to give a right of way for the street opening, and this was confirmed by a by-law—No. 393—passed by the town council of Windsor on the 20th of November, 1882.

Work on the improvements was commenced at once. A three-store, two-storey brick building and basement stood just across the proposed extension of Ouellette Avenue to the river. A Chicago firm of expert house movers was employed to move the building, which they did, taking it 150 feet west of where it then stood, and without any mishap whatever, which was considered a great engineering feat at that time, the operation being watched by crowds as the work went on. The right of way being then clear, the town filled in and graded the street to the river. A dock was built and waiting rooms, custom house, etc., erected, and in the latter part of the year 1883 the ferries commenced running from that dock, then abandoning both the upper and lower docks.

All boats running from a central dock proved to be a most satisfactory arrangement, and since that time boats have been landing at the Ouellette Avenue dock in Windsor and at the east side of Woodward Avenue in Detroit. In 1880 the screw-wheel steamer *Garland* was brought out by John Horn. of Detroit, and added to the ferry fleet. Soon after coming out the *Garland* met with an unfortunate accident while coming up the river near Wyandotte. She ran down a yacht having on board an excursion party of little children in charge of a priest. The accident resulted in the loss of a number of lives.

Shortly before the opening of the Ouellette Avenue dock the steamer *Hope* was the scene of a tragedy which, on account of its sensational features, was given much prominence. On Sunday night, August 19, 1883, while on the trip to Windsor, the passengers were startled by seeing a man, with a revolver in his hand, chase a woman around and shoot and kill her. The man proved to be a citizen of Detroit and the woman he shot was his wife. Being jealous of her, he had followed her to the boat and taken his revenge. When the boat landed in Windsor the man was arrested. A very fine point of law was raised in the case as to whether the shooting took place in American or Canadian waters. But it was finally decided that it had taken place in Canadian waters, and he was subsequently tried and convicted and hanged in the jail yard at Sandwich.

The steamer *Hope*, originally a side-wheel boat, had been changed to a screw-wheel, and later on was sold and taken to Fort Erie, on the Canadian side, opposite Buffalo, N.Y., there to be used as a ferry on the Niagara River between Fort Erie and Buffalo.

The steamer *Essex* was taken into the Ferry Association in 1878 and withdrawn from the ferry service and laid up for a while; but later on, about 1880, was taken over by the Walkerville Ferry Company to open up the ferry service between Walkerville and the opposite Detroit shore. After a short time she was sold and taken to Sarnia to be used as a ferry on the St. Clair River between Sarnia and Port Huron, and later on was destroyed by fire. The steamers *Ariel, Sappho* and *Essex* (No. 2), all screw-wheel steamers, were added to the Walkerville Ferry Company.

The steamer *Sappho* was afterwards bought by the Detroit & Windsor

HISTORY OF WINDSOR AND DETROIT FERRIES

Ferry Company, her present owners. On February 11th, 1881, the Windsor town council passed a by-law granting a lease to the Detroit, Belle Isle & Windsor Ferry Co. (the company which succeeded the Detroit & Windsor Ferry Association), the lease being for the term from April 1st, 1881, to September 29th, 1888, the latter date being the one on which would expire the lease given by the Province of Canada to the Town of Windsor in 1863 to run for a term of twenty-five years. On the 3rd of October, 1888, the ferry company was given a renewal of the lease direct from the Dominion Government to run for a period of five years. About a year later this was extended for a further term of five years, and the lease has been further renewed in 1895 and 1905.

The ferry business has been growing steadily during the years, and other and larger boats have been built, among those being the steamer *Promise*, built in Detroit in 1892, and the steamer *Pleasure*, built in West Bay City, Michigan, in 1894. The steamer *Fortune* was sold and taken to Sault Ste. Marie, Michigan, to be used in the ferry business there. Since 1894 three

Ferry Boat Britannia.

still larger boats have been built by the company. These are the steamers *Columbia*, *Britannia* and *Ste. Claire*, making altogether one of the finest fleets of ferry boats to be found anywhere.

Nothing could illustrate the growth of the ferry company better than the increased size of the later built and larger boats, as shown by the number of passengers they are licensed to carry, as compared with the smaller boat, the *Victoria*, the *Columbia* being allowed to carry 3,544 passengers and the *Victoria* 600 passengers.

During the past thirty-five years the company has developed a large summer excursion business. For a while boats ran to the Sandwich mineral springs, during the period of 1876-1886. The Sandwich springs were situated on the Canadian side, about four miles below Windsor, and were noted for a flow of sulphur water which was supposed to have curative properties for certain diseases. The water was so strongly charged with sulphur that if a silver coin was dropped into it it would almost immediately turn black. Bath houses were erected, and for a number of years the springs were well patronized until finally the flow of water stopped.

In 1885 a Mr. Geo. C. Buchanan, of Kentucky, opened an amusement park on the river front, just below the springs, and called it Brighton Beach. This only remained open for two or three seasons, and during that time the boats ran to both the Mineral Springs and Brighton Beach. Among the novelties of the Beach was a roller coaster, one of the first to be operated in this locality. Another feature was the staging of the then popular opera, " Pinafore," from the deck of a large sailing vessel anchored on the river front there. In the act where Dick Deadeye is thrown overboard (on the regular stage), in this case he was actually thrown overboard into the river.

In the early nineties there was open for a few seasons a summer resort on Fighting Island, a few miles further down the river, under the name of " Des-chree-shos-ka," an Indian term meaning " a place to catch good fish." A large casino was built for the summer trade and for a few seasons the resort was well patronized. The ferry company ran a line of boats to the island until the place was closed.

The Steamer Ste. Claire.

The last resort opened up was that of Bois Blanc Island. " Bois Blanc " is from the French, meaning " white wood." During the war of 1812-13 the celebrated Indian chief Tecumseh and his warriors encamped at Bois Blanc. It is now owned by the ferry company, and was opened to the public in 1898. A large casino and dance hall were built and the grounds improved and beautified. Since then a larger stone and steel dancing pavilion, with 20,000 square feet floor space, has been built; also a bath house, a women's building for the use of women and children only, and a modern cafe. The grounds have been still further improved by the laying out of play grounds for children and athletic fields, including six baseball diamonds. The island is situated eighteen miles below Detroit, at the head of Lake Erie, and the trip down the river is a most enjoyable one.

Belle Isle Park, owned by the City of Detroit since 1879, is a wooded island, two miles long, and contains 707 acres. It is situated three miles above the Woodward Avenue dock. In 1768 a Lieutenant George McDougall bought the island from the Ottawa and Chippewa Indian tribes for the value of about $975, and in 1879 the City of Detroit purchased it from the Barnabas Campeau heirs for $200,000. Belle Isle is noted throughout the country for its location and its beauty, and is always visited by a great number of tourists who come yearly to Detroit during the summer season. The City of Detroit has spent large sums of money in beautifying the grounds and building an aquarium, conservatories, filled with plant life from all parts of the world, and also laying out a zoological garden, covering fifteen acres, and public play grounds, the latter being located near the centre of the island. Belle Isle has for a long time been the play ground of Detroit and Windsor as well. The ferry company has for years run a line of boats to the island, with a steadily increasing patronage, so that for some time past during the summer months boats between Detroit and Belle Isle have been run every twenty minutes during the days and evenings.

It must be said to the credit of the ferry company that during all of the years past, and with the multitude of passengers carried year after year, that its record has been singularly free from accidents.

NOTE.

[The foregoing instructive article is reprinted, with revisions, from the "Silver Jubilee" number of the Windsor "Evening Record" of May 23, 1917, Windsor being then 25 years a city.—ED.]

VII.

THE FOUNDING OF KIRKFIELD, ONT.*

By A. F. Hunter.

The circumstances connected with the founding of Kirkfield, a village of some importance in Victoria County, are worthy of a place in the annals of the Province.

In the autumn of 1859, three settlers from the vicinity of Queensville, in the Township of East Gwillimbury—Jacob Dixon, Jacob Belfry, and Silas Smith—took up locations on the site of Kirkfield, built log houses, and moved their families thither, and these became the first families within the village. Dixon started the first tavern, and Silas Smith opened a general store. At this time contractors were building the Victoria Road, and this made it necessary to have a place of accommodation and trade, as the nearest place on the west was Beaverton, several miles distant. Contractors and sub-contractors and jobbers of various kinds swarmed around the new village.

Dixon's public house was a hewed log structure with one room, serving as dining-room, kitchen and bar-room, where the township council meetings of the day also were held. Smith's store had the addition of an upstairs or loft where some other gatherings took place, as for example a Good Templar's Lodge. The doorway of Belfry's house was lacking in altitude, so much so that a person of ordinary height had to bend down to enter it.

A short way south of the corners at which the new village took its rise, when the above-mentioned settlers located here, there was an old clearing near the foot of the hill, overgrown with second growth pines, with the remains of two log cabins, dwelling and stable, where the pioneer of the place, Mr. Munro, had first settled some twenty-three years earlier, but he had afterwards erected more commodious buildings on another part of the farm and had moved his family to the new home. It was while this family lived in their first abode that the first white child was born on the site of the future village in 1839—John Munro, who is still living about a mile south of the village. It was Mr. Munro, Sr., who named the village. The first white child born in Kirkfield after the beginning of the village was Robert Frederick Smith, who was born May 7, 1860, and is still living in the State of Pennsylvania, U.S.A. At the time of the origin of the village, there was a good farming settlement on the top of the hill southward.

The McKenzie family, of whom Sir William is a member, were also early residents; in fact, they owned some of the land (as a farm) upon which the village is now built.

Kirkfield is at the intersection of the Portage Road (from Lake Simcoe to Balsam Lake) and the eighth concession of Eldon. The first settlers in the

---
* In the compilation of this article the Secretary is indebted to Lt.-Col. Geo. E. Laidlaw for some interesting facts gathered from Mr. Samuel Truman, and to others.

vicinity were largely Highland Scots, both Protestant and Catholic, with a few Irish and French families.

The first schoolhouse was built in the neighbourhood, on the sixth concession of Eldon, in 1851, and the settlers built a new schoolhouse at the village about 1857.

The late Rev. John MacMurchy, Presbyterian, was the first minister to preach in the vicinity, and afterward, about the time of the starting of the village, a Methodist Church and cemetery were begun.

At first, the Kirkfield settlers got their mail at Eldon post office, which was kept by a farmer named Macready on the Portage Road, three miles west of Kirkfield, but later (in or about 1860) Silas Smith got Kirkfield post office in his store, and was the first postmaster at the new village.

Some time later Smith took the contract for corduroying a stretch of the Carden Road, and also took out spars and masts, having as many as seven timber shanties at one time, but fire burnt up the whole work before it was off his hands and paid for, and he was a heavy loser. On account of his misfortunes Smith left Kirkfield in the spring of 1865, and settled at Sugar Creek, near Franklin, Pa., where he opened another store. In that vicinity he remained for the rest of his life, and died at Franklin so recently as March 13th, 1918.

Other settlers in or near Kirkfield at the time were Patrick Mooney, who lived close to the village at its northern end, on the Carden Road, and his son-in-law, Macdonald, who opened a beer tavern in the village shortly after its beginning.

The environs of Kirkfield had then, as now, some natural interest. Grass River, whose water flows to Lake Simcoe, and along which the Trent Valley canal now runs, was known by this name in that day, and then also had abundant water, enough for boating with canoes and punts. At Balsam Lake, where the family of Mr. McInnis lived, fish, including eels, were caught in abundance, and the lake opened the way into the wide country to the northward, and also along the Trent Valley chain of lakes.

Ontario Historical Society

PAPERS AND RECORDS

VOL. XVII

TORONTO
PUBLISHED BY THE SOCIETY
1919

CONTENTS

I. Leaves from an Unpublished Volume. (President's Address, 1919.) GEO. R. PATTULLO, ESQ. 5
II. The Retreat of Proctor and Tecumseh. JUDGE C. O. ERMATINGER 11
III. History of Presbyterianism in the County of Oxford. REV. W. T. McMULLEN, D.D. 22
IV. Women in Pioneer Life. MISS AMELIA POLDON 25
V. The Six Nations Indians. MISS A. I. G. Gilkison 30
VI. Old Stage Coach Days in Oxford County. MR. W. B. HOBSON 33
VII. The Former Names of the Thames River. MR. JAMES SINCLAIR 37
VIII. The Amishman. JUDGE GEORGE SMITH 40
IX. Waterloo County History. W. H. BREITHAUPT, C.E. 43
X. Williamstown, an Historic Village. MISS JANET CARNOCHAN 48
XI. Some Unusual Sources of Information in the Toronto Reference Library on the Canadian Rebellions of 1837-8. MISS FRANCES M. STATON 58
XII. Canada's Part in Freeing the Slave. FRED. LANDON, M.A. 74
XIII. The Mosquito in Upper Canada. HON. JUSTICE RIDDELL 85
XIV. Gananoque's First Public School, 1816. MR. FRANK EAMES 90
XV. British Naval Officers of a Century Ago. LT.-COL. D. H. MACLAREN 106
XVI. A Concise History of the Late Rebellion in Upper Canada to the Evacuation of Navy Island (1838). GEORGE COVENTRY 113

I.

LEAVES FROM AN UNPUBLISHED VOLUME.

By Geo. R. Pattullo.

The President's Address, June 16th, 1919.

Settlement first began in the County of Oxford during the last five years of the eighteenth century. Lots were sold in the township of Blenheim, and in one or two other sections of the county, as early as 1797. Naturally settlement was slow and straggling for a number of years. It followed pretty closely the centre line of the county, since known as the Governor's Road or Dundas Street, and along the River Thames between Woodstock and Ingersoll. It was not until between 1820 and 1840 that there was any considerable settlement even in what have since become the City of Woodstock and the Town of Ingersoll.

There were then practically no transportation facilities whatever. Communication between isolated settlers and settlements was by trail and in many cases the distances covered were great. The usual routine common to pioneer life in Canada followed, though slowly, on foot, by oxen or horseback, by waggon, next buggy, next by stage coach, next by steam cars, now by auto, and lastly by aeroplane. The latter is not yet in general use, but the writer is still young enough to hope to see it.

Of the topographical features of the county it may be said that the land is generally undulating and rolling. There are no very high hills, although the ridge running north and south from Woodstock is part of the watershed in Western Ontario. The Thames flows westward from here to Lake St. Clair, while the River Nith joins the Grand River and flows eastward. These are our only rivers.

The County of Oxford has been usually described as the "Garden of Canada," a name first applied to it by the Hon. George Brown on an election tour. But this description, since generally appropriated, may perhaps be due to local pride. The truth is that there are many counties in the Province of Ontario, whose fertile fields, fruitful orchards, sleek and lowing herds, great and varied manufacturing establishments, prosperous and progressive business men, and, above all, the numerous school houses that dot the landscape, entitle them to that description equally with the County of Oxford.

We owe much to the early settlers of the county and of the Province for the place names that they have brought with them from the old land. These names link the old world with the new. The surrounding counties of Norfolk, Middlesex, Perth and Waterloo suggest Old Country counties and memories. Oxford itself reveals Britain's famous university, while the County of Brant very appropriately stands as a monument to the great Canadian Indian Chief. The names of Norwich, Woodstock, Tavistock, Blandford, Blenheim, remind us of England and of England's great duke; Embro,

Braemar, Golspie, Strathallan and Peebles recall Scotland, from which so many Oxford pioneers came. Milldale reminds us that the English Quakers were also early and most worthy residents in Oxford County; Cassel in the township of East Zorra denotes the presence of a large and highly respected German element—the Amishman about whom our friend, Judge Smith, has recently written a volume.

Zorra, oddly enough, though the home of the large Highland settlement in the County, is of Spanish origin. Early Canadian pioneers are represented by Ingersoll, Tillsonburg, Brownsville, Plattsville, Oliver, Gobles, Wolverton and others. Eastwood recalls especially the large settlement of gentlefolk, representatives of the army, navy and official life of England, who followed Governor Simcoe to Canada, and whose wealth, education and culture and withal Old Country characteristics and habits, have left a refining impress on the life of the community. The village of Eastwood was named after Mrs. East, a sister of Admiral Vansittart.

Such are some of the material and general characteristics of Oxford County. They are important, but, after all, not the most important essentials, however generously bestowed. Things material do not make a community or a country. It is the people, the good, honest, high-minded, God-fearing men and women. In this respect, too, Oxford County is fortunate.

Her population is typical of many other Canadian communities: Numbering about fifty thousand of the several chief English-speaking nations, the Scotch—both Lowland and Highland—were probably the most numerous. The Lowlanders are more scattered, but in the aggregate probably outnumber the Highlanders, the latter being located in an almost solid block in parts of East and West Zorra. Next come the English, followed by the Germans, Irish, United Empire Loyalists, and a considerable element from the United States and the Maritime Provinces, particularly New Brunswick. These are the sources whence came the early pioneers of Oxford and their children. The present population are the human amalgam which represent them, and which constitute the brain and brawn of our citizenship to-day.

The early achievements of the men and women of Oxford are chiefly those common to pioneer life in Canada. Though in a measure commonplace, they were nevertheless heroic. Unlike some frontier communities, they could boast but little of martial glory. Their victories were rather those of peace, than of war. Hard work and high purposes and an abiding faith were their weapons of victory; by them they felled the forests, made the wilderness to disappear and caused the fields to "bloom and blossom as the rose." By them municipal institutions were founded. courts of law established, churches and school houses built, and the blessings of law and order and of the gospel and of education were thereby secured for their children. Those are high achievements—the highest attainable in the history of the County or the Province during the last century.

Few counties have contributed more of their sons to the church—four moderators of the Presbyterian Church: Dr. McMullen, Dr. Robertson, Dr. J. L. McKay (Formosa) and Dr. R. P. MacKay; four bishops of the Anglican Church: Sweatman of Toronto, Fauquier of Algoma, Farthing of Montreal and Mills of Ontario; and there is still much first class material for one or more additional bishops in this fruitful field of ecclesiastical and episcopal promotion. Another of her sons has indeed already had a very narrow escape from episcopal distinction—mayhap he was spared for a bigger and even more important work. McLaurin, of the Baptist College, became a great preacher and successful missionary in India for many years, while Crosby of the Methodists was one of the pioneer missionaries to British Columbia.

The great Methodist body too—notwithstanding its system of itinerancy—has contributed some half dozen or more presidents of Conferences from the County of Oxford. The bench, the bar, college halls and professors' chairs, medicine, engineering, journalism, literature have also worthy representatives from the old county, as also the army and navy and the great business world. Two, at least, of her sons were among the great missionaries of the last century—Robertson of the Canadian Northwest and McKay of Formosa, representatives respectively of the home and foreign mission interests of the great Presbyterian church. Scores of prominent clergy of various denominations have gone forth from the County's borders. Some of her sons have occupied and are now occupying seats on the Bench and in the High Courts of the country, from Ottawa to Victoria. Some have held high military positions in India and elsewhere; while three of her gallant sons, McKenzie, Leonard and Findlay—have sealed with their blood their love for British freedom at Ridgeway, Haartz River and Paardeburg. The United States Senate and Congress in many States of the Union have drawn largely from the County of Oxford for high statesmanship, while several of the millionaires of the United States, not an enviable distinction at present, look back with pride and pleasure to the County of Oxford as their birthplace.

A not unimportant characteristic of Oxford, is healthfulness. This is shown by the numbers of years so many of the pioneers have lived. There died recently, one aged 95, who was able to discharge the duties of his office until the last week of his life; and an old lady aged 90, both of whom had lived for three-quarters of a century in the County. And one old and worthy pioneer—Mr. Maurice Egan, died at the age of 100. In the county House of Refuge for aged people, there were at one time three inmates over 90 years of age, one of them being 98, and no less than twenty-three over 80 years of age.

But long public service, as well as long life, seems to be a rule in Oxford County. One of our most prominent ministers retired nine years ago after a faithful pastorate of forty-five years in the same church. He is now Pastor Emeritus, in the enjoyment of excellent health at the age of 87, and it may be doubted if there are many younger clergymen who to-day surpass him in clarity of thought, strength of statement and purity of diction. You have to-day had evidence of his continued vigor of both mind and body.

There is another side, however, to this characteristic of life in Oxford which to some people may not be quite so satisfactory. In a political sense the longevity of public officials is deeply discouraging to those who wait. Once in office an Oxford official declines either to die or retire. There have been thus far only four Judges, three Registrars, four Crown Attorneys, five Sheriffs and four Surrogate Clerks, in a period extending over nearly a century. Thomas Horner, who was one of the first parliamentary representatives of the County, was also the first Registrar. My predecessor, the late Colonel James Ingersoll, held the position for 52 years and I for over 33, leaving a comfortable margin yet for me. A Deputy Registrar of Colonel Ingersoll and myself died after 35 years of service. There were recently in the County six Chief Officials whose terms of service are as follows: 60 years, 57 years, 40 years, 34 years, 39 years and 26 years respectively. Some of these have lived through the lives of both Conservative and Liberal Governments and some of the younger of them have high hopes that they will have equally good luck!

The political influence of Oxford has been unduly great. In this respect it ranks with only two or three counties—Kingston, whose life-long representative with only a single break, was the Right Hon. Sir John A. Mac-Donald as Prime Minister—Lambton, so long continuously represented by the Hon. Alexander McKenzie, also a prime minister, and Quebec West, the constituency of the Right Hon. Sir Wilfrid Laurier, Prime Minister.

Oxford has had for its representatives no less than three prime ministers: Sir Francis Hincks, Hon. George Brown, and Sir Oliver Mowat. Of cabinet ministers it had also Hon. Dr. Connor, Hon. Wm. McDougall, Hon. Adam Crooks, Right Hon. Sir Richard Cartwright, and Hon. James Sutherland. Other cabinet ministers who sought, but in vain, the suffrages of the constituency, were: Hon. J. C. Morrison, Hon. Stephen Richards and Hon. Isaac Buchanan; these were not of Oxford's political faith.

Among other representatives of the County, apart from those who now occupy those positions, may be mentioned the late E. V. Bodwell, Lt.-Col. Skinner, Thomas Oliver, Adam Oliver, Andrew Pattullo, Dr. Angus McKay, Col. Munroe and Dr. Andrew McKay. It is suspected also that another distinguished representative of Oxford County was the Hon. N. W. Rowell, president of the Privy Council, in the Union Government. When leader of the Opposition in the local legislature he wielded an exceptionally powerful influence, and had he remained in the legislature, there is little doubt that a second premier could have been claimed for Oxford County.

Politics in the early days of Oxford were exciting. There was open voting and two days' polling, followed a week later by the official declaration, which was generally made the occasion of a political parade, with bands of music and flying banners by the victorious party and its friends.

George Brown and his paper, *The Globe,* were the predominant political influences in Oxford in the 50's. No one who has not seen or heard him can imagine Mr. Brown's extraordinary influence over a political audience and the tremendous political power that he wielded throughout the County, and indeed over the whole Province. As a boy, I have seen him face a turbulent meeting and in five minutes have it completely under his control, so that at the close the audience rose en masse and refused to listen to the opposing speaker. Eloquent Brown undoubtedly was; his oratory was of the torrential order and his tremendous enthusiasm bore down everything before it. His discussion of "Rep. by Pop.," which at that time was the great question championed by him in Upper Canada, was most forcible and convincing, and always excited enthusiasm among both friends and foes—so that in Upper Canada both political parties gradually came to favor Mr. Brown's opinions.

As a representative of North Oxford in the legislature for nearly 25 years, while premier of Ontario, Sir Oliver Mowat practically formulated and carried out the policy of the Liberal party during all that time, while one of his colleagues, Hon. Adam Crooks, was also a very able man, who carried on successfully and with necessary changes, the good work of the founder of Ontario's educational system, the Rev. Dr. Egerton Ryerson.

Right Hon. Sir Richard Cartwright represented the same constituency for many years in the House of Commons; he was perhaps the strongest parliamentarian Canada has ever had, and exercised a great influence upon the politics of his party and of the Dominion.

In the 30's the Oxfords, North and South, were only one political division and it extended considerably beyond the bounds of the present county—almost from Dundas to London. There was then open voting, and an electoral contest lasted for five days. The polling place was on the height of land midway between Woodstock and Ingersoll, at the fork of the Governor's Road, known as Marin's Stand. There was little or no money going at the elections, perhaps for the reason that there was little or no money in the country. But there was plenty of whiskey. It cost only 10 cents a gallon, and later a shilling. Each party supplied its friends with all they wanted. A barrel on each side of the road was tapped and tin cups supplied. At a later date, when Sir Francis Hincks was a candidate in North Oxford, the late F. R. Ball, K.C., who recently died, after fifty years of service as Clerk of the Peace for the County, was selected as election agent by Sir Francis. The latter forwarded him a blank cheque with which to cover the necessary election expenses.

The thrifty young agent, however, simply sent out a barrel of whiskey to the polling place, and after the return of Sir Francis he sent back the cheque unused, advising Sir Francis that the only expense incurred was the purchase of a barrel of whiskey.

Cynics and temperance extremists may deplore such election methods, but it must be remembered that there was no corruption or purchase of votes, in thus supplying whiskey for the electors at that time. It was merely the customary and recognized form of entertainment, and though there might be many a "bad head" next morning, the conscientious and intelligent electors went their way with no guilty consciousness of having sold a freeman's franchise for a few dirty dollars—as too often is the case in present elections.

But perhaps the personal reminiscences and associations of Oxford boys are recalled with even more pleasure than their substantial achievements at home and abroad. It may be that one thinks kindly of the old church to which he was accustomed to go on Sunday morning, or of the old clergyman—Donald McKenzie of Embro, William Robertson of Chesterfield, Canon Bettridge or Rector Revell of Old St. Paul's, Beardsall, Geary or Bates of the Baptists, Griffin or Russ of the Methodists, Daniel Allen, Dr. McMullen or Dr. W. A. McKay of Woodstock, Dr. Fyfe, Principal of the C. L. Institute, now Woodstock College, and several of his successors, and others familiar to our fathers and ourselves. Or it may be perhaps the old school house, or the teachers, George Strachan or D. H. Hunter of the old grammar school, Henry Izzard or Goodwin of the public schools in Woodstock, McLean and Ainslie of Blenheim, Carlyle and others. It may be the sacrament at Embro—a really great occasion, and attended by hundreds from far and near. It may be the mid-week prayer meeting, though then as now there were among the male portion of the community those who would fain neglect it. Or it may be that one thinks gratefully of his favorite physician, Dr. Watt, Dr. Turquand, Dr. Beard or Dr. Scott of Woodstock, Drs. Clark and Rounds of Blenheim, Dr. Duncan of Embro, Drs. Cook and Carrol or Thrall of Norwich, and others.

The comradeship of the Oxford Rifles may recall many pleasant memories to not a few. Its first commanding officer, Col. W. S. Light, Brigade Major of the Western District, an exceedingly handsome officer, Col. Hugh Richardson, Col. Thos. Cowan, Col. H. B. Beard, K.C., Col. James Munroe, Col. Fred McQueen, Col. John White and others.

Or it may be the delights of sugar-making time in the early spring when both lads and lasses joined in the fun and the taffy pull, or the sleigh ride with jingling bells and sleigh boxes filled with straw, blankets and robes, and when sleighing lasted not for a week or a month, but for three or four months continuously; or the logging bee, or the barn raising when neighbor gathered to help neighbor as well as to enjoy the social gathering, which usually ended up with a dance; or the fall threshing. Then there were the spelling matches and the singing schools and debating clubs—delightful evening gatherings during the winter months—while in the summer the local horse races, without race-track or professional training, cricket matches and baseball games, including those of the then champions of Canada, the celebrated young Canadians of Woodstock. These things and many more served to brighten the lives of the early pioneers and their children, and they will revive many a pleasant recollection in the minds of their successors.

II.

THE RETREAT OF PROCTOR AND TECUMSEH

By His Honour Judge Ermatinger.

We are prone to contrast the reputed words of Tecumseh when he first saw General Brock—" This is a man !"—with his language addressed to General Proctor, when the latter decided that a retreat from the western front was necessary, taunting him with lack of courage. " Father," he is reported to have said, " you have got the arms and ammunition which our great father sent for his red children. If you intend to retreat give them to us, and you may go and welcome for us."

Nevertheless Proctor had won distinction and a Brigadier-Generalship by his conduct of the Battle with Winchester's forces at the River Raisin on the 22nd of the previous January, and earned the encomium of Chief Justice Woodward in his intercepted letter to Secretary Munroe in which he wrote: " The operations of the British Commander are marked by the same minute correctness of judgment in this instance, and the same boldness of conception and execution which distinguished in the former instance his illustrious predecessor, General Brock. It is a military movement of equal and in fact of greater splendor."

Proctor's conduct subsequent to his victory at the River Raisin has been the subject of much discussion and animadversion ever since. Chief Justice Woodward's encomium concerning his conduct of that action was so strong as to suggest, (coupled with the fact of the letter having fallen into British hands) an endeavor on the part of the writer to ingratiate himself with the British Commander for some ulterior purpose. The encomium, however, was not altogether undeserved. Proctor had acted with boldness and promptitude, though he had a force inferior in numbers and nondescript to some extent in character—though augmented by almost as many Indians.

His movements and actions during the spring were by no means discreditable when the great disparity between his forces and those at the command of General Harrison is considered. Proctor had crossed the lake, nevertheless, in April and attacked the enemy's entrenchments in the beginning of May—with disastrous results to a considerable part of Harrison's force on May 5th, a loss of some 1200 men in killed and prisoners who had taken part in a sally. Proctor's conduct, however, throughout—both before and after the retreat from Amherstburg began—has been the subject of so much adverse criticism by military men as to make a defence of it by one unskilled and inexperienced in such matters a hopeless task, even if evidence to justify a defence were available.

I find in the appendix to Casselman's edition of Richardson's " War of 1812," a brief note of the career of Major-General Harry Proctor, in which the author of the edition states:—" In opposition to the general verdict of most historians of this war, I have come to the conclusion that Proctor was used disgracefully. No account has been taken of the valuable services he performed; with less than 1000 whites and a very unreliable Indian following he destroyed three American armies as large as his own. Reinforcements he asked for were not sent. His soldiers became stale and dispirited because of neglect from headquarters. The defeat at Moraviantown was the inevitable result of this neglect."

The destruction of these armies (so small in comparison with present day forces) was nevertheless unavailing, it may be replied. Of what value then were his services? may be asked.

Richardson himself, who was present throughout the campaign, is unsparing in his denunciation of Proctor's conduct or lack of same—not only on the Thames, but in the second expedition, and he even criticized adversely his generalship at the commencement of the Raisin River battle. "In this affair," he wrote, "which, if properly conducted, would have been attended by little loss to the assailants, we had 24 rank and file killed and 11 officers and 158 rank and file wounded, exclusive of sergeants whose number is not recorded."

Lieut. Bullock, the senior and only officer of the 41st regiment who escaped from the field of Moraviantown, in his report to a superior officer, gives a detailed account of the retreat from Amherstburg to the close of the battle at Moraviantown, giving facts and circumstances apparently quite inconsistent with proper supervision of his troops by Proctor, through continued absence and lack of orders, while the disposition of the force under his command, to receive the enemy's attack, has been generally condemned. Lieut. Bullock closes his report with the following significant sentence: "Having been thus far particular in stating everything to which I was an eye-witness and which has come to my knowledge, I beg leave to remark that, from the well known character of the regiment, any observations emanating from those whose interest it is to cast a direct or indirect reflection upon its conduct, cannot be received with too much distrust."

This closing warning no doubt refers to observations made by General Proctor himself.

Lieut. Bullock had been requested to "state most minutely the nature of the ground on which the regiment was formed for action, the manner in which it was formed, the number then of the regiment actually in the field, etc., if it had received provisions regularly, was complete in ammunition and could have got supplies when required and, in short, every circumstance that happened from the commencement of the retreat from Amherstburg relative to the regiment."

Bullock was moreover warned of reports afloat, disgraceful in the extreme to the regiment and every individual with it that day, and that Proctor's report highly censured the conduct of the regiment.

Lieut. Bullock replied to this as follows: "As a platoon officer, I cannot positively say whether the whole regiment was complete with ammunition or not, but this I can say, a number of men who escaped from the enemy that day were not complete before the action commenced, and this I am inclined to think was the case with many of those killed or taken, and in the event of expending the ammunition in their pouches they could not have received a fresh supply, the whole of the spare ammunition being taken by the enemy some hours before the action, which circumstance was known to many of the regiment. I now proceed to give every other information required in your letter as correctly as my rank and situation on various occasions enabled me to observe.

"The force under Major-General Proctor, consisting of the 1st Batt., 41st Regiment, a few of the 10th Veterans (about 18 or 20), some artillery and a body of Indians retreated from Amherstburg in September last to Sandwich, from whence we retired on the 27th of the same month to the River Thames, the banks of which at a place called Chatham (54 miles from Sandwich and 70 from Amherstburg) General Proctor had promised the Indians to fortify with a view to await the enemy. On this retreat I commanded the grenadier company. We arrived within three miles of Chatham at a place called Dolson's, on the 1st of October. On the 3rd General Proctor was at Moraviantown, 26 miles from us, on the road leading to the head of Lake Ontario when information was received that the enemy was within 4 or 5 miles of us, and we retired 1½ miles by order of Lieut.-Col. Warburton, and formed on the bank of the river in expectation of an attack. At the expiration of half an hour we retired to Chatham. The Indians were encamped on the opposite bank of the river, and on our arrival sent to me to say that we should not proceed beyond the ground we then occupied— that Gen. Proctor had promised them to await the enemy on that ground and fight them, and had also promised to erect fortifications there. After endeavoring to reason with them Lieut.-Col. Warburton was compelled to remain there for the night and informed the Indians through Colonel Elliott of the Indian Department that whatever had been promised by Gen. Proctor should be fulfilled as far as he (Lieut.-Col. Warburton) had it in his power. I was then ordered on picquet with the grenadier company and at the same time received such particular instructions from Lieut.-Cols. Warburton and Evans that I have no doubt they expected the enemy that night. Captain Chambers of the Qr.-Mr. General's Department accompanied me and pointed out the ground my picquet was to occupy, which was one mile and a half in advance towards the enemy. Early next morning the picquet was called in. On arriving at Chatham where the rest of the regiment had passed the night, provisions were issued; the meat was raw and before it could be divided we were ordered to march in consequence of the approach of the enemy. We retired about six miles when we were joined by Gen. Proctor on his return from Moraviantown. We marched all day; the roads were excessively bad. About eight o'clock in the evening Capt. Muir's company was halted at Richardson's, six miles from Moraviantown, and the grenadier company was left with it to support it in the event of an attack; the remainder proceeded on, the advance being at a house called Shearman's one mile from where the rear guard had halted. At daybreak next morning (the 5th) the rear guard and grenadier company moved to Shearman's where the whole regiment collected. At this place, after having halted for some time, a few head of cattle were shot, but before the meat could be divided, the enemy were reported to be close at hand and we were ordered to march. We proceeded to Moraviantown and when within 1½ miles of it were ordered to halt. After halting about five minutes, we were ordered to face to the right about and advance toward the enemy in files, at which the men were in great spirits. Having advanced about 50 or 60 paces we were halted a second time, at which the men appeared dissatisfied and over-hearing some of those nearest me express themselves to the following effect, " that they were ready and willing to fight for their knapsacks, wished to meet the enemy, but did not like to be knocked about in that manner doing neither one thing nor the other," I immediately checked them and they were silent. About this time several of the regiment came up without arms or accoutrements, who had escaped from boats cut off by the enemy's cavalry. From these men we learnt that the enemy was within a mile of us and had a large force of cavalry.

"We had halted about half an hour when the Indian alarm was given that the enemy was advancing; most of our men were sitting on logs and fallen trees by the side of the road. On the alarm being given we were suddenly ordered to form across the road. From the suddenness of the order, apparently without any previous arrangement, the manner in which it was given, the way in which it was given, which was to 'Form up across the road,' and from the nature of the ground, the formation was made in the greatest confusion, so much so that the grenadier company was nearly in the centre of the line and the light company on the right. A second order as sudden as the first was given for the grenadiers and No. 1 to march to the rear and form a reserve. The grenadiers and part of Capt. Muir's company accordingly formed a second line about 200 yards in rear of the first under command of Lieut.-Col. Warburton; the left of it about 8 or 10 yards to the left of the road extending to the right into the woods formed at extended order, the men placing themselves behind trees and consequently much separated. The first line I could not distinguish but from what I have been informed by Lieut. Gardner, 41st Regiment, commanding a six-pounder, it was formed in the following manner: A six-pounder was placed in the road having a range of 50 yards, the 41st Regiment drawn up on its right extending in the wood; on each side of the limber of the six-pounder were some of the Canadian Light Dragoons. From the men of the regiment who escaped from that line, I understand they were not formed at regular extended order but in clusters and in confusion. To the left of the road in which the six-pounder was placed and parallel to it, ran the River Thames. To the left of the road was a remarkably thick forest, and on the right where we were formed free from brush wood for several hundred yards and where cavalry could act to advantage. My position at this time (being on the right of the second line) and the thickness of the forest precluded me from noticing the manner in which the enemy attacked the first line. The attack commenced about two hours after the order was given to form up across the road. I heard a heavy firing of musquetry and shortly afterwards saw our dragoons retreating together with the limber of the six-pounder placed on the left of the first line. About a minute afterwards I observed that line retreating in confusion, followed closely by the enemy's cavalry who were galloping down the road. That portion of the first line which stood fast fired an irregular volley obliquing to the right and left which appeared to check the enemy. The line having commenced firing, my attention was directed to that part of the enemy moving down directly in my front. Hearing the fire slackening I turned toward the line and found myself remaining with three non-commissioned officers of the grenadier company. The enemy's cavalry had advanced so close before the reserve could commence firing from the number of trees that before a third round could be fired they broke through the left and the rest not being formed in a manner to repel cavalry were compelled to retreat. The number of the regiment actually in the field were one Lieutenant-Colonel, six Captains, nine Lieutenants, three Ensigns, three Staff, twenty-six Sergeants, eighteen Corporals, four drummers, 297 rank and file. In what manner the rest of the regiment was distributed, you will be made acquainted with by the enclosed statement signed by the adjutant of the regiment. The number of Indians we had in the field was 800. The number of the enemy, I cannot positively affirm, but from the information obtained from individuals of the regiment taken prisoners on that day and who afterwards escaped could not have been less than 6,000, of which 1,200 to 1,500 were cavalry and mounted riflemen. The number of our dragoons did not exceed 20. Our loss on this occasion was 3 sergeants and 9 rank and file killed and 36 wounded, that of the enemy 15 killed and from 40 to 50 wounded."[1]

His closing sentence I have already quoted. I give his statement in extenso as that of an apparently fair-minded officer who was on the spot.

Staff Adjutant Reiffenstein, in an apparently more precipitate flight from the scene than his commanding officer, had spread reports which were afterward characterized by Major-General De Rottenburg, in command of the upper Province, as "false and scandalous"[2] and by Sir Geo. Prevost, commander-in-chief, as gross exaggerations, though the latter appears to have regarded Reiffenstein's statement as "confirmed in all the principal events which marked that disgraceful day."

In the general order issued by the Commander of the forces from which the foregoing words are quoted, he said: "The subjoined return states the loss the Right Division has sustained in the action of the fleet on Lake Erie on the 10th September, and in the affair of the 5th October. In the latter but very few appear to have been rescued by an honorable death from the ignominy of passing under the American yoke, nor are there many whose wounds plead in mitigation of this reproach.

"The Right Division appears to have been encumbered with an unmanageable load of unnecessary and forbidden private baggage, while the requisite arrangements for the expeditious and certain conveyance of the ammunition and provisions, the sole objects worthy of consideration, appear to have been totally neglected, as well as all those ordinary measures resorted to by officers of intelligence to retard and impede the advance of a pursuing enemy.

"The result affords but too fatal a proof of this unjustifiable regret. The Right Division had quitted Sandwich in its retreat on the 26th September, having had ample time for every previous arrangement to facilitate and secure that movement. On the 2nd of October following the enemy pursued by the same route and on the 4th succeeded in capturing all the stores of the division and on the following day attacked and defeated it almost without a struggle."[3]

The result was a Court Martial held at Montreal, according to Order in Council dated at the Horse Guards, 9th September, 1815—the Court Martial having sat in the previous December and January.

[1] Cruikshank's Documentary History, Part 8, 254-7.
[2] De Rottenburg to Sir Geo. Prevost, 18 Oct., 1813, Cruikshank's Doc. Hist., Part 8, p. 80.
[3] Ibid., p. 231.

The charges were in brief:

1. That Proctor did not evacuate Amherstburg so soon after the loss of the fleet on Lake Erie (10th September) as military arrangements could be made, but delayed retreat until 27th September.

2. That he did not use due expedition, encumbered the division with large quantities of useless baggage, halted for several whole days and omitted to destroy bridges behind him.

3. Did not take necessary measures to prevent ammunition, stores and provisions falling into the enemy's hands or being destroyed and troops were without provisions a whole day previous to attack.

4. That he did not carry out promise to the Indian warriors to fortify the forts of the Thames at Chatham and neglected to occupy the heights above Moraviantown although he had previously removed his ordnance with the exception of one six pounder, nor throw up works there, but halted the Division in a highly unfavourable position, but two miles away, to receive attack.

5. That he did not make the best military dispositions to meet attack, nor attempt to rally and encourage the troops nor to co-operate with the Indians.

The Court acquitted Proctor wholly on the first charge.

As to the second, found him guilty of not taking proper measures for conducting a retreat and acquitted him as to the rest of the charge.

Found him guilty of not taking proper measures to protect the boats, etc., laden with stores, ammunition and provisions, but nothing further on the third charge.

Acquitted him of neglect to fortify the forts at Chatham, but found him guilty of neglect to occupy the heights above Moraviantown, although he had previously removed ordnance there and halted the Division within two miles of the village, etc.

His Royal Highness the Prince Regent, on behalf of His Majesty, confirmed the finding of the Court on the 1st, 3rd, 4th and 5th charges, but expressed surprise that the Court should find the prisoner guilty of the offence alleged, while at the same time acquitting him of all the facts upon which the charge was founded and that they were by a " humane but mistaken lenity " induced by the general good character and conduct of Major General Proctor to ascribe the offences found proved to error in judgment and passed sentence " inapplicable to their own finding of guilt "—to be publicly reprimanded and suspended from rank and pay for six months. The public reprimand was confirmed by the Prince Regent who ordered the charges, finding and sentence and his own confirmation to be entered in the general order book and read at the head of every regiment in His Majesty's service.

Major General Harrison's lengthy report of October 9th, to the Secretary of War serves to corroborate the charge of neglect to destroy bridges until too late, and the consequent loss of a large quantity of arms, munitions and stores, by Proctor.

The choice of a battle ground was not unwisely made, especially where the attacking force was mounted. " A moment's reflection, however, convinced us," wrote Harrison, " that from the thickness of the woods, and swampiness of the ground, they would be unable to do anything "—i.e. to turn the Indians' right flank—" and there was no time to dismount them and place their horses in security. I therefore determined to refuse my left to the Indians and to break the British lines, at once, by a charge of the mounted infantry. The measure was not sanctioned by anything that I had seen or heard of, but I was fully convinced that it would succeed. The American backwoodsmen ride better in the woods than any other people: a musket or rifle is no impediment to them, being accustomed to carry them on horseback, from their earliest youth. I was persuaded, too, that the enemy would be quite unprepared for the shock, and that they could not resist it."

The sequel showed that he was right.

Harrison stated his force aggregated 3,000 " certainly greater than that of the enemy " to quote him again—about double the number as a matter of fact. His casualties he stated were 7 killed 22 wounded, five of whom afterwards died. The British casualties, 12 killed and 22 wounded with 33 Indians left on the ground " besides those killed on the retreat."

I think it but fair to read Proctor's later and more succinct statement of the whole affair, before concluding this branch of my subject. It is contained in a letter written from Burlington to General De Rottenburg, dated 16th November, 1813, which I give in full:

" Sir, I have the honour to acknowledge the receipt of your letter of the eighth inst., and shall endeavour to comply with what is required. I regret that I should not have been able to make myself understood or that in endeavouring to be clear I should have been diffuse. I did not fail to give to the Port of Michilimackinac a due portion of my attention. Had it been otherwise in my power I could not have sent troops there, lest I might thereby have increased the want of provisions. Repeated communications was made to the officer in command there, of the Loss of the Fleet and the intended retreat to the Thames which had in consequence become requisite, with assurance also that the sending of pork especially by way of Mashedash should be strongly urged. For a detail of the precautionary measure to rid my Force of every incumbrance ere the retreat from Sandwich to Dover on the Thames, I beg leave to refer to my former letters being unable to give a clearer account than what has already been furnished. I have mentioned my determination to have made a stand in the first instance at Dover, a measure which was necessary for the protection of the craft, naval and ordnance stores, etc., brought from Amherstburg, and placed as high up the river as the navigation would then admit of. During a second attempt to reconnoitre the country in my rear, the troops were on the approach of the enemy moved from Dover to the Forks, a measure that early the next morning caused a determination in the Indian body to commence an immediate retreat to Moraviantown, and which I found on my arrival was carried into effect, and the requisite disposition made by Lt.-Colonel Warburton. These unfortunate circumstances left no option but the immediate sinking and destruction of the vessels and stores that would not be brought off from the want of time and transport. I trust it is unnecessary to repeat the capture of the boats with the stores and men therein. I most firmly believe that no article whatever of private baggage of any individual attached to the army was saved, at the expense of, or whilst the provisions and ammunition fell into the hands of the enemy. As already stated, finding that the enemy approached too near, I determined to meet and give him battle in a wood below the Moraviantown, as he was in considerable force, and particularly strong in Mounted Infantry and Cavalry. The position I had taken I also conceived to be favourable, as it reduced the enemy to a small front and secured my flanks, my right being on an impenetrable swamp, and my left on the river. The 41st Regiment occupied the space between the river and the Indians who were on their right, with their right thrown up. The troops had a reserve and marksmen near the six pounder on the road, for its further security. It was under the direction of Lieut. Gardner of the 41st Regiment who, on a former occasion had been found very useful when attached to the artillery. The gun, when taken, was loaded with canister and a sphente case shot, laid, and the port fire light; a plan of co-operation was cordially established with the Indians, who were to turn the left of the enemy, whilst the troops should resist the right. The Indians did turn the left of the enemy and executed their part faithfully and courageously. If the troops had acted as I have ever seen them, and as I confidently expected, I am still of opinion notwithstanding their numerical superiority the enemy would have been beaten; all ranks of officers exerted themselves to rally the men though ineffectual. Though retreating was the furthest from my thoughts I had caused as far as time and circumstances would admit every impediment to a retreat to be removed, and had also placed the field ordnance under the orders of Lieut. Thornton of the Royal Artillery, so as to defend an important point by which the Indians had retreated to us, and also to cover the retreat of the troops, whilst order was retained by them. The Indians, after the troops were broken, retired through the woods: and brought with them those who escaped in that direction. On the evening of the 5th of October provision was made for the feeding of the Indians and troops who should arrive at Delaware: the commissariat were also stationed on the route to Ancaster for the same purpose, as well as parties of Dragoons to aid and assist those who had effected their retreat on their way to Ancaster. I proceeded to the Grand River and endeavoured to prevent individuals proceeding who might create false alarms, and immediately communicated with the officers in command at Long Point, Burlington, and with Major General Vincent, commanding the Centre Division.

I have the honour to be Sir,
Your most obedient humble servant,
HENRY PROCTOR,
Major General.

We can scarcely at this date sit in appeal from the judgment of the Court Martial and the Prince Regent's general order of almost 104 years ago but may cast the mantle of charitable criticism over the memory of an officer who evidently felt keenly his position and suffered much. His death at Bath, at the comparatively early age of 59, may have been hastened by this suffering—for which I confess a feeling of sympathy.

It is a relief to turn from the branch of my subject with which I have been dealing, the fate of the unhappy Proctor, to that of the hero Tecumseh, whose end was tragic, his life heroic throughout, the subject of universal admiration.

Tecumseh was one of the two greatest and most heroic figures of the native races of this continent. Both Brant and Tecumseh preferred the

British as allies. Brant acquired a home for himself and his people here. Whether Tecumseh acquired even a grave to rest in is still questioned.

Tecumseh was a patriot in the truest sense. By some American historians Tecumseh's activities among the native races of the South—the Creeks and others—were attributed to British intrigue. This was a mistake.

Tecumseh or Tecumthe'—the name is said to signify "a shooting star"—was of the Shawanoes or Shawuness (Southerners) of the Delaware race, who removed from the south to the region of the Ohio and the Miami where Tecumseh was born in or about 1768. He is said to have been one of three brothers, born of a Cherokee mother at the same time. Tecumseh's activities were stirred up at finding the Americans were acquiring the Indian lands with the consent of certain tribesmen whom he deemed irresponsible, and he sought to form a vast confederacy of native races to resist these encroachments. Tecumseh's brother "the Prophet," acted with him, but relying more upon his powers of enchantment than upon the valour and discretion which characterized his brother, he in the latter's absence, attacked General Harrison's forces at Tippecanoe, with disastrous results. Tecumseh was much dissatisfied with his brother for his too precipitate attack, which wrecked their plans. An invitation was, by General Brock's order, sent to Tecumseh by the Superintendent of Indian Affairs through the agency of the Hurons to confer with him and them—to counsel Peace between him and the Big Knives (the Americans) apparently, judging from the "Speech of the Shawanoes, Kickapoos and Winibagoes delivered by Teckumthie at Machetie, on the Wabash, in answer to the message I (Mr. Elliott, S. I. A.) sent to them by the Hurons last winter." The closing sentences of this speech (received in June, 1812) are as follows:

"Brothers;—We Shawanoes, Kickapoos and Winibagoes hope you will not find fault with us for having detained you so long here: we were happy to see you and to hear your and our Father's words: and it would surely be strange if we did not listen to our Father and our eldest brothers.

"Father and Brothers.—We will now in a few words declare to you our whole hearts—if we hear of the Big Knives coming towards our villages to speak peace, we will receive them, but if we hear of any of our people being hurt by them, or if they unprovokedly advance against us in a hostile manner, be assured we will defend ourselves like men. And if we hear of any of our people having been killed, we will immediately send to all the nations on or toward the Mississippi and all this Island will rise as one man. Then Father and Brothers it will be impossible for you or either of you to restore peace between us."[1]

In the following month (July, 1812) Lieut.-Col. St. George, then in command of Amherstburg reported "a grand council of chiefs, etc., from the neighborhood." "Tecumtha (the Prophet's brother) acted a conspicuous part on the occasion."[2]

This was apparently his first appearance on this side of the Lake. Thereafter followed the various operations, including the taking of Detroit by Brock, the River Raisin, and the subsequent events of Sandusky, etc., culminating in the naval battle of Lake Erie in which the gallant Captain

[1] Mich. Pioneer and Historical Collections Vol. 15, p. 90.
[2] Ibid., pp. 98-9.

Barclay lost both his ships and the use of his only arm remaining to him after Trafalgar, as well as the only officer properly qualified to fill his place when wounded (Capt. R. Finnis), the enemy having treble the number of seamen and double the weight of metal* as well as a change of wind at the most critical moment of the day in his favour.

We have seen how reluctant Tecumseh was to retreat fiom Malden—I need not further dwell upon the details of the retreat, or of the battle.

The following seemingly truthful account of our hero's death is given in the Michigan Pioneer Collections, Vol. 10 (p. 160), as having been narrated by Noonday, an Ottawa Chief, to a Mr. Cook, whose diary runs thus "After rehearsing the speech which Tecumseh made to his warriors previous to the engagement, and how all felt that they fought to defend Tecumseh more than for the British he was asked:

"Were you near Tecumseh when he fell?"

"Yes, directly on his right."

"Who killed him?"

"Richard M. Johnson."

"Give us the circumstances."

"He was on a horse and the horse fell over a log, and Tecumseh with uplifted tomahawk, was about to dispatch him, when he drew a pistol from his holster and shot him in the breast and he fell dead on his face. I seized him at once and with the assistance of Saginaw, bore him from the field. When he fell the Indians stopped fighting and the battle ended. We laid him down on a blanket in a wigwam, and we all wept, we loved him so much. I took his hat and tomahawk."

"Where are they now?"

"I have his tomahawk and Saginaw his hat."

"Could I get them?"

"No: Indian keep them."

"How did you know it was Johnson who killed him?"

"General Cass took me to see the Great Father, Van Buren, at Washington. I went to the great wigwam, and when I went in I saw the same man I see in battle, the same man I see kill Tecumseh. I had never seen him since, but I knew it was him. I look him in the face and said: 'Kene Kin-a-poo Tecumseh,' that is, 'you kill Tecumseh.' Johnson replied that he never knew who he was, but a powerful Indian approached him and he shot him with his pistol. 'That was Tecumseh: I see you do it.'

"Noonday finished his story of Tecumseh by telling of his noble traits, the tears meanwhile trickling down his cheeks. There is no doubt of the truth of his unvarnished tale."

More poetic, if less authentic, is the account given by Charles Mair in his noble poem, who places in the mouth of the dying chief the words:

> "The hour is come; these weary hands and feet
> Draw to the grave—Oh, I have loved my life
> Not for my own, but for my people's cause.
> Who now will knit them? Who will lead them on?
> Lost! Lost! Lost! The pale destroyer triumphs.
> I see my people fly—I hear their shrieks,
> And none to shield or save! My axe! My axe!
> Ha—it is here! No, no, the power is past.
> Oh, Mighty Spirit, shelter, save my people."

---

*Sir James Yeo to Sir John B. Warren, 10 Oct., 1813, Can. Archives, and Cruikshank's Documentary History, 220.

In the basement of the Corcoran Gallery at Washington there reposes a marble recumbent statue of "the Dying Tecumseh" chiseled by a Spanish sculptor of some note. It once had a place in the Capitol building, but has been relegated in later years to comparative obscurity. I have looked upon it not without emotion and to it might be addressed, not inappropriately, the closing words of Mair's poem,

> "Sleep well, Tecumseh, in thy unknown grave,
> Thou mighty savage, resolute and brave!
> Thou Master and strong spirit of the woods,
> Unsheltered traveller in sad solitudes,
> Yearner o'er Wyandot and Cherokee,
> Couldst tell us now what hath been and shall be?"

III.

HISTORY OF PRESBYTERIANISM IN THE COUNTY OF OXFORD.

By The Rev. W. T. McMullen, D.D.

The pioneer Presbyterian settlers of a locality were, as a prevalent usage, accustomed to assemble on Sabbath for social worship without Minister or Missionary. This usage was followed in the early days of the settlement in the County of Oxford. In 1833 the Rev. George Romanes, an ordained Minister from the Presbytery of Glasgow, Scotland, visited Canada and preached in Zorra, July 21st, and reported to his presbytery on his return home that he found a log church built, in which regular Sabbath services were held and well attended, though they had no minister. The Rev. Donald McKenzie visited Zorra in 1834, dispensed gospel ordinances there, and in many of the new settlements in this section of the province; and in 1835 he became settled pastor of the Zorra congregation, now known as Knox Church, Embro. From the time of Mr. McKenzie's settlement in Zorra he conducted an occasional service in Woodstock. The Rev. George Murray came from Scotland about the same time as Mr. McKenzie, and settled in the Township of Blenheim. He also conducted an occasional service in Woodstock.

But the planting of Presbyterianism in Woodstock, as in Zorra, must be credited to a "Laymen's Movement" in the strict and proper sense of the expression. Two names stand out prominently in connection with Sabbath services held three or four years before the settlement of a minister in Woodstock. The names are Mr. David White and Mr. John Bain, both of whom came to Woodstock in 1834, and up to a ripe old age served in the office of eldership.

The first Presbyterian minister settled in Woodstock was the Rev. Daniel Allan, who in 1838 became pastor of the united charge of Woodstock and Stratford, but there was at the time no road between the two places, and the journey had to be made on horseback through unbroken forest, with the added difficulties of swamps and quagmires towards Stratford. Mr. Allan preached two Sabbaths in succession in each place and with heroic endurance continued the arrangement for two years, and then resigned Woodstock and confined his labours to Stratford and North Easthope. Those three venerated fathers of the church, Rev. Donald McKenzie, Rev. Daniel Allan and Rev. George Murray, left lasting impress on the religious life of the County of Oxford and rendered unutterably valuable service to the cause of the Presbyterian church, not only within their respective spheres of labour, but throughout Canada, and even beyond the bounds of Canada. It was to Mr. McKenzie's congregation in Zorra the church was indebted for the great foreign Missionary, the Rev. George Leslie McKay, D.D., founder of Oxford College, Formosa, the man whose praise is in all the churches. There is probably no congregation in Canada that has made such a distinguished record as regards the giving of young men to the Gospel Ministry, as Knox

Church, Embro. Some years ago the Ladies' Aid Society of the congregation prepared and had printed a handsome Register in which are entered thirty-eight names of young men of Knox Church, Embro, who devoted themselves to the Gospel Ministry; and since that date eight more at least have to be added, making a total of forty-six.

Oxford College, Formosa, to which reference has been made, takes its name from this County, the Presbyterians of Oxford having provided the funds for the erection of the building. That which inspired the generous giving was the gratification felt in the fact that the great Missionary, Dr. G. L. McKay, was a native of the County. Two other sons of Oxford Presbyterianism, Dr. Robert Chambers and Dr. W. N. Chambers, devoted their lives to foreign Missions, and for the past twenty years or more have laboured in Turkey, under the American Board. The former is now transferred to Constantinople to take oversight of College and Mission work, and the latter is engaged in Mission work at Adana, the scene of the great massacre. If what the County of Oxford has done in the way of giving men and money to Foreign Mission work deserves honourable mention, a like record must be credited to her in connection with Home Missions. The Rev. Dr. James Robertson, the great Home Mission Superintendent, was one of Oxford's sons. He thought big things, aimed at big things, and did big things for the Church of Christ, and for Canada.

Another of her sons is our efficient and devoted Foreign Secretary, the Rev. R. P. McKay, D.D.

Having illustrated the claim that the pioneer fathers of Presbyterianism in the County of Oxford left an impress that has told powerfully on both the Home and Foreign Mission work of the Church, we now resume the local history at the point of digression, viz., Mr. Allan's resignation of Woodstock in 1840. In 1841, the building of St. Andrew's Church on Graham Street was commenced under the brief pastorate of Rev. F. P. Sims, who succeeded Mr. Allan.

The disruption which took place in Scotland in 1843 extended to Canada in 1844. A large proportion of the Presbyterians of Woodstock took sides with the Free Church, resulting in the formation of the congregation of Knox Church, and the erection of the Old Knox Church on Perry Street in 1849 under the pastorate of the Rev. W. S. Ball, B.A. Chalmers Church was built in 1852, also in connection with the Free Church and for the accommodation of those in Woodstock and vicinity who desired one service on Sabbath in the Gaelic language. It thus came about that in 1860 there were four Presbyterian congregations in Woodstock with settled pastors, viz., Erskine Church connected with the United Presbyterian Church, St. Andrew's Church, and Knox and Chalmers Churches.

But days of union were at hand. The first great union came in 1861 when the United Presbyterian and Free Church formed the Canada Presbyterian Church. The second great union came in 1875, consolidation of all the Presbyterians in Canada and Newfoundland in what is now known as the Presbyterian Church in Canada. The local effect of these unions was that the four congregations in Woodstock became consolidated in the two now existing.

In Ingersoll also, as the outcome of the union of 1861 the congregations of Knox Church and Erskine Church united, forming the congregation now known as St. Paul's Church. Associated with the early history of Presbyterianism in Ingersoll stand the names of Rev. Arch. Cross, Minister of Erskine Church, and Rev. Robert Wallace, Minister of Knox Church from 1849 to 1860. Long pastorates were the rule fifty years ago. The Rev. Donald McKenzie was minister in Zorra 38 years. The pastorate of Rev. Daniel Allan, in North Easthope, covered a like period. The Rev. George Murray made a similar record in Blenheim. The Rev. Wm. Robertson was minister at Chesterfield 32 years. Two other ministers in our Presbytery, Dr. Cochrane in Brantford and Dr. Thompson in Ayr had pastorates of 36 and 40 years respectively. The writer of this sketch was pastor of Knox Church, Woodstock, 46 years and nine months. Oxford and vicinity were not peculiar in this regard. The same permanency in the pastorate prevailed everywhere throughout the Church. In illustration of this it is only necessary to mention as samples, Peterborough, Galt, Fergus, Stratford, London, Chatham, Sarnia. Unsettledness and change have now become the rule, and the long pastorate the rare exception. How has this change come about? This question is more easily asked than answered. In all departments of human life great changes have taken place in the past fifty years. In the main these changes are for the better, however opinions may differ as to certain details and incidental effects. There is in the Church, the permanent and the variable. Fluctuation in the variable is not to be interpreted as a sign, much less accepted as a proof, that "the former days were better than these."

IV.

WOMEN IN PIONEER LIFE.

By Miss Amelia Poldon.

It is said that "the Pilgrim Fathers" of New England were the sifted wheat of the pioneer colonists of the United States, so, also the pioneers of Ontario may be termed the sifted wheat of the early colonists of Canada. Many of them were U. E. Loyalists, who emigrated from the United States after the War of Independence, and through their loyalty to the British Government were willing to brave the dangers, and to suffer the hardships and privations incidental to life in the woods of Canada. They left homes of comfort and luxury, were separated from their friends, a long distance from any post office, had to drive many miles to find a store to purchase necessities, or a market for their produce, no doctor nearer than twenty-five or fifty miles, and they had to live on the scantiest fare. The country was an unbroken forest with no roads; only occasionally, a path made by the surveyor, with a few blazed trees to indicate it; this path was called a blazed trail. Wolves, bears, and other wild animals were in abundance, and the wolves especially were a dangerous enemy at night and a few cases were known where they had devoured settlers, and many had narrow escapes from this terrible death.

Sir G. W. Ross said of the early pioneer, "No better stuff climbed the heights of Alma, or charged the Dervishes at Khartoum."

All honour to the brave men and women, who performed heroic deeds in resisting the invaders of Canada; we reverence their memories, we build monuments to commemorate their bravery; books after books have been written and published, so that the generations following and those to come will also honour and revere their names and the nobility of their character and know and remember their great achievements.

But we also owe a great debt to the pioneers of our country, and their names and their persistent efforts, and their bravery in enduring the privations and vicissitudes of the early pioneers of a new country should be remembered; the history and the records of their work should be preserved for the generations to come.

> "In the temples they founded, their faith is maintained
> Every foot of the soil they bequeathed is still ours,
> The graves where they moulder have not been profaned
> But we wreathe them with verdure and strew them with flowers."

A pioneer life was certainly a strenuous one. The pioneer's first work was to take his axe and chop down the trees for a space to build a house, then he must build a barn and enclosure to protect his stock. But if the men led a busy life it would seem as though the women lived a busier life if possible, and their privations and difficulties were almost beyond human endurance, but they trained up a generation of noble men and women. Many of the pioneer women had come from homes of culture and refinement and were accustomed to comfort and luxury. Their first experience was the process of moving, for there were no ways for transportation only by waggons drawn by teams of horses. Mr. Moses Mott wrote a sketch describing their moving trip in the fall of 1810 from Duchess County, New York, to the Township of North Norwich. They had three teams, were twenty-one days on the road, resting on the Sabbath and some rainy days. Mr. and Mrs. Mott brought with them their family of five sons and one daughter. The country was new, very few settlers, roads very bad, several of the small streams had no bridges, and had to be forded, sometimes their waggons were stuck in the mud, would have to be pried out, and it would take two teams to draw them out. They crossed the Niagara River at Black Rock; the craft they crossed in was something like a scow, with four oars and two men at each oar. It took nearly all day to get each team across, one at a time.

When they arrived at the Grand River, they had to ford the river as there was neither bridge nor ferry boat. A man rode a pony ahead as a guide, and the team followed closely behind, the water coming up to the horses' sides some of the way. This experience was common to all who travelled one hundred years ago, and certainly was not comfortable for the womanhood of the company.

The home of a pioneer woman was her kingdom and she presided over it like a queen. It was constructed of logs; some of them had two rooms, one the living room, the other a sleeping room, and an attic above. If only one room, it had to combine both sleeping and living necessities. The sleeping apartment had usually two beds and trundle beds for the younger children, the older boys sleeping in the attic, for in those days there were children in the home, "like olive plants around the table." The heating of the home and the cooking was done by a fireplace. From the top of the chimney a chain was suspended, to which was attached two hooks, on which the busy housewife hung the iron kettles for cooking and for heating water. The bread was baked in a covered iron kettle, the dough was put into the kettle, which was placed upon the hearth and covered with coals, where it remained until the time was sufficient to bake it. After a time an oven would be built outside and in it large batches of bread, cake, and pies could be baked at once. This lessened the tediousness of providing food enough for the family but often storms made it very inconvenient; stoves were introduced later on. Lights were not plentiful, usually a couple of pine knots and the fireplace furnished the light in the evening; a tallow candle was quite a luxury until later years, when there were cattle to kill to provide the tallow. It was no easy matter to keep the family comfortable in such limited circumstances. The mother had to spin the flax and the wool into yarn to weave into cloth to clothe the family. In every neighbourhood there would be a home in which there was a loom and some woman skilled in weaving cloth. The housewife would dye the yarn; the dyes in those days were homemade, not the dye preparations of these days which require so little effort to use them: the pioneer dyes needed days often to complete the colouring. Souvenirs of the dress goods prepared in those days are some of them beautiful and compare favourably with those of to-day, and there were no shoddy goods either. They also fulled the cloth, termed full cloth;

it was thicker and warmer for men's wear, and outer garments for women. After the cloth was prepared, the mothers had to be the dressmakers and the tailors. Stockings and socks had to be knit for the family; the father would tan his own leather and in the evening or stormy days would make the shoes for the family. Then with all the home cares, there was much social life, " the latch string was always out," everybody was welcome in the homes.

In the pioneer days it was impossible to get medical attention, doctors were from twenty-five to fifty miles distant from most districts, but these busy housekeepers did not forget their duty to those about them. It can truthfully be said of the pioneer woman:—

> " She layeth her hand to the spindle and her hands hold the distaff.
> She stretcheth out her hands to the poor, yea
> She reacheth out her hands to the needy."

These women responded to every call and in early days it was often a perilous journey. Now in North Norwich, Mrs. Adam Stover was the only physician until 1831, when Dr. Cooke settled on Quaker Street. She was a capable and skilful nurse, having received special training before they moved into Norwich in 1811. She was in great demand, going early and late, travelling on horseback over rough roads, through storms, braving danger, for at night the forest was infested with wolves. Mrs. Stover found in her first visits to the sick and those to whom she ministered that they were frequently without clothing and comforts, so she always kept a satchel ready, filled with clothing for sickness, also for the little one, if one was to be ushered into the world. Many a young mother had no opportunity of getting cloth for little garments, there being no store nearer than fifty-five miles. So in every county we find these records of noble deeds in sickness by its womanhood. In our own limited experience we could add scores of names of women who lived for " Others," and to help the suffering ones.

> " The sweetest lives are those to duty wed,
> When deeds both great and small
> Are close knit strands of an unbroken thread
> Where love ennobles all
> The world may sound no trumpet, ring no bell,
> Tho ' Books of Life ' the shining records tell."

Many mothers educated their children at home, schools were often a long distance, and sometimes the teachers were not very efficient, usually some one in the section and when circumstances did not require the children to be taught entirely in the home, the strong personality of the mother, her noble ambitions, her strict adherence to the principles of honour and justice, her persistent efforts for the uplift of her family and the community in which she lived were a noble heritage for her children, and in the majority of the citizens of Canada to-day, who are descendants of our pioneer families, we find them men and women who live to make the world better; they are loyal to God and country, and those principles of Righteousness and Freedom that uplift a nation.

About twenty-five years ago I was intimately associated with a mother who educated her family at home until they were ready for college. When I knew her she had two or three maids to assist in her elegant home. In conversation with her on educational problems I inquired how she had managed to educate her family at home. She said when her two eldest boys were small she lived on a farm, made butter and raised poultry and eggs for the market, usually had two men to board, her husband, and four children, and no maid, could get help for washing and cleaning. " The school was some distance, and not a desirable association for my family. I had a good English education, with some knowledge of Latin and French. I felt that my boys had been given me to train and mould into good men, and as they evinced a desire and a capability for becoming educated men, I had a small table in the kitchen and while I was attending to domestic duties I taught them. They were among the first pupils in Ontario County to write on the Entrance Examination and after another year at home, we sent them to Cobourg University, then to Johns Hopkins University at Baltimore. Both became very successful barristers, and the eldest one represented the U. S. Government in every court in Europe on some phase of Political Economy." He was in London, England, when the late Edward VII. was Prince of Wales, and was at a banquet at which the Prince presided, and her son gave his address in pure French. His picture and that of our own De L. F. Barker of Johns Hopkins were illustrated in the *Globe* as the two eminent Canadians. The younger son and daughter received the same education at home; the son is one of the prominent judges in a large Canadian city, the daughter died just after her graduation. This is only the brief record of one of the hundreds of mothers in our Canada, who helped to make its greatness by donating such a noble citizenship.

All over our province we find records of grand and noble deeds accomplished by our pioneer women. I shall just give a brief reference to one of these splendid women, Dr. Emily H. Stowe, who was born in the wooded country of South Norwich in 1831 and who accomplished great things for the womanhood of our country.

Dr. Emily H. Stowe was the daughter of Mr. and Mrs. Solomon Jennings, her mother was the granddaughter of Peter Lossing, the North Norwich pioneer. She was one of the leaders of Canadian women, who believe it is their duty to do their part, in every sphere of public and private life, where they may promote the welfare and advancement of humanity. She began her public life as a teacher, at the age of fifteen and continued to advance in her profession, until she became the first female High School or Grammar School teacher in the Dominion. She married, was the mother of three children, was an excellent wife and mother, a model housekeeper, so her intellectual qualifications and aspirations did not unfit her for domestic life.

After she had been married a few years her attention was directed to the fact that women were needed in the medical profession. She decided to enter into it, but like all pioneers on any path of human progress, she encountered unreasoning prejudice, great obstacles and had to face strong opposition from those even from whom you would have expected approval, and also found much social and professional antagonism.

As there were no opportunities for women to obtain a medical education in Canada, this courageous woman attended the New York Medical College for Women, and graduated from that institution in 1868, and commenced to practice in the city of Toronto, and thus became the first woman to enter the medical profession in the Dominion. The subsequent struggle for a right to practice in Toronto left no trace of bitterness or animosity. Women who now choose the medical profession in Canada, and find every facility provided for the various courses of study, can never know how deeply they are indebted to this great pioneer, who opened the path now so easy to follow.

Dr. Emily H. Stowe was a wise and untiring worker in the long struggle for the admission of women into the University of Toronto. The man-monopolized world in the early part of the 19th century did not believe in the higher education of woman. There was a strong opposition against girls entering the high schools. In 1826, the town of Hatfield, Mass., discussed the question of taxing it to provide a high school for girls or of enlarging the one they had for that purpose. One indignant citizen exclaimed "School she's!" "Never!" The extension of the Franchise to women and the Married Woman's Property Act were among the results of her persistent efforts.

Dr. Emily H. Stowe possessed intellectual courage, clear convictions, steady unswerving purpose, a composed philosophical mind, and these were the qualities that won success in the long struggle against the opposition to girls having the right to receive the higher education.

V.

THE SIX NATIONS INDIANS.

BY MISS AUGUSTA I. G. GILKISON.

You cannot forget that this continent of America and Canada first belonged to the Indians. How they came into this land, where they came from, has not been found out. A remark made by a chief in the early days was: "The Great Spirit gave this big Island to the Red Man, and the land across the big waters he gave the White Man, but the white man was not content with what he got, but must come over the big waters and take ours from us."

When the first white men sailed up that beautiful river, (now the St. Lawrence) they saw nothing but brown and red men, wearing deer skins, and feathers on their heads. You can imagine how astonished the Indians were, to see a large ship with sails, and white men. Fortunately for the white men, they happened to be a peaceable tribe. They received Cartier with astonishment and hospitality. Most noted of the Indians were Brant, Tecumseh, Pontiac, Splitlog and Red Jacket. Indian chiefs and warriors were in all the battles in Canada from 1620 to 1814. These battles were at Quebec, Prescott, Chrysler's Farm, Toronto, Hamilton, Niagara frontier, Detroit and Amherstburg.

The centre of all the ties which bind Canada together can be found about the grey old rock of Quebec, so full of historic memories of Cartier, Champlain, Levis, Montcalm, Wolfe, and others. It was to this spot that Cartier came, followed by Champlain, the soldier, the sailor and the statesman. It was from Quebec that Christianity was first given to Canada. Jacques Cartier sailed up this beautiful river in 1534, with his three ships and 162 picked men, passing the river Saguenay, landed at Stad-a-co-na, now Quebec: meeting the well known chief Donn-a-co-na, he sailed on and next stopped at Hochelaga (now Montreal) and was well received by throngs of Indians.

The last letter addressed by Champlain to Cardinal Richelieu set forth the importance of subduing the hostile tribes of the Five Nations and bringing them into sympathy and friendship with the French. Conflicts occurred between the English and French, until the British won, with the death of Wolfe, Montcalm and others. In June 1760 Sir Wm. Johnson brought to General Amherst one thousand of the Six Nation Indians, (by this time including the Tuscaroras admitted in 1714.) This was the largest number of Indians ever seen in arms at one time in the cause of Britain. At the close of the war in 1783, the Six Nations almost to a man, under Brant's leadership, left their beautiful valley on the Mohawk River and retired to Canada. What Brant was to the British in the revolutionary war, Tecumseh was in the war of 1812, and the memory and the services of those two great Indian warriors would, with other motives wanting, of themselves constitute a reason why the Indians of British America should be treated with justice, consideration and respect. Tecumseh turned to his braves and pointing to Sir Isaac Brock said "This is a man." Sir Isaac Brock took off his red sash, put it on Tecumseh, and the chief received it with much pleasure.

In 1783 the Six Nations (U.E.L.) headed by Brant, took up the lands in the neighborhood of Brantford, presented to them by the British Government, six miles on each side of the Ouse or Grand River from above Elora to Port Maitland on Lake Erie. Captain Brant, who was in England in 1784, brought out a bell, which was the first bell that rang for church service in Upper Canada. He brought out also the royal coat of arms of King George the Third. This coat-of-arms is a very rare one. The Lord's Prayer, the Ten Commandments and the Creed in the Mohawk language he also brought out. Brant built the church in 1784, which started the Mohawk village.

In February, 1793, Lieut.-Governor Simcoe and suite were the guests of Chief Brant at the Mohawk village, coming from Niagara and Fort George. On their arrival the Indians hoisted their flags and trophies of war and fired a cannon. They then gave the Governor an Indian name, Dey-on-quh-o-kawen, meaning "One whose door is always open." Chief Brant and his warriors accompanied Governor Simcoe to the Delaware Reserve, below London, Ont., on his way to Detroit, which then belonged to the British.

The Six Nations are now nearly all Christians, and have splendid schools, many churches on the reserve, and at a village called Oshweken, about ten miles from Brantford, Ont., a brick council house, the corner stone of which was laid by the superintendent, Colonel Jasper T. Gilkison, in October, 1863, whose Indian name was "Shaonwenyaw-anck," meaning "One Who Governs." (Mohawk). Miss Gilkison (his daughter) was adopted October, 1913, and given the name "Go-ih-Wih-Sacs, meaning "One Who Makes a Research," (Cayuga, Wolf Clan.)

This village of Oshweken has exhibition grounds, post office, high school, two churches, frame houses nicely furnished and a hotel. The Indians are musical and sing very softly and sweetly. The first clergymen were Rev. Mr. Luggar, Rev. Mr. Nelles and Rev. Mr. Elliott, who ministered to them fifty years. The Indian reserve has had many distinguished visitors: The Duke of Connaught, Lord and Lady Dufferin, Lords Lisgar, Aberdeen and others. Beautiful addresses were sent to Queen Victoria, King Edward and King George V. He is the head warrior chief of the Six Nations, with the name On-Onti-yah, meaning Pleasant Mountain. Prince Arthur (now the Duke of Connaught) was made chief in 1869, at the Mohawk church and Indian Institute, and given the name Ka-rah-kon-tye, meaning The Sun Flying, of the Mohawk tribe, Wolf clan. He was only twenty years old. I myself witnessed the ceremony.

Brant was tall, with fine oval face, not dark, and was very highly respected by all the high officials of that day. The Duke of Northumberland, Earl of Warwick, Marquis of Hastings and others of the nobility were friends of Brant. He was also a captain in the British army.

Over three hundred of the Six Nations have gone to the front in the present Great War, and the first that paid the supreme sacrifice was Lieutenant Cameron Brant, a descendant. The monument which is erected to chief Brant is the finest on this continent; the casts of the faces were taken from living men on the reserve—a Mohawk, Cayuga, Seneca, Onondaga, Oneida and Tuscarora.

Brantford was laid out as a village in 1830. The council had a dispute about a name—some wanted Birmingham, another Biggarsville, etc., but there happened to come into the room a man named Dutton, whom they thought something of, and they asked him what name he would give this new village. "Why," he said, "is not this place known as Brant's Ford?" They said yes. "Then call it Brantford." They all agreed, so the trouble was settled.

Tuscarora, means "hemp gatherers," Indian hemp being a plant of many uses among the Carolina Tuscaroras. In 1708 they had 15 towns and about 1,200 warriors, with a population of two thousand. They were an important people and possessed many amiable qualities and behaved better to the white people than the whites did to them, for they kidnapped their children and sold them into slavery. They were so illtreated by the whites and the other Indian tribes that in 1714 the Tuscaroras came to the Five Nations for protection, and they with the Five Nations came to live on Grand River Reserve in 1784.

Tutelo Heights, 2 miles from Brantford, where the Bell Telephone was invented, was named after the Tutelo tribe, which came with the Six Nations in 1784 and settled by themselves on these heights. The Tutelo tribe dwelt in 1671 in Brunswick County, South Virginia, then afterwards with the Tuscaroras they moved to Pennsylvania, afterwards to New York, where they joined the Five Nations and with them moved to the Grand River Reserve. Their tribal ensign consisted of three arrows: their chiefs were allowed to sit in the Great Council. The Tutelos were tall, likely men with large robust bodies: they were cultivators of the soil. The last full blood Tutelo died in 1871—Nikonha, John Tutelo, as he was known on the reserve, aged 82.

VI.

OLD STAGE COACH DAYS IN OXFORD COUNTY.

By W. B. Hobson.

Years ago I collected a large amount of stage-day reminiscences and data, but have found on reviewing it lately that it contained so much repetition and sameness that I have decided to give a short paper on the old Stage Road with a few of the essential facts. The old Stage Road was the leading highway of Ontario in early days, with many branch lines leading from it along the way.

Staging is merely a substitute for the term coaching, and coaching dates back to the twelfth and thirteenth centuries.

In England during the eighteenth century the coaches were great, lumbering affairs drawn by six horses, and it was conceded that a good walker could make better time. The passengers, it would appear, were usually either rich, lazy, fat or cripples. In the year 1718 the first contracts were given to the coachmen for carrying the mail. Up to that time the mail had been carried by post boys. Staging was introduced in America as soon as the country was sufficiently populated to warrant it, and the stage routes spread with the people, or rather, the people spread with the stage until they had reached all points of importance in North America.

It is my intention at this time to deal with stage days in Oxford, and as my information has been gathered from many sources it will necessarily be somewhat fragmentary.

In my youth I heard many stage stories from my uncle, George Hobson, who, in his early life, had the mail route from Hamilton to London, and ran stages on the old Stage Road for many years, and later on through Woodstock after the Governor's Road was finished. One little incident I remember him telling. The stages passed through Woodstock on sleighs on the 10th day of May, 1844—an old letter furnished me with the correct date. Winter was surely lingering in the lap of spring that time. I find that one Jed Jackson, in the year 1832, got the first contract for carrying the mail from Brantford to London over the old Stage Road, and from that road into Woodstock with a light rig, although there was no post office in Woodstock until the year 1835. Just at this point in my investigation I made a discovery. I cannot very well understand why the stages had been running over the old Stage Road for many years before the Government gave a contract for carrying the mail. The question is, how did the people do business or get the mail?

Dorman was one of the first stage proprietors of importance, but I cannot find that he ever carried the mail. Dorman's stables at Sydenham, now Cathcart, were noted for their large number of high class stage horses. Two years was the average life of a stage horse.

Up to about 1836 the stages carried nine passengers inside and a goodly number outside. There was always room for one more. About the year 1853, when Babcock & Co., Hiram Weeks, George Hobson and others were staging, the stages were more commodious and carried as many as sixteen passengers. They were known as Concord stages, as they were at that time all built in Concord, New Hampshire. The old Stage Road between Niagara and London was considered the most beautiful drive in the country, winding through varied and ever-changing scenery the entire distance, passing a few miles south of Woodstock, and it is said, of which there is no doubt, that this old historic road was originally an Indian trail from Niagara to Windsor.

Eighty years ago, in the year 1839, Woodstock had become of much importance, or imagined so, having many retired military and naval officers living in and about it, who, having influence with the Government, succeeded in having work commenced in the year 1840 on the road leading from Sydenham to Eastwood to join the Governor's Road, through Woodstock. This road was well graded and planked with three-inch pine lumber. It was finished in the year 1843 and for a number of years nearly all the traffic passed through Woodstock, although the old Stage Road was never abandoned; it still had its attractions which led many that way. About the year 1847 the planking and grading on the Governor's Road had become much worn and the traffic reverted very largely back to the old Stage Road.

During the construction of the Great Western Railroad there was very heavy traffic over both roads. Often as many as six four-horse stages passed each way every day. Stages travelled at the rate of eight to ten miles an hour, and usually changed horses about every fifteen miles. Some stage lines had relays of horses at Putnam, Beachville, Eastwood, and so on, while others ran from London to Ingersoll, from there to Woodstock, and from Woodstock to Sydenham. It seems that each stage proprietor allotted relays to suit himself, which was not a difficult matter, as there were over thirty taverns between London and Brantford, twenty of which were between Woodstock and Brantford, and all did a flourishing business. Many of the old-time landlords were noted characters, and all seemed to be the very soul of hospitality. The stages made a practice of stopping at every tavern, business or no business. It took but twenty-five cents to treat the crowd, no matter about the number. Jokes and songs were the order of the day, and light-hearted merriment seemed to prevail everywhere. The old-timer would be considered illiterate and coarse now-a-days, but he at least seemed to live as long and get as much pleasure out of life as the people of to-day. Our better education would appear to be but the mother of discontent, and our bigoted social conditions are leading us into chaos. The old-timers tried to keep the ten commandments, but we have added ten times ten to the ten and break most of them. I fear our laws are becoming so drastic and fanatical that liberty has lost its meaning. The poor, uneducated pioneer in his stage coach would compare favorably, mentally, morally, physically and religiously with the educated masses who travel in Pullman cars to-day. The better education and Christianity do not appear to be working in harmony.

The old-time stage proprietor was looked upon as the salt of the earth, not that he had any outstanding qualifications as a rule any more than our modern M.P.P. or bank managers, but people who hold favors in the hollow of their hands are always treated with great deference. All the proud virtue of this vaunting world fawns on success and power. The highest ambition of the young man in early days was to be a stage driver, not that the remuneration could have been any inducement as they received ten or twelve dollars per month, but the exciting life seemed to overcome the many hardships.

During the construction of the Great Western Railroad the fare from London to Brantford was $5.00, or $3.00 from Woodstock to Brantford, but this had not been the rule. In earlier days the competition was at times so great that they had rate wars and frequently carried passengers from London to Hamilton free and fed them on the way and treated them at each tavern. It was a common thing for stage drivers of opposing lines to meet at stage stations and fight like wild cats, and a man of pugilistic fame often drew double the pay of an ordinary peaceful driver, and fighting qualifications were recognized as a mark of efficiency.

A rather laughable incident is told by one of the stage drivers: being stuck in the mud on one occasion he ordered all the passengers out, and all obeyed excepting one big, burly fellow, who sat still. When the driver caught sight of him he said: " Look here, my good man, if you don't get out of there, I will serve you as I did a man here yesterday." The big fellow started to pull his coat off, saying: "How did you serve the man yesterday?" "Oh," replied the stage driver, " I just let him sit still."

Another pathetic incident I remember my uncle telling. On one occasion he was driving himself, and overtook a poor weary woman, near Martin's Tavern, and having room, he took her on. She had a small sack of flour on her shoulder, and she said she lived somewhere north of Ingersoll, and had walked nearly all the way to Hamilton with one bushel of wheat, and was returning with the flour. She had no money, but had not suffered for food or lodging on all the trip. The hospitable tavern keepers along the way gave her food, bed and a sup of whiskey, as she called on them, and the stage drivers gave her a lift when they had room.

Very likely this poor woman was the grandmother of some of the fanatics in our midst to-day who would not allow us to bet a nickel on a horse race or drink a glass of ale, yet would doff their hats to the promoters who fleece the public out of millions, and overlook the thousand greater evils that are leading the world into Bolshevism.

When the stage proprietor was put out of business there was no McKenzie & Mann, or Merchants Bank, to call upon the Government and force them to make good; railroad magnates and banks and big interests had no strangle hold on the throat of the government at that time.

But the stage proprietor and the stage driver, and the old-time tavern keeper and the toll gate, have all gone, never to return.

THE THAMES RIVER ROAD.

Long gone with the past are the pioneer days
When the riverside road was only a blaze,
And the Indian lurked like a beast of prey,
While the ox teams went lolling along the way.
But the ox team, and red man, and birch bark abode
Are passed like a dream from the Thames River Road.

Then came the stage coach with its rumble and din,
Full bulging with passengers outside and in,
All fresh from the motherland over the sea,
In search of new homes in the land of the free.
They chopped and they cleared and they plowed and they sowed,
And passed in their turn from the Thames River Road.

The railway came next and thus ended the age
Of the pioneer inn, the toll gate and stage,
And the landlord, that soul of mirth and good-will,
Long since with the stage driver sleeps in the hill.
All gone,—after doing the duty they owed,
Old mother in toil, by the Thames River Road.

The valley now echoes with whistles and wheels,
Of railways and tram-cars and automobiles;
A merciless, mercantile, serve-me-and-go,
Days coming and going with no after glow.
A money-mad, pleasure-bound, top-heavy load
Profanes the dream scenes of the Thames River Road.

Could we but turn back a few pages of time,
And see the old hills in their primitive prime.
But past locks the doors upon all that has been,
And Future is something no mortal has seen.
To-day 'tis our duty to lighten the load
Of the weary who travel the Thames River Road.

VII.

THE FORMER NAMES OF THE THAMES RIVER.

BY JAMES SINCLAIR.

It has appeared to me that there are few sections of Ontario that can present material for historical consideration to a greater extent than the valley of the Thames, whether we consider it in connection with our Indian period, or as the centre from which radiated an influence which did much to stamp upon our earlier settlers those characteristics that have made Ontario as a whole, the premier province of our Dominion. The Indian trail, or as it was more generally known, the River Trail, which margined the river from this point westward had the effect of bringing our earlier settlers into more intimate contact with the natives, who, in many cases, rendered valuable service in the primitive pioneer period. This river had been for centuries prior to the advent of the white man an established highway across the western peninsula, connecting Lake Ontario, the Grand River Valley and the western lake front. It seems to have been a settled custom with the natives to select the river valleys of the country for their more permanent places of residence, which is explained when we consider their mode of life, and in the valley of the Thames all their requirements were abundantly supplied. For forty miles of the distance on the western point of the trail, an unbroken wilderness existed on both sides of the river. Here a band of Moravian missionaries established themselves 127 years ago (1792) and it is to these men we are indebted for what written records exist.

Perhaps it would be well at this point to give the principal source of my information as to what follows. I do not intend to repeat what is already on record as accepted history of events of the later military experiences, in this connection. It was my good fortune to meet at a very early period of my life an old Indian, known as Chief Tim, who frequently visited the home of a relative of mine, and as one who could claim to be contemporary with Simcoe and Brant, was always an interesting visitor, while the old man was always willing to recall the past, and was considered the oracle of his tribe. His knowledge of the history of his race was wonderful, and conflicted in many cases with the commonly received statements, which often proved correct on investigation, one of which was that Brant was the son of a chief. This he contradicted, and our evidence proved him correct. He also had a different version of the selection of the site of Ingersoll, and, as he stated, it was military matters that prevailed; and also of the naming of the river as recorded. And instead of exploration, as he presented it, it was for the purpose of exploitation, as the beavers were numerous and the trade profitable. They had only entered the river when they were forced by the natives to return. The name LaTranche was never recognized by the natives, although it passed into the records. *Picturesque Canada* (p. 502) gives the statement of Bellin, map maker of Louis XV's Department of Marine, that the river was explored for 80 leagues without the obstacle of a rapid. Now there is something wrong about this statement of 80 leagues on a river of 135 miles long. The word trench is almost identical with the French word La Tranche, and in plain English means ditch. It is not a distinctive name; it is a term used to differentiate between a natural and an artificial water course, and is in fact a contradiction.

The statement that this river did not possess a name at that time, anyone at all conversant with Indian history will recognize at once as incorrect—one of their outstanding characteristics being their habit of applying names to objects of vastly minor importance. This river had a name, and an exalted one at that. While the name has been lost, the meaning has been preserved, and is "The Gift of the Manito of the Waters," and is the subject of a legend which has been written presumably by the Moravian missionaries.

There is another matter in connection with the naming of the St. Clair, with respect to which our Canadian historians are not in evidence, while our friends in the U. S. have not overlooked it. In 1765, when the revolutionary pot was beginning to simmer, it was deemed advisable that some one in the interest of our country should be somewhere in the neighbourhood of our western front. The appointee to the situation was a British officer named Patrick Sinclair, who had been prominent in the campaign under Wolfe. Arriving at the western front, he decided to purchase a tract of land from the Indians, and which had to be done with the consent and assistance of the leading members of the tribe, as the situation was in almost direct connection with the River trail. Brant at this time was about 22 years of age, and acting chief of the tribes, while his predecessor, Abram, was still Titular Chief, which permitted him to conduct the diplomatic business with the revolutionary commissioners. With the following brief reference by the American chronicler:—"St. Clair, a river called Sinclair in honour of Patrick Sinclair, a British officer, who in 1765 purchased from the Indians a tract of land along the river," all reference to the matter ends so far as it concerns the establishment of Patrick Sinclair on the western front, which had the effect of securing to the British the river trail as a complete line of defence. At a later period our friends in the U. S. claimed the naming of the river for Arthur St. Clair, who was also a British officer but resigned his commission in 1762, joined the revolutionists and opposed the British. He was defeated by the Indians at the Miami villages. There were therefore three sources from which this river (St. Clair) has derived its name:—from LaSalle in 1689, Patrick Sinclair in 1765, and Arthur St. Clair in 1800.

Governor Simcoe in all his activities was first of all a military man, and in his position as governor of the province, the selection of a more suitable situation for the seat of government was necessary. His initial step in this direction was renaming the river, and by a proclamation which he issued July 16th, 1792, it received the name of the "Thames River," having for its prototype the world's famous stream. Nor did he fail to accompany his proclamation with the dignity of appropriate ceremony, his own party, together with many others, assisted by the chaplain, singing God Save the King, a practice he followed whenever justified.

The delay in naming London at this time was no doubt due to political consideration in other quarters, as there is no question of his own desire to name London as the capital of the province. However, in 1794 the site was selected, and London placed on the map. Immediately followed the naming of the counties, with Middlesex naturally following the naming of London, from its situation on the River, "Chatham," from its position on the River corresponding to that in the motherland in the County of Kent. Oxford was named in 1793, for in that year settlement had taken place, and Woodstock with Blenheim—the home of the Marlboroughs. Thus we behold the very heart of the empire recreated, in embryo, in the yet unbroken wilderness of Canada, and with its foundations laid in the valley of the Thames.

The foregoing is but a summary of a subject that lends itself to more extended treatment. Could we but visualize the mind of Simcoe at this supreme moment, what would we behold? His sentiment in the naming of places had a reality behind it that justified every forecast he made, and as Robert Gourlay (an Oxford man, and the stormy petrel of our early political life) said, the removal of Simcoe to another field of action put back the development of Western Canada for 50 years. By his system of naming places a dual purpose was served—it intimated to the English-speaking immigrant where, under the same flag, he would find the same laws and usages, both civil and religious, and with the same environment as in his native land.

VIII.

THE AMISHMAN.

BY HIS HONOUR JUDGE GEO. SMITH.

As the Amish is distinctly a religious sect it may not be amiss to view them first from this point of view. Puritanism, as the word implies, originated in an effort to purify the Protestant Church. The reforms aimed at were almost as drastic and radical as were those of the Protestant reformers. One of the tenets of the Independents in England was that "any gifted brother, if he find himself qualified thereto, may instruct, exhort and preach in the Church." George Fox was the leader and founder of Quakerism. The sect grew and multiplied.

Besides the Papist and Churchman there were Presbyterians, Independents, Baptists or Ana-baptists, Old Brownists, Antinomians, Familists, Millenaries or Chiliasts, Expecters or Seekers, Divorcers, Anti-sabbatarians, Traskites, Soulsleepers or Moralists, Arians, Socinians, Anti-scripturists, Sceptics or Questionists, Atheists, Fifth Monarchy men, Ranters, the Maggletonians, Boehmists, and Quakers or Friends.

As it was in England so was it in Europe whence came the Mennonites. In such a transition period fanaticism played a conspicuous part. Prynne, for example, ridiculed the Church choir in set terms. He said, "Choristers bellow the tenor as it were oxen, bark a counterpart as it were a kennel of dogs, roar out a treble as it were a sort of bulls and grunt out a bass as it were a number of hogs." (Quoted in Cort's Puritanism, p. 455). This criticism shows their lack of appreciation of the artistic. Even the great Milton was as extreme. Carlyle recognized Fox as a religious genius and reformer. He felt that the Mission revealed to him was "to turn people to that *Inward Light*—even that Divine Spirit which would lead men to all truth." This doctrine of the *Inward Light* was the corner-stone upon which Fox built and upon which Quakerism rests.

There was more latitude among the Friends than within the narrower limits of other sects. They considered war "an evil as opposite and contrary to the spirit and doctrine of Christ as light to darkness."

The early Friends' marriage ceremony for solemnity and tender touching simplicity is incomparable. After an impressive silence each in turn repeats, "In the presence of the Lord and this Assembly I take thee to be my wife (or husband), promising with Divine assistance, to be unto thee a loving and faithful husband (or wife) until death shall separate us." If anyone desires to feel and realize the presence of God in a public or private gathering let him attend a Quaker wedding.

The term Quaker was applied to them in derision, but they called themselves *Friends*.

Though the foregoing has special reference to the English Quakers it is applicable equally to the aims and doctrines of the German Quaker or Mennonite.

I quote here from the introductory chapter in *The Amishman*, a little book I wrote just before the war, now ended.

"They derive their name from their founder, Jacob Amman, a Mennonite preacher of Berne, Switzerland. Amman was very conservative in his views, and advocated "avoidance," or the practice of "shunning" those placed under the ban. He prescribed a dress of a particular cut and material, and the use of hooks and eyes. The German word for hook being *haft*, they got the name of Haftler, in contradistinction to the Mennonites, who used buttons, and were called "Knopfler," a word derived from the German word *knopf*, a button.

"He revived the practice of 'feet-washing' at the communion service. It may be noted in passing that the Pope on occasions practices the ceremony of feet-washing, as does also the Greek Church.

"Emigrants from Switzerland carried the division to Alsace-Lorraine and the Palatinate, whence they came to America chiefly from 1820 to 1850, owing to the hardships resulting from the Napoleonic wars. Many came to Ontario from Pennsylvania, being attracted by the cheaper lands available for settlers."

The history of the Canadian Amish begins with the wanderings of Christian Nafzigger, a Bavarian who came to America in 1822 and landed at New Orleans. Thence he went by foot to Lancaster County, Pennsylvania, thence to Ontario, where in the fall of 1822 he secured a tract of land in Wilmot township, Canada West. He went back to Bavaria and returned with his colony in 1826.

In the meanwhile he had been preceded by several families who reached central Ontario by way of Lancaster County, Pennsylvania. Among these were John Brenneman, John Gingerich, Jos. Becher.

The first church was organized in 1824 with John Brenneman and Joseph Goldschmidt as the first ministers. This colony has since developed into four large congregations near the original settlement: one being in the Township of East Zorra (16th Line) in the County of Oxford, and one near Lake Huron, founded in 1849.

The Mennonite immigration antedated this Amish one. A small group of men from Plumstead, Black's County, Pennsylvania, left for Canada in 1786. Kulps, Albrights and Hahns located in Lincoln County, about twenty miles from Niagara Falls. Later several small scattered settlements were made in South Wellington, Welland and Haldimand.

Joseph Schoorg and Samuel Betzner in 1799 and 1800 bought bush lands on the Grand River, east of Doon and Betzner on the west side, near Blair. These men wrote encouraging letters home to Pennsylvania, and several more families from Lancaster County emigrated to Canada. Among them Dave Gingerich, (1801) later Bechtels and Biehns followed, also Michael Baer from New York County. Some treked on horse back, some with Conestogo waggons with four horses. They crossed the Alleghany Mountains, went up the Susquehanna River through New York State and struck Niagara below Buffalo.

Thence they proceeded via Hamilton to Dundas, through the Beverley Swamp to the settlement on the Grand River. They bought land from

Richard Beasley, who owned most of Waterloo Township, at from $1.00 to $4.00 per acre.

In 1803 it was found that there was a mortgage for $20,000 on Beasley's lands. Through the advice of Hans Eby they formed a stock company in the United States which bought up the township and assumed the mortgage. Samuel Bricker was appointed agent for this company with Daniel Erb as his assistant. $20,000 in silver was taken in a light waggon and given to Beasley when the company then got a clear title to 60,000 acres of land in Waterloo County.

In the same year (1803) a settlement was made near Markham in York County. In 1807, 45,000 acres were bought in Woolwich Township, north of Waterloo.

In the second decade of the 19th century immigrants flocked in. Soon much of South Waterloo Township was occupied by the Mennonites, that is, near Doon and Preston.

Berlin was once called Ebytown, and since the war, Kitchener. In 1827 it was given the name Berlin upon the suggestion of Bishop Eby. Bishop Eby was appointed in 1812 and exerted a strong influence in the community till his death in 1835. He wrote a short history of the Mennonites.

In 1909 there were thirty congregations in these districts in Ontario, mostly in Waterloo. There would likely be a total membership in 1913, of about 2,000.

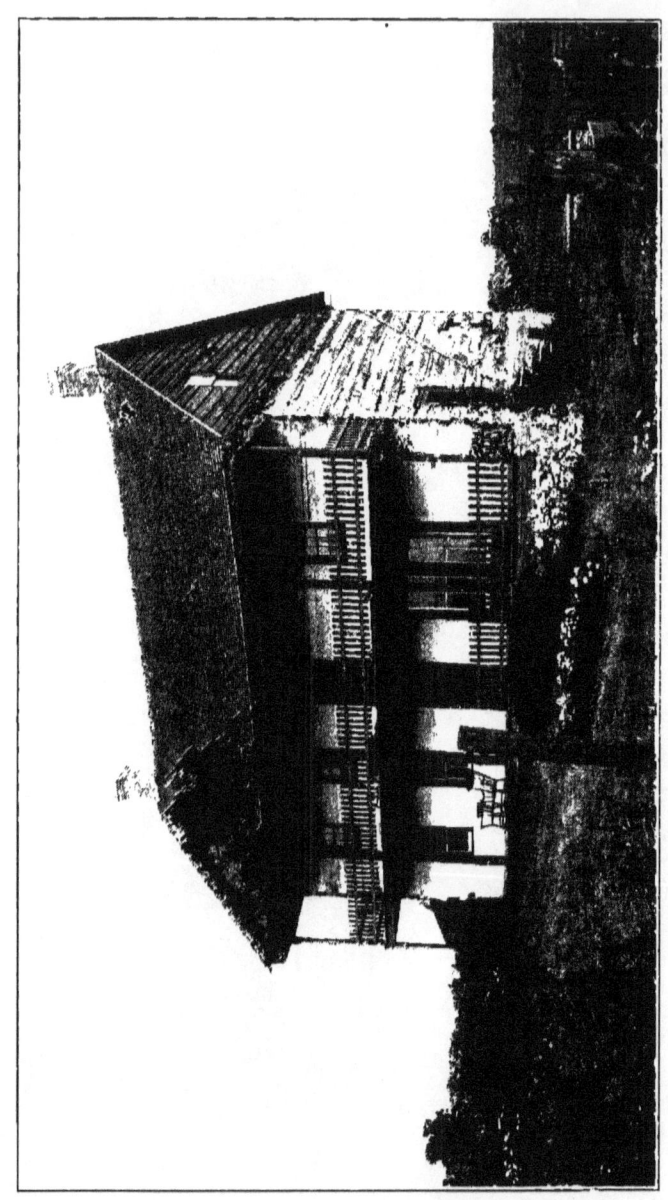

House near Doon, Waterloo Township, built by Christian Schneider 1807.

IX.

WATERLOO COUNTY HISTORY.

By W. H. Breithaupt, C. E.

Waterloo County is in the heart of the peninsula of south-western Ontario. It is watered by the beautiful Grand River and its three principal tributaries, the Conestogo, the Speed, and the Nith Rivers, the first two uniting with the main stream within the county and the third a little below its southerly boundary.

Before its settlement the stretch of country of which the county forms a part was one of the most densely wooded sections of the continent. Magnificent hardwoods, maple, beech, elm, ash, oak, and others were interspersed with great pines. Oak trees three to five feet in diameter, and pine up to five and six feet in diameter, were not uncommon. Some pine were as much as six and a half feet in diameter and two hundred feet high. The clearing of these lands by the settlers, the removal, at great labour and with only slight utilization, of the dense forestation, the development of numerous water powers, the building of saw mills and other industries operated by the waterpowers, is an interesting story by itself.* One hundred and twelve larger and smaller waterpowers have been traced as in operation within the county at some time. Some of them, comparatively few, still remain.

The County was on the northerly edge of the Attiwandaronk or Neutral Indian Country.† Little evidence of continuous aboriginal residence is found within its borders. Tree growth was too dense and continuous to afford suitable lands for the agriculture of the Indian. It was however a fine hunting and fishing country. There are remains of Indian encampments at various places along the Conestogo River, and at Breslau and below Galt on the Grand River. Flint arrowheads and spear heads, stone axes, tomahawks, etc., are well in evidence. No ossuaries or other large Indian burial places have been found within the county.

There is little mention of the settlement of Waterloo County in general Canadian History, nor did the early map makers know of this Pennsylvania colony. John Cary for instance, a noted map-maker of London, showed on several maps, 1806 to 1808, London, Upper Canada, and Dundas Street extending therefrom to well east of Kingston, and the Waterloo district as Six Nation Indian Reservation, while the fact is that neither London, Upper Canada, nor much of Dundas Street existed at the time, while Block 2 Home District, as it was called, was already fairly occupied by settlers.

There have been several county historians in Waterloo. Hon. James Young, published in 1880 his History of Galt and North Dumfries. Ezra Eby, himself a Pennsylvania descendant, brought out in 1895 two large volumes, somewhat on general county history, but, in the main, being a biographical dictionary of 8495 individuals, Pennsylvania settlers in Waterloo County and their descendants. The best account of the settlement of the county appears in Vol. VII of the Ontario Historical Society publications, in a paper by the Rev. A. B. Sherk, who was in his time the foremost authority

---

* E. W. B. Snider, 1918 Annual Report, Waterloo Historical Society.
† "Indian Occupation of S.W. Ontario," James H. Coyne, LL.D., F.R.S.C., 1916 Report, W. H. S.

on early Waterloo history. Mr. Sherk was born near Breslau, Waterloo Township, in 1832, and died in 1916. He personally well remembered the two first (1800) settlers, who were his granduncles; and thus in a manner spanned the entire period, well over a hundred years, up to the time of his death, of the history of Waterloo County.

At the close of the eighteenth century we find the Grand River valley one of the grants made, at the end of th Revolutionary War, by the British Government to its Indian allies, the Six Nation Indians, who came here from Central and Western New York State. The Indians soon sold in parcels or blocks a large part of the lands granted to them. Block 1, of Grand River lands, 92,160 acres, was sold to Philip Stedman of " Fort Erie Tp., in the County of Lincoln," in 1795; and Block 2, of the same lands, 94,012 acres, was sold to Richard Beasley, James Wilson and John B. Rousseau; these two most concern us.

The first settlers in what became Waterloo County were what were called Pennsylvania Germans, and this was the third, and soon became the largest, colony of these people in Upper Canada. The first to come appears to have been the Niagara Colony, somewhat scattered from near Port Colborne to Campden, Lincoln County; the second the Markham Colony, east of Yonge Street, not far from Toronto. A traveller in 1794 relates that "on the east side of Yonge Street, in the rear of the townships of York and Scarborough, is the township of Markham, settled principally by Germans." Elsewhere he states that "these Germans came in this season, furnished with everything to make their situation comfortable." This was the Markham colony of Pennsylvania Germans.

Germans of the Mennonite faith formed a distinct body, as do their descendents to this day, in Pennsylvania, to where they began to migrate in 1683, on the invitation of William Penn, to escape religious persecution and to find entire freedom of conscience. They continued to come to Pennsylvania for over half a century, partly from Switzerland, largely from the Rhine Palatinate, as is reflected in their dialect, and some from Holland, the original home of their religious denomination. The records of the earlier emigration to Pennsylvania are meagre.

Influenced by the example of the United Empire Loyalists and by their preference for the stability of British Government they came to Upper Canada where they were promised freedom, in the full exercise of their religious tenets, one of which was not to bear arms in war. In this connection there may be mentioned that some of the Grand River settlers served as teamsters, and otherwise in the supply service, in the war of 1812.

Waterloo County has the distinction of being the first larger settlement in the interior of Upper Canada. Up to their coming, settlement had been mainly along the border and lake shore; the Pennsylvanians struck out boldly for the interior of the country.

The pioneers midway along the Grand River were Joseph Schoerg and Samuel Betzner, brothers-in-law, farmers from Chambersburg, Franklin County, Pennsylvania. They crossed the Niagara by the Black Rock Ferry in the fall of 1799, and located on the Grand River early in 1800, all as related by the Rev. A. B. Sherk in the Ontario Historical Society paper referred to. Tidings went back to the home country, three more families came out in 1800, seven in 1801, and more in 1802. These vanguard comers obtained what they thought was sufficient title to their lands from Richard Beasley, who appears to have withheld from them knowledge of the mortgage covering the whole of Block 2, Home District, Upper Canada, which was the legal name of the territory. On discovery of the mortgage the settlers were in great distress. However, a mission to Pennsylvania, supported no doubt by the fact of the good quality of the lands in question, resulted successfully in the formation of a Company with sufficient capital to purchase and discharge the mortgage on 60,000 acres, comprising not far from the whole of the present Waterloo Township, of the 94,012 acres of Block 2. The deed conveying this tract, thereafter known as the German Company Tract, and still so referred to in land transfers in the Township, to Daniel Erb and Jacob Erb as trustees, is dated June 29th, 1805.

The first four-horse team driven from Pennsylvania to the Grand River settlement came in 1800, the first year of the colony. The driver was George Clemens who later attained to wealth and importance in the community. The regulation settler's waggon, known as the Conestogo waggon, had a long high box, with graceful longitudinal sweep somewhat on the lines of a ship, with a canvas cover on wooden ribs or hoops, and the ends closed in by gathering cords,—the prairie schooner type familiar in pictures. This was the means of transportation for the bulk of Waterloo County settlers from Pennsylvania. One of these waggons driven by Abraham Weber, from Lancaster County, Pennsylvania, to the site of the later village of Berlin, now the flourishing city of Kitchener, where the driver located in 1807, is in the Waterloo Historical Society's museum.

A grist mill was built in 1807, by John Erb in what became the village, now town, of Preston, of which he was the founder. Eby gives a circumstantial account of a small earlier mill, built for one John Miller, at the site of Galt. But as to this the evidence is conflicting. Abram Erb, brother of John Erb, built the grist mill in Waterloo in 1816. Both of these mills, improved, enlarged and rebuilt from time to time, have practically been in continuous operation from the beginning, and are to-day among the largest flour mills of the county.

Benjamin Eby visited the Grand River settlement in 1806, and the following year came to stay. His lands comprised a large part of the village of Berlin, so named about 1829 as nearly as has been ascertained. Eby was made Mennonite preacher in 1809, and Bishop in 1812. For about forty years he appears to have been the principal man of affairs, both spiritual and temporal, in Waterloo township. He was the founder of Berlin, where he encouraged manufacturers and mechanics to make their homes and begin their industries. The first furniture factory in the village, begun by Jacob Hoffman about 1828, was directly due to his support, as were other industries. The first church in the county was built by Bishop Eby on his own land in 1813. This is the old Mennonite church, now in its third building, at the east end of King Street, Kitchener. It is characteristic of the historical modesty of the Mennonites that this first church of Waterloo County exhibits no other date on its name tablet than that of the construction of the present building, 1902. Bishop Eby also started the first school in the village, in connection with the church. A spelling book compiled by him and printed by his son, Henry Eby, is extant.

The first school in the county was started near the present village of Blair as early as 1802, and had a Rittenhaus, a name noted in the educational history of Pennsylvania, for teacher.

An interesting historical fact in connection with Bishop Eby is that his great-great-grandson, in line of descent of oldest sons in each generation, Ralph Alexander Eby, was the first Waterloo County man to be killed in action in the Great War. He enlisted from Swift Current, Saskatchewan, and was killed at Neuve Chapelle, March 20th, 1915. Enlistments from Waterloo County in the Great War were 3,706. Of these 486 were killed or died of wounds or disease; 112 received military 'decorations.

Up to about 1820 settlement was almost entirely by Mennonites from Pennsylvania. About this time European Germans and others began to come. One of the first of these was Frederick Gaukel, the first hotel-keeper in Berlin. He built what was then considered a large hotel in 1835, on the site, continuously occupied as a hotel since that time, of the present Walper House, Kitchener. Gaukel donated the land for the Court House, when Berlin was made the County Town in 1852.

In the thirties of the last century, the village of Preston was a thriving business centre. Active there, were Jacob Hespeler, a native of Wurtemburg, Jacob Beck from the Grand Duchy of Baden, Otto Klotz from Kiel on the Baltic, who was noteworthy in the educational and general intellectual progress of his village and county, and others. Hespeler later removed to New Hope which was renamed after him in 1857 in recognition of his public service in the large industries he started there. Beck founded the village of Baden, in Wilmot Township, where he developed a considerable water-power and various industries, notably a foundry and machine shop, which had a wide range of business.

North Dumfries Township was next taken up after Waterloo. On restoration of peace and normal conditions after the war of 1812, there was a renewed tide of prosperity and immigration in Upper Canada. The Honourable William Dickson of Niagara, whose attention had first been directed to the Grand River colony by the fact that he acted as the legal adviser of the Pennsylvanians in their purchase of lands, and who had no doubt watched their progress with interest, decided to invest in Grand River lands himself. In 1816 he purchased from the Hon. Thomas Clarke of Stamford, Lincoln County, who then held the title, Block 1, Home District, already referred to, 92,160 acres. the greater part of the township of North Dumfries in Waterloo County and South Dumfries in the County of Brant for the sum of roundly £24,000, this including a mortgage of £8,841 which had remained against the property from the Stedman purchase. Mr. Dickson at once engaged as his agent, to reside on and administer the lands, a young Pennsylvania German, Absolom Shade, then living in Buffalo, whom Dickson had known as a carpenter contractor. Together they set out to explore the lands, and to locate a town site, as they did at a well adapted place on the Grand River, which in due time became the village of Galt, so named in 1827, for John Galt, the author, then commissioner for the Canada Company in Guelph, a friend of Mr. Dickson. Settlers were attracted, largely from Scotland, and were given liberal terms of purchase and payment, the price of land being generally about four dollars an acre. Galt soon became a prosperous trading and manufacturing centre. was incorporated as a village in 1850 and as a town in 1857. It was for many years the principal place of business not only in the county, but for a section of country extending as far as Goderich. In 1846, and before, it had lines of daily stages to Hamilton and Guelph and tri-weekly to Goderich.

The township of Woolwich was also taken up largely by Pennsylvania Germans, later comers, and some of the younger generation from Waterloo. In Wilmot Township many settlers were directly from Germany, among them a body of Amish, an early offshoot of the Mennonites, for whom their leader, Jacob Nachtsinger, had obtained a grant from the British Government. Around Haysville in Wilmot there was a considerable colony of settlers from England, and some from Ireland. The Canada Company had a tract comprising four concessions in the southern part of Wilmot. Wellesley Township was in greater part settled by Scotchmen and partly by German Catholics who predominate around St. Agatha in Wilmot, where they have a fine church, orphanage, etc., and extend to Bamberg and St. Clements vicinity in Wellesley. Another large settlement of original German Catholics is around New Germany in Waterloo Township.

The first newspaper of the county was the *Canada Museum und Allgemeine Zeitung,* printed mostly in German and partly in English, of which the first issue is dated August 27th, 1835. It continued for only five years, when its editor and proprietor, Henry William Peterson, was appointed registrar of the new county of Wellington, and moved from Berlin, the domicile of the *Museum,* to Guelph. The *Museum* was followed by the *Deutsche Canadier,* published by Henry Eby, a son of Bishop Eby, and Christian Enslin as editor. Henry Eby was also a book publisher, bringing out Mennonite devotional books and others. In Galt the *Dumfries Courier* first appeared in 1844, and was published for three years. Next came the *Galt Reporter,* whose editor Peter Jaffray, had been active on the *Courier.* The *Dumfries Reformer* began publication in 1850.

The building of railways to and through Waterloo County marked the transition to more recent conditions and progress. At the beginning of Canadian railroading the Grand Trunk Railway Company, with its main line from Montreal to Toronto, its seaport connection to Portland, Maine, and its extension westward to Sarnia, was by far the largest and most important company. Next in importance was the Great Western Railway Company with main line from Niagara to Detroit. Both of these companies built to Waterloo County at the beginning of their operation. A branch of the Great Western Railway from Harrisburg on the main line to Galt was opened for regular traffic on the 21st of August, 1854. The Hamilton to Toronto branch was not opened until December, 1855. An extension to Guelph through Preston and Hespeler was built as a separate enterprise, 1855 to 1857. It was leased to the Great Western Railway and eventually forfeited by reason of deficits in operation which grew into a mortgage which was foreclosed. There was also an extension to Berlin from Preston, built in 1856-1857, as part of the Galt-Guelph Railway. The Preston-Berlin branch had a short career. It was opened for traffic, November 2nd, 1857, and ran for three months only when its bridge across the Grand River, above Blair, was wrecked by high water. The bridge was not rebuilt, and the Preston end never again used. The main line of the Grand Trunk Railway, built through Waterloo County as the Toronto-Sarnia extension, in 1853 to 1856, traversing the townships of Waterloo and Wilmot, with principal stations Berlin and New Hamburg, was opened through to Stratford on Nov. 17th, 1856. And thus Waterloo County began its more rapid development, particularly in manufactures, which has kept pace with the most progressive sections of the Dominion of Canada.

X.

WILLIAMSTOWN, AN HISTORIC VILLAGE.

By Miss Janet Carnochan.

Although I had spent some weeks in this little village many years ago, I had no idea till lately that it was such a wonderful village, with such a remarkable history, with no larger a population than two hundred, a little river running through the midst, the people of different races,—Scottish and French speaking different languages,—English, Gaelic, French; of two different religions,—Presbyterian and Roman Catholic; with traces of Sir John Johnson, of his father Sir William Johnson, of Lord Selkirk, of Sir Alexander Mackenzie, of David Thompson, of Simon Fraser, these great geographers and explorers, of Bishop Macdonell, of Bishop Bethune and his venerable father, Rev. John Bethune, of U. E. Loyalists, of Hudson Bay factors, of the Northwest Company, of soldiers who had fought in the Revolutionary war and in distant countries, a village with an endowed church, an endowed High School, a church built in 1812, the manse in 1823, the first manse built about 1787, or shortly after 1787, when Rev. John Bethune came. A centenary of the settlement of the County of Glengarry was held in 1884, when many interesting reminiscences were printed in the *Montreal Witness*, and many relics of the early days were shewn. A centenary of the building of the present church was held in 1912, and my friends, who know that I always uphold the name of Niagara, wondered much to hear me say that the centenary celebration held in Williamstown was far ahead of either St. Mark's or St. Andrew's in Niagara in 1892 and 1894 respectively. And it is true, for the celebration lasted a week instead of three days, and besides being the centenary of the church was also that of the U. E. Loyalists. Many distinguished sons of Williamstown came from distant homes to speak; many valuable gifts were donated to the church by loving and loyal members.

And first, of how Williamstown received the name. When the United Empire Loyalists, or those who remained loyal to the king and British Institutions, left their possessions and came to what was then a wilderness, the British government, to partly compensate them for their losses, gave them grants of land. Sir John Johnson, who was the largest land owner in the American colonies, fled to save his life, with some faithful followers, through frightful dangers. He was given large grants of land, and perhaps the selection of the site was from its position on the River Raisin, being suitable for mills from the water power, and the place was at first called Milltown. The inhabitants wished to call it Johnstown from Sir John Johnson, but he declined the honour, and wished it called Williamstown from his father, Sir William Johnson. The Manor House, still standing, was the property of Sir John Johnson; the centre part was built in his time, but additions were made later. He parted with his Williamstown property in 1821.

WILLIAMSTOWN, AN HISTORIC VILLAGE

So much for the name, but whence came those early settlers, and how and why? I have always found the story of those who came out with Bishop Macdonell very confusing, as sometimes they are spoken of as soldiers from Scotland, again as a regiment from Ireland, and again as those ejected from lands in Scotland. Another statement is that they were U. E. Loyalists; another as Hudson Bay Factors, or from the North West Company. And remarkable to say, these statements are true of the different settlers coming at different times from different places. The best explanation was given by Bishop Macdonell himself, that wonderful man with the ability of a business man, the tact and skill of a diplomat, the piety of a soldier of the cross, in an address at a farewell dinner given to him at Kingston in 1838, where he told of his efforts for those of his own faith. But the people of Glengarry were not all Catholics from Scotland. It is rather difficult to sort out all the different groups which came. The Protestant Highlanders who came to South Carolina in 1772 form the first emigration from Scotland, and when trouble arose a ship load left for Prince Edward Island, but afterward came to Nova Scotia, and in 1774, on the breaking out of hostilities, formed the 84th Regiment, of which Rev. Jno. Bethune became the Chaplain, and many received grants of land in Glengarry. This formed one group.

The 2nd of Highlanders, chiefly Macdonells, at the invitation of Sir William Johnson, came to the Mohawk Valley in 1773. When war broke out, Sir John Johnson with friends and neighbours, fled to Montreal through dangers dire, in 1776. He raised a battalion at his old home in Tryon County, among his followers, and called it the King's Royal Regiment of New York, and they and their families came to Canada in 1783.

3rd. The first emigrants who came direct from Scotland came in 1786 under Alexander Macdonald, 520 in number. 4th. In 1792, Macdonell of Greenfield came from Scotland with followers. 5th. In 1803 the last large emigration came through Bishop Macdonell, the discharged soldiers of the First Glengarry Fencibles under Macdonell of Glengarry, and these had been under the charge of Alexander Macdonell, afterwards Bishop Macdonell.

To explain why so many left Scotland is a sad story. From 1782 to 1790, tenants were turned out to make room for large sheep farms, and when these tried to emigrate, all sorts of restrictions were used to prevent them, even ships of war guarded the harbours to board emigrant vessels and press into the Naval Service every able-bodied man. In spite of this, many came with their families. In 1784, land surveyors arrived, lots were drawn, and the name Glengarry given to the county from Glengarry in Scotland.

The material for this paper I have gained from many sources. From the pamphlet giving an account of the Centenary Celebration of St. Andrew's Church, Williamstown, I have learned much; from "A Retrospect of the first Catholic Diocese of Upper Canada" much has been gleaned; in a paper read by Mrs. Foran before the Women's Canadian Historical Society of Ottawa. (Transactions of that Society, Vol. VII, 1917), "My native County—Glengarry," many interesting facts were found. In an old copy of the *Montreal Witness*, headed "Lochiel," the celebration in 1884 of the settlement of Glengarry, most interesting accounts were given of the early settlers, pictures of relics exhibited, anecdotes grave and gay, and names of clans represented. In all these articles the two most outstanding persons are Rev. John Bethune and the Rev. Alexander Macdonell, both staunch Scots, with all the best qualities common to the race, as the military phrase we have so often heard of late—" carrying out the best traditions of the army." And they both, we may say like St. Paul, "fought with beasts at Ephesus." Both were clergymen, but of different faiths, stalwart supporters of the same, yet tolerant to others, loved and admired by their people, and the public generally. To give the story of Williamstown much must be told of the former and incidentally of the latter, but the account of the centenary touches on almost every point of the history of the settlement. The celebration was from August 25th to September 2nd, including services on two Sundays, the intervening days being given to addresses by prominent speakers and distinguished and loyal sons of Glengarry who had come from distant points to do honour to their birthplace. The Rev. John Bethune was born on the Island of Skye in 1751 of a family tracing their descent as far back as the Norman Conquest. Cardinal Beaton was of the same family. He went to South Carolina and was the chaplain of a regiment there, but in the first years of the Revolutionary War was made a prisoner and suffered much for his loyalty. Being exchanged he came to Nova Scotia and there organized a regiment, the 84th or Royal Highland Emigrant Regiment of which he became the Chaplain of the First Battalion. When that was disbanded he organized a congregation in Montreal,—St. Gabriel's church, in which he preached May 6th, 1787. His grant of land as an officer in the army being in Glengarry, he removed to Williamstown, then the leading settlement, and laid the foundation of the Church, also of congregations in Cornwall, Martintown and Lancaster, and was the first Presbyterian minister in Upper Canada. It is told of him that he performed 2379 baptisms in this district, and must have been a good organizer as his records, all in good shape, show. Two of his sons became Anglicans, one the second Bishop of Toronto, the other Dean of Montreal. The inscription on his monument by his six sons attests his fine character. A remarkable tribute was paid to him by Jno. A. Macdonald, K.C. "I am not, as you know, of your religion. I am a Catholic, as my people have ever been, but I may say with no impropriety that Mr. Bethune was a faithful and zealous missionary, and to this day the fruits of his vigour and efficiency remain; indeed the epitaph of Sir Christopher Wren in St. Paul's Cathedral might, in Williamstown, be well applied to Mr. Bethune *Si monumentum requiris circumspice,* (If you seek his monument look around.)

The inscription on his monument in the cemetery is creditable alike to the father and his sons; thus—

"Sacred to the memory of the Rev. John Bethune, pastor of the congregation of the Kirk of Scotland in Glengarry. He departed this life at Williamstown, 23rd September, 1815, in the 66th year of his age and the 44th of his ministry.

"That he was a faithful steward, the peace and happiness of his flock are the most certain proof. That he was eminently endeared by those conciliating, endearing qualities which united Society in the closest bonds of unanimity and friendship, his numerous congregation who shed the tribute of unfeigned sorrow over his grave have borne the most honourable testimony.

"That he was open, generous and sincere, those who participated in his friendship can afford the most satisfactory evidence.

"That he was a kind and affectionate husband, a tender and indulgent parent, the love and unanimity of his numerous family furnish the most undeniable proof.

"This monument is erected as a mark of filial affection to his memory by his six sons, Angus, Norman, John, James, Alexander, Donald."

A very remarkable document is the Pastoral Letter directed to his congregation a few days before his death, in which he urges them strongly, as he had done before, to look out for a successor to himself as he feels his health failing. Very plain language is used in the advice given with regard to finances, to the choice of a minister, to the manner of conducting their meetings, all shewing the good common sense, the fervent piety, the wish for their spiritual prosperity.

The next minister was the Rev. Jno. Mackenzie, M.A., a native of Fort Augustus, Scotland, who remained with them for thirty-seven years. He too was a loyal subject, as in the Papineau Rebellion, the men of Glengarry were called out, and Mr. Mackenzie was with his people at the front. The next minister was the Rev. Peter Watson, a native of Inverness, Scotland. He too was a faithful and eloquent pastor, succeeded by Rev. Alexander MacGillivray, D.D., their first Canadian born minister, 1877—1888. The present pastor, Rev. Arpad Govan, B.A., has served from 1888, to the present time, a period of thirty-one years. St. Andrew's has been very fortunate in its ministers; in a period of 132 years there have been only five ministers, an average of over twenty-six years for each. It is not likely that any other congregation can furnish a parallel.

To Bishop Macdonell we now turn. Many tributes have been paid, alike by Catholics and Protestants, the most remarkable perhaps being that by the Orangemen. Born in Inverness-shire in 1760, educated partly in Paris and also in Spain, he did noble work in Scotland, in Ireland, in Canada, and died in Dumfries, Scotland, in 1840 at the age of eighty. His was a long life full of strenuous work, first for the tenants ejected from their homes, obtaining employment for them in Glasgow, then forming them into a Highland regiment, the first Catholic one formed, remaining with them in Guernsey and Ireland eight years, next procuring land for them in Canada, with much trouble obtaining 160,000 acres of land, next for his church. On his arrival he found only two Roman Catholic clergymen in Upper Canada and only two wooden churches and one stone one. He travelled from one end of the province to the other, on foot, or on horseback, in canoe or rough waggon, without roads or bridges. In the war of 1812 he formed the Second Glengarry Fencible Regiment. Next he repaired to England twice, as he had on former occasions, this time to obtain help to build churches, and pay salaries; this with much delay and trouble he obtained. In his address to the Catholic and Protestant freeholders he says "I address my Protestant, as well as my Catholic friends, because I feel assured that through the long period of four and forty years intercourse with some of you, and two and thirty years with others, no man will say that in promoting your temporal interests I ever made any difference between Catholic and Protestant and indeed it would be both unjust and ungrateful in me if I did, for I found Protestants upon all occasions as ready to meet my wishes and second my efforts to promote the public good as the Catholics themselves, and it is with no small gratification that I here acknowledge having received from Orangemen unequivocal and substantial proofs of disinterested friendship and generosity of heart."

At the centenary of Glengarry in 1884 it was told of him that he had sometimes been called in to the dying beds of Protestants whose minister could not be procured. Many a fervent prayer in his own loved Gaelic he offered.

and he had been heard to declare that he knew many good Protestant prayers. Mr. Bethune too, was sometimes called in to a Catholic bedside in a similar emergency.

The address of Bishop Macdonell given at the farewell dinner to him in Kingston in 1838, explains clearly what seemed to be contradictory statements. He says "The only claim I have to the good will of my countrymen was the warm interest I took in the welfare of a great number of poor Highlanders who were ejected by their landlords before the close of the last century, and they and their families set adrift in the world. These poor people to the number of several hundreds I conducted to Glasgow and procured employment for them in the manufactories where I remained with them myself till in consequence of the French Revolution, and the stagnation of trade on the continent, the manufactories were ruined and the Highlanders thrown out of employment. It was then that I represented their condition to the Government, got them embodied into a Fencible Corps, and accompanied them myself to the Island of Guernsey, and to Ireland, and attended them for the period of eight years till they with all the other Scottish Fencibles were disbanded in 1802. Seeing them thus a third time set adrift without home or habitation I applied to Government and obtained lands for them in Canada, came with them myself and resided with them in the County of Glengarry for twenty-five years."

Bishop Macdonell had thus travelled twice to London in the interest of his people, first to consult with Dundas, Secretary of War, to form the Glengarry Regiment, and second to consult with Premier Addington as to obtaining land in Canada, and his influence gained his request in each case. His modest statement tells nothing of the difficulties he met with in these journeys, nor of his patience and perseverance in urging the claims of his people.

A tribute paid to him in the obituary notice in the *British Whig* of Kingston was this: "His loyalty to the British Crown was never surpassed; by word and deed he proved how sincere was his attachment to British institutions, and he infused into the hearts of his fellow countrymen and others an equal enthusiasm." The tribute of J. A. Macdonell K.C., will be a fitting close: "The business capacity of this extraordinary man distinguished him who was a most loyal and faithful subject of his Sovereign, a most loyal and true-hearted friend of the Highland people of this County of Glengarry without distinction of class or creed."

It is remarkable that both Rev. John Bethune and Rev. Alexander Macdonell, although as clergymen supposed to be men of peace, each helped greatly to form regiments whose duty it was to fight; in each case it was to protect their country, each acted as chaplain to a regiment. Someone used the phrase, "With the Sword in one hand and the Bible in the other." As the names are mentioned together, it may be told that on one occasion a difficulty had arisen between Rev. J. Bethune and his congregation. A happy thought was to submit the matter for settlement to Bishop Macdonell. He gave his decision in favour of their clergyman, and at the same time gave the congregation a stern rebuke, ordering them to submit to their pastor, this in choice Gaelic to which due submission was given.

At the Centennial many interesting historical items were brought to light. At the Social Reunion at the home of Col. D. M. Robertson, the Manor House, it was told that the central part of the dwelling was built during its ownership by Sir John Johnson over a hundred years ago, the Rev. A. Govan gave an historical sketch telling of the first church built about 1787, an unpretentious log building, the furnishing of which was very primitive, the seats being planks resting on cedar blocks. Besides serving as a church, it did duty during the week as a school and afterward served for many purposes. It stood till quite recently. The present church of stone was started in 1812. There are in existence the minutes carefully kept; the earliest contributions were made in 1809. The walls were built by Francis Rochileau of Kingston; his contract was for £205; all material was found him, and all unskilled labour. Owing to the war it was not finished till 1815. The steeple was built by Pierre Poitras of Montreal at a cost of £212 and £10 additional for the copper weathercock, gold leafed. The bell still in use has the following inscription: "1806 Thomas Mears & Sons of London, Fecit. The gift of Sir Alexander Mackenzie, to the Presbyterian Church of Glengarry, Province of Upper Canada, North America. The Rev. John Bethune, Minister." The total cost of the church was £2000 and each member of the congregation contributed £20 before he was entitled to a pew. In 1818 the first division of pews was made by lot, after setting aside a pew for the minister's family, and pews for the elders, one for Sir Alexander Mackenzie and for the North-West Company.

A singular thing was that the title to the church and burying ground had been given to Mr. Bethune personally. By his will all his Williamstown property was left to his wife. She sold the glebe to Mr. David Thompson, the noted geographer and explorer and inadvertently the title to the church and cemetery was included, but this was returned and given in 1819 to six trustees of the church. The Manse built for Mr. Bethune is still in good repair, and is owned and occupied by Mr. Farquhar Robertson of Montreal. The rooms are large and the house commodious.

On Sunday afternoon there was a service in Gaelic conducted by two young clergymen, Rev. D. Mackenzie of Moose Creek, Ont., and Rev. J. B. MacLeod of Martintown, Ont. It was a surprise to the congregation to see two young men so thoroughly conversant with the language in which in the early days the services were regularly conducted, sometimes one service being in English and the other in Gaelic, while now only the older generation of Glengarry retains a perfect knowledge of the Gaelic. The explanation was that both came from Prince Edward Island where Gaelic is still used extensively.

All the old Bibles and Psalm books that were available were gathered for the occasion and a large percentage of those present were able to join intelligently in the service and with appreciation. At all the services of the centenary celebration was observed the old time custom of singing the psalms and hymns without musical accompaniment, the tunes being started by the Precentor. At the Gaelic service the clergymen acted as Precentors. Many came long distances to have the privilege of taking part in the service, in one case driving forty miles in a buggy.

On Empire Loyalist day a beautiful service was held in the cemetery when the graves were decorated, particularly those of U. E. Loyalists and those who formed the first congregation. Mr. Donald McMaster, K.C., D.C.L. a member of the British Parliament, who was born and spent his early years in Williamstown, paid a tribute to those who had gone before and whose remains now lie in this sacred soil. Beautiful floral wreaths were placed on the graves of the three ministers buried here, Rev. Jno. Bethune, Rev. J. Mackenzie and Rev. P. Watson. Flowers were also placed on the graves of McDonalds, Grants, Dingwalls, Fergusons, Chisholms, Camerons, McLellans,

McKenzies, McLennans and many others. The 59th Regt. Highland Pipe Band played "The Land o' the Leal," Donald McMaster spoke eloquently of those who had chosen to sacrifice lands, position, wealth and comfort and had to leave the graves of their ancestors. He quoted the words of an American writer, Mr. Vantyre: "They had been obliged to accept at par the depreciated money and had stood in terror of the law. Finally a Test Act had demanded of them an oath which they could not take, and refusal had brought upon them fines, disabilities, special taxation and even imprisonment and whipping. When the partisan struggle was the hottest the persecutors had resorted to proscription, outlawry and confiscation."

John A. Macdonell K.C., of Alexandria, who has written so much on the history of the two counties, paid a splendid tribute to the U. E. Loyalists giving an interesting history of their coming, paying a tribute to Sir John Johnson's loyalty, quoting from the American historian, Stone—"He voluntarily gave up domains in what is now the United States, larger and fairer than had ever belonged to a single proprietor in America, William Penn only excepted." Upwards of ten thousand acres of the most fertile land in the Mohawk Valley was the sacrifice he made for a United Empire. He also paid a high tribute to the Rev. John Bethune, and incidentally to Bishop Macdonell, and the utter absence of intolerance between those of different creeds, speaking of the kindly relation between them. He had made a close study of Lord Dorchester's list of U. E. Loyalists, and in the fifty-one names mentioned, there are thirty-three clans; of these names there are thirty-three Mac's ranging alphabetically from McAlpine to McPherson, ranging through McIntyre, McLeod, McMartin, McNairn: those also who are not Mac's are Campbells, Robertsons, Stewarts, etc.

In speaking of a very extraordinary document, an address of the Orange body of Toronto to Bishop Macdonell, shewing the absence of party feeling, he closed with the words: Your committee have indeed shown a continuance of that spirit, when they invited me, a Roman Catholic, known by everybody in our county to be such, to participate in your festivities, upon the centenary of St. Andrew's Church. I appreciate your courtesy and kindness, and descendants of these Loyalists, I take my leave of you with this wish—the best that I may—May you and your children be loyal as they."

St. Andrew's congregation has been particularly fortunate in the character of its ministers, their ability, their faithfulness, their long term of office; fortunate, too, in the possession of goodly elders who gave time and talent to the building up of the congregation, and who were the able assistants of the ministers; fortunate too in the possession of valuable documents, deeds, etc., which have been carefully preserved. Not many congregations are so fortunate, as I could mention churches and high schools which, although they date back as far or nearly as far as Williamstown, have no records further back than 1860, the changes of secretaries, and the carelessness of officials, causing this lamentable loss.

Williamstown is one of the few congregations which possess Communion tokens. They had the inscription, "Revd. John Bethune, Glengarry, 1794." Among the documents preserved are the Rules and Regulations of the proprietors of the church, of which there are fourteen, chiefly relating to the office bearers, of the temporalities, of the rights of pew holders, and payment of salaries. To this are appended eighty-two names, 10th July, 1808. Another is a list of pew holders of whom there are twenty-eight in 1818 and a most remarkable pastoral letter of Rev. Jno. Bethune in 1815. There is also the deed of St. Andrew's church site of Martintown, April 10th, 1811. A very curious document in the possession of Mrs. Barbara McKenzie, Williamstown, is called: Black River tithes, 1791, being so many bushels of wheat, with thirty-three names, mostly two, one being four of oats, and several giving peas. To this are attached little notes explanatory signed by John Bethune or simply J. B. as: " N. B.—Mr. McKenzie will please exempt also from this list—of the late 84th Regt. provided he will promise not to swear any more or play the fool.—J. B." Another, a regimental discharge, to John Mackenzie, dated 24th December, 1783, signed: John Johnson, showing that the bearer had served honestly and faithfully and was entitled to the portion of land allotted to each private. It begins " His Majesty's Provincial Regiment called the King's Royal Regiment of New York, whereof Sir John Johnson, Knight and Baronet, is Lieut.-Colonel Commandant."

The contract for the erection of the present Manse is dated 1822, and is for the sum of £239 Halifax currency, one third to be paid in produce, the second third in cash and the remaining third, February, 1824. The Manse still stands with a large lawn in front, with spacious rooms, and it has the appearance of a modern house although nearly a century old.

Another remarkable thing is the valuable gifts received at the Centenary Celebration; a pulpit by Rev. A. MacGillivray, D.D., of Toronto, a former pastor: Communion table, Col. D. M. Robertson; Elder's chairs, His Honour Judge James McLennan; Individual set, Henry Hunt, M. D., Toronto; Bible and Book of Praise, Bonar Congregation, Toronto; Velours Curtains and Fixtures, Mrs. Farquhar Robertson: One thousand dollars endowment, David Grant, South Branch.

But a word must be said about the old Manse now known as the "White House," and its owner for some time, a most remarkable man, perhaps the most remarkable inhabitant of Williamstown. David Thompson, the noted geographer, explorer and astronomer. Born in London, England, of Welsh extraction, he received lessons in navigation and at the age of fourteen was apprenticed to the Hudson Bay Company for seven years. In 1797 he wrote in his journal, May 23rd. " This day left the service of the Hudson Bay Co., and entered that of the Company of Merchants from Canada. May God Almighty prosper me," Till 1812, he remained in the employment of the North West Company, surveyed their posts, and explored from sea to sea as he says when at the mouth of the Columbia River. In 1816, he was employed by the British Government to survey the boundary line between the United States and Canada from Maine to the Lake of the Woods. The maps made by him still govern. In some respects he was indeed remarkable for those days, as he never used alcoholic liquors, and while other posts were bar-rooms of the lowest type no liquor was allowed in any post under his charge. Also to the Roman Catholic Frenchmen in his charge, he often read chapters of the Old and the New Testaments with explanations, they listening attentively. In an article in the Geographical Journal by Mr. J. B. Tyrrell, F.G.S., called " David Thompson the Great Geographer," a fine tribute is paid to him: " His work was detailed and exact. It has been my fortune to follow Thompson's course for thousands of miles, and to take observations in the same places, where he took them, and it is impossible for me to speak too highly of the excellence of these surveys and observations. Both morally and scientifically he was a man of the very highest type. As a discoverer and explorer he stands in the highest rank."

Another noted man, if not a resident, made at least a visit to Williamstown—Lord Selkirk, that philanthropic nobleman who did so much to help his countrymen with an unstinted hand, and who met with so much opposition from the elements, fire and frost and famine, freshets and locusts, and still more from the North West Company, and who retired brokenhearted from the struggle. But many of the descendants of his settlers now reap the fruits of his toil, in prosperous and happy homes in Manitoba. In his diary in 1803, he says, reaching Williamstown: " I went to see the Presbyterian minister, Rev. John Bethune, and stayed with him. He gave me an account of the Highland settlement, and referred to the good people who came out from the old country."

A word, indeed, a good many words should be said of the cemetery. Never has it been my lot to see in a small village the resting place of the dead kept in such beautiful order. On my inquiry—How do you do this? the answer was, Oh! there is an endowment. Think of it, ye who leave those sacred spots without care, given over to briars and weeds, an endowment of $3,000, of which $2,000 was given by Mrs Grant who gave liberally for two scholarships for four years for the High School.

And that brings us to the history of the High School, also a remarkable one, and that has to me a personal interest. As there are only two high schools in the county, Williamstown and Alexandria, they have a large constituency from which to draw pupils. Of what benefit the scholarship founded by R. R. McLennan M.P. is, I happen to know that one widow had two of her children who gained the scholarship educated so as to enter Queen's University and obtain the degree of B.A. And the good example set by the "Laird," as he was called, has been followed by others, Margaret Grant giving two scholarships of the value of $400 and $360 respectively. That of Laird McLennan was for $440. Another scholarship, or bursary as they are called in Scotland, was given by Marion Stewart McDonald. Can any other village High School tell of such generosity as there are now four scholarships. Men's good deeds do live after them. How many in after years will bless the memory of these founders of scholarships which will help them in the pursuit of education, which reminds me of the Snell Scholarships in Scotland founded 300 years ago, and in this year is to be unveiled a monument to its founder. In a little village is a monument to the old blacksmith, Andrew Snell, whose son John Snell saved the life of Charles Stewart, after the battle of Worcester, and on his restoration to the throne advanced his preserver, who left a large sum of money to found scholarships for his countrymen. A public spirited man now living in Ayr hunted up the whole history, circulars were sent to those who had gained the scholarships or their descendants living in different continents. Money was given, a site, an architect gave the plan and in September, 1914, the monument was to have been unveiled, but the war prevented, and now after four years the good deed will be commemorated and others incited to similar generosity.

Of my personal recollections of Williamstown, as it was, over forty years ago, I have said nothing, but I remember the two square pews in the front of the church for the use of the elders, the confusion of names, to distinguish one Macdonald from the other. At the Post Office most bewildering mistakes might occur, except that many of the odd descriptive names were known. Sheriff McMartin was always called "The Sheriff" and all his family called thus "Maggie the Sheriff;" "Jimmy the Sheriff;" and so on. Mrs. McDonald was called "The widow Nellie" and her son "Angus the widow." Why should Alexander Grant be known as Alick Jim Roy? Two of the McMartins were "Mac on the Mill" and "Curly Mac." A MacDonald was always called "Black Angus," and his daughter "Betsey Black Angus." The son of Colonel Angus Macdonell was called "Alex. Colonel Angus," and another woman was called "Betsey Black Angus." Among other names were "Sandy Ocean" and Sandy Sank, Johnnie Bush and Archie Squire. I remember a mistake I made which caused a laugh at my expense. There being a James Macdonald and a John Macdonald each of whom had a daughter Annie, to distinguish them one was called Annie John the other Annie James. Hearing the name, on being introduced, I called her Miss John.

XI.

SOME UNUSUAL SOURCES OF INFORMATION IN THE TORONTO REFERENCE LIBRARY ON THE CANADIAN REBELLIONS OF 1837-8.

By Frances M. Staton.

When about three years ago we decided, after some consultation on the subject, to publish, at intervals, a series of bibliographies of material available and readily accessible in the Reference Department of the Toronto Public Library, our object was two-fold:

In the first place, to bring to light many of the treasures of which we were possessed, and in a general way to make known to the public the vast resources of material on Canadian topics with which our library is so richly endowed.

Our object, secondly, was to endeavour by these means to aid the student and other readers who were desirous of pursuing some particular course of study, by removing as many impediments as possible out of their paths, and to make their fields of investigation as interesting and as fruitful as possible.

The value of a library and especially a reference library, is increased manifold if its consultation, by the readers who frequent it, is made easy and attractive. Therefore, special bibliographies bringing together all the resources of the library on a particular topic, cannot fail to make pleasant the paths of those who wish to venture into the long avenues of research. In this way, too, the student is not only guided in his reading, but receives much encouragement and incentive to further efforts in his chosen branch of study.

Again, when our clients come to the library with the object and hope of obtaining material on a certain subject, their chief desire is to find out what books and other material can be provided there and then.

While general bibliographies are not to be despised or under-valued, giving, as they do, many numerous sources of information on particular subjects, they are, as a rule, confined to lists of books, and do not convey to the reader, where those references are accessible; whether or not they are available in their own town library—they are utterly silent in this regard. They merely mention there are certain books on that topic to be had on the "Beautiful Isle of Somewhere." It does not interest or help readers to be told what books have been published, nor to be informed that material may be obtained in the library of New York or Boston. What they do want to learn is, what their own city or town library can produce. Therefore the value of a special bibliography on a special subject, in our own particular library, cannot be over-estimated.

To this end then, we planned a series of special bibliographies on Canadian topics, and the first of these undertaken and compiled by the speaker, was a list of all the early Canadian printed books in the Reference Library, dating from 1764, when the first printing press was established in Canada, to the year 1837, which in a way, gives us a very good idea of the progress of printing and publication in Canada during that period.

This list is chronologically arranged, and is comprised of about 600 entries, which include books, pamphlets, periodicals, almanacs, directories and government documents. The title of the bibliography is: "Books and pamphlets, etc., published in Canada up to the year 1837, copies of which are in the Public Reference Library in Toronto." As stated in the preface, "the date of ending the list is purely arbitrary, having no connection with book production, but marking an historical event which was influential in shaping the destinies of our country."

That our first effort was somewhat successful, was evidenced by the many congratulatory letters, received by the Chief Librarian, Dr. Locke, and the favourable comments of the newspaper press and book reviews, not to speak of the use made of it by our readers, and the number of copies that were sold—all of which it is needless to say was very gratifying, and encouraged us to go on with the good work.

Our next attempt was rather more ambitious, as we decided the next contribution to our series would be a bibliography of one of the most salient points in the history of our country—that of the Canadian rebellion of 1837-8, both in Upper and Lower Canada.

This work being assigned me, I felt at first that it was no easy task, and at times was rather appalled at its magnitude, and that it was impossible to do adequate justice to so important a subject. But fortunately it was a favourite theme in Canadian history, which made the work more congenial, and the interest in it soon grew to be a labour of love, and when the task was ended, I felt amply repaid by the knowledge that it was indeed, not "Love's labour lost."

Now the title of this paper suggests a special bibliography on a special topic—The Canadian Rebellions of 1837-8.

Some time ago, in looking through an old volume of the *Library Journal*, published many years ago, I came across an article on bibliography, in which the writer states, that bibliography may be divided into two branches, the first having reference to the contents of books, and which may be termed intellectual bibliography, the second treats of the external characteristics of books, their names, prices, dates and places of publication, and to this class may be applied the term material bibliography. This last class will not claim our attention to-day, but to the former—intellectual bibliography, we shall devote our consideration for a short time.

Having decided on the subject, the next thing to consider was the plan of campaign in regard to the research work. Although the undertaking was an arduous one, no trouble was anticipated so far as the general material was concerned, for the Canadiana of our reference library, is one of which Toronto may be justifiably proud, being as a general collection, the finest in America, and some have gone so far as to say the best in the world.

Of course, we had several histories of the rebellion, and numerous histories of Canada which dealt in detail on the subject as an epoch in the history of our country, but a history, unless very attractively written, is a rather dry and uninteresting source of material to put into the hands of the budding historian.

General histories of course, have their place, as all things have, and indeed contain a mass of valuable information, but there is very little that is bright or attractive to be found in their pages. They do not convey to the reader the spirit of the times unless he is possessed of an uncommonly vivid imagination. Then again, he is apt to see things from the viewpoint of the historian, becoming biased in his judgment, not having sufficient scope for independent thought.

So I thought I would try to lead the student to more interesting sources of the fountain of knowledge, than at the dried up springs of the ordinary history.

I then arranged to begin the bibliography, by doing the easiest part first, which was to collect and make a list of all the histories of the rebellion, then books dealing with the rebellion, then the most important histories of Canada which dealt with the subject to any extent. This in itself presented quite a goodly list.

I next turned my attention to pamphlets, in which we are very wealthy. In regard to pamphlets dealing with Canada in some phase or another, it is not an exaggeration to say that we have to the number of about 6,000. Now a word on the use of pamphlets as an aid to the study of history. No one can deny that their value is inestimable. It is generally written on some important topic, or some event or question, political or social, that is agitating the minds of the people at the time; and its interest is enhanced by the fact, that it only relates to present day questions. As an instrument in shaping and moulding the opinions of the people in times of political storm and stress especially, it is, as a rule, very keen and convincing. Pamphlets, like some periodicals, do not enjoy a very long existence. Many of them, like human beings, are only born to die. They are seldom reprinted —hence the importance of preserving them as aids to research, and the study of history for the future generations.

Let me quote what Disraeli in his "Amenities of Literature" says of pamphlets: "We must not consider pamphlets wholly in a political view, their circuit is boundless, holding all the world of man, they enter into every object of human interest. The silent revolution in manners, language, habit, are there to be traced; and indeed it is the multiplicity of pamphlets on a particular topic or object, which appear at a particular period, that offer the truest picture of public opinion."

So much for the importance of pamphlets as an aid to historical study.

Another interesting source was the magazine literature, and though not quite so productive of results as the pamphlets, a good deal of valuable material was brought to light. Our collection of bound periodicals is very extensive, comprising several thousands of volumes, many of our sets dating back, as far as, and some beyond, the rebellion period. This literature too, like the pamphlets, is an expression of the thought and opinion of the writers on the various vital and important questions of the times, and was, to some extent, influential in shaping the destinies of nations and peoples. Therefore we cannot overlook the fact of their importance, they having always proved a reliable and unfailing friend in need.

Then scrap books were searched, but as we did not possess many of these, that is of clippings of that period, the exploration of that source was soon over. My efforts, however, were not in vain, for some very interesting matter was secured.

The next field of investigation was the Transactions of Learned Societies of which we have over 5,000 vols. Of these, of course, there were only certain ones that would likely contain any of the desired references. These were searched, with the result that several interesting papers were unearthed. Thus we see that the Transactions of Learned Societies are also desirable mediums for history study.

Then an excursion was taken into the realm of books, seeking hither and thither for incidental chapters, for odds and ends and out of the way information, which search was very satisfactorily rewarded. Government documents too, was another by-path to the high road of history, and their importance also is universally recognized, recording as they do the events, the heated discussions and debates, that took place in parliament in those far off stormy times.

Next to be entered was the field of romance, cherishing a hope to glean there at least a few tales and stories founded on such an exciting and interesting a topic as the Canadian rebellion of 1837-8. The reward was not commensurate with the labour, but I felt very well satisfied at having secured three or four works of fiction. These are of interest, from the fact that they throw more or less light on the life of the people at that time.

Last but not least, and the most interesting and prolific of all our sources, were the newspapers, of which we have a very representative collection, dating from 1830, to the end of the rebellion period.

The task of examining them was a rather formidable one, involving a good deal of eye and nerve strain and brain fatigue, but on searching through the files, turning over one by one the musty yellow leaves, such a mine of wealth was revealed, that I only realized for the first time, the immense value of the newspaper as an historical source. More so than periodicals and pamphlets are they a revealer of public sentiment and opinion. Much more vividly do they chronicle the daily events of the times, and by a thorough search cannot fail to bring to light many important facts and much curious information, which it would be impossible to find elsewhere.

Through the medium of the press, the people in those days, as now, voiced their grievances and opinions of affairs, political and social, thus exerting a wide and far reaching influence, and in this way too, we get at the pros and cons of many important questions that exercised the minds of the public. From the newspapers also, we obtain a much more graphic and accurate picture of the period than we can possibly do from other sources. Here, as may easily be seen, the student of history has abundant scope and opportunity for securing unusually interesting material for his work.

As previously stated, our collection of early newspapers is fairly representative, and while we cannot boast many complete sets, what we have is sufficient to meet all reasonable demands.

It is not within the scope of this paper to enter into any of the details of the causes and agitations that led to the rebellion, nor to comment on any of the events connected with it. The purpose now is to show what our different sources can produce; therefore a few examples from each will be given by way of explaining the nature of the bibliography.

The first source to be noticed are the books—and to begin at the beginning, it will be understood that in order for the student to arrive at a fair and accurate knowledge of the causes which led to the rebellions of 1837-8 it will be necessary to read, mark, learn and digest the Quebec Act of 1774, and the Constitutional Act of 1791. The text of these acts may be found in "Documents of the Canadian Constitution," by Wm. Houston, and "Documents of the Canadian Constitution," by Professor W. M. P. Kennedy. Examples of the other material are "The Quebec Act of 1774," by Gerald E. Hart, "Account of the proceedings of the British and other Protestant inhabitants in the Province of Quebec, in North America, in order to obtain a House of Assembly in that Province," London, 1775, and "Debates of the House of Commons in the year 1774, on the bill for making effectual provision for the Government of the Province of Quebec, drawn up from the notes of Sir Henry Cavendish."

Again, in order to learn the causes of the rebellion we should not like to omit the works of the famous Robert Gourlay, that much abused Scotsman, who came to Canada in 1817, as land agent, with a view to promoting immigration, and was the first to agitate against the many abuses which had sprung up in the country under the tyrannical rule of the Family Compact, the then dominant party. Everyone is familiar with his story, of his treatment by the Family Compact, his unlawful imprisonment, and lastly his exile from the Province. His writings are worthy of consideration, and are as follows: "The Chronicles of Canada, being a record of Robert Gourlay, No. I, concerning the convention and gagging law, 1818;" "The Banished Briton" and "Neptunian;" "The unpublished papers of Robert Gourlay to 1818;" "Statistical Account of Upper Canada," 3 vols.

Examples of histories of the rebellion are: "Story of the Upper Canadian Rebellion of 1837," by J. C. Dent; "The Canadian Rebellion of 1837," by D B. Read. In general histories of Canada, those that give fairly detailed accounts are: "History of Canada," by William Kingsford; and "The History of Canada," by John McMullen. The latter is particularly good. Other fruitful sources are: "A Narrative," by Sir Francis Bond Head, giving a full account of the rebellion and its causes.

"The Seventh Report from the Select Committee of the House of Assembly on Grievances," W. L. Mackenzie, Chairman, 1835.

"Annals of Canada for 1837-8," by David Chisholm.

"Papers relating to Sir Francis Bond Head, ordered by the House of Assembly to be printed." 1837.

Lord Durham's "Report on the affairs of British North America," 1839.

"Lithographic views of the Military operations in Canada, under His Excellency Sir John Colborne, during the late insurrection," by Lord Charles Beauclerk, accompanied by notes, historical and descriptive.

"The Canadian Farmer's travels in the United States of America, in which remarks are made on the arbitrary Colonial Policy, preached in Canada, and the free and equal rights and happy effects of the liberal institutions and astonishing enterprise of the United States, by Robert Davis, Buffalo, 1837." "The relation of the United States with the Canadian Rebellion of 1837-8, by Orrim E. Tiffany."

After the quelling of the rebellion, many of those who took a prominent part, were banished to Van Dieman's Land, there enduring a long captivity, and the story of those political prisoners during their exile in that country, told by themselves, is extremely interesting. It would take up too much time to give any review of these books, or to name all of them, but the titles of a few will explain their contents.

Among others, are the following:

"Letters from Van Dieman's Land, written during four years imprisonment for political offences committed in Upper Canada," by Benjamin Wait. Buffalo, 1843.

"The Exiles' Return; or Narrative of Samuel Snow, who was banished to Van Dieman's Land for participating in the patriot war in Upper Canada in 1838." Cleveland, 1846. This book is now very scarce.

"Recollections of life in Van Dieman's Land" by Wm. Gates. One of the Canadian Patriots. Lockport, 1850.

"Canada in 1837-8, showing by historical proofs the causes of the late attempted revolution and of its failure, together with the personal adventures of the Author, and others who were connected with the Revolution," by E. A. Theller, Brigadier-General in the Canadian Republican Service. Phil., 1841.

"A Narrative of the adventures and sufferings of Captain Daniel Huestis and his companions in Canada, and Van Dieman's Land during a long captivity, with introduction. The Canadian Movement, by Benjamin Kingsbury." Boston, 1847.

"A brief review of the settlement of Upper Canada, by the U. E. Loyalists and Scotch Highlanders in 1783, and of the grievances which compelled the Canadians to have recourse to arms in defence of their rights and liberties in the year 1837-8, with an account of the Military executions, burning and sackings of towns and villages by the British in the Upper and Lower Provinces during the commotion of 1837-8, by D. M. McLeod, Major-General, Patriot Army, U. C. Cleveland, 1846."

"A letter to Her Majesty, the British Queen, with letters to Lord Durham, Lord Glenelg and Sir George Arthur, to which is added an appendix embracing a report of the testimony taken on the trial of the writer, by a Court Martial of Toronto, in Upper Canada," by Thomas Jefferson Sutherland. Albany, 1841.

"Report on the case of the Canadian prisoners, with an introduction to the writ of Habeas Corpus," by Alfred Fry, one of the counsel in the case.

Our next source—chapters from books—is a very interesting one, obtaining as we do, the view points of the different authors, and securing many odds and ends of information, and items of local interest, that we do not find in the general history.

The following are a few examples:

"Events of a Military life," by Walter Henry, Esq., Surgeon to the Forces. London, W. Pickering. 1843. Vol. II, chaps. 44-55.

"Account of the Rebellion of 1837-8." In the History of Galt and Dumfries, by James Young. Chaps. 13-14.

"Incidents of the Rebellion of 1837-8." In "Upper Canada Sketches," by Thomas Conant. Chap. 6.

"Pickering and the Canadian Rebellion." In "Past years in Pickering," by W. R. Wood. Chap. 4.

"Political Affairs of the Province and the Rebellion of 1837." In "The Talbot Regime," by C. O. Ermatinger. Chaps. 26-29.

"The Rebellion of 1837." In "Twenty-seven years in Canada," by Major Strickland. Chap. 16.

"Reminiscences of the Canadian Rebellion of 1838, by one who was an eye-witness and shouldered his musket at that time." In "Canadian Pen and Ink Sketches," by John Fraser. Chaps. 5-9.

A very full account of the rebellion may be found in "Canada as it was, and is, and may be," by Sir Richard Bonneycastle, 2 vols.

"The Canadian question and the principal causes of the late insurrection," in "A Dairy in America," by Capt. Marryatt. Chaps. 1-6.

"The Patriot War of 1837-40." In "History of St. Lawrence and Franklin Counties," New York, by T. B. Hough. Chap. 10.

An unusually good book, containing many interesting incidents of the rebellion, is "Three Years Residence in Canada, from 1837-1839," by T. R. Preston. In this work is found some out-of-the-way material, for instance, he gives an uncommonly good account of the Hunters' Lodges and Associations, with the object of their foundation; the names and nature of the various signs, and the wording of the oaths in the various degrees of the lodges, also the mode of initiating persons to the different degrees of membership. Vol. I, chaps. 3-5.

The next source to be noticed is the pamphlets. The collection on, and relating to, our subject is an interesting one, comprising, as it does, a great wealth of material on the rebellion, and the causes and events connected with it. The titles of some of these will give some idea of their contents as it will be impossible, in this paper, to remark on their nature or merits:

Statement of facts relating to the trespass on the printing press of Mr. William Lyon MacKenzie, in June, 1826, addressed to the public generally, and particularly to the subscribers and supporters of the *Colonial Advocate*. York, 1826.

The Legislature Black List of Upper Canada, or Official Corruption and Hypocrisy Unmasked, by William Lyon MacKenzie. York, 1828.

First report on the state of the representation of the people of Upper Canada in the legislature of the Province. Members of Committee. Messrs. Lyons, Buell, Shaver, Howard and MacKenzie. York, 1831.

The celebrated letter of Joseph Hume, Esq., M.P., to William Lyon MacKenzie, Esq., Mayor of Toronto, declaratory of a design to "Free these provinces from the baneful domination of the Mother Country" with the comments of the press of Upper Canada, on the pernicious and treasonable tendency of that letter, and the speeches, resolutions, and amendments of the Common Council, of this city, which were the result of a motion of that body, to disavow all participation in the sentiments of Mr. Hume. Toronto, 1834.

MacKenzie's own narrative of the late rebellion with illustrations and notes critical and explanatory; exhibiting the only true account of what took place at the memorable siege of Toronto in the month of December, 1837. Toronto, 1837.

A canvass of the proceedings on the trial of W. L. MacKenzie for an alleged violation of the neutrality laws of the United States, with a report of the testimony. The charge of the presiding judge to the jury. The arguments of the United States Attorney, and a petition to the Presidency for his release, by T. Jefferson Sutherland. New York, 1840.

Proceedings had in the House of Assembly on the subject of an address to His Excellency Sir F. B. Head, for certain information on the affairs of the Colony. Toronto, 1836.

Letters addressed to the people of the Canadas, on Elective Institutions. Coburg, 1835, by an East-Anglian (M. S. Bidwell).

Message from His Excellency Sir Francis B. Head, in answer to the address of the House of Assembly, of the 5th February, 1836, with sundry documents requested by the House in said address. Toronto, 1836.

There are also a number of interesting pamphlets on the Clergy Reserves, one of the most agitated topics of the time, and one of the principal causes of the rebellion. The term "Protestant Clergy" being interpreted "Church of England" by that body, aroused a great storm of protest from people, both lay and clerical. Titles of the following pamphlets will throw some light on the nature of the discussions and dissensions that took place between the clergy of the different denominations:

The exclusive right of the Church to the Clergy Reserves defended, in a letter to the Rt. Hon. the Earl of Liverpool, being an answer to the letter of the Protestant of the Church of Scotland to His Lordship.

An apology for the Church of England in the Canadas; an answer to a letter to the Earl of Liverpool, relative to the rights of the Church of Scotland, etc., by a Protestant of the Church of Scotland. By a Protestant of the Church of England. Kingston, 1826.

Speech in the Legislative Council, Upper Canada, 6th March, 1828, on the subject of the Clergy Reserves, by the Venerable John Strachan, D.D.

Reply of William Morris, member of the Legislative Council of Upper Canada, to six letters addressed to him by John Strachan, D.D., Archdeacon of York, 1838.

A pastoral letter from the Clergy of the Church of Scotland, in the Canadas, to their Presbyterian brethren, on the subject now agitated between them and the Clergy of the Church of England, relative to the appropriation of the lands reserved for the support of the Protestant Clergy in these provinces. 1828.

A circular letter from the Bishop of Quebec to the Clergy and Congregations of the Church of England, in the diocese of Quebec, in relation to some existing difficulties of opinion respecting the Clergy Reserves, and certain other points, cautioning the congregations against the claims of the Presbyterians to a participation in the Clergy Reserves. Quebec, 20th Dec., 1827.

Celebrated speech of Dr. J. Rolph, then member for Norfolk, delivered in the Upper Canada House of Assembly, in the year 1836, on the bill for appropriating the proceeds of the Clergy Reserves to the purposes of education. Toronto, 1836.

This speech is without parallel in the annals of Parliamentary debate.

The Clergy Reserve Question as a matter of history—a question of law and a subject of legislation: in a series of letters to the Hon. W. H. Draper. M.P.P., Member of the Executive Council, and Her Majesty's Solicitor-General of Upper Canada. By Egerton Ryerson. Toronto, 1839.

The above pamphlets are very representative of our collection.

Then come the Periodicals, but this literature being much akin to that of the pamphlets, their articles written chiefly with the object of expressing

5 H.P.

the views and opinions of the writers on some outstanding question of the day, time will not be taken up with many examples, but it may be of some interest to mention the magazines contained in the bibliography where material on our subject may be obtained:

The Annual Register; Acta-Victoriana; Blackwood's Magazine; Canadian Christian Examiner; Canadian Magazine; Colonial Magazine; Dublin Review; Dublin University Magazine; Eclectic Review; Fortnightly Review; Fraser's Magazine; Littell's Living Age; Magazine of American History; Mirror of Parliament (English); New Dominion Monthly; Nile's Register; Nineteenth Century; North American Review; Quarterly Review; Rose Belford's Canadian Monthly.

The following are a few examples of the articles:

"Canada: False Principles of Government, the cause of its suffering." *Colonial Magazine.* Vol. I.

"Causes of the Rebellion in Canada." *Dublin University Magazine.* Vol. II, 1838. "War in Canada: Its Causes and Consequences." *Eclectic Review.* Vol. 67, 1838. "Remarks on the Proceedings as to Canada in the Present Session of Parliament," by one of the Commissioners. April 10th, 1837. *Quarterly Review.* Vol. 61.

"The Canadian Revolt; a short history of its causes, progress, and probable consequences." *United Service Journal,* May, 1838.

"Canada and Ireland; the strict analogy of the Whig Policy in regard to these countries clearly traced." *Blackwood's Magazine.* Vol. 43, 1838.

"Personal Narrative of the Escape of W. L. MacKenzie from Toronto to the United States." *Littell's Living Age.* Vol. 16.

"Speech of Mr. Menefee of Kentucky, on the reference of the President's message relating to the attack on the Caroline, delivered in the House of Representatives, January, 1838." *Nile's Register,* January 27th, 1838.

Among the transactions and proceedings of learned societies, entries have been made from the following:

Niagara Historical Society Publications; Transactions Royal Society of Canada; Michigan Pioneer & Historical Society; Transactions Canadian Institute; Johns Hopkins University Studies; Buffalo Historical Society; Lundy's Lane Historical Society and Ontario Historical Society. By way of example, in paper No. 13 of the Niagara Historical Society, there is a very interesting paper "A wife's devotion, a Canadian heroine of sixty years ago." (The story of Maria Wait, the wife of Benjamin Wait, the exile), by Miss Carnochan.

In *Papers and Records* of the Ontario Historical Society, Vol. XVI, 1918, we find an interesting account of "The Books of the Political Prisoners and Exiles of 1838," by Mr. J. Davis Barnett.

Of the publications of the Buffalo Historical Society in Vol. V, 1902, we have an excellent general bibliography of the Upper Canada Rebellion of 1837, by Mr. Frank Severance, which is the best we have yet seen published.

From the source—Government documents, examples need not be given, as every one is quite familiar with the nature of the contents, comprising as they do, Parliamentary debates and discussions, Reports of Select Committees, Petitions, Memorials, Proclamations, etc.

Among our scrap books, are two which deal particularly with the Rebellion. One composed of extracts from the *Montreal Star,* which deal almost wholly with the insurrection in Lower Canada. The other is one which Dr. Locke was fortunate enough to secure in London, England, when on a visit there some years ago. It consists of copious clippings from American papers of that time, such as the *Herald and Sentinel,* Philadelphia; *Ledger and Daily Transcript; Rochester Democrat; The Pennsylvanian,* etc. These cuttings contain many interesting items we have not found elsewhere, and are particularly valuable because of the light they throw on the subject of American sympathy and opinion.

From the source—the Field of Romance—the examples are not many, but the titles may be of interest:

"The Empress of the Isles; or, the Lake Bravo, a romance of the Canadian struggle in 1837," by Charley Clewline. The scene of this story is the Thousand Islands, in the St. Lawrence. The heroine of the romance is Kate, the daughter of the notorious Bill Johnson, the smuggler.

"The Prisoner of the Border; a tale of 1838," by P. Hamilton Myers. Published in New York, 1857. In this story also, Bill Johnson figures very conspicuously.

"Rose and Minnie; or the Loyalists; a tale in 1837." No author given. One of the series of historical tales (No. 28), published in London, Eng., 1868. pp. 106.

"The Volunteer's Bride; a tale of the Canadian Rebellion," by C.P.T. (Catharine Parr Traill?). Rice Lake, 1854. This is a short story contained in a magazine *The Maple Leaf.* Vol. II.

"Two and Twenty Years Ago; a tale of the Canadian Rebellion," by a Backwoodsman (Dr. William Dunlop). Toronto, 1859. pp. 112.

We have now arrived at the Newspaper Sources, where I am compelled to hesitate. Their contents proving a veritable embarrassment of riches renders it impossible, by giving only a few examples, to convey an adequate idea of the matter contained in the volumes, and the difficulty is increased by the number of the different papers that have been examined. The following are those from which entries have been made: *New York Albion.* This paper is full of excellent material, containing many official documents and despatches, accounts of battles, and particularly the frontier troubles. Other papers are: *The Loyalist; The Canadian Courant; Western Mercury; Quebec Gazette; Coburg Star; The Vindicator; British American Journal; Canadian Correspondent; Brockville Recorder; Upper Canada Courier; Dundas Weekly Post; Correspondent and Advocate; Montreal Transcript; The Traveller,* or *Prince Edward Gazette; Toronto Mirror; The Church; The Examiner* and the *Globe.* From this list will be seen that our library contains a fairly good number of newspapers, on and around the rebellion period. We find them a true mirror of past events; their contents are unusually interesting, receiving, as we do, a delightfully clear and vivid account and description of the occurrences of those bygone days. Through their medium may be traced a complete and accurate history of the revolt, and of the events and incidents relating to it. Some idea of the nature of the material may be gained by saying, that in these may be found discussions and debates in the Houses of Parliament on many vital questions concerning the province. Despatches, messages and instructions of the Imperial Parliament to Governors of the Provinces, the replies in return, etc.

There are the accounts of the organization of various societies, both

Constitutional and Reform, their reports, meetings, etc. Then a wealth of interesting matter may be culled from the proceedings of the numerous public meetings that were held in almost every section of the province in order to attest loyalty to the crown or otherwise. The resolutions read and adopted, and the speeches, almost invariably ending with an address to the King, expressing their unyielding allegiance, or presenting a petition of grievances. There are interesting editorials, letters from citizens and residents in the province, each voicing his opinion on the events and troubles of the day. We find also, accounts of the battles and skirmishes that took place, in connection with which there is a mass of official correspondence. There are also many proclamations and messages of the United States Presidents, relative to the troubles on the Frontier, besides addresses, and militia orders, as well as detailed reports of the trials of some of the political prisoners, the charge of the Judge to the Jury, and his speech on passing sentence.

Then too, as now, many bouquets were thrown at each other through the medium of the press, by individuals who unhappily held different opinions on certain agitated questions. Only in these days they would be made up of old-fashioned flowers.

The amount of material selected from the papers is rather a formidable one, consisting, as it does, of almost a thousand entries, many of them curious and amusing. The task was no easy one, but I felt rewarded for the labour, by the fact of having amassed a great deal of information on the rebellion that was quite foreign to me before.

Out of so many entries it has been very difficult to select examples, as almost all are interesting, and time will not allow to give more than a few, neither would I tax your patience.

By way of example, after the title will be given the name and date of the paper that contains the article. These examples are arranged chronologically:

Debate in the House of Commons Imperial Parliament on the Civil Government of the Canadas, May 2nd, 1828.

The Loyalist, York, U.C., June 14th, 1828.

Report of the Select Committee to the House of Commons, Imperial Parliament, appointed to inquire into the state of the Civil Government of Canada, in regard to several petitions from the inhabitants of the two provinces which had been referred to them by the House, July 22nd, 1828.

The Loyalist, York, U.C., Sept. 27th, 1828.

Letter to the Farmers residing in the County of York, who have ranged under the banner of W. L. MacKenzie, Esq., Editor of the *Advocate*, York, Upper Canada.

By A. Freeholder of the County of York, Oct. 20th, 1831.

The Western Mercury, Nov. 24th and Dec. 1st, 1831.

Mr. MacKenzie's grievances! His Meetings!! and his addresses!!! Notice of some of the movements which this missionary of the Christian Guardian, and of the old Central Junto, is now making throughout the Province to obtain signatures to the list of "grievances" which were fabricated by the said Guardian, and the said Junto, at this town some months ago. With copy of a letter to the members of Chinquacousy Committee, by W. L. MacKenzie.

The Western Mercury, Oct. 27th, 1831.
A detailed account of the proceedings of the meeting convened at St. Thomas, on the 17th inst., for the purpose of addressing the King and obtaining a public expression of the people, on the subject of grievances so strongly urged by the revolutionary party in the country, by A Bystander. St. Thomas, March 19th, 1832. *Western Mercury,* 1832.

Despatch of Lord Goderich to Sir John Colborne, regarding communications and statements of Mr. MacKenzie upon the subject of grievances said to exist in Upper Canada, and for redress of which various petitions have been addressed to His Majesty, Nov. 8th, 1830. *Cobourg Star,* Jan. 30th, Feb. 6th, 13th, 20th, 1833.

Letter to the Freeholders of the County of York, discussing the charges against Mr. MacKenzie for Libel and Mr. MacKenzie's defence in the House of Asembly, By an Elector of the County of York.

Western Mercury, Jan. 12th,-19th, 1832.

Debate in the House of Assembly of Upper Canada, on the expulsion of Mr. MacKenzie from the House of Assembly, Dec. 16th, 17th, 1833.

Election address of Mr. T. D. Morrison, to the Free and Independent electors of the Third Riding of the County of York.
Signed T. D. Morrison, Toronto, 19th Sept., 1834.

The Vindicator, Oct. 10th, 1834.

Resolutions adopted at the formation of the Canadian Alliance Society, and a statement of the objects for the attainment of which the Society is established. Motto of the Society:—" Where bad men conspire, good men must unite." *Cobourg Star,* Dec. 24th, 1834.

" To my own true blues." A letter to the Alliance Societies of Upper Canada, by Patrick Swift. (William Lyon MacKenzie). *Corres. and Advoc.,* July 30th, 1835.

Letter to Egerton Ryerson, Andrew Bell, John Wilson, and the rest of the bribed parsons in Upper Canada, by an English Reformer. Toronto. May 27th, 1835. *Corres. and Advoc.,* May 29th, 1835.

Letter to A. N. McNab, and the rest of the loyal itinerant reformers of the Gore and Home districts, by " A hater of the factious hypocrites." Boston, Nov. 3rd, 1834. *Corres. and Advoc.,* Feb. 5th, 1835.

Letter to William Lyon MacKenzie, Esq., late M.P.P., Knight of the most ignoble order of agitators, corresponding secretary to the Machiavelian Anti-British Societies in North America, Grand Promotor of discontent and Anarchy therein, Commander-in-Chief of the Radical Malcontent Forces of Upper Canada, etc., etc., etc., on the subject of his political tergiversation. by James McMillan. Toronto, July 20th, 1836.

The Patriot, July 29th, 1836.

Proceedings and resolutions passed at a meeting held in the Free Church, Dundas, 30th March, 1836, to give an expression of Public Opinion at this important crisis. *Corres. and Advoc.,* 4th April, 1836. John Patterson, Chairman.

What has Parliament done for us this winter? Why were the supplies amounting to about £5,000 refused? Letter to the Electors of the Second Riding of the County of York, from William Lyon MacKenzie, Queenston. 2nd May, 1836. *Corres. and Advoc.,* May 4th, 1836.

Resolutions adopted at a meeting held at the Alliance Societies Chambers, in the City of Toronto, May 5th, for the purpose of taking into consideration the state of the province at the present critical juncture; and of devising some mode of attesting public esteem and gratitude for the invaluable services of Daniel O'Connell, Esq., M.P. *Corres. and Advoc.*, May 11th, 1836. T. D. Morrison, Chairman.

Meeting at Finch's tavern, Yonge St., for the notice of which the following hand-bill was posted: York Township Meeting.

The Gore of Toronto Meeting that was to be held at Charles King's store, East Toronto, is postponed for a few days, then to be called in a more central situation. The meeting of the township of York, to choose delegates, enroll the names of members of societies, and take efficient steps for the numbering and classing the Reformers, so that they may act with unison and system in their effort to get justice for Canada, will take place at Finch's tavern, Montgomery Town, Yonge St., at noon, on Friday, August 18th, 1837, with an account of the proceedings, and the resolutions adopted at the meeting. Robert Moodie, Chairman.

Finch's tavern, Yonge St., 18th Aug., 1837.

The Patriot, August 22nd, 1837.

A letter to Dr. O'Callaghan, Editor of the *Vindicator,* Montreal,

Toronto, Aug. 25th, 1837.

Signed: "Yours to the shoe tie," William Lyon MacKenzie, of the Rebel race.

The Patriot, Sept. 12th, 1837.

Short letter from W. L. MacKenzie to the Editors of the Buffalo *Whig* and *Journal,* informing them that the reformers of Upper Canada, have taken up arms in defence of the principles of independence of European domination:

"We are in arms near the City of Toronto, 2½ miles distant."

Signed "William Lyon MacKenzie,"

Yonge St., Dec. 6th, 1837.

Quebec Gazette, Dec. 27th, 1837.

Proclamation by William Lyon MacKenzie, Chairman Protem of the Provincial Government of Upper Canada, setting forth a list of grievances, etc., and offering a reward of £500 for the apprehension of Sir Francis B. Head. Navy Island, Dec. 13th, 1837.

Cobourg Star, Jan. 3rd, 1838.

Proclamation by Sir Francis Head, offering £1,000 for the apprehension of William Lyon MacKenzie, and £500 for the apprehension of David Gibson, Samuel Lount, or Jesse Lloyd, or Silas Fletcher.

New York Albion, Dec. 23rd, 1837.

Resolutions passed at a public meeting of a numerous and respectable body of the citizens of Buffalo, held in the Ball Room of the Buffalo Court House, expressive of sympathy for our neighbors of the Provinces of Upper and Lower Canada.

John O'Meara, Chairman.

From the *Buffalo Commercial Advertiser.*

Cobourg Star, Dec. 27th, 1837.

Copy of a letter from Captain Drew, Commander Royal Navy, to the Hon. Col. A. N. McNab, reporting the capture and burning of the *Caroline.* Chippewa, 30th Dec., 1837.

The Patriot, Jan. 5th, 1838.
Account of the rebellion near Toronto, by William Lyon MacKenzie. Navy Island, U.C., 14th Jan., 1838.
The Patriot, Feb. 16th, 1838.
Special message of Governor Marcy, to the Legislature of Upper Canada on the subject of the burning of the *Caroline.*
Cobourg Star, Jan. 10th, 1838.
Address of the Hon. Chief Justice Robinson on passing sentence of death upon Samuel Lount and Peter Matthews, 29th March, 1838.
The Patriot, April 6th, 1838.
Narrative of facts connected with Frontier Movements of the Patriot Army of Upper Canada, with a copy of the correspondence between Renss-Van Rensselaer, and W. L. MacKenzie.
The Patriot, April 10th, 1838.
Address of Dr. Theller at his trial for treason, on being asked by the Judge why sentence of death should not be passed upon him.
The Mirror, April 14th, 1838.
Report of the trial of David Morrison for High Treason. 24th April, 1838.
The Patriot, May 4th, 1838.
Report of the trial of Charles Durand for High Treason, before Mr. Chief Justice Robinson. 7th May, 1838.
The Patriot, May 15th, 1838.
Copy of a proclamation recently issued by the leader of the gang that destroyed the Steamboat *Sir Robert Peel,* obtained for Governor Marcy.
Signed " William Johnson."
10th June, 1838.
The Albion, June 16th, 1838.
A letter from Elizabeth Lount, widow of the lamented Judge Lount, to the Hon. John Beverley Robinson, Chief Justice of Upper Canada.
Pontiac, Mich., June 12th, 1838.
The Toronto Mirror, July 14th, 1838.
Biographical and character sketch of Bill Johnson, the Lake Buccaneer, leader of the gang of Refugees, on the " Thousand Islands " in the St. Lawrence, and known also as the leader in the recent destruction of the *Sir Robert Peel.*
The Patriot, July 17th, 1838.
Battle of Windmill Point. Result of expedition to Prescott under Colonel Dundas, and an account of the attack on the mill with the number killed and wounded.
Cobourg Star, Nov. 22nd, 1838. (From the Kingston Chronicle).
The arrest of Bill Johnson. *Cobourg Star,* Dec. 12th, 1838.
Resolutions passed at a meeting of the Ladies of the City of Buffalo, held at the Ladies' parlor of the United States Hotel, on Saturday, the 29th day of December, for the purpose of forming a society in aid of the suffering Canadian Patriots now struggling to free themselves from the yoke of tyranny and oppression, and to relieve, so far as possible, the suffering of those families who have been driven destitute from their country and their homes, and compelled to seek refuge among us.
Mrs. Burgess, President.
(From the *Buffalonian*) *Cobourg Star,* Jan. 9th, 1839.

Report of the trial of William Lyon MacKenzie for breach of the Neutrality laws. From the *Rochester Democrat*, of June 21st, 1839.

Quebec Gazette, July 1st, 1839.

The charge of Judge Thompson to the Jury, on the occasion of the trial of William Lyon MacKenzie for breach of the neutrality laws, at Canandaigua. Ont. Co., N.Y.

June 20th and 21st, 1839. *Nile's Register*, July 6th, 1839.

MacKenzie the rebel and the Colonial Office. Motion by the Earl of Ripon in the House of Lords, for the production of certain papers relative to the correspondence which, in 1832, had taken place between himself, then secretary for Colonial affairs, and an individual by the name of MacKenzie. March 12th, 1839.

Cobourg Star, May 1st, 1839.

The case of William Lyon MacKenzie: What sort of a man is MacKenzie, and what is his real character? An article from the *New York Reformer*.

Toronto Mirror, Oct. 25th, 1839.

MacKenzie and our British relations: An article on the imprisonment and punishment of MacKenzie by the Government of the United States. From the *New York Reformer*.

Toronto Mirror, Nov. 1st, 1839.

We now pass over the interval of a decade, when we find Mr MacKenzie, in the winter of 1849, taking a trip through the Canadas. He says "After an absence of twelve years, I availed myself of the provisions of the Amnesty Act, passed in February, 1849, to visit Canada."

While in Montreal, he writes the following: "A letter to the Editor of the *Montreal Herald*, giving a true account of the death of Colonel Moodie, in refutation of the charge that he was personally responsible for Colonel Moodie's death."

Signed "W. L. MacKenzie," Montreal, March 7th, 1849.

The Toronto Mirror, March 16th, 1849.

The Examiner, March 21st, 1849.

Mr. MacKenzie next pays a visit to Toronto, where he evidently was not very cordially received, at least by the Tories, as our entry reads thus: "Account of the Tory riots in Toronto, 22nd March, 1849, on the occasion of Mr. MacKenzie's visit to the city.

The Examiner, March 28th, 1849.

While on his trip through the Canadas, Mr. MacKenzie writes a series of very interesting articles for the *New York Tribune*, entitled "A winter's journey through the Canadas," in which he reviews the state of the affairs of the country, and the events and causes connected with the rebellion. We have never seen these articles published in book form, and if not already done, that work would be well justified of the labour and expense. Evidently few are aware of their existence, for we know definitely that one, at least, of Mr. MacKenzie's descendants had no knowledge of them until they were brought to his notice. This series of articles was taken from the *N. Y. Tribune*, and published by the *Examiner*, and may be found in *The Examiner* from April 25th, to July 25th, 1849.

Some time after his return to New York, Mr. MacKenzie writes a long address to his old friends of the County of York, which is entered as follows: Copy of the highly interesting address written by William Lyon MacKenzie to the inhabitants of the County of York; " A County he represented, so long, so faithfully and with so much ability in Parliament."

The address is signed "W. L. MacKenzie," New York, Nov. 6th, 1849.

We are very pleased to have as our final entry, the following just and well-deserved tribute to our hero:

" A letter to the Editor of the *Examiner* on Mr. MacKenzie's address to his old friends, and on the incalculable services that he has rendered to the good cause of civil and religious liberty in Canada," by "Justice." Dec. 3rd, 1849.

Examiner, Dec. 12th, 1849.

Having come to the last of the examples from our sources, given, as has already been stated, with the object of describing the nature and arrangement of the bibliography, it only remains to be said that it is a very exhaustive one, containing at least, 1,700 entries: Books, about 200; pamphlets 150, and periodical entries, about 100, besides over 1,000 newspaper items.

It will be noticed that no examples have been given of the entries for the Lower Canadian Rebellion, judging that it would make too lengthy a paper, but the material, though not quite so exhaustive, is no less interesting and valuable.

XII.

CANADA'S PART IN FREEING THE SLAVE.

By FRED LANDON, M.A.

Historians of the anti-slavery movement in the United States have, for the most part overlooked the very great measure of assistance that came to that cause from the geographical location of the free British provinces to the north and from the attitude of mind of the people of those provinces with regard to the blacks escaping out of bondage. To those in this country who lived during the years immediately preceding the Civil War, or who since that period have had anything to do with older coloured people, the term "Underground Railroad" is not the mysterious term that it is to a younger generation. When Prof. Siebert, of Ohio State University, one of the eminent historians of the United States, can make the statement that "the underground railroad was one of the greatest forces which brought on the Civil War and destroyed slavery," we on this side of the border may properly add that during a large part of the period of its activity Canada was practically essential to the success of the underground system.

Though slavery was legal in all the thirteen original states of the union at some time or another, it was natural that in the group of northern states it should die out quickly. It was excluded by Congress from the old northwest territory by the ordinance of 1787, thus creating a group of states around the Great Lakes that were never to know slavery. By 1820 the republic had been divided by a more or less irregular geographical line, north of which were the free states and south of it the slave states. It was in that year that the first state was created west of the Mississippi River, Missouri, and though lying as far north as southern Illinois, free, it came in as a slave state. From that time until the end of the Civil War one of the great issues in the nation's politics was the control of the new west, should it be free or slave. Prior to 1830 or 1835 there had been many in the south to whom the evils of slavery were something to be rid of and abolition societies actually existed in the south before they did in the north. But from 1830 on there came a new teaching in the south, the doctrine that slavery is a positive good, ordained of God, for the benefit of the black race. Economic conditions were changed, too, by the spread of cotton growing. The old domestic slavery, bad though it might be, was a mild evil compared with the conditions that came when huge cotton plantations demanded vast hordes of slaves and there grew up the domestic slave trade. Virginia, the mother of presidents, became a vast breeding ground and her aristocratic families made fortunes in the selling of men, women and children to the far southern plantations.

From the very earliest days slave owners had experienced severe losses by their slaves running away. As early as the first half of the seventeenth century there are found laws and regulations for the return from one colony to another of fugitives. In the Federal Constitution adopted at Philadelphia in 1787 there is a clause which reads:—

"No person held to service or labour in one state under the laws thereof, escaping into another, shall, in consequence of any law or regulation therein, be discharged from such service or labour, but shall be delivered up on claim of the party to whom such service or labour may be due."

The first federal law providing for the return of a runaway slave was passed in 1793. The law was none too effective from the southern standpoint and was amended at various times until the passage of the famous Fugitive Recovery Bill of 1850 which proved a powerful influence in creating antislavery sentiment in the north. Under this act the question of ownership was determined by the simple affidavit of the person claiming the slave. The testimony of the slave himself was not to be received. There were heavy penalties for harbouring or interfering with the arrest of a runaway. Federal commissioners were paid ten dollars for every slave returned and only five dollars if the fugitive was discharged. Thus a direct premium was paid to convict fugitives. But the clause that particularly irritated the north was that which declared that the federal commissioners might call "all good citizens" to aid and assist in the execution of the law. It was at once pointed out that this made every northern citizen liable to be a slave-catcher. Added were such other injustices as denying jury trial, resting liberty on ex-parte evidence, making habeas corpus ineffective and offering a bribe to the federal commissioner to return the fugitive to slavery.

"The passage of the new law," says one writer, "probably increased the number of anti-slavery people more than anything else that had occurred during the whole agitation."

The period from 1850 to 1861 is filled with incidents arising out of this fugitive slave law. The most famous probably is the case of Anthony Burns, who was arrested in Boston on May 24, 1854. Boston blazed with indignation and a riot broke out in which blood was shed. On the 2nd of June Burns was formally remanded to slavery. The authorities felt it necessary to line the streets with troops and place cannon in the squares on the day that Burns was taken from jail to the boat that was to carry him south. Fifty thousand people standing with bared heads watched the grim military procession pass. Business houses for blocks were draped with black cloth and at one prominent corner a coffin hung suspended over the street. It is not to be wondered at that the *Richmond Examiner* commented: "A few more such victories and the south is undone."

The later life of Burns has a Canadian interest. His stay in the south was brief, money being subscribed to purchase his freedom and provide him an education. He became a clergyman, came to Canada and lived for many years at St. Catharines as a missionary among his own people.

Canada had known slavery at an earlier date but had long since cleared herself of the blot. The French introduced slavery into Canada in an effort to meet the ever prevalent shortage of labour. It existed all through the Old Regime and was not changed by the passing of the country into the hands of the English. Indeed it was not until the beginning of the nineteenth century that slavery disappeared, though at no time and in no locality was it ever existent on a large scale. The early disappearance of slavery in Canada had the effect of creating an anti-slavery sentiment at an early date. In 1829, when the Negroes of Cincinnati were threatened with ruin by the enforcement of the Black Laws, they sent a deputation to York to interview the governor, Sir John Colborne, and find out if they would be allowed to take refuge in Canada. "Tell the republicans on your side of the line" replied the governor, "that we royalists do not know men by their colour. Should you come to us you will be entitled to all the privileges of the rest of His Majesty's subjects."[1] This position was taken by all of the later governors and on the very eve of the Civil War Sir Edmund Walker Head declared that "Canada could still afford homes to the fugitives."[2]

From a very early period there had been those in the northern free states who felt it their duty to give aid and comfort to the blacks making their way north. This was particularly true of the Quakers who at all times were friends of freedom. Gradually there grew up a strangely organized system of aiding the fugitives and to this was given the name of the Underground Railroad. As the slave owners remarked, the slave disappeared at some point in the south and reappeared only in Canada as if he had gone through a long tunnel. The underground is the most romantic highway this new world has known. It followed certain definite routes that have been charted by Prof. Siebert, and the small army of people that were engaged in its operations formed a sort of freemasonry of freedom that brings them the tribute of all who love liberty and hate oppression. A railroad "jargon" grew up. The places where fugitives making their way north could obtain temporary shelter, food and clothing were known as the "stations." Those living there and aiding the runaways were "station agents." More daring individuals travelling with the runaways and guiding them to freedom were "conductors," while in Canada, ready to receive the new comers were "freight agents." A code for messages was used. An innocent telegram, stating that two cases of hardware were being forwarded, meant to the recipient that two slave men were on the way, while reference to cases of dry goods referred to women. Sometimes these phrases had very special meaning, for there are instances where men and women were actually boxed up and shipped in freight cars to the north.[3]

With a Fugitive Slave Law that made freedom impossible even in Boston there was danger for the fugitive after 1850 except in Canada. From 1850 to 1860, therefore, the negro immigration that had been a trickling stream ever since the war of 1812 became a regular torrent and thousands of coloured people crossed the border every year. Prof. Siebert has charted the main routes by which the fugitives made their way to Canada and his map shows most clearly the important influence which the free British provinces exerted upon slavery through their geographical location. Along the northern boundaries of the states of New York and Pennsylvania there were ten main points from which the runaways crossed into Canada, the more important of these being on the Niagara frontier. On Lake Erie and the Detroit River there were eight points at which entry was made into Canada, the Detroit River, of course taking first place. At Fort Malden (Amherstburg) as many as thirty a day entered in the period after 1850.[4] On Lake Erie proper, a considerable number seem to have come in by Kettle Creek (Port Stanley), thence making their way to London or Ingersoll.

Slavery had scarcely disappeared in Canada before runaways from the southern states began to make their appearance, and that in considerable numbers. Isolated instances of negroes reaching Canada can be found, of

---
[1] Drew. North Side View of Slavery, pp. 244-245.
[2] Mitchell. Underground Railroad, pp. 150-151.
[3] The best account of the workings of the underground system is Prof. W. H. Siebert's "Underground Railroad," New York, 1899. He has an excellent chapter on the life of the negro refugees in Canada before the outbreak of the Civil War.
[4] Siebert: Underground Railroad, p. 194.

course, at a very early date. As early as 1705 an act was passed in New York, and renewed in 1715, to prevent slaves running away to Canada from frontier towns like Albany,[5] and there was also frequent trouble between the French and the English or the French and the Dutch over the runaways who came to Canada. It was not, however, until the beginning of the 19th century that Canada began to be known to any degree among the negroes in the southern states. It was really the period of the discovery of Canada to the negro mind. The War of 1812 exercised powerful influence in directing negro thought to the free country to the north. Kentuckians and others who fought in the War of 1812 must have been surprised to encounter negroes among the Canadian forces opposed to them. But back in the south, when the news of the war began to penetrate there, the negro might fairly conclude that his master's enemy was likely to be his friend, and it was not long before the fact that Canada offered real asylum to the runaway had permeated the slave population throughout the border states at least. As early as 1815 negroes were reported crossing the western reserve in Ohio in large numbers, and one group of underground railroad workers in Southern Ohio is stated to have passed on more than 1000 fugitives before 1817.[6] Dr. S. G. Howe, who made one of the best investigations of the condition of the refugees in Canada, states that the arrivals, few in number at the start, increased rapidly early in the century, with special activity between 1830 and 1840, and greatest activity of all between 1850 and 1860, when the drastic Fugitive Slave Law was in operation.[7]

There were many ways in which the reputation of Canada was spread abroad among the negroes. The effect of the war of 1812 has already been noted. In this connection the slaveholders themselves probably helped to make Canada known by spreading the most foolish stories with regard to its cold climate and the hardships that were endured by the people there.[8] The shrewd negro mind saw through this, and was the more determined to reach the place that his master derided. Black men from Canada were a second influence in making the country known. Many a refugee slave, successful in his break for liberty, would afterwards return to the slave states to assist relatives or friends to freedom. Such an one would serve to plant the germ of freedom in the minds of those with whom he came in contact and thereby increase the number of runaways. White men, too, went from Canada to spread the news of freedom and to aid slaves in reaching their Canaan. James Redpath, the biographer of John Brown, writing in 1860, said that five hundred men went south from Canada annually to assist others in securing their freedom.[9] Slaves who were sent from the south into the border states to work would likely hear of Canada there and so in many and devious ways there was a certain amount of acquaintance with Canada all through the slavery area.

By 1826 the South was feeling the loss of its human property to such an extent that an effort was made to reach an agreement with Great Britain on the subject. But Britain was not responsive. In the troubles of 1837-8 the citizens of the U. S. who tried to create trouble along the border received

[5] Northrup: Slavery in New York, pp. 258-259.
[6] Birney: James G. Birney and His Times, p. 435.
[7] Howe: Refugees from Slavery in Canada West, pp. 11-12.
[8] In a speech in the U.S. Senate on May 5, 1858, Senator Mason, of Virginia, said of the fugitives, "They perish with cold in Canada." See also Ward: Autobiography of a Fugitive Negro, p. 161.
[9] Redpath: Public Life of Captain John Brown, p. 229.

another shock like that of their compatriots of 1812, for again negroes were found defending their new home. All through the forties there was a steady influx of negroes into Canada, the *Western Citizen* of Chicago stating in its issue of Sept. 23, 1842, "there are over $400,000 worth of southern slaves in a town near Malden, Canada."

"It (slave abduction) threatens to subvert the institution in this state," said a Missouri newspaper of the period,[10] while another authority estimated that between 1810 and 1850 no less than 100,000 slaves valued at $30,000,000 were abducted from the south.[11] After 1850 the situation, from the southern standpoint grew worse and worse. Senator Polk, of Missouri, said in 1861: "Underground railroads are established stretching from the remotest slaveholding states clear up to Canada.[12] The *New Orleans Commercial Bulletin* of Dec. 19, 1860, estimated that 1500 slaves had escaped annually for 50 years past, a loss to the slaveholders of $40,000,000.[13] A vigilance committee at Detroit is stated to have assisted 1200 negroes to freedom in one year.[14] A similar committee at Cleveland is stated to have assisted over 100 a month.

Estimates of the number of refugees in Canada on the eve of the Civil War vary greatly. The Canadian census figures have been shown to be quite unreliable and the estimates made by contemporary observers range all the way from 20,000 to 75,000. The bulk of the refugee population in Canada was located in the western part of the province of Upper Canada, where many of their descendants are to be found to-day.

The fugitives who came into Canada during the half century before the Civil War were a continual object lesson to the people of Canada of what slavery meant in the degradation of the black race. Homeless, friendless, destitute, their bodies marked with the lash and the still more brutal punishment of the "paddle," their feet torn, bleeding, frozen often as the result of a flight north in the dead of winter, these products of the slavery system made their own mute appeal to the compassion of a free people. Older people in Canada to-day still speak with emotion of the impression that was made upon their minds sixty years ago by the coming into their community of negro fugitives. The escaped negro was himself one of the powerful influences operating to create in Canada, as in the free states of the North, a sentiment hostile to slavery. The Canadian newspapers of the fifties contain many narratives of fugitives reaching Canada, so that those who did not come into actual contact with the negroes were made acquainted with their condition. The negroes themselves also published newspapers at Chatham and at Sandwich that were agencies in creating anti-slavery sentiment in Canada.

Another influence that was powerful in creating anti-slavery sentiment in Canada, as it did on a tremendous scale in the northern states, was the publication of Mrs. Stowe's famous novel "Uncle Tom's Cabin." First published serially in the *National Era,* an anti-slavery paper printed at Washington, it was issued in book form in March, 1852, the first Canadian edition appearing in the same year and having a large sale. Above all else the book brought home the conviction that slavery was injustice, opposed both to the

[10] *Independent,* Jan. 18, 1855, quoted in Siebert, Underground Railroad, p. 194.
[11] Claiborne: Life and Correspondence of John A. Quitman, vol. II, p. 28.
[12] *Cong. Globe,* XXXVI Cong., 2nd sess., 356.
[13] Quoted in American Anti-Slavery Society annual report for 1861, p. 158.
[14] Mitchell: Underground Railroad, p. 113.

law of God and the best interests of mankind. Many who were careless of the issue were brought to a consciousness of the evils of the slavery system by the reading of this book, or by the dramatic presentations of it that soon followed its first publication. Even to-day, with the issue it presented settled a half a century ago, Uncle Tom's Cabin remains one of the most widely read books in Canada, as it is also one of the most widely read books in the United States.

Towards the enslaved race the Canadian people performed remarkable service during the years 1815 to 1860. The Canadian hatred of slavery found its most spectacular outlet in abduction of slaves from the south, both by native Canadians and by Negroes who had settled in the country. Dr. Alexander Milton Ross tells in his memoirs [15] of more than 30 blacks whom he assisted to freedom. Josiah Henson, himself a fugitive, claims that he brought out 118 slaves. [16] William Wells Brown says he took 69 over Lake Erie in six months; [17] and the famous woman, Harriet Tubman, is credited with having assisted more than 300 fugitives to liberty, making repeated trips into the slave states for that purpose. [18]

A second work that was performed by Canadians was that of receiving the fugitives at the end of their flight and assisting them to get on their feet in the new country. Missions were established at Malden, Sandwich, Toronto, and elsewhere, and the material as well as the moral side of the Negro was cared for. Rev. Isaac Rice, a graduate of Hamilton College, laboured for many years at Malden. He had been well situated in Ohio as the pastor of a Presbyterian church, and with fine prospects, but he gave it up in order to aid the helpless blacks who crowded over the Canadian border. At his missionary house in Malden he sheltered hundreds of the fugitives until homes could be found for them elsewhere. [19]

Of another character was the work done by men like Rev. Wm. King, Henry Bibb and Josiah Henson in the founding of distinctly Negro colonies, with schools and churches and effort directed to improving the whole social status of the race. Interesting observations have been recorded in connection with these colonies. The constant violation of domestic relations, under a slave system was bound to react on home life and take away the incentive to constancy, yet one of the first things married slaves did on arriving in Canada was to have their plantation union reaffirmed by the form of marriage legal in Canada. It was observed that the refugees tended to settle in families and to hallow marriage, and that sensuality lessened in freedom. Their religious instincts were manifested in charity to the sick and to newcomers and in their attitude towards women. The general improvement was well summed up by one competent observer, who wrote: "The refugees in Canada earn a living and gather property; they build churches and send their children to school; they improve in manners and morals—not because they are picked men, but, because they are free men." [20]

---

[15] Ross: Recollections and Experiences of an Abolitionist.
[16] Henson: Father Henson's Story of His Own Life, pp. 149-150.
[17] Brown: Narrative of William Wells Brown, p. 109.
[18] Bradford: Harriet, the Moses of Her People, p. 88.
[19] Coffin: Reminiscences, pp. 249-250.
[20] Howe: Refugees from Slavery in Canada West, p. iv. For Howe's general conclusions with regard to the improvement of the race in Canada, see pp. 101-110 of his report.

Here, then, was a most important truth that Canada was showing forth to the people of the United States, namely that slavery was not necessary to the welfare of the black race, as the south claimed. Canada was also showing that, though brutalized by slavery, the best instincts of the Negro race were reasserted in freedom and the degraded bondsman developed morality and intelligence. In short Canada steadily gave the lie to the plea that slavery was the state best suited to the Negro, and the one best calculated to raise him intellectually and morally.

But Canadians were not satisfied to be merely passive agents in the larger phases of the long struggle against slavery. Early in 1851 there was organized in the city of Toronto the Anti-Slavery Society of Canada which continued active until the Emancipation Proclamation had been made effective and the United States had itself removed the blot from its fair name. The objects of the Anti-Slavery Society of Canada were declared to be "to aid in the extinction of slavery all over the world by means exclusively lawful and peaceable, moral and religious." Rev. Dr. Willis, principal of Knox College, Toronto, was president of the Society all through its history and among others who associated themselves with its work were George Brown, the editor of *The Globe*, and Oliver Mowat, afterwards premier of this province. From Toronto the work of the Society was spread out to the leading centres of Negro population, branches being formed and a steady campaign carried on. *The Globe* under Brown proved a stout ally, and gave much attention to the Society's work. Working relations were entered into with the Anti-Slavery societies in Great Britain and in the United States and a large amount of relief work was looked after by the Women's Auxiliaries. Though the churches generally, with the exception of the Presbyterians, held somewhat aloof from the work of the Society, recruits in plenty were drawn from the clergy. It was a Presbyterian clergyman who was president of the Society all through its history; the first secretary was a Methodist minister, and on the committees appointed from year to year there was always to be found a good representation of the clergy. [21]

The Canadian law gave the Negro fugitive all the rights of citizenship and protected him in their enjoyment. The Negro was encouraged to take up land and it gave him the franchise the same as his white neighbour. Negroes were enrolled in the Canadian militia and bore their share of service during the troubles of 1837-8. "The colored men," says Josiah Henson, "were willing to defend the Government that had given them a home when they had fled from slavery." [22] Under the Canadian law the fugitives were allowed to send their children to the common schools or to have separate schools provided for them out of their share of the school funds. [23] Separate schools were established in some places where prejudice existed and religious agencies also established schools at a number of points. Visitors noted that a surprisingly large number of the Negroes learned to read and write after coming to Canada and in the University of Toronto a number of prizes were taken by coloured youths. Principal McCullum of the Hamilton Collegiate Institute was quoted as saying that his teachers agreed that the blacks were the equal of the whites

---

[21] For a fuller account of the Anti-Slavery Society of Canada see Landon: The Anti-Slavery Society of Canada, *Journal of Negro History*, Vol. IV, No. 1, January, 1919, pp. 33-40.

[22] Henson: An Autobiography, p. 176.

[23] Howe: Refugees from Slavery in Canada West, pp. 77-78; also, Woodson: Education of the Negro Prior to 1861, pp. 248-255.

in mentality. The best educational work seems to have been done by the schools which were established by the Negroes themselves, the mission schools and those located in the Negro colonies.[24] Government interest was shown by the incorporation in 1859 of the "Association for the Education of the Coloured People of Canada," the object of which was to secure educational advantages for the younger people of the race.[25]

The attempts at planting distinctly Negro settlements in Western Ontario form one of the interesting phases of Canada's relation to the slavery issue. Most interesting of all probably was the work of Rev. William King, who was the founder of the Elgin Association or Buxton Settlement. King was an Irishman, a graduate of Glasgow College, who came to America and was made rector of a college in the state of Louisiana. There, by marriage, he became the owner of fifteen slaves of an estimated value of $9,000. For a time he placed them on a neighbouring plantation and gave them the proceeds of their labour, but that did not satisfy his conscience, and in 1848 he brought them to Canada, thereby, giving them their freedom. But his work did not end there, for he felt it his duty to look after them, to educate them and make of them useful citizens. With some prominent Canadians he organized what was known as the Elgin Association which was legally incorporated "for the settlement and moral improvement of the coloured population of Canada, for the purpose of purchasing crown or clergy reserve lands in the township of Raleigh and settling the same with coloured families resident in Canada of approved moral character." The aims were met with decided opposition from certain elements in Kent County, but this did not impede the progress of the Association, a tract of about 9000 acres south of Chatham being purchased. This was surveyed into small farms of 50 acres each, which were sold to the colonists at $2.50 an acre, payable in ten annual instalments. Each settler bound himself within a certain period to build a house, at least as good as the model house set up by the Association, to provide himself with necessary implements and to proceed with the work of clearing land. Roads were soon cut through the forest, and the work of clearing up the country began. The slaves who had been freed by Rev. Mr. King formed the nucleus of the colony, but others came as soon as the land was offered, so that within four years there were 400 people located, and in 1857 it had 800 population. Dr. Samuel Howe gave the warmest praise to what he saw at the Elgin Settlement:

"Buxton is certainly a very interesting place," he wrote. "Sixteen years ago it was a wilderness. Now good highways are laid out in all directions through the forest and by their side, standing back 33 feet from the road, are about 200 cottages, all built in the same pattern, all looking neat and comfortable; around each one is a cleared place of several acres which is well cultivated. The fences are in good order, the barns seem well filled, and cattle and horses, and pigs and poultry, abound. There are signs of industry and thrift and comfort everywhere; signs of intemperance, of idleness, of want, nowhere. There is no tavern and no groggery; but there is a chapel and a schoolhouse. Most interesting of all are the inhabitants. Twenty years ago most of them were slaves, who owned nothing, not even their children. Now they own themselves; they own their houses and farms; and they have their wives and children about them. They are enfranchised citizens of a govern-

[24] Howe: Refugees from Slavery in Canada West, pp. 79-81.
[25] Statutes of Canada, 1859, cap. XXIV.

ment which protects their rights. The present condition of all these colonists, as compared with their former one, is remarkable. The settlement is a perfect success. Here are men who were bred in slavery, who came here and purchased land at the government price, cleared it, bought their own implements, built their own houses after a model and have supported themselves in all material circumstances and now support their schools in part. I consider that this settlement has done as well as a white settlement would have done under the same circumstances." [26]

Interchange of effort between the abolitionists of Canada and those of the United States was noticeable all through the course of the movement. The Canadian negroes did their part, of course, chiefly by going south and helping relatives and friends to escape to freedom. In this they were given the active assistance of a few white Canadians, Dr. Alex Milton Ross being the most noteworthy example of this daring kind of work. From the United States there came in workers on behalf of the fugitives whose efforts deserve every tribute that has ever been paid to them. Hiram Wilson and Isaac Rice, missionaries to the negroes, are names that should never be forgotten by the coloured race and like tribute might be paid to the work of such black men as Rev. S. R. Ward, Austin Steward, Rev. J. W. Loguen, Fred Douglass and Henry Bibb. Bibb was a worker on both sides of the line, putting in several years as a speaker for the anti-slavery forces in Michigan before coming to Canada to attempt a colonization venture in what is now Essex County. Benjamin Lundy, the most prominent of the pioneer abolitionists, was an early visitor to Canada and wrote an account of his trip in The Genius of Universal Emancipation. Noticeable, too, is the fact that the American abolitionists took deep interest in the condition of the fugitives in Canada. Men like Levi Coffin, and more particularly Benjamin Drew, made careful investigations of the results that had attended emancipation by coming to Canada.

Abolition was a common cause for Canadians and their neighbours. Boundary lines did not separate in this fight for the freedom of a race that went on during half a century. The Anti-Slavery Society of Canada entered into working relations with the American Anti-Slavery Society at its inception. Newspaper comment interpreted the movement in the United States to Canadian readers and few American editors had a surer grasp of the direction in which events were heading after 1850 than did George Brown of *The Globe*. His paper not only reported the activities of the Canadian abolitionists but as well kept them in close touch with what was going on across the line. Perusal of *Globe* files, particularly in the fifties, shows that newspaper always aggressive in the support of the cause of the slave. It is quite true that not all the Canadian press was of like mind, but a pro-slavery attitude, or scornful indifference, was never quite so marked as Brown's ceaseless anti-slavery agitation through the columns of his newspaper. The actual attitude of the Canadian parties was quite clearly indicated by their newspapers. The Tory press was usually scornful of the abolitionist movement in the United States and treated the Canadian effort with more or less contempt. The Reformer in Canada naturally fitted abolition into his programme and gave to it some of the same enthusiasm that he directed to the curing of distinctly Canadian

---

[26] For a fuller account of the Buxton Colony, see Landon: The Buxton Settlement in Canada, *Journal of Negro History*, vol. III, No. 4, October, 1918, pp. 360-367. An unpublished history of the colony, based on the papers of Rev. William King, is by Mrs. Annie Straith Jamieson, of Montreal.

abuses. Prof. A. B. Hart has drawn attention to the fact that the thirties and forties in the United States were a period in which religious life had as its characteristic the sincere effort to make religion effective, "to make individual and community correspond to the principles of Christianity." This ideal led to the organization of various reform movements, "causes," each of which took the form of a national society, with newspaper organs, frequent meetings and appeals to the public. Some of this same spirit was manifest in Canada at the same period and the anti-slavery cause gathered to its support a few people who practically devoted their whole lives to its ends, while many others contributed of their time and money as opportunity afforded. The anti-slavery movement had about it an atmosphere of crusade that gave it a spiritual power with many people. Nor must it be overlooked that to some Canadians of the time, there was a secret pleasure in striking a blow at the institution that seemed to be the chief power at Washington. Not that the average Canadian loved the northerner or despised the southern slaver. The opposite would be nearer the truth, but, when the north permitted its laws to be used to arrest runaways in the streets of northern cities and to drag them back to slavery, the Canadian of the time was not far out when he associated the north with south in the guilt of slavery. That belief was nurtured by the constant attempts at compromise, and it was not until towards the end of the fifties that there was a clear understanding in Canada as to where sympathies should lie. To Thomas D'Arcy McGee is due in part the credit for setting Canadian opinion aright in this respect. He saw and described the southern Confederacy as a "pagan oligarchy" and strongly championed the cause of the north.

John Quincy Adams wrote in his diary in 1820: "If slavery be the destined sword in the hand of the destroying angel, which is to sever the ties of this Union, the same sword will cut in sunder the bonds of slavery itself." It took forty years for that prophetic utterance to be fulfilled, and there were many agencies at work during that long period working to the one end of destroying the system of human bondage that had been planted in the new lands of the western hemisphere, and that sapped its life for so many years. Not all these agencies working for the destruction of slavery were apparent on the surface. A contrast of conditions as between 1830 and 1860 might have seemed to indicate that the future of the Negro was darker than ever before on the eve of the Civil war. The area given up to slavery in 1860 was larger than at any previous time, the slaves were more numerous and the slave codes and Fugitive Slave Law the most rigorous the country had ever known. Steps were even being taken to revive the African slave trade.

All this existed after 30 years of debate on the issue. It is doubtful if either side made converts to its own particular views. Indeed, by 1860, the South had reached the point where denunciation of slavery had ceased, when no further efforts were being made to ameliorate the slave's condition, when justification of slavery had become praise of the system, and to speak ill of the institution was regarded as treason. Naturally, the South desired to see the area of slave territory increased and never ceased its demands for expansion; but as individuals, the slave-holders were more powerfully affected by two other considerations, both related to their property, namely, the constant fear that the slaves would rise up and murder them, and the constant loss suffered by the slaves running away or being spirited away. In a sense the Civil War began when the first Negro slave was abducted, and every loss added to the steadily growing division in the country. The climax came when the people of the North rebelled against being made slave catchers by a Fugitive Slave Law, and instead gave assistance, as never before, to aiding the slaves to gain their liberty. There was a war raging between North and South for ten years before the first gun was fired at Sumter, and in that conflict Canada had become an ally of the free states. With the opening of the Civil War the Canadian Government assumed an attitude of neutrality, but of her citizens at least 35,000 joined the Northern armies and played their part in war, as they had already played it in peace, to the end of making the Negro race free.

XIII.

THE MOSQUITO IN UPPER CANADA.

BY THE HONOURABLE WILLIAM RENWICK RIDDELL, LL.D., F.R.S.C., ETC.

The Insect has been called the "Outlaw of Creation;" and some have not hesitated to say that the great fight ahead of man is with the Insect, and that if he does not conquer the Insect, it will conquer him and civilization together.

Whatever truth there may be in these somewhat alarming statements, there can be no doubt of the tremendous amount of misery and mischief done by some kinds of insects. And the mosquito is not the least noxious. Her activities are almost as varied as the methods of spelling her name; Murray gives twenty-six spellings and the mosquito has at least a score of ways of being a nuisance.

All writers on early Upper Canada agree in their account of the extraordinary number of mosquitoes in that new land;—apparently the Arctic regions in the summer are the only places which could be cited as a rival in that respect. Dr. Howison who spent a few years in this Province in the second decade of the last century tells of visiting the Gaelic settlement in Glengarry, and says that on going up to his bedroom at that place the moment the door was opened a cloud of mosquitoes and other insects settled on the candle and extinguished it. While such an occurrence must have been unusual, every one who lived even half a century ago in rural Ontario must have seen swarms not much if at all less thick. The "rain barrel" without which the farm mistress could not do her washing was placed at every corner of the house and almost invariably was full of "wigglers" or baby mosquitoes, larvae. Offensive as the mosquito was and is, her music annoying, her bite irritating and poisonous to man and beast, until recently she was not blamed for more. And yet it is quite certain that what we now call malaria is due to the mosquito. In olden Upper Canada, fever and ague, ("fevernager" was the common pronunciation,) remittent fever or "fever of the country," was an almost intolerable curse. The cause was generally considered to be the bad air of swamps or low lying undrained lands, and if one here and there suggested the mosquito as the real offender he had no hearers. It was not until the closing years of the 19th century that it was scientifically established that the real cause is a very minute parasite in the blood and introduced by the Anopheles mosquito—that kind of mosquito which stands on a window pane with the proboscis and body in a straight line at an angle and not parallel with the surface, and "the female of the species is more deadly than the male."

The Anopheles has been busy in this Province ever since it was a province and it would be impossible to set out all her deeds. We shall speak of only two or three.

After the foolish and fratricidal war of 1812 had been waged for two years and a half, the contending parties agreed to quit as they began. By the Treaty of Ghent they also agreed to refer to two Commissioners, one appointed by each party, the determination of the middle line of the international waters which was the boundary agreed upon in the Treaty of 1783 (which acknowledged the independence of the United States.)

General Peter Buel Porter, who had served with some credit in the War of 1812 and who was to be Secretary of War in Adams' Cabinet, was selected as the American Commissioner, and John Ogilvy of Montreal, the British Commissioner. Their duties led these men into the St. Clair Flats where the deadly Anopheles swarmed. Porter survived the attack, but Ogilvy, bitten by the insects, was stricken with fever and died at Amherstburg, September 28, 1819, the doctors all attributing the fatal infection to the miasmic air of the lowlands.

A little before the St. Clair mosquitoes plied their deadly beaks on John Ogilvy, their sisters were busy with equally nefarious if not equally fatal work at the other end of the peninsula.

In June, 1817, there entered the Province of Upper Canada a Scotsman over whose head forty winters had passed and who was to become almost by chance one of the most noted men in our whole Provincial history. Robert Gourlay—he later adopted his mother's maiden name "Fleming" as a middle name—was born in Fifeshire of a moderately wealthy family; he devoted himself to farming but quarrelled with almost everyone but his devoted wife and children. Well educated, a man of good principles, honest, generous, ever mindful of the poor, he had peculiarities which were sometimes not far removed from insanity; he seems always to have been anxious to put some one in the wrong, not for any advantage to himself but for chastisement of the wrongdoer; he quarrelled on trivial pretexts with his neighbour the Earl of Kellie, his landlord the Duke of Somerset and several of his friends. At length he made up his mind to come to Upper Canada where he had land. He did not intend to remain more than six months, but purposed to return to his farm in Wiltshire. But *l'homme propose;* he visited his wife's kinsman, Thomas Clark, at Queenston in July 1817 and there he was laid up for two months with a fever caused by the stinging of mosquitoes. This misfortune entirely ended his plan of a speedy return to England.

He had sent out printed enquiries to various parts of the Province; and had received certain answers as to the state of the various townships.

Gourlay remaining in the country published an Address to the Resident Land Owners of the Province, advising the drawing up of a full statistical account of the Province and for that purpose the holding of meetings throughout the country to draw up answers to questions which he framed. The last of these attracted most attention: "What in your opinion retards the improvement of your Township in particular or the Province in general and what would most contribute to the same?"

Gourlay most emphatically states—and apparently with perfect truth—that he did not intend Parliamentary Reform and that he had no political object in view; he published the address in the official organ of the Government, the Upper Canada Gazette, after having consulted the Administrator, the Chief Justice and many of the leading personages of the little capital. Only one Councillor saw anything wrong in the Address; the Reverend Dr. Strachan as soon as he saw it in print, considered it of an inflammatory and dangerous nature. Gourlay was annoyed and angry. He took no pains to be conciliatory but rather the reverse, he wrote articles in the Press which aggravated his supposed offence and confirmed Dr. Strachan's bad opinion of him. The view spread amongst the official classes, and it was spread by them that Gourlay was seditious and desirous of overturning the existing order of government and society; he was even charged with being pro-American, an imputation at that time quite as serious as that of being a pro-German at the present.

There is no reasonable doubt that both Gourlay and Strachan were perfectly honest; both desired the best advantage of the Province; both were Scots, both "dour," both fixed in their views—what one's enemies call stubborn, one's friends, firm—both intolerant of opposition and both of perfect courage of conviction. The contest for awhile lay between these two implacable countrymen, the divine suspecting the farmer, the farmer despising the divine.

But Gourlay could only talk and write; Strachan could act. In a short time the Province was stampeded, the Legislature forbade certain meetings which had been projected to carry out Gourlay's scheme, and the patriotic and philanthropic Gourlay was branded all over the Province as a traitorous self seeking intruder.

Prosecuted for seditious libel at Brockville and at Kingston, he was twice acquitted but there was a weapon in the existing law more effective than the law against libel.

In 1804 owing to the large number of disaffected Irish who were entering the Province, a Bill which had been at first intended as a protection against Americans hostile to our monarchical system was enlarged in its passage through the Legislature to cover the case of British subjects as well. As finally agreed to, it authorized certain officials, Judges, Executive and Legislative Councillors and others—to cause the arrest of anyone who was not an inhabitant of the Province for six months or who had not taken the oath of allegiance, and if not satisfied with his words or conduct to order him to leave the Province—if he did not leave the Province within the time given he could be tried for so doing and if found guilty he could be again ordered to leave the Province. If he disobeyed he was liable to the death penalty "without benefit of clergy."

This Statute had seldom been appealed to but it was in full force when the enemies of Gourlay failed in their prosecutions of him for seditious libel. Two magistrates of Niagara had him arrested; he was ordered to depart from the Province; he refused and was cast into the Niagara Jail to await his trial at the Assizes. In the Fall of 1819 he was tried and convicted; ordered to leave the Province, he passed through the State of New York and the Province of Lower Canada for the Old Land.

There oscillating between England and Scotland he remained for nearly fourteen years, three of them in prison because he refused to give bail when required; he horse-whipped Henry (afterwards Lord) Brougham in the Lobby of the House of Commons because (as he claimed) Brougham had neglected a Petition which Gourlay wished presented to the House of Commons; he worked on the road as a pauper; he showered petitions on the House of Commons, the House of Lords, the King; he drew up plans for the improvement of Edinburgh, for the settlement of New York State, and had the luxury of law suits both in the English and the Scottish Courts—and at length in 1833 he returned to this continent. He refused William Lyon Mackenzie's advances but ultimately returned to Upper Canada in 1838. From that time on, the "Banished Briton," as he called himself, kept pestering the Provincial Parliament with petitions about his wrongs and demanding an admission that he had been wrongly banished. At length he was given a small pension which he refused and a pardon which he protested against; he lived in Upper Canada, the United States and Scotland until 1863 when he died in Edinburgh.

Gourlay is one of the most striking figures in our whole history: he just failed of being a great and a useful man; his prosecution which, while within the law, was really persecution, had some influence in uniting the forces opposed to "Family Compact" rule, although he himself always despised Responsible Government.

If the mosquitoes had let him alone, he would doubtless have returned to his English farm and quarrels with his landlord and his neighbours, and the world would have never heard of the Banished Briton and Neptunian.

The next victim of the Anopheles—which word, by the way, means in Attic Greek, worthless or injurious—to be mentioned is a dignified Judge of His Majesty's Court of King's Bench for the Province of Upper Canada— the Honourable Levius Peters Sherwood, the son of a Loyalist father who in 1784 came to Upper Canada with his family and slaves, locating about two miles below Prescott in the Township of Augusta. Levius Peters, the second son, joined the Law Society of Upper Canada in 1801, being the second Student at Law on its Rolls: he was called in 1803, and soon attained eminence at the Bar. He was a Member of the Legislative Assembly for Leeds in the Sixth and Eighth Parliaments and Speaker in the latter; he was a consistent and active supporter of the Government and after being Judge of a District Court, he became a Justice of the Court of King's Bench in 1825. His health even at that time was undermined and he was liable to give way under any undue strain.

It became the duty of Mr. Justice Sherwood to preside at York in 1828 at some of those semi-political trials which convulsed the Province and its little capital, and which were symptomatic of a deep-seated and far-reaching discontent with the Government and its officials, the best known exponent of this discontent being William Lyon Mackenzie. In 1826 some young men of the official class showed their resentment against Mackenzie by raiding his printing office and throwing his type into the Bay: he sued for the trespass and was given damages many times greater than his real loss; then Mackenzie began making personal attacks on Sheriff Jarvis, calling him a murderer— basing the charge upon his having killed young Ridout in a duel some years before. Jarvis published statements of those present to show that the duel had been perfectly fair on his part: then Francis Collins an enthusiastic Radical Irishman, who claimed descent from the old Irish Kings, began making similar attacks in his newspaper the *Canadian Freeman* on Henry John Boulton, the Solicitor General, who had been Jarvis' second in the duel: the Solicitor General called upon the Attorney General, John Beverley Robinson, to prefer a Bill for Criminal Libel against Collins which he did: the Grand Jury found a True Bill whereupon Collins attacked them also: they found a True Bill for that libel also: Collins was to be arraigned on the two Bills but he asked an enlargement which Mr. Justice Sherwood granted; afterwards there was apparently a misunderstanding—Robinson not acceding to Collins' request for an adjournment of his trial, Collins was convicted; he then published an article reflecting on Robinson's "native malignancy" and was again indicted for Criminal Libel. This trial also was before Mr. Justice

Sherwood; his health always poor was at the time very bad; the mosquitoes had tortured him and he was suffering from indisposition and great debility occasioned by a severe attack of the "fever of the country." After having charged the jury he became so ill that he was obliged to retire from the Bench; before doing so he stated to Collins and his counsel that Mr. Justice Hagerman would receive the verdict if they assented; this they did and Mr. Justice Hagerman took his place. The Jury brought in a verdict of "Guilty of a libel on the Attorney General"—the clerk entered a verdict of "Guilty" on the Indictment, but Dr. Rolph, Counsel for Collins, objected and Mr. Justice Hagerman then told the Jury that if they found the defendant guilty of any part of the Indictment, they should return a general verdict of "Guilty"—which they did.

It is probable that the more experienced Sherwood would have acted differently and in such a way as not to be open to objection. Much complaint was made against Hagerman's direction and more against Sherwood's very heavy sentence of a fine of £50, imprisonment for one year and to find sureties for good behaviour for three years.

The sentence was approved by Sir Peregrine Maitland and his Executive Council; but the House of Assembly took a different view. Collins was sent to jail where he complained of the Sheriff, Mr. Jarvis, not supplying him with bread, the Sheriff contending that this was an indulgence extended to indigent persons only and not a legal right; as a matter of fact, Collins had given his allowance of bread to the wife of an absconded jailer who had to support herself and her nine children. Collins did succeed in forcing the Sheriff to supply him with wood but there is no record of success in his claim for free bread.

The citizens of York and others petitioned for his release, but unsuccessfully; at length, the Lieutenant Governor asked for instructions from the Home Authorities, the Law Officers decided that the trial had been conducted in accordance with law but thought the sentence too severe, recommending its reduction by one half, and after ten months imprisonment the editor was released without bail.

The examples given may perhaps suffice to indicate the evil effect of the mosquito in this Province in early days—but who can estimate the toll of misery, disease and death taken by the tiny pest? The use of quinine has much mitigated the trouble for many years, but it is by no means got rid of. In the country to-day we see the fretful babe, with its swollen face writhing in torture from the irritation of the poisonous bites, the hardworking mother deprived of needed rest and sleep, the toiler of the field affecting to despise but in reality dreading the plague which saps his strength and dissipates his energy—the list is unending. In simple self-defence "the mosquito must go."

XIV.

GANANOQUE'S FIRST PUBLIC SCHOOL, 1816.

By Frank Eames.

To perpetuate and honour the names of certain pioneers who founded Gananoque's first Public School; to present as far as possible complete transcriptions of the early documents recovered concerning that work, and to impress upon the principals, the school boards, and the local teachers of to-day their duty of bearing in lasting remembrance those pioneers who laid so good a foundation, are the chief objects of this paper.

Any item concerning the initial step of civilization's noblest movement—education—is of great importance, and eminently worthy of permanent record. By the reproduction of some original documents concerning the step taken in Gananoque one hundred years ago, the writer hopes to rescue some important historical facts before the fast fading characters of a most beautiful handwriting become wholly illegible.

Blown about by the winds, the first paper was salvaged from the street (Brock Street), one early morning. A short time after, others were obtained from children who had found them on a "dump." Some thirty or forty odd papers and letters, all dealing with Gananoque life of a century ago, were obtained in this way, by one who fully realized their great importance to the community.

The documents referring to the early school were copied and then presented to His Honour Judge Herbert Stone MacDonald, for it was from the old homestead they had been wantonly discarded as "trash." The Judge, appreciating their value, sent them to the press for publication, which was partly carried out; but other school papers equally important came to hand later, and the whole were again collected for the present effort. Light thus falls across the first milestone in a century of educational endeavour in Gananoque. The names of worthy men again appear to the view of a well established community. State documents may reveal state history, but for local history within the state go to the pioneers.

First mention of the actual locality known as Gananoque is to be found in the "New York Colonial Documents" where the entries kept by Frontenac on his journey up the St. Lawrence to Kataroqui—Kingston—are published verbatim.

Two men sought the grant of land whereon stands the town of to-day; these were Sir John Johnson and Colonel Joel Stone. Both men were deemed worthy of consideration for the land grant, which was evenly divided by the Gananoque River passing along its centre. The grant, which was roughly triangular in shape, was bounded on the south by the River St. Lawrence, on the northeast by the Gananoque River to the mouth of Mud Creek, and by a line running from there southwesterly to the River St.

Lawrence at Lindsay's Point of to-day. The Point at that time was known as Shiriff's Point, a man by the name of Shiriff having settled there. When Shiriff died his wife went to live with Carey and his young daughter, Mrs. Shiriff being Carey's sister. Carey's daughter married a Mr. Jamieson whose name appears in the list of proprietors of the schoolhouse later. Jamieson's family consisted of two daughters and a son, whose families are included among Gananoque's population of to-day.

Colonel Stone was a direct descendant of William Stone, who sailed from London, England, with twenty-five others in May, 1639, landing and settling in Connecticut. In this state Colonel Stone was born, at Gilford, in August, 1749. After helping his father on the farm until he grew to manhood, he developed inclinations for business in which he became a success. He lost his winnings from this source through his British loyalty, which caused the revolutionary element to become suspicious of him.

A "Gananoque Souvenir" published by the late Treasurer of Gananoque, Mr. Freeman Britton, a brother of the learned Judge, tells us that he rode off one night for New York, where he joined General Wentworth's forces on June the 20th, 1777. In 1778 he was commissioned to recruit for the forces of Sir William Howe, a brother of the equally famous "Black Dick" or Richard, Lord Viscount Howe, who at that time was Commander of His Britannic Majesty's fleet in North America, and who later, as first sea lord, took command again and broke the blockade of Gibraltar on the "Glorious First of June."

The Colonel, while engaged on his recruiting mission, was surprised and taken by the rebels at night; he escaped, however, and being in ill health went to the sea to recuperate; returning to New York he was assigned to a Lieutenancy in Company 22, New York Militia.

On the twenty-third of March, 1780, he married Miss Leah Moore, the daughter of an ocean skipper, William Moore.

The Colonel then made application to England for recognition of his services, and later went over there personally to arrange his affairs to the best advantage. For three years he remained in this endeavour, and finally had to prearrange matters and leave for the west and his new home in Upper Canada. The Colonel's wife, by appointment, met him at Quebec, in 1786, and after a brief stay there they went on to New John's Town, or Cornwall of to-day. He arrived there in 1787 with his family of four persons, himself and wife, with two children, William and Mary Stone, the latter becoming eventually the wife of Charles MacDonald, uncle to the present learned Judge MacDonald. A leatherbound handbook of William Stone's which bears his signature and date of purchase in Montreal, is now in the possession of the writer.

It was Lieutenant-Governor Gore who later gave the rank of Colonel to Joel Stone when he was posted to the command of the 2nd Regiment of Leeds.

Joel Stone landed at Gananoque in 1792 and erected a temporary abode on "The Point" which is now the coal and lumber yard.

A Frenchman named Carey answered a signal hung in front of Stone's camp, and they eventually became partners, but the partnership was of short duration. It seems to have terminated when the camp took fire and destroyed practically all of Stone's effects. After this Carey went outside of Stone's boundary line to the west and settled with his young daughter, previously mentioned.

Stone, by remaining, became the first settler and founder of Gananoque. His letters of application for privileges are addressed from Cadanoryhqua and Ganenoquay, respectively, in 1792. The town is situated in the extreme southwest corner of the County of Leeds, and in the township of that name. It is 18 miles from Kingston East and 32 miles from Brockville West. Of such great beauty is this charming location that the natives upon the first arrival of the French were found to be calling the locality "Manatona," or "The Garden of the Great Spirit," and such it may well be called. No grander or more scenic aquatic playground exists than the Thousand Islands. They are not only beautiful; they are sublime in the fullest sense. Canadians generally, know very little of their magnificence. A more glorious heritage never fell to a worthy people than the Thousand Islands to Canadians.

Many forms and renderings of the name Gananoque have fallen under the observation of the writer, and for the sake of its interest he has retained them and they are presented here. Variation in spelling such a name might very well be traced to its ready adaption in various forms; again, it might be attributable to the loose, guttural and very difficult articulations of the aborigines from whom it passed through the French pronunciation into English. We are sure that the chief interests of the early comers were centred in the more lucrative peltry bales, or the more material log heaps and fallow fires, than in the spelling and definition of the name. A count shows 15 different renderings of the name of which Count Frontenac's comes first in an excerpt from his diary; he tells us that: "On the eleventh a good day's journey was made, having passed all that vast group of islands with which the river is spangled, and camped at a point above the river called:

1. On-non-da-qui, up which many of them go hunting.
2. Gan-non-o-qui. From the Huron, "Oughseanto," a deer.
3. Kah-non-no-kwen. "A meadow rising out of the water." Leavitt's History of Leeds and Grenville.
4. Ca-da-no-ghue. "Rocks in running water."
5. Ga-na-wa-ge. From Morgan's Map of the St. Lawrence.
6. Ga-na-na-quy. Ontario Archives, 1905, pp. 504 and 512.
7. Co-na-no-qui. Ontario Archives, 1905, p. 511.
8. Ca-da-noe-qui. From Colonel Stone's application to the legislature for bridge and ferry privileges, 1801. Granted this, he carried out his plans and charged toll as follows: Horse and one man, one shilling; one man, threepence; one boatload, one shilling and sixpence. The Colonel passed his privileges on to one Silas Person in 1802.
9. Ca-da-no-ry-hqua. From Colonel Stone's letters.
10. Ga-nen-no-quay. From an old account book of the Colonel's, 1819.
11. Gau-nuh-nau-queeng. "Rendezvous, or Place of Residence." From "History of the Ojebway Indians" (p. 164) by Rev. Peter Jones (Kakewaquonaby).
12. Ga-na-no-qui. Not Iroquois, but supposed to be Huron.
13. Ga-na-no-coui. Chewett's Plan of Upper Canada, 1793.
14. Gar-an-o-que. Proclamation of Counties in Public Archives. Sess.

Papers 29. C. Page 79, Constitutional History Canada. This form is admittedly a misprint.

15. Ga-na-no-que. The accepted form of to-day which first appears (to my knowledge) in an old account book in the early twenties.

Regarding Sir John Johnson, he was a son of Sir William Johnson who figured so prominently in colonial wars. Sir John commanded a regiment of some eight hundred men; the post of Isle aux Noix was held by him and it was from thence, at the north end of Lake Champlain, the discharged fighters under him came to Canada where they had secured grants by drawing lots. It was one of these men, in the person of Thomas Howland, who eventually became one of the first trustees of Gananoque's school, that Sir John put in charge of his interests at Gananoque. Mr. Howland cleared a piece of land and erected a home near Skinner's factory of to-day. Sir John, who never lived upon his Gananoque grant, chose to make his abode in the Province of Quebec, at Argenteuil, and later he became its seigneur. Sir John never developed his holding, nor its water power privileges, and all eventually passed to Joel Stone and Charles MacDonald.

To retrace our steps backward a little, we find that the first substantial habitation was a log house built to accommodate hired help as well as Colonel Stone. It stood, we are told, where Church and Tanner Streets meet at King Street, practically in the middle of the highway of to-day. Here Stone cleared land first. It was a part of his clearing that later became the site of the first schoolhouse, as it was afterward the site of at least two others, as well as a church.

In the growth of the community the first essential was some form of civil government for law and order, and the establishment of improved conditions for both old and young. The recording of such activities are a natural outcome of their adoption. In that early and primitive day, a chest, cupboard, or open shelf became the repository of many important documents. The most natural enemies to papers of importance, under such conditions, are dust, fire and dampness. It is not much to be wondered at that many of the more valuable of our early records are lost; and yet we have to be thankful that our records are as complete as they are, under such conditions.

To the painstaking and methodical care of two of our pioneers and the manner in which they kept their records, our gratitude is due; for while these papers were almost lost through later neglect, yet their neatly folded appearance and careful annotation reveal the sign of scrupulous care. To them we owe our thanks for the carefully guarded information now at our disposal. They were Charles and John MacDonald.

Charles, who married the Colonel's daughter Mary, became one of Gananoque's first business men, in 1812. He opened a store which stood upon the street about midway between the Spring and Axle Company's warehouse and their foundry; the building was a stout frame one, and was sold eventually to a Mr. Henderson, who utilized the timber for barn construction.

John became a partner with Charles in 1817, he having just arrived from Troy, New York.

Charles seems to have been very active in the settlement from the first. He did an extensive business, and carried on a sawmill and gristmill, as well as conducting a general lumber trade in which he went so far as to supply materials for the King's ships at Kingston. It was Charles who carried out the construction of some blockhouses for the Government of that day; he built one on what is known as Chimney Island, so called from the chimney of the blockhouse, which remains standing. Another one he built on Blockhouse Hill, within the town limits. The door of the latter structure faced the western approach of the King Street bridge. According to one source of information, the blockhouse was in command of Mr. Hiel Sliter in 1812. (See Sliter's Memoirs in Leavitt's Hist. of Leeds and Grenville). He says: "In 1812 I joined a rifle company and entered upon my first duties at Gananoque. While in charge of the blockhouse at that time I learned the multiplication table; as no slates were to be had, my companion and myself obtained some chalk and by using the top of the stove as a slate succeeded in mastering the first simple rules of arithmetic."

The last remaining timbers of the blockhouse at Gananoque were taken away in 1859 by Mr. William Edwards, who told me they were used in factory construction. Whether the building was erected before Forsyth's raid upon the settlement from Sackett's Harbour, or after, I have no knowledge, but probably after, for according to a recent article in the Alexander Bay *Sun*, Capt. Forsyth did great damage there. This is questionable when compared with our own version of the affair; besides, if Forsyth did effect the damage stated, then the blockhouse was either not built or he could not take it, which seems hardly likely, for that raid is admitted to have been the first American success in the campaign of 1812; in fact, the first success of the war. The raid was made September 9th, 1812. Capt. Forsyth made his landing at Lindsay's Point, about two miles west of the settlement. Outposts had been mounted by the settlers, two in number, between the village and the Point; these were taken by Forsyth's party, who numbered some ninety-five; the mounted outposts, according to the American version, endeavoured to escape and give the alarm, one only succeeded and the other was shot. It is known that the capture of the Colonel was much desired, and a visit was made by the marauders to the Colonel's house. They, in the belief that it was empty, satisfied themselves with firing a shot into the building haphazard, the ball striking Mrs. Stone in the hip; they did not capture the Colonel, however.

Mr. Sliter informs us that in 1803 there were three dwellings only in the settlement, the Colonel's, that of a Capt. Bradish and one belonging to Seth Downs. Mr. Howland's must have been a shack, or he had not arrived at the building stage. However, the number had increased by 1818 to forty-six, and the population was then three hundred and nineteen. This is important, since it shows to what extent the need for consideration of the young, and their welfare along educational lines, had become apparent.

The nearest schoolhouse in Johnstown District to Gananoque was at Halleck's, some little distance west of Brockville. Halleck's school was active in 1811.

Squire Stone and others formed at first a body to consider the construction of a schoolhouse. This they concluded to do by forming among themselves a proprietary body in which each member should assume a certain portion of the burden, according to his means or inclination. The cost of such a building arrived at, they made a division of the total into eighty-five shares: these were disposed of at approximately twenty-two shillings per share. The contract says the cost was to be ninety-four pounds.

GANANOQUE'S FIRST PUBLIC SCHOOL

The following list of names, with each man's number of shares opposite his name, is presented in exactly the same form as on the original sheet:

NAMES OF THE PROPRIETORS OF THE SCHOOL.

(The side-notes are those of the writer.)

Name.	Shares.	
Joel Stone	10	Founder of the settlement and donor of school site and books.
*Thomas F. Howland	8	Sir John Johnson's agent.
*Andrew Bradish	8	A military captain.
*Charles MacDonald	15	Merchant and millowner.

(* The preceding three were Gananoque's first school trustees.)

John Brownson	7	
Seth Downs	10	Contractor and builder of the school.
Neal McMullen	6	
E. Webster	3	Merchant.
John S. MacDonald	3	Surveyor.
F. Firman	1	Yeoman.
Harvey Stratton	1	
H. A. Delamatter	4	Delamatter's name is indistinct on the list, being only partly legible, but the two or three last letters were made up from the name in the first store ledger of Charles MacDonald.
Leman Crans	1	Yeoman.
N. M. Miller	1	Yeoman.
John McNeil	1	Yeoman.
John Howard	2	
Nathan Fish	1	
D. Jamieson	2	
J. A. Jeffers	1	
	85	

The site is next to be considered; the exact location of it is not set forth in the copy of the deed which we are able to present. The Squire's first clearing, at the junction of the present Church and Tanner Streets with King Street, seems to have been the spot chosen and presented by him for the school; much circumstantial evidence can be shown in favour of this site.

COPY OF THE DEED.

This indenture made the .... day of .... in the year of our Lord One Thousand Eight Hundred and Fifteen Between Joel Stone Esqr of the Village of Gananoque in the County of Leeds in the District of Johnstown and Province of Upper Canada of the one part, and Thomas F. Howland, Andrew Bradish, and Charles MacDonald, Trustees nominated by the inhabitants of the said Village of Gananoque and its vicinity for the purpose of erecting a Public School House in the said Village. Collecting Subscriptions to carry the same into effect and of receiving a deed in fee simple of a Lot of Ground upon which the said School House is to be erected. of the other part, witnesseth that the said Joel Stone considering the importance and utility of Public Schools and willing as far as he is able to facilitate (so worthy) an object Doth for himself and (his heirs) in Consideration of three pepper Corns and for the purpose hereinafter specified, Give, Grant, Convey and Confirm by these Presents for Ever unto the said Thomas F. Howland, Andrew Bradish and Charles MacDonald and to their Successors, One Quarter of an acre of Ground situated in the Village of Gananoque aforesaid Butted and Bounded as follows, that is to say (The boundaries are not filled in).

And the said Trustees Thomas F. Howland, Andrew Bradish and Charles MacDonald for themselves and their successors annually chosen Doth hereby promise and agree to have Erected upon the aforesaid lot of Ground as soon as convenient after the date and execution hereof a School House, and that the said Lot shall not be appropriated to any other use or purpose whatever but what is connected with the aforesaid School and Schoolhouse. In Witness whereof the Parties to these Presents have hereunto set their Hands and Seals the day and year first above written.

The boundaries and necessary signatures have been omitted by the person drawing the copy of the deed, they having been set forth in the original for registration. This paper was evidently copied from the original by the Colonel himself, to judge by the handwriting.

Although the Town of Gananoque has spread, covering both sides of the Gananoque River to-day, we know that the first or original village mentioned by the Colonel in the deed of gift was situated on the west side of the River Gananoque. This statement may seem superfluous to present inhabitants of the town, but the fact will pass some day from memory, and those who follow will appreciate this record. The Colonel naturally settled on his own land on the west side of the river. He cleared his first land, as stated, where he built his first house, viz., on King Street. At least three schoolhouses occupied the site at the east corner of Church and King; we have evidence to that effect, a church, too, having been built there. The Squire recorded the fact that the schoolhouse was used as a church for different denominations in turn. Mr. Britton, in his "Gananoque Souvenir," says that the first church was built near the first school house, although Mr. Britton gives the date of the first schoolhouse as 1831. Whether John S. MacDonald surveyed the school site or not cannot be said; he was surveyor, however, and it was he who surveyed the section of Gananoque called the West Ward; this was done in 1824; the North and South Wards were not surveyed until about 1847. The reprint of Reports and Minutes of the Counties Council, Brockville, shows that Mr. John Robinson, surveyor, resident in Leeds, made his report of the survey that year, and his report also gives the lines of demarcation, streets and lanes.

John S. MacDonald, the surveyor, must not be confused with John MacDonald, the partner of Charles. He had not yet arrived from Troy, New York, to join his brother Charles. Neither was John S. any relation of the two brothers, John and Charles. (Smith's "Canada.")

It may be well to mention that Mr. Firman, or Fairman, the father of Daniel and William Fairman, who lived to a very old age in this locality, was heard to say that he could remember the ruins of the original School in his early boyhood days. This was also the statement of two others who lived to a good old age—Mr. Robert Bulloch and Mr. John Lasha. These remarks were noted in 1898 as well as those regarding the blockhouse and the position of its doorway. Another feature worthy of note also was the statement of Mr. William Kidd and Mr. William Edwards (the latter still living) in reference to the stockade around the blockhouse. Both gentlemen concurred in the statement that the stockade was of cedar pickets and followed the crest of the bank along the River Gananoque toward the present rear of the High School, and thence over to Stone Street, almost following Stone to King, thence along the rear of the present row of business houses, and back toward the river bank again. The blockhouse stood upon, or nearly upon, the site of the present standpipe.

Our next document takes us back to the schoolhouse again and is the draft of the contract with Seth Downs:

CONTRACT.

Contract, or agreement, entered into by Seth Downs of the Village of Gananoque in the County of Leeds of the one part.

And Thomas F. Howland, Andrew Bradish & Charles MacDonald of the said place (Trustees for building a schoolhouse at the aforesaid village) of the other part.

The said Seth Downs on his part, by these presents, agrees to build or cause to be built, a school house on the plot of ground in said village marked out and appropriated for that purpose of the following dimensions and materials, and to finish the same in the manner herein mentioned, viz.:

The aforesaid building to be constructed and finished conformable to the directions agreed upon by the Proprietors as specified in writing in a paper hereunto annexed,—part of which is herein explained and the articles necessary thereto to be made as herein described.

In the first place by way of explaining the above mentioned annexed writing the chimney to be carried up through the centre of the roof in a frame made for that purpose.

Secondly: A porch of convenient size with door to be made in the front of the said building.

Thirdly: A necessary office to be made of the following dimensions and in the manner herein mentioned, viz.: the height, seven feet; breadth, four feet, and length, eight feet; square roofed, covered with shingles, and the sides, etc., clapboarded; a jointed partition in the middle of the same, with two conveniences and a door to each division.

The Teacher's writing desk: Breadth, 28 inches; length, 3 foot 7 inches; ledge on the top of this desk, 7 inches wide; height 10 inches; height of lower side or front, 4 inches, which gives 21 inches for the leaf or fall of the desk; to be fixed with hinges and a lock and key, to contain papers.

A plain framed table in lieu of a stand for the said desk; height, 2 feet 4 inches; the length and breadth to suit with the size of the desk.

A seat or form for the abovementioned desk—18 inches long, 13 inches wide and 17½ inches high.

The scholars' writing desks as follows: to suit in length the sides of the room (except the front side) which makes three in number—Height, 2 feet 10 inches and four inches in front; 3 feet 6 inches wide, leaving a

7 H.P.

ledge on the top of 7 in. wide; three sufficient stands for these desks of framed work, 2 foot four in height.

Six forms, or seats, to the above desks of lengths suitable to the desks, 17½ inches high, one foot wide or wider.

A row of pegs fixed in a board or plank on the wall, on the whole length of the side of the room containing the door (except for the space of the door itself), a row of 10 or 12 pegs on each side of the room.

And the aforesaid Seth Downs agrees to build and finish the whole of the forementioned in a workmanlike manner, and to have the same completed by the first day of December, 1815.

And the aforesaid Trustees, viz.: Thomas F. Howland, Charles MacDonald, and Andrew Bradish, agree by these presents to pay unto Seth Downs aforesaid, the sum of Ninety-four Pounds, Current Money of this Province, as soon as the aforementioned building is completed, and finished in the manner herein specified,—as Witness our hands and seals at Gananoque aforesaid this eleventh day of November in the year of our Lord One Thousand Eight Hundred and Fifteen.

Signed and sealed   SETH DOWNS.
in presence of   T. F. HOWLAND.
E. MACDONALD.   ANDW. BRADISH.
PHILIP WIELCRAVE.   CHARLES MACDONALD.

The paper on which the above contract is written bears a watermark with the name, "J. Ansell, 1812." Being a folded sheet, the opposite page bears a watermark showing Britannia holding a spear, not a trident, and with a shield, oval, bearing the Cross of St. George. The handwriting is beautifully executed, and this paper is in a fairly good state of preservation.

The question of the erection of a schoolhouse having been disposed of, the next step taken was the appointment of a committee to discuss the question of suitable books. Any movement in conjunction with the founding of a system, and especially an educational system, requires much preliminary study before any acceptable course of procedure presents itself. Men of ability who have undertaken educational problems in an endeavour to produce results often only find partial success for their labours. There is no department of civil organization where close application and ability are more essential than in education; nor are the objects more difficult of attainment or more disproportionately appreciated than in this. Many declaim against any increase of money grants for the maintenance of their schools. These men usually have no material, or rather personal, interests in schools. Their children may have grown up and dispersed, while they themselves are able to retire through thrifty habits and may feel inclined to keep down increased taxation. This is a fallacy, and a detriment, not only to the whole community but to themselves as well. Take away the schools and the population will move away; increased facilities and encouragement of better and more refined schools will redound to the credit of any community. No one will deny that the latter course will find due reward in increased growth of the community. How many parents distress themselves to move nearer better opportunities for the education of their families.

Joel Stone clearly foresaw the need of this inducement to settlers, and furnished that need in the best sense. Heads of families would not be willing in many cases to send their young children to Kingston, Brockville or other localities favoured by educational advantages, and the only thing to do was to furnish them with a school at home.

At this very early period of Upper Canada's existence, when steps were to be taken to educate the children of pioneers, it devolved upon the very few men of exceptional gifts and education to be the advisers and directors. Few as they were in the sparsely settled districts, thanks to their forethought they rose to every occasion, realizing that education must become the foundation of the future.

It is not too much to say that at least eighty per cent. of those who would receive their education in the common school, and end it there, would be obliged to assume manual labour at a very early age. Teachers then taught seldom more than six months in the year. Of the pupils receiving this scant education some few exceptionally bright ones would perhaps attend the Grammar School in Kingston or York. Under these circumstances it became natural that sharp scrutiny should be made of all strangers who were likely to be in direct association with the schools, as well as of the school books. Questions such as the nationality of a teacher were put to those who sought to teach. Swearing allegiance to the king was also a frequent requisite. The origin and authorship of school books were enquired into. All these were common preliminaries of those sturdy pioneer trustees of the time. Gananoque men were no exception in this regard; they held views in common with all others throughout the country when it came to choosing definitely either teachers or books.

These precautions were but the natural outcome of sharp lessons born of war. Upper Canada had just passed through the throes of invasion and strife. Only eight months prior to the signing of the contract for the school at Gananoque, the news of the Treaty of Ghent, signed on December 24th, 1814, had reached Upper Canada.

But the Treaty had not been sufficient to wholly withdraw the sting of bitterness and distrust. Mark closely the wording of the following and observe the deep-rooted desire to guard and protect the young from insidious and anticipated mischief:—

REPORT OF THE COMMITTEE ON BOOKS.

Gananoque, March 23, 1816.

The Committee appointed by the proprietors of the School House for the purpose of selecting proper books for the use of the School having met, and seriously considered the utility of having proper books used in school, and the confusion attending tuition of pupils by not having similar books used by each scholar, as well as the dangerous effects that may result from the introduction of the works of American authors into schools in the provinces of Canada by having a tendency to alienate the juvenile mind from a proper attachment to the Government, and weaning their affections from a love to their mother country, we therefore earnestly recommend to the proprietors of the school to lend their aid and support by signing the following subscription for the purpose of purchasing the following schoolbooks which we impartially recommend as being the most proper compilations that can be introduced into schools in this part of the country, viz. :—

List of School Books recommended by the Committee, viz. ;

  Dilworth's Improved Spelling Books .... 12 copies.
  Murray's Grammar, abridged .... 12 "
  Murray's Introduction to English Reader .... 24 "
  Murray's English Reader .... 24 "
  Murray's Sequel to English Reader.......... 24 "
  School Testaments .... 24 "
  School Bibles .... 12 "

We the subscribers concurring in the sentiments of the Committee and for the encouragement of the School promise to pay to the Trustees of said School the several sums annexed to our several names on demand to be appropriated by them to purchase the above books:—

Gananoque, Mar. 23, 1816.

              £   s.   d.
Joel Stone 5   0   0

A neatly ruled form of account, containing the above subscription, concludes this document, which is written on fairly well preserved paper. It shows once more the debt of gratitude owing to the " Squire's " generous disposition and kind heart. Once more the sponsor guaranteed the first item for an equipment for many poor children of his little colony, and no names followed his.

While upon the subject of books I will insert an item of much interest. Prior to the handing over to the Town of Gananoque of the substantial brick mansion which was formerly the home of the Hon. John MacDonald's family, and while it was in the hands of a local gentleman pending action on the part of those transferring the property to the Town for a Municipal building, some miscellaneous material had been brought together in cleaning up and dispensed with so as to prepare the premises for other uses. Among this flotsam and jetsam were a number of books. I looked over perhaps thirty-five or forty, and selected a Murray's Grammar in full leather binding and in first-class condition. I obtained the book with some others for a small sum, and upon examination discovered upon the fly-leaf written in feminine hand the following:

    Miss H. Mallory's Book. March 15th, 1825.
And on the coverlid within:
      Abraham Mallory's Book
        March 29th, 1817.

The book was published by Samuel Swift, of Middlesbury, Vermont. Its original price was eight shillings. The lady whose name appears above was married to the Hon. John MacDonald in 1831, and was consequently the mother of the learned Judge MacDonald of Brockville. The book was no doubt used in the schoolhouse at the time.

Several months elapsed after receiving the Report of the Committee on Books before any action was taken toward opening the school. The next step we have any record of is to be found in the

PROPOSALS FOR TEACHING A SCHOOL.

By John S. McDonald.
Gananoque, October 8th, 1816.

He will engage to teach for a space of time not less than one year for Two Hundred and Fifty Dollars per year exclusive of board.

His board and lodging must be procured by the Trustees in a convenient place within half a mile of the School.

The above sum of Two hundred and fifty dollars to be paid in four equal quarterly payments and the payments made to him within fifteen days of the expiration of each quarter.

He will engage to teach five days and a half for a week, estimating thirteen such weeks a quarter.

He will teach six hours each day.

If accounted ineligible to teach under the existing School Act on account of residing in the States during and prior to the late war (being already a British born subject) he will (provided he will be continued in the capacity of a Teacher during good behaviour and provided that the school be organized according to law) engage to swear allegiance to His Majesty, provided that it can be done without going personally to the Governor's place of residence.

He will abide by the above engagements for the space of one year during which term if the school be entitled to any money from Government the same when received he will accept as part of his above mentioned annuity and after the first year he will engage to teach for such an additional sum to the yearly annuity from Government as he and the Trustees of the School shall agree to.

He will engage to teach the term of one year without any intermission, but if required by him the Trustees must permit him to be absent from school a space of time not exceeding four weeks during the space of one year, which space he is afterwards to teach in order to complete his term of one year.

He will commence his said School at such time as he and the Trustees can agree to, which time however must not exceed the 15th of November next.

Gananoque, October 8th, 1816.

JOHN S. McDONALD.

It should be noted that in the last paragraph of Mr. McDonald's proposal, there is set forth a specified time at which the School shall commence; indeed this is the only clue we have of any set date. We may be sure, however, that the time was very near to that event since everything appears to have been in readiness except the selection of the Teacher, which selection, I am inclined to think, fell upon Mr. Andrew Bradish.

The following draft of proposals from Mr. Bradish prompts this belief, for he makes it apparent that he was displeased with the proposals set forth by Mr. McDonald "on a former night;" to remove this attitude was the task set for Mr. Abraham Fulford. However, let the Bradish paper speak for itself:

THE PROPOSALS OF ANDREW BRADISH. OCTOBER 23, 1816.

Mr. McDonald by withdrawing the Proposals made by him to the Trustees of the Gananoque School having removed the causes of my silence on a former night, and Mr. Fulford in the name of all the Trustees having called upon me to request my Proposals might be delivered at their next meeting in case I should be inclined to undertake the direction of the school[1];
I submit the following for consideration—

First:—I will attend the customary hours and give instruction to day scholars in the usual branches of a plain English Education for £87 10/— same payable quarterly—and whatever money may be awarded by the Board of Education to the Teacher of the said school shall be considered a part of the above sum.

Second:—Any boarders, not children of Proprietors, that may be sent to my house to be educated under my superintendence shall be permitted to attend at the School House at School hours and the fees for their tuition shall be included in the above sum of £87 10/.[2]

Third:—Receipts from me presented by any subscribers to the Trustees shall be accepted by them in payment of their subscriptions.

To the Trustees of the Gananoque School.

ANDW. BRADISH.
23rd October, 1816.

This last document seems to have been all that was submitted for the consideration of the Trustees, and we may assume that the "opening" followed shortly after, for the Squire, in a later meeting, makes reference to the activity of the school by a citation of the salary of the teacher for the preceding year.

Present at a meeting to answer certain queries by Robert Gourlay regarding the District of Johnstown, Colonel Stone stated: "One good Frame Building erected and finished for a School House in Gananoque, also to serve as a place for Divine Worship, free for ministers of different denominations. There are no regular preachers resident, but those of the Baptist and Methodist Congregations preach every alternate Sabbath, and occasionally those of the Presbyterian persuasion."

The Squire, with his own generosity, aided by the labours of others, presents the school at last in perpetuity to the youth of the place, who down through a whole century have gathered their knowledge from the institution.

From the portals of this modest edifice the youth of the future were to emerge with an all too scanty equipment for their entrance into Life's vast uncertainties. Yet with all its meagreness, what a boon it must have proven for many of them! What a debt they owed to the philanthropic Squire and

---

[1] Owing to the decay of this portion of the paper by dampness, to follow the words "direction of," the writer suggests: "the school."

[2] The words "not children of Proprietors" have been struck out of the original document, evidently at the time of its consideration. Also the words "and the fees, etc.," (to end of clause), for which is inserted: "and that one half of the fees of tuition shall go in part payment of the above sum of £87, 10/, and the other half to my benefit."

his company of Proprietors! Do we see the group about the door of the structure? hear the key rattle in the lock? See the Squire proudly, perhaps slightly moved with emotion, throw wide the door and mentally bid the child enter.

> Within these portals Knowledge dwells;
> Salutes thee first.
> Give heed to that which falls
> From Wisdom's lips,
> And fill youth's golden hours
> From this rich harvest.
> Glean here, and garner zealously each grain,
> For by the yield, Time gauges all Life's profits.
> Within, I charge thee take thy choice of roads—
> The best, the worst. Be nothing loth
> To take the best. With heavier loads
> Sound training takes the race from sloth.
> Seek and advance. Shun idleness as sin.
> Invite besides a worthy and pure, reasonable ambition
> To share thy friendship;
> Work and win.

Having now fairly launched the craft upon its long voyage, let us take up the last remaining records dealing with the new School.

First available to the writer comes the reference from history already published concerning the meeting at which the Colonel officiated as President in 1818. This is in connection with the replies to Robert Gourlay.

Verbatim it is as follows:—" Number of Schools, one; under the patronage of the Board of Education for this District, viz.: Johnstown, comprehending two Counties—Leeds and Grenville. Salary, £20, 6/3 per quarter, currency, including an allowance of £5, 0, 0 per quarter.

In 1819 we have Mr. McDonald's proposals: " For the ensuing year."

PROPOSALS FOR TEACHING THE COMMON SCHOOL AT GANANOQUE FOR THE ENSUING YEAR, BY JOHN S. McDONALD.

1. He will engage to teach six hours in each day and five and a half days in each week, and instruct his pupils in the various branches of common English Education for the sum of Eighty-one Pounds, five Shillings H.C. per year.

2. The said sum (except what part of it may be awarded by the Board of Education) is to be paid to him by the Trustees of said School in four quarterly payments; that is, one payment at the end of every quarter.

3. If the said payments be not made within fifteen days after the expiration of every quarter, then the said Trustees jointly and severally shall give him their Note of Hand for what may be due to him of said payments or either of them.

4. All receipts from him to any subscribers, if tendered, shall be accepted as payment for their subscriptions.

5. He will commence by the first day of March next, but would not wish to before that time on account of other arrangements.

JOHN S. MCDONALD.

Gananoque, January 9th, 1819.

The foregoing constitutes the last of such century-old documents which the writer has been able to gather together, and with a reference to the Grammar School of 1859, our documentary evidence will end. The reference mentioned is contained in a letter from the Hon. John MacDonald to his son, then attending college at Kingston. The latter is the present esteemed Judge MacDonald of Brockville.

Brief excerpts are only given from this letter, dealing with the schools of the day; a Mr. McCoomb and a Mrs. King are mentioned as having taken scholars, as they evidently have taken them for the advanced branches of the Grammar School, which School, according to the letter: "Has dwindled down to eight scholars, so Mr. Fraser informed me Saturday night. When there is a small attendance of scholars, the Government money is small in proportion. I don't think it to be Mr. Fraser's fault, but from the circumstances and the low price in the Common School—sevenpence halfpenny per month—with what is called a good teacher, and I presume he is for the common branches, under those circumstances the Trustees cannot incur the responsibility of engaging a teacher just now. When the new school is up the two schools will probably be joined."

(Signed) JOHN MACDONALD.

From the modest fees quoted by McDonald and Bradish of a century ago the local school maintenance has reached the sum of approximately $15,000 a year, all devoted to securing for the youth of the place that grandest of all life's noblest attainments—a sound education.

From beneath the lintels of Gananoque's schools her youth have passed for a hundred years into the many phases of life; some to fame and fortune, others to assume their places in the ranks of the masses, but all prepared with the elementary essentials of success, by means of which we step from our narrow chamber into the broad highways of the world.

Statistics tell us that the number of Schools in Upper Canada in 1827 was 340, with twelve to fourteen thousand on the lists of attendants.

The following list of names taken from the first cash book of the MacDonald Bros. dating from the commencement of their partnership in 1817 and extending to 1826, represent the settlement fairly well at the time.

Charles MacDonald	O'Connor	Wm. Phillips
John MacDonald	Zebulon Bass	Mr. Hilliard
Joel Stone	Seth Downs	Mr. Chisholm
Samuel Beerman	Abe Fulford	Mr. Marshall
Robt. Cheetham	Fayette Cutting	Mr. Ansell
Riverus Hooker	James Collinge	Mr. Richards
Silas Ward	McNiel	Mr. Wood
Wm. Hough	Henry Cross	Mr. Bell
Elias Teed	Justin Grant	Mr. Lawton
John W. Lidyard	Urana McNiel	Fredk. Firman

Daniel Howe	Elihu Bidwell	James Mallory
Geo. Wilkinson	Mr. Rutter	Charles Bockus
John Gilmore	Mr. Sheldon	David Bockus
Nicolas Sliter	Mr. Harnwood	Wm. Robinson
Hiel Sliter	Mr. Parks	Josiah Rogers
Wm. Dinsmore	Mr. Purvis	John Niblock
Wm. Sturdivant	Mr. Chipman	Thos. Emery
David Jamieson	Mr. Fulford	W. H. Landon
Neal McMullen	Mr. Eaton	Henry Cross
Nathan Fish	Mr. Moore	John S. McDonald
John Brownson	Mr. Root	Colin MacDonald
George Cook	H. A. Delamatter	J. C. Potter
James Halsted	Nicolas Rosbeck	Sid Jones
Avery Smith	Peter Seeley	Mr. Macpherson
J. C. Cameron	R. M. Millar	Dr. Breckenridge
Amos Dimming	H. Plumb	Mr. Allis.
Joshua June	David Tolman	

Mr. Ephraim Webster and also the Lloyd family should be mentioned as one of the Lloyds participated in the 1812 affair. The name appears with some thirty or more in the Report of Militia Affairs for 1875, in which, among the long list of those survivors of the war of 1812 to 1815 still living, they are mentioned as entitled to the Government gratuity.

From the blazing pine-knot torch and rush dip candle the schools are now lighted by the switch and magic button of electricity. The log cabins have made way for the substantial structures of brick or stone. The old schoolhouse has passed with some others into oblivion, and organized educational activities show three good schools for the common branches, and the High School—a splendidly equipped edifice—as the culmination of the united labours of the pioneers.

Over the old camp site of Colonel Stone's first dwelling, where in 1792 his lonely fire sent out the only gleam from the north shore, the nights now reveal the glow of illuminant. Thus has the old rendezvous of the Indians been transformed: "The Garden of the Great Spirit," where the River Gananoque meets the St. Lawrence at the Thousand Isles. Here beauty abounds on every hand, on the broad bosom of one of the world's most mighty and glorious rivers. The River is a scene of grandeur, only the slow-moving current amidst beautiful isles, with here and there a white-winged yacht or swiftly-darting motor-boat—or at night with only the call of the lonely loon, as it patrols some little nook among the islands. But of the founder of Gananoque nothing is left to show where stood his halting place to the stranger. Of the great explorer and pioneer, Count de Frontenac, who halted at this place and noted the fact, nothing is here to keep the event in memory. What better for the Gateway of the Thousand Islands than a pair of pillars bearing plaque or tablet with suitable legends, which may set forth the facts concerning the two men who dared so many dangers " and camped at a point above the river called the Onnondaqui."

XV.

BRITISH NAVAL OFFICERS OF A CENTURY AGO.

BARRIE AND ITS STREETS—A HISTORY OF THEIR NAMES.

BY LT.-COL. D. H. MACLAREN.

(*Sheriff, Simcoe County.*)

(A paper read before the Simcoe County Pioneer and Historical Society, April 28, 1908.)

Earl Grey when Governor-General accomplished many good things for Canada, and took a foremost part in all schemes for the welfare of our country, among which the nationalizing of our great battlefields into public parks is worthy of special mention. And while we commend this project most heartily we should remember that the army did only one half the work of winning Canada and of holding it for Britain later on in the war of 1812. In each of these campaigns the army could have done little without the assistance of the navy, and yet we have no National Park in Canada laid out in honour of the senior branch of the service—as the Navy is—to remind our citizens of the debt we owe to those gallant sea-dogs.

We are proud to say, however, that in the names of our town, its streets, and its surroundings, we have a memorial to the British Navy more noble, more beautiful and more lasting than any other could be. All these names are redolent with memories of gallant seamen and brave deeds of British sailors.—

"Admirals all, for England's sake
Honour be yours, and fame.
And honour as long as waves shall break
To Nelson's peerless name.

"Admirals all, they said their say
(The echoes are ringing still).
Admirals all, they went their way
To the haven under the hill.
But they left us a kingdom none can take,
The realm of the circling sea,
To be ruled by the rightful sons of Blake,
And the Rodneys yet to be."

Barrie, as first surveyed in 1833, was comprised within the area of Berczy Street on the East, Bayfield Street on the West and Grove Street on the North. At the same time as the town was laid out and designated Barrie, these streets received their names, being nearly all in honour of naval officers of the war of 1812-1814. From Berczy Street to Duckworth Street is the Berczy Survey; and from Duckworth Street to the eastern limits of the town, the great admirals of Britain are remembered in the streets of this portion of the present town.

Before taking up the town itself we would say that Lake Simcoe, as *The Gazeteer* of 1799 informs us, was so named by Lieutenant-Governor Simcoe in respect to his father, Captain John Simcoe of the Royal Navy, who died in the operations for the taking of Quebec in 1759. It was Captain Simcoe who piloted the British Fleet up the St. Lawrence River in this campaign. For a time Captain Simcoe had for lieutenant the great navigator, Captain Cook, and in his honour Governor Simcoe named the southern bay of our lake, Cook's Bay; and our own western bay was named Kempenfeldt in memory of the disastrous end of the Royal George, sinking in Portsmouth Harbour with Admiral Kempenfeldt, and nearly 800 officers and men.

Barrie was so named in honour of Commodore Robert Barrie, R.N. who at that time occupied one of the highest offices in Canada, being Acting Commissioner of His Majesty's Navy on the Great Lakes from July, 1819, until its abandonment. Robert Barrie was born in Forfarshire, Scotland, in 1772. He was a nephew of Admiral Lord Gardner, Commander of the Channel Fleet, and entered the Royal Navy at an early age. He served as midshipman under Captain Vancouver in 1791, in his voyage of exploration and discovery on the Pacific Coast. In 1795 he was made lieutenant. In 1801 he was strongly recommended to the Admiralty for promotion on account of his gallant conduct in a fight with a French squadron "where though dangerously wounded he disdained to quit the deck." He received this promotion in 1804 when he was made Captain of the Brilliant—a ship of 24 guns. In 1806 he was promoted to the command of the Pomone—a ship of 38 guns—a large vessel in those days. On 5th June, 1807, he valiantly attacked a French fleet with a convoy—in all seventeen vessels, and completely defeated them, sinking three men-of-war and capturing and bringing to England fourteen war vessels and store-ships,—and doing this all with his one ship the Pomone, and her brave crew. For this feat he received great and well merited praise. He was sent next to join Lord Collingwood's fleet on the Mediterranean, where shortly afterwards he captured a French privateer commanded by De Boissi, Adjutant General of France. In 1809 he captured, unaided, a French man-of-war and five transports laden with provisions for the French army. In 1811 he captured without assistance a strong Corsican fort and three French men-of-war in the harbour. In the same year he captured a French war vessel upon which was Lucian Buonaparte with much booty plundered from every country in Europe upon it but Captain Barrie would not touch it nor allow his men to take it as booty.

In 1813 Barrie was appointed to the command of H.M.S. Dragon and employed on the east coast of America until the end of the war of 1812-14. He blockaded the Chesapeake River and greatly assisted in the capture of Washington. During the remainder of the war he harassed the American commerce, and captured many of their war-vessels. At the conclusion of the war he left the Dragon, and in 1815 was decorated as a C.B. and in 1819 was appointed Commodore of His Majesty's Navy on the Great Lakes in Canada, with headquarters at Kingston, where for many years he was a notable figure. Commodore Barrie was an open-hearted generous man, unflinchingly brave and kind to all who served under him, both officers and men, and was therefore beloved by all.

Barrie's first visit to our town was before it had received its name, viz., in June, 1828, when he passed through on a journey from Toronto to Penetanguishene on a tour of inspection of the Naval Depots on the Great Lakes. Dunlop Street was so named in honour of Captain Robert Dunlop and such a seaman deserves such a worthy remembrance. Son of a Scotch laird, he entered the Royal Navy at thirteen years of age. He took part in ninety-three engagements and was over one hundred times under fire. At the siege of Fort Cornelores he was dangerously wounded in three places and was carried through the breach into the fort on the boarding pikes of his sailors. During his first nine years' service in the navy he slept on shore only seven nights. Transferred for temporary service with the army, he was in charge of a naval battery at the siege of San Sebastian. He was recalled to the navy to command the Garonne and sent to cut out a flotilla of gun boats and store ships intended for the relief of Bayonne. He captured the whole flotilla, including Bonaparte's Imperial Barge. Half a hundred such gallant deeds could be told of him but it would make our article too long. Dunlop came with his vessel to Halifax in 1814. Soon after his arrival, the war was over and his ship was ordered home. He then retired upon half pay, and went to Edinburgh University to educate himself. He came to Canada in 1828, joining his brother Dr. William Dunlop ("Tiger Dunlop") who was one of the leading men of western Ontario, and who (by the way) superintended for the Government the first cutting out the Penetanguishene Road from Kempenfeldt Bay to Penetanguishene in the winter of 1814-1815. Capt. Dunlop was the first member of parliament for the County of Huron, and continued so until his death.

Collier Street recalls Sir George Collier, who, entering the navy in 1796, served under Lord Nelson until Trafalgar. He was sent to Canada in 1812 and commanded the Princess Charlotte, one of the largest man-of-war vessels on Lake Ontario in 1813 and 1814. He built a frigate for H.M. Navy at Penetanguishene, in 1814. Returning to England at the close of the war, he was made an Admiral in 1850.

The next street north of Collier, running east and west, is Worsley, so named from Capt. Miller Worsley, R.N., who was chief in command on Lake Huron in 1814. He assisted in the defence of Fort Michilimackinac, and later with one vessel captured two U.S. war schooners, the Tigress and the Scorpion. In the official despatches he is praised for his ability and activity in this matter having first suggested the attack and carried it out with signal success,—Oct. 7, 1814.

Capt. Archibald MacDonald saw many years' service under Collingwood before he was sent to Canada. He commanded H.M.S. Onondaga, which was wrecked in 1797. In the war of 1812-14, he commanded H.M.S. Moira. After him MacDonald Street is named, and his lieutenant, afterwards Commander, James, is commemorated in James Street.

Taking next in order the streets running north from the Bay in the original survey of Barrie, commencing at the western boundary we have Bayfield Street, named after Admiral Bayfield, a native of Norfolk County, England, who served through the Napoleonic wars under Lord Collingwood, as lieutenant of his flagship, and afterward commanded a vessel on Lake Huron during the war of 1812-14. To this most efficient and distinguished officer the people of Canada are very deeply indebted, as he made the first hydrographic surveys of all our Great Lakes from the extreme western shore of Lake Superior, to the outlet of the Gulf of St. Lawrence, the Straits of Belle Isle, around Prince Edward Island, Cape Breton and Nova Scotia. In this stupendous work he had only one assistant and two to four labouring men and one or two small boats. He was a painstaking indefatigable worker, and the accuracy of his charts are still a wonder to all navigators and until a very few years ago they were the only ones in use on the Great Lakes. In this hydrographic work he was engaged from the close of the war in 1814 to 1856, when he retired after more than sixty years service in the Royal Navy.

Clapperton Street is called so, for Commander Hugh Clapperton, R.N., who was lieutenant in Admiral Lord Cochrane's flagship, Asia. He commanded a gun boat on the Great Lakes in the war, 1812-14. He afterwards was one of the pioneer African explorers, dying in the centre of Africa upon his second expedition in 1827.

Admiral W. F. Owen, and for whom Owen Street is named was a native of Nova Scotia and brother of the greater admiral Sir Edward Owen; he also fought under Admiral Lord Cochrane. He commanded a large vessel on the lakes during the war of 1812-14. In 1815 he made a partial hydrographical survey of Lake Ontario, in which he was assisted by Lieutenant Bayfield, who completed the work. In 1816 Captain Owen became Commodore of the Lakes, and remained such until succeeded by Commodore Barrie in 1819. Owen Sound is also named after Admiral Owen.

Mulcaster Street recalls a name well known in the navy from 1790 to 1814, that of Capt. Sir W. H. Mulcaster, C.B. He served under that brave old sea dog, Admiral Jarvis, Earl of St. Vincent. In 1806, Captain Mulcaster with two vessels captured five Spanish men-of-war in Finisterre Bay. He did splendid service and was severely wounded at the capture of Cayenne in 1809. He captured seventeen American privateers in 1812-13. He commanded the Princess Charlotte, 42 guns, on Lake Ontario in 1814. In this year he was very dangerously wounded at the storming of Fort Oswego from which he never fully recovered.

Poyntz Street commemorates Capt Newdigate Poyntz, who served under Lord Nelson through all the Napoleonic struggle, and later was sent to Canada in the war of 1812, during which he commanded a vessel, and in 1813-14 he was chief in command of the navy on Lake Huron. In the latter year he made the first hydrographical survey of Penetanguishene Harbour.

Sampson Street is the next street east and parallel with Poyntz. This is named after Captain Sampson, R.N., who in the war of 1812-14 commanded H.M.S. Simcoe. In this vessel Captain Sampson brought from Niagara to Toronto the American prisoners taken at the battle of Queenston Heights, and at the same time brought to the citizens of Muddy York the first news of the great victory and of the death of Sir Isaac Brock.

Berczy Street commemorates Wm. Berczy, a Prussian, who came to Toronto in 1794, and first cut out and opened up Yonge Street as far north as Gwilliamsbury as well as the road into Markham. His son Charles was afterwards the third Postmaster of Toronto, and owned the Berczy Block, Barrie. He named the streets therein after his wife and daughters. But Berczy had too many daughters for the number of streets in the block, so the last one was called Harriet and Melinda Street, after the remaining two of the family not already honoured. This street which runs north from Blake Street, was a short time ago renamed Dundonald Street in honour of Admiral Cochrane, the tenth Earl of Dundonald, whose brilliant naval career is second only to that of Nelson, and who has been justly termed the greatest naval commander of the 19th century. His wonderful genius brought victory upon victory to the navies of Britain, Chili, Brazil and Greece, in all of which he held, at various times, the chief command.

Admiral Sir John Duckworth, who, in 1799, with his single ship captured and brought to port eleven Spanish vessels laden with gold and silver, is commemorated in Duckworth Street.

Kempenfeldt Street which is really a continuation of Dunlop Street to the east derives its name from the same sailor as our Bay.

In Blake Street, we have the name of him, who divides with Nelson the honour of being the greatest of all British admirals, Admiral Robert Blake, whose success is without a parallel in naval warfare. Given command of the fleet by Cromwell, he sailed out against the Dutch who appeared in the Downs, with 45 ships of war under their great admiral, Van Tromp. Blake had only 20 ships of the line, but, by able seamanship defeated them. Next year (1653) Van Tromp wishing to retrieve his defeat appeared off the south coast of England with a fleet of 100 battleships. Blake put to sea with 70 vessels to meet him, and there was fought one of the greatest naval actions in the world's history, lasting three days, contested with the utmost courage and stubbornness by both sides but ending in a complete victory for Blake. Later on he waged incessant and equally successful war against the Spaniards, the inveterate enemies of Britain in those days.

The sea is the element on which British glory has ever ridden in triumph and in Rodney and St. Vincent Streets we recall the brilliant genius of Admiral Rodney, who in the reign of George III. swept almost from off the seas in succession the hostile fleets of Spain, France and Holland, and of Admiral Sir John Jarvis, Earl of St. Vincent, who utterly defeated a Spanish fleet of twice his strength, off Cape St. Vincent in 1797.

The next street east on Blake Street is Cook Street, so named after the celebrated Captain Cook, R.N., explorer and navigator.

In Codrington Street we have remembered Admiral Codrington, the hero of Navarino. In this, one of the great naval battles of the nineteenth century, Codrington with 24 ships under his command defeated more than twice that number and in fact utterly destroyed the entire combined navies of Turkey and Egypt.

Napier Street is named for a famous British admiral, Sir Charles Napier. In 1807, Napier, then a junior captain, in his one little vessel captured three French men-of-war, one of which was of 74 guns. To this latter he was appointed captain and it became a British man-of-war. He served in the war of 1812-14, on the Atlantic Coast Squadron in 1813.

In Vancouver Street and Puget Street, we have the names of two well known navigators and officers in the Royal Navy.

In Monk Street, we have the name of Cromwell's greatest general, who was afterwards Admiral Monk, successfully filling the highest rank in both branches of the service.

Collingwood Street, Nelson Street and Nelson Square, recall the greatest naval battle in the history of the world,—the battle of Trafalgar, when the fleets of these two admirals destroyed the combined navies of France and Spain and thus gave to Britain the title of the Mistress of the Sea, which she still holds undisputed for more than a century. The history of both of these great seamen is so well known that we will not touch on any other of their great deeds.

Three streets in the extreme eastern portion of the town are named after officers of the Royal Navy who lived in Barrie or its neighbourhood in its early days. Oliver Street, called after Captain Oliver, R.N., who first owned the Raikes' farm, and later the town plot of Barrie. Steele Street was named for Capt. Elmes Steele, R.N., who was member of Parliament for Simcoe County, 1841-44. O'Brien Street was named after Capt. Robt. O'Brien, R.N., afterwards Admiral O'Brien, who lived at Tollendal and owned a sawmill there about 1832. He left there about 1836, to rejoin the navy.

Nor are Britain's Arctic explorers from the Royal Navy forgotten for in the east we have Parry Street, and Davis and Back Streets named after Captain Parry, Captain Davis and Lieutenant Back. In the west end we have Ross Street running from Bayfield Street westward. This street was one of the earliest named in the town, and so called from Sir John Ross, R.N., the Arctic explorer. Franklin Street (once called John St. West) was named in honour of the most celebrated of Arctic explorers, Sir John Franklin, R.N. Franklin passed through Barrie on his second Polar expedition in the spring of 1825. His party camped on the spot now covered by the King Block, near the G.T.R. Station, afterwards walking over the "Nine Mile Portage" to the Nottawasaga River, &c. On this journey he was accompanied by Lieutenant Back R.N., above mentioned.

Thus we have run over the names of about thirty-five of the streets of Barrie, telling for whom they were named and briefly stating something about each of these men.

As I walk along our streets and see these illustrious names I always think very kindly of our unknown friend who so fittingly named them, for we must acknowledge that it was the British Navy that not only largely made the British Empire of to-day but also that the British Navy alone made such an Empire possible. And we all believe, as Alfred Austin writes:—

> "Across the trenches of the deep
> Unflinching faces shine
> And Britain's stalwart sailors keep
> The bastions of the brine.
> Though all the world together band
> Not all the legions of the land
> Can ever wrest from England's hand
> The sceptre of the sea."

I think a fitting close to this article is found in a short poem printed in Blackwoods Magazine many years ago, as it expresses the feeling of every true Canadian and also brings in the names of many of our streets:—

> "If o'er that dreadful hour should come—but God avert the day,
> When Britain's glorious flag must bend and yield old ocean's sway,
> When foreign ship shall o'er that deep where she is Empress, lord,
> And the cross of red from boltsprit head be hewn by foreign sword,
> When foreign foot her quarterdeck, with proud stride treads along
> And her peaceful ships meet haughty check from hail of foreign tongue—
> One prayer, one only prayer is mine, that ere is seen that sight,
> Ere there be warning of such woe I may be whelmed in night.

"If ever other prince than ours wields sceptre o'er that main,
Where Howard, Drake and Frobisher the Armada smote of Spain.
Where Blake 'neath Cromwell's iron sway swept tempest-like the seas
From north to south, from east to west, resistless as the breeze.
Where Russell tamed great Louis' power, which bent before to none,
And crushed his arm of naval strength, and dimmed his rising sun—
One prayer, one only prayer is mine, that ere is seen that sight,
Ere there be warning of such woe I may be whelmed in night.

"If ever other keel than ours triumphant plough that brine
Where Rodney met the Count de Grasse and broke the Frenchman's line,
Where Howe upon that first of June met the Jacobins in fight,
And with old England's loud huzzas broke down their godless might.
Where Jarvis at St. Vincent's felled the Spaniard's lofty tiers,
Where Duncan won at Camperdown, and Exmouth at Algiers—
One prayer, one only prayer is mine, that ere is seen that sight,
Ere there be warning of such woe I may be whelmed in night.

"And, oh, what agony it were when we should think on thee,
The flower of all the admirals that ever trod the sea,
I shall not name thine honoured name, but if the white-cliffed isle
That reared the Lion of the deep, the hero of the Nile.
Him who at Copenhagen's self o'erthrew the faithless Dane,
Who died at glorious Trafalgar o'er vanquished France and Spain,
Should yield her power—one prayer is mine that ere is seen that sight,
Ere there be warning of such woe I may be whelmed in night."

XVI.

A CONTEMPORARY ACCOUNT OF THE REBELLION IN UPPER CANADA, 1837.

BY THE LATE GEORGE COVENTRY, ESQ.,

WITH NOTES BY THE
HONOURABLE WILLIAM RENWICK RIDDELL, LL.D., F.R.S.C., ETC.,
JUSTICE OF THE SUPREME COURT OF ONTARIO.

INTRODUCTION.

The following History of the Rebellion of 1837 is from a manuscript left by the late George Coventry of Cobourg who died in 1870.

The manuscript was procured for me through the kindness of Andrew J. Hewson, Esq., of Cobourg, who takes a deep interest in the early history of this Province.

The style is reasonably clear, though affected; it displays the pen of a ready writer, which, indeed, Coventry was.

I have added a number of notes to clear up and explain certain points, and I have been favoured with information by Mr. A. F. Hunter, Secretary of the Ontario Historical Society, which will be found at the proper places.

Coventry's vituperation is characteristic of the language almost universally used by the Loyalists of the "Rebels." A somewhat diligent student of the constitutional history of our own and other English-speaking communities, I may be allowed to say that it is time such language should cease and Mackenzie recognized as an honest (if mistaken) lover of his country. No one, however, who knew Coventry will doubt his perfect sincerity.

William Renwick Riddell.

Osgoode Hall, September 29, 1919.

GEORGE COVENTRY.

George Coventry was born at Copenhagen Fields House, at Wandsworth Common, Surrey, July 28th, 1793, in the house "at the corner near the city road" and "within the sound of Bow Bells." His father was a ward of Baron Dimsdale, of Thetford, and was placed by his guardian with Jones, Havard & Jones, merchants, in London. His mother was Elizabeth Thornborrow, from Lupton Hall, Westmoreland, who was visiting Sir Joshua Reynolds, when she was won by Coventry. Coventry, Senior, afterwards was a member of the firm of Junson & Coventry, and seems to have been a man of considerable ability and literary tastes. The son had the misfortune in early life to lose his mother, who died of cancer when he was three years old. The lad was then placed in a Ladies' School, at Peckham, Surrey, kept by Mrs. Freith and her three daughters, one of whom the elder Coventry afterwards married.

George Coventry was then sent to a Boys' Boarding School at Hitchin, Hertfordshire, kept by Mr. Blaxland, where he stayed for about three years. On the death of Mr. Blaxland, his undermaster, Mr. Payne, started a school near Epping Forest, which young Coventry attended until his fourteenth year, when he was sent to Dover, where he completed his education. He afterwards engaged as an employee in his father's firm, and in that capacity travelled over the greater part of Great Britain. He also visited France, where he thinks he saw at Fontainbleau some flowers, the offspring of certain plants which he had seen leaving Dover, a present from the Queen of England to the Empress Josephine. He came to Canada in the fourth decade of the 19th century, was an eye-witness of some of the occurrences of the rebellion of 1837, and returned to England in 1838. Returning to this Province he lived for a time in St. Catharinees; afterwards he was in Cobourg, then in Picton as editor of a paper there, then he returned to Cobourg, and made that his home for the remainder of his life. He died at Toronto, February 11, 1870, and was buried in the St. James' Cemetery, Cobourg.

He left at his death a considerable mass of manuscripts, one being "A Concise History of the Late Rebellion in Upper Canada."

Coventry also left a considerable mass of poetry, more or less good; amongst the manuscripts is one seemingly based on Chaucer, which purports to be a fishing and hunting party at Rice Lake; it brings in a great many persons who were well-known in Cobourg, Port Hope, and the township of Hamilton, and each one of these is made to tell a story. At the present day the stories are rather vapid and of little interest to anyone except those who were acquainted with the persons to whom they are attributed. (I knew most of them by sight and all by name.)

He also left a manuscript, "Reminiscences," which contains an account of his life up to the end of the second decade of the last century. He gives an interesting story of John Wesley, and also the following:—

"I was at Vauxhall the night that George IV died. Everyone was in full black dress, which gave the Gardens a most remarkable appearance. Such a sight will never be seen again, for they are now abolished."

Coventry was employed by the Government of Canada to collect material for the History of Canada, and it was through his efforts that the "Simcoe Papers" were obtained.

According to my recollection, Coventry was a man of fine presence and dignified bearing and with the courtesy of an English gentleman.

Mr. A. F. Hunter has kindly furnished me with the following notes concerning Coventry.

From the Biography of the Hon. Wm. Hamilton Merritt, M.P., by J. P. Merritt, St. Catharines, 1875, I glean these items regarding the life of George Coventry:

P. 186. In 1838 Coventry assisted in the inspection of the Grand River with a view to the sale of the Welland Canal to the Government.

P. 191. In 1838 he was clerk for Mr. Merritt in the milling business at St. Catharines, and late in the same year he visited his friends in England.

P. 214. He was clerk on the Welland Canal in 1840.

P. 252. Coventry drew up the memoirs of W. H. Merritt's father, Thos. Merritt, who died in 1842, to be deposited in the Archives of Upper Canada.

P. 380. The Appendix to the Journal of the Assembly for 1851 has an 80-page history of the water communications of the country, nominally Merritt's, but probably Coventry's (at least partly).

P. 398. A pamphlet of 48 pages—"Historical Record of the Welland Canal" (1852)—also probably Coventry's compilation, in part at least.

P. 424. The Coventry documents in the Parliamentary Library at Ottawa contain 10,000 folio pages of manuscripts. It is interesting to note on the same page that W. H. Merritt, in 1858, interested himself in the historical material of Upper Canada, and in view of the work done by the Literary and Historical Society of Quebec in 1860 attended a meeting in Toronto to establish a Historical Society, probably the first serious attempt of the kind in Ontario.

P. 429. When at Port Hope in 1862, W. H. Merritt visited Coventry there, or in the vicinity, by this time.

MEMORANDUM.

In the notes contractions will be employed as follows:—

"Dent"—The Story of the Upper Canadian Rebellion by John Charles Dent, Toronto, 1885. This work is more than usually accurate in the account of the *Caroline* episode. I have not referred to "The Cutting Out of the *Caroline* and Other Reminiscences of 1837-38," by Robert Stuart Woods, Q.C. (afterwards Judge Woods), Chatham, Ont., 1885; everything of value in that work has been utilized by Dent.

"Head"—A Narrative by Sir Francis B. Head, Bart., 2nd Edn. London, 1839. I have not quoted Head's "Emigrant"; it does not afford any useful material.

"Leg. Ass."—Journal of the House of Assembly, Upper Canada, Session 1837-8, Toronto, 1838. (Official.)

"G. T. D."—The Burning of the *Caroline*, by G. T. D. (George Taylor Denison, Sr., father of the Police Magistrate of Toronto of the same name). *The Canadian Monthly and National Review*, Vol. 3, 289 (April, 1873), The head note reads: "The following narrative is by a Canadian officer who served against the rebels and their American sympathizers." It does not appear that Denison took part in the cutting out.

"Trial"—Gould's Stenographic Reporter, Vol. II, Washington, D.C., 1841. This contains a full stenographic account of the trial at Utica, N.Y., October, 1841, of Alexander McLeod, charged with the murder of Amos Durfee at Schlosser at the cutting out of the *Caroline*. It was satisfactorily proved that McLeod was not in the expedition at all, although both he and his friends had claimed that he was.

"Kingsford"—The History of Canada, by William Kingsford, LL.D., F.R.S.Can., Toronto and London, 1898, Vol. X.

"Lindsey"—The Life and Times of Wm. Lyon Mackenzie, by Charles Lindsey, two volumes, Toronto, 1862.

[Mr. Hunter is responsible for the notes marked H., Mr. Justice Riddell for the others.]

A CONCISE HISTORY OF THE LATE REBELLION IN UPPER CANADA, TO THE EVACUATION OF NAVY ISLAND.

"Unthread the rude eye of rebellion and welcome home again discarded faith."

King John, Act V, Scene IV.

BY GEORGE COVENTRY.[1]

The reader is here presented with an authentic narrative, written in a familiar style, by the author, to his sister in England. The current, vague reports of the day have been scrupulously avoided, as they would, if countenanced, embrace a far larger volume than the present, were he to commence the insertion of any ridiculous stories, which have, from time to time, been the theme of conversation since the commencement of the rebellion.

Chippawa, near Navy Island,
    Upper Canada.
                                  Chippawa, Upper Canada, 1838.
My dear sister :—

I little thought when we last parted[2] that it would fall to my lot to record an event which has lately happened in this rising colony. I refer to a cruel and unnatural rebellion which has broken out in Upper Canada.

An event of this nature might have been anticipated in Lower Canada, from the general proceedings of Papineau and his adherents, but that the seed of discontent should be sown in this happy province was an event totally unlooked for, and not even contemplated by any of the respectable settlers.

I see your curiosity is awakened to ascertain the cause, and to know by whom these iniquitous proceedings were perpetrated. In due time, with a little patience (which I know you to be gifted with) I will a tale unfold, almost as portentous as the one described by Shakespeare in his Hamlet.

You must know then that, as a young and rising colony, it is extremely difficult for any Government to be selected by the Mother Country[3] who can please all parties, either by suavity of manners, conciliation, or the redress of grievances. In the nature of things he must give offence to some of the disaffected, particularly to those who are looking out for some of the loaves and fishes, when in reality, all the fragments are taken up. From the observations I have made, since my very pleasant residence in this country, I can find

---

[1] On the upper right-hand corner of the front page of the MS. the following address is written in ink, apparently at the time the MS. was originally written, which may connect it with Coventry's visit to England in 1838: G. Coventry, Esqr., Care of Messrs. Hunter & Coventry, Whitehart Court, Lombard Street. With the exception of Coventry's lavish use of capitals and his punctuations, which have been made to conform to current usage, the text is an exact transcript of the MS., in which spellings of proper names, often various in the original, have been made uniform. (H.)

[2] I have not been able to ascertain definitely the time at which Coventry left England.

[3] Of course in those days the Governor did actually take a great part in "governing" the Province, and the personality of the Governor was of great importance.

but little that any moderate-minded man could, with propriety, complain of. This I have endeavoured to impress upon the minds of all those who, in social converse, I have at various times visited. Not that my own private opinion, as an individual, is of any weight or importance, yet every grain in the balance of argument tends to ameliorate and soften down the minds of those who look with a jaundiced eye on any supposed maladministration.

On maturely reviewing the cause of the late disturbances, it appears to me that had the people been compelled to pay more taxes toward the general improvement of the Province in the construction of bridges, roads, &c., there would have been less leisure time for fostering complaints. By complaints, you are not to understand that there were even these among men of sense and discernment. It was wholly confined to unlettered mechanics and farmers who, if no cause of distrust existed, would, in all human probability, have quarrelled among themselves.

A country so bountifully enriched by Heaven, with woods, forests, rivers, lakes and quarries only wanted the genial hand of industry to cultivate, so as to render the settler in a short time independent. This has been carried into effect to an immense extent throughout various districts, to the delight of the enquiring traveller, interested, as I have been, for one, in the growing prosperity of the human family. Nothing in fine was wanting but peace of mind to obtain for Canada the name of Utopia, so eloquently described by that great and learned man, Sir Thomas More. But no country under Heaven can become Utopian where the seeds of anarchy and confusion are sown by a few miserable strangers whose sole object appears to have been to reduce mankind to the same abject level as themselves. This I endeavoured to explain in a few letters which I wrote to Toronto two years ago. At that period there certainly was a restlessness and uneasiness springing up among many who, before the appearance of Mackenzie's writings, were good citizens and respectable members of the community. Alas, their minds became contaminated and poisoned.[4] They exchanged their once happy firesides, their farms and their families, for the noisome pestilence of low taverns, where politics were freely discussed. But few of them understood the purport until explained by a rebellious faction to suit their own notion of things. Thus, events for which there was no real cause of disapprobation gradually spread into discontent; the fire was kindled by a few sparks, but gradually enlarged until it broke out into a flame which, for a short period, threatened to endanger the peace and happiness of the loyal part of the community.

[4] That the agitation ultimately resulting in rebellion was factious, unfounded and due to malignity and ignorance was the honest opinion of the Governor and the governing classes; they did not believe, for they could not understand, that there were any real grievances; but there were others equally honest and equally intelligent who did understand.

> The toad beneath the harrow knows
> Precisely where each sharp point goes;
> The butterfly upon the road
> Preaches contentment to the toad.

We still have those who can see no merit in any of the claims of the Radicals, and can think of Mackenzie only as a despicable little apothecary.

One great bone of contention was the question relative to the Clergy Reserves.⁵ To men of no religion this was a fruitful topic. It has often reminded me of the charge against our Saviour for using some precious ointment which the Pharisees contended ought to have been sold and given to the poor. Not that they cared an iota for the poor, but they wanted to find fault and raise contention, precisely similar to the demagogues here. You may remember that a very large portion of land in this country was voted by the Legislature for the use of the Clergy, in lieu of the odious system of tithes. This land was to be appropriated for the maintenance of the Clergy. and, in my opinion, a wise provision, provided it had been located in solid blocks of land, where it would not have interfered with the different settlers throughout the Province. But unluckily, where any great improvements were made throughout the Province, these neglected lands have been an eyesore to any further improvement in that district. They could not be sold; neither could they be exchanged or improved. On this account I consider the appropriation injudicious. You are not to infer that there has been no solitary instance of any improvement; but to take the observation on a broad scale by considering that these lands for the most part are lying idle in the midst of other improvements.

Session after session, various schemes have been submitted to bring this momentous question to some issue. But where the forms of religion are so divided and subdivided into various denominations, it has been totally impracticable to please all parties. Thus, year after year, time has rolled away, and instead of lessening the evil has invariably increased it, from the circumstance of men's minds having been unhinged by other topics. For the peace and harmony of society it would have been fortunate had the whole appropriation been swamped, similar to the land contiguous to the Grand River; but there the trees stand in all the stateliness of primeval nature, no sturdy peasants being allowed to let in the sun's rays preparatory to cultivation, when the earth would yield her increase in corn for the kindly use of the people.

I should weary your patience were I to enter into further discussion on the subject. Suffice it to say, that the last scheme agitated seems to me the most reasonable and most likely to give general satisfaction—the lands to be reinvested in the Crown, for the Legislature at home to appropriate for the best interest of the country. which will probably be done in the following manner:—

A certain proportion for general education, this necessary branch of economy at present being greatly neglected.

A certain proportion for dissenters of various denominations.

The remainder to the Church, either to be sold for a perpetual fund, or leased out to such settlers best calculated to improve the property.

---

⁵ The question of the Clergy Reserves is somewhat vaguely stated here, though with some fairness. The Constitutional Act of 1791, which brought the Province of Upper Canada into existence, provided for "the support of the Protestant clergy," and as each new township was surveyed, every seventh lot of land was set apart for the purpose. The Church of England claimed the lands thus sequestrated, notwithstanding that a large majority of the population of the Province belonged to other Protestant denominations. After many years of political dispute on the subject, the Act, passed December 18, 1854, finally appropriated the Clergy Reserves for municipal purposes; Appendix (LL) to the Journals of the Legislative Assembly for 1854-5 contains the statistics of the funds. (H.)

There being a clause in the original grant, not generally known, giving the House of Assembly the discretionary power to amend the appropriation, nothing short of the above arrangement will satisfy the people, who, deriving no benefit from the lands as they remain at present, may be literally said to have sown the wind and reaped the whirlwind of contention.

I fear I have tired you with this dry subject, so pass we on to the chief engine of discontent—William Lyon Mackenzie. Demagogues like him, who leave their own country in disgrace and take refuge in another, where they have no character, to obtain for themselves an honest livelihood, either turn thieves, rogues or incendiaries.[6] The latter is the course he has invariably pursued since his arrival in this Province; first, by inflaming the minds of the ignorant, and latterly, because he could not succeed in his rebellious views, putting the strict meaning of the word into effect, by setting fire to and burning Dr. Horne's house.[7]

This degraded being first turned libeller, thinking he could shake the foundation of social order in society, but as this scheme did not succeed where he could never gain admission, he made a few industrious mechanics, who have thriven by their industry, the scapegoats to further his degraded views. They unfortunately listened to his sophistry and ultimately became the deluded victims, while he ignominiously left them in the lurch by running away to the States, laughing in his sleeve at their credulity.

That the mind of man is capable of being egregiously imposed upon I readily admit. It has been so through all ages; but that an industrious people who have settled in the country, and thriven by its advantages, should have been led away by so notorious an adventurer, staggers every calm observer of men and manners. In the history of the buccaneers of South America, there are frequent traits of some noble manly feeling, but in the wandering of the archrebel Mackenzie, we neither hear of or discover one redeeming virtue for even the sympathizing to applaud.

I was of this opinion soon after my arrival in the country, on perusing his writings, and I entertain the same opinion now, after a calm survey of his atrocities.

The following documents alluded to in the former pages will shew you the low opinion that was even then entertained of his character and proceedings. Unluckily, however, for his poor deluded victims, they have cause to curse the hour they ever listened to the voice of a viper who has entangled

---

[6] This is a sample of the abuse then—and sometimes now—levelled at political reformers by those whose principle is *Quieta non movere*. It is grossly unjust to Mackenzie, whose personal character was above reproach both in Scotland, his birthplace, and in Canada; any crimes he committed were political. Most Canadians at the present time are of the same opinion as was he whose memory I hold in the utmost reverence; he who carried a musket against the Mackenzie rebels frequently told me that what Mackenzie sought was right, but his methods were wrong.

[7] Dr. Robert Charles Horne, a somewhat prominent physician; he was at one time King's Printer and published the *Upper Canada Gazette* at York (Toronto); he got into trouble by publishing matter offensive to the Government really written by his reporter, the well-known Francis Collins. Retiring from this position, he became Assistant Cashier in the Bank of Upper Canada. He was an active member of the Medical Board of Upper Canada who examined and licensed students of medicine, authorizing them to practise. He detested and despised Mackenzie, and Mackenzie during the short campaign of 1837 burnt his house on the east side of Yonge Street, nearly opposite the Davenport Road. This act of Mackenzie's seems to have been wholly without excuse; and he never satisfactorily explained it.

them in the net of destruction by his venomous writings.[8] Immersed in jail, away from their once happy homes, deprived of the comforts of their domestic firesides, their wives, children and social acquaintance, the ultimate confiscation of their farms and property, these deluded victims through the instrumentality of a miserable renegado, forfeit their future peace of mind and happiness, perhaps their very existence, for a visionary project which could never benefit them one farthing, it being impossible, from the known loyalty of nine-tenths of the inhabitants here, for it ever to be brought to maturity. But I digress from the subject I alluded to, which I now forward for your perusal;—

'An individual, signing his name W. L. Mackenzie, has put forth a rhodomontade in the *Advocate* newspaper, which he addresses to the people of Upper Canada. He quotes a motto from the satirist, Churchill, which he thinks applicable to his subject, but, alas, in his blind zeal for the fulfilment of his wishes, the downfall of all institutions in which he has no share, unfortunately for him, applies to himself, viz., "to spread destruction o'er the land." Native does not include him for he is an exotic that can bloom in no country.

The genial land of his forefathers, which fostered men of principle, and gave birth to promoters of institutions for the benefit of the country at large, is too fair a soil for his reception. He therefore seeks an asylum in this land of freedom, and addresses his philippics to an intelligent race of men whom he calls fellow countrymen. He may rest assured they are no countrymen of his, for they will not own him. He is too spurious a breed to be engrafted on so honest a stock. Instead of improving the fruit, the tree would wither, as by a pestilential blast. He is comparable to a blight wafted by an eastern breeze that destroys whatever it touches. Yet this outcast from his native land has the audacity to frame rules of advice for this people's government and sets himself up as an oracle of the first order to be consulted. He may rest assured, however, that none but fools and madmen listen to his nonsense. Men of sense scorn his principles, laugh at his follies, and spurn his advice if a jumble of declamation may be classed under so comprehensive a word. His style is coarse, his bombast low and vulgar, indicative of the society he must formerly have kept; his reasoning, fallacious; his effrontery, unparalleled. Yet this rude inhabitant of Scotia's hills has the vanity to think that his farrago is clear as law and comprehensive as the Gospel.

Like Dionysius formerly, he is surrounded by his satellites, who applaud his compositions and submit to his dogmas, but they will find to their sorrow that when his leaf is in the sear, they will wither as quickly and fall equally unregarded.[*]

His own operations being a bubble, he concludes all institutions like them. Needy in pocket, he envies his more fortunate possessors of a circulating medium called money, and would wish to level all the industrious and thriving

---

[8] It would be difficult to conceive of a more delightful collection of "Hibernicisms." A *viper* deludes his victims by his *voice*, and thereby *entangles* them in a not by his *venomous writings*—and Coventry was an Englishman! The *Advocate* mentioned just below is, of course, *The Colonial Advocate*, founded by Mackenzie, published at Dundas, the first issue being May 18, 1824; he removed it to York in the following November, when he changed his residence to that city, and continued its publication till the time of the Rebellion.

[*] Since fully realized.

to his own scale of penury. He compares a paper currency to a grist mill and the issuers to fashionable rogues, forgetting that when he has discounted himself, the old adage applies that the receiver is as bad as the thief.

Like a weathercock, he is blown about from north to south, from east to west, all institutions now eyeing his name with a suspicious eye. A quietus, however, from any of the banks would long ago have been sufficient to lure his restless spirit to repose, and cause him to adore any establishment which would enrich his finances. A needy adventurer in a young colony can never be encouraged, unless he is found to possess the intrinsic virtues of an honest, honourable man, which he can never aspire to. Hence his epithet "scourge of the colony" which he may bear in mind applies with more force to himself than to the Bank which falls under his censure and reproach.

Like Lucifer, he introduces religion when any particular end is to be accomplished, and talks to the mechanic and farmer with as much effrontery as tho' they were as devoid of talent and foresight as himself. He dives into the private affairs of intelligent men with as little caution as he exposes his own ignorance. One minute, his watchword is—"Away with paper currency"; the next, he proposes the establishment of a Bank on a foundation as firm as a rock. He tells us that the old Bank, as well as the new ones, keep the merchants in chains and the farmers in fetters; but that the bank which he proposes to sanction will break their yoke. What delightful news! This shallow brained individual forgets to tell you that he has found out the philosopher's stone whereby you can live without any trouble. According to his statement, the Upper Canada Bank is in a bad way as well as all others; therefore, what a fine opening for the firm of Mackenzie & Co. Farmers, prepare for a storm, for it is approaching, and when you see the sky above this silly financier look black, which it frequently does, and the Bank once announced as about to be opened, look to your wheat, for it will then want housing.'

Again

'The wolf that has for several weeks quietly slept in his lair is again on his rambles. With a hungry appetite and glaring eyes he is not dainty about his prey. A limb of a parson, a lawyer, a judge or a civilian,* all serve him in turn to pick, and this he does with very little mercy. Like the eastern serpent, he tries to charm his prey before he seizes it, and commences his attack by treating his readers with a quotation from the powerful pen of the prophet Micah. Instead of referring to Dean Swift he should have perused the whole chapter from the original, as well as the previous one, wherein he would have found the following applicable to himself;—

"Woe to them that devise iniquity and work evil upon their beds; when the morning is light they practise it because it is in the power of their hand."

He also quotes an extract from a country paper, applauding a country preacher for diverting the minds of his congregation from their religious duties, and for turning the house of prayer into a Compting House, or rather into a den of thieves to hear him preach sedition. This he imagines will

---

* Probably the parson was the Hon. and Rev. Dr. John Strachan, afterwards Bishop of Toronto—the lawyer, Henry John Boulton, Attorney-General, or Christopher Alexander Hagerman, Solicitor-General, both afterward raised to the Bench—the Judge, Sir John Beverley Robinson, Chief Justice of Upper Canada—the name of the civilian was Legion.

tickle the reader's fancy. All this is a circuitous route to reach this sign post, with the name of McNab[10] written upon it, and to level his abuse at that gentleman as well as all lawyers. If he had been named one of the commissioners, all would have gone on right for a time, and Chief Justice Robinson would then have been a man of discernment, but that honest judge knew the *Lyon* too well to allow him to lie down in the same lair. So he growls and thinks the law very wickedly concocted.

The truth is;—he envies all thriving men and upholds them to the world as a parcel of rogues and rascals as devoid of principle as himself. His sole object is to stir up confusion in the land, as his writings too plainly testify. But never let him show his face again in the Gore District after the horse-whipping he so justly received.

Whither then can this restless, unhappy, degraded mortal retire?[*] If he wend his way to Hamilton, the finger of scorn is pointed at him. In the west, his name is a byword of detestation and reproach, and at home he is too contemptible for notice any further than as a miserable object of compassion for his follies. He has placed himself on a level with a common incendiary[†] who eyes with jealousy the fruits of industry that he cannot partake of, and sends forth a firebrand to reduce his neighbours to that abject condition he is himself condemned to.

Reckless of his own character, his bosom harbours all the furies of Cerberus, which he lets loose upon the public to suit a bewildered and chagrined imagination. He possesses none of the graceful qualities of man, as justice, verity, bounty, mercy, lowliness, courage or fortitude. but like Malcolm in Macbeth

> ". . . . . . abounds
> In the division of each several crime
> Acting it many ways. Nay, had I power I should
> Pour the sweet milk of concord into Hell,
> Uproar the universal peace, confound
> All unity on earth."

This scion of so loathsome a stock fancies his low scurrilities acceptable to the people. A very sorry opinion they must have of any stranger who derides all institutions and belies his Governor by asserting that the meaner the individuals are who approach him, the better he likes them, who libels all government officers by asserting that they are "tipsy fools." None but cowards and villains dare make use of such gross epithets, since they shelter themselves under the mask of the lowest rank of rebels, who aim at the destruction of society altogether. Such bravadoes never fight, because they have no innate feeling of honour, and they are too contemptible for prosecution as every respectable individual pities a wretch so debased in the scale of human nature.

Blind to his own degraded station, he talks of brazen faces and a blackguard press, forgetting that no one bears so close a resemblance to the former and no press possesses the title of the latter but the one polluted by his

---

[10] Of course, Hon. (afterward Sir) Allan Napier MacNab.

[*] Since absconded to the States, where he has been fostered and protected by a race of men as devoid of principle as himself. Men of integrity would not countenance his proceedings, nor have they.

[†] Now proved by his actions in December last.

own letters. Hence, the tyranny he speaks of engendered by his own venom, and this he calls a responsibility that he never shrinks from. Men of no principle claim this as a privilege, having no responsibility to offer, yet this tyrant of the press stigmatizes the whole Gore District as the meanest set in the colony. They are not so mean, however, but they can appreciate his good opinion of them in a proper way by the application of a horsewhip at a cart's tail on his next appearance there. A man must be gifted with a consummate impudence to utter so foul a slander, but he knows no better, not having been brought up in the school of propriety. Wrapped up in his own mercenary views, he is too callous to see his own distorted image in the mirror of life. Yet this empty-headed individual has been heard to say that "Every man has his price" as a bait for the Government. But, thank God, it is composed of men of too clear a discernment to harbour a serpent who, when warmed by the fire, would instantly turn round and bite them with his venomous teeth.

How fully many of the above insinuations have come to pass, you will perceive as we enter further into our narrative. Suffice it here to draw your attention to two facts;—the first, wherein his conduct since, has fully justified the severe censure passed upon him at that period, and his recent cowardly conduct in running away to the States, leaving his *infatuated* friends, as he termed them, to fight their battles in their own way. Numbers of these having property at stake in the country, (which he has not), returned to their disconsolate homes and have since been incarcerated in jail to await trial, in consequence of information by their own party. So true it is, as Shakespeare justly observes, that rebellion seldom prospers,[11] first, by reason of its being a bad cause, and secondly, by disunion among the leaders and perpetrators. The subjoined letter to Mackenzie himself terminates the interest I have hitherto taken in his proceedings. I considered that by endeavouring to stem the torrent of his incendiary writings was no more than a duty which everyone owes to a liberal government interested in the happiness and well being of the colonists. The hour has arrived when it is gratifying to reflect that

"His treasons now sit blushing in his face,
Not able to endure the light of day,
But, self-affrighted, tremble at his sin."

—*Richard II*, Act iii, Scene ii.

---

[11] "There's such a divinity doth hedge a king
That treason can but peep to what it would."—*Hamlet*, Act 4, Sc. 4.
"Thus ever did rebellion find rebuke."—*1 Henry IV*, Act V, Sc. 1.
"Rebellion in this land shall lose his sway."—*1 Henry IV*, Act V, Sc. 1.

There are several like passages in *Richard II* and *2 Henry IV*. Possibly Coventry was thinking of Sir John Harrington, who gives the true reason of treason's want of prosperity:

"Treason doth never prosper: what's the reason?
For if it prosper, none dare call it treason."

—*Epigram, "Of Treason."*

To William Lyon Mackenzie.

Toronto, October, 1835.

"I make no apology for commenting on your extraordinary outrage upon society. Your palpable falsehoods betoken a heart devoid of all principle. Not content with attacking the institutions of the country, you descend to private individuals with a scurrility that none but the lowest dregs of society would ever countenance. This you style Patriotism, and set yourself up as the high priest of reformation, a word that I very much doubt you know the meaning of. I would seriously recommend you to set about reforming yourself. For this one act, the world might perhaps give you credit, provided you shew any sincerity, but, alas, it is contrary to your very nature. No credit can ever be due to a driveller who sits down to sap the foundation of order and good government, and who endeavours to stir up confusion among an honest, peaceable and industrious yeomanry. If you anticipate any result by your inflammatory and incendiary writings, you will be disappointed. The aggregate of the community are not such fools as you take them to be; they are men of sober, calm reflection and reject your dogmas and advice with scorn. You may ape the politician and man of intellect in a low tavern, a place you seem particularly partial to, to circulate your opinions; but even there, your follies are discussed after your departure; whichever way you turn, your hopes are frustrated. All the low cunning you possess will never turn to account, because you have no principle in your plans. They are visionary, chimerical and foolish, fit only for Robespierre or Danton, not for a respectable community.

Your vanity leads you to suppose you are lord of the ascendant, and that the name of Mackenzie is a tower of strength. Poor, frail man, you are not the first to swim on empty bladders. Conceit has been the stumbling block of thousands besides yourself, therefore you by no means sit solitary in the annals of tomfoolery. Your chief juggler in politics behind the curtain makes you the scapegoat and is no doubt delighted that you are a willing instrument to bear the brunt of popular derision. Recollect that this is not the reign of folly as once was the case in France. The people now think and act calmly for themselves and are not so easily led away by demagogues and low raillery.

Your time has been profitably employed in feeding yourself during the summer months at the expense of the public in looking over the Welland Canal books, an arduous undertaking truly to a man like you, so little skilled in accounts, but which an accomptant of the commonest capacity would have accomplished in one-fourth the time. But this did not suit your finances. You must be kept, and pretty well too. Yet you turn round when your laboured task is completed and bite the very hand who has fed you. To render your name the more infamous, you betray the trust confided in you, and slily convey items of *private* expenditure to a distant paper, thinking it would not be supposed that you were the aggressor. This is the quintessence of baseness, but quite consistent with the depravity of your mind.

The page of history can scarcely furnish an instance of such barefaced treachery, with the exception of Caesar Borgia, of whose dark and lowering soul you are the very type. This is indeed a pitiful extremity for any man to arrive at, especially one who has the audacity to call himself a patriot, and one who has secretly been trying to stir up rebellion, whereas your private character ought rather to be faultless like Sydney's to give confidence to your adherents. Not so with you. On the contrary, you appear to possess all the various and black passions of Caracalla's soul. You write with the anguish of a tortured mind and a disordered imagination. Were you conscious of one spark of humanity, you would shudder at the palpable falsehoods you circulate to the world. But this spark, if ever you possessed it, appears for ever extinguished, leaving you the possessor of a tenement that no one can envy you possession of. But the hour of reckoning must arrive, when all the horrors of a guilty conscience will arise in judgment against you. This alone will be a sufficient punishment for the barefaced assertions you have promulgated. Remember that, although you may flee from the punishment you so justly merit, yet you cannot avert the retributive power that inevitably pursues the liar, the treacherous and the ignoble. You will then retrace your ambitious footsteps to the path of obscurity from whence you emanated, a fatal lesson to forlorn adventurers like yourself."

How far this prophetic declaration is verified, you will be made acquainted with hereafter. One assertion I may boldly make, that the latter part is not far from the truth, when we know to a certainty that he at present is a fugitive and a vagabond on the opposite shore. The people in that quarter will soon find to their cost that they have cherished and countenanced the proceedings of an individual in every respect unworthy the confidence of even a nation of savages.

From the general tenor of his writings, it required but little discernment to see through his ostensible object. Not content with undermining the foundation of the government, by denouncing all proceedings connected therewith, he launched out into invectives against every public establishment throughout the country. Banks, canals, in fine, every institution of public utility was censured and abused.

That he was a hireling connected with some rebels in the mother country and the States, I have always thought, and now firmly believe from correspondence that has been found in the fugitive's papers. Their main object appears to have been to create distrust in the government and weaken the power of the country in every possible way.

In the English House of Parliament, the outcry against profuse expenditure was made the subterfuge for removing the Naval Establishment here. Having succeeded in that, the object of their wishes, they then proceeded to further extremities. I was extremely sorry to find, when I had the pleasure of seeing Commodore, now Admiral, Barrie, at Montreal, that he was called home, and that the Establishment was to be abandoned. This was the most unwise, injudicious proceeding that was ever carried into effect by the colonial policy. It was conducted at a small expense and at all times a valuable check against any insubordination. The present results have proved the truth of this assertion.

In a country abounding with such fine navigable lakes and rivers. there was fine scope for their movements from one end of the colony to the other.[12]

[12] The abandonment of the Canadian Naval Establishment in 1831-2 by the British Admiralty was the result of several causes, viz., the successful operation of the Rush-Bagot Agreement of 1817 by which Great Britain and the United States were each to maintain no more than one gunboat each on Lake Champlain and Lake Ontario and no more than two on the upper lakes, the introduction of steamboats and the development of steam navigation by the St. Lawrence, Ottawa and Rideau routes

Gunboats have been tested in all countries as most formidable engines of war. In this province most essentially so, either for the conveyance of troops suddenly from one district to another, from Lake Ontario to Lake Erie or elsewhere, or for the destruction of piratical vessels. They require no harbour in their evolutions, as they can run into any creek, or anchor close along the shore in case of emergency. An Establishment managed by sailors of intrepid courage, as they have unanimously been proved to be, should be fostered and protected even in the days of profound peace, particularly so when located in the vicinity of a country liable at all times to encroach upon our borders. Not that I would have you to imagine the restless temperaments of its inhabitants would do so with impunity. But the question relative to the boundary line, not having been amicably settled, always afforded a pretext for some national squabble, and until that important question was finally adjusted, there was the greater need for an Establishment of observation. The propriety of this remark is now generally admitted, and with just cause, since the late outrageous proceedings by American citizens, with whom we have for many years been on terms of good fellowship and communion. On perusing the details of the late conflict, you will be made fully acquainted with the services which some of those disbanded gallant fellows rendered in the cause of their country and which justly entitled them to the thanks of their government. The framers and plotters of the rebellion were well aware of their utility, and on this account laid their plans and succeeded in having them removed from service. All this was done under the mask of befriending the people by a reduction of the expenditure of the nation. You are aware that I am averse to every species of warfare but, until the nations become more nearly allied on true Christian principles, war and all its concomitants appear as necessary evils which society has to endure to cement it together.

Not only was the country deprived of assistance from this valuable Naval Establishment, but the army was reduced to a part of three regiments which had been removed to Lower Canada on the breaking out of the rebellion there. Steamboats, schooners, scows, boats and every description of craft were laid up for the winter, icebound, none of which were contiguous to Chippawa, where they were afterwards most wanted. Under these circumstances never was a more favourable opportunity for Mackenzie's party to create confusion, although the plans were visionary in the extreme. They were considered so by the Governor* himself, who knew all their movements and who even allowed them a full opportunity of making the experiment. So contemptible did he consider the party that he even took no measures to prevent their private drilling, and allowed the leader to circulate his seditious writings.[13] Free scope for action was afforded, thinking that the deluded people who

---

in 1826, etc., the approaching completion of the Carillon, Greenville and Rideau Canals, begun in 1827, and the opening of the Welland Canal in 1829. These changes had a profound effect upon the naval situation in Canada, yet Coventry seems to ignore all of them in forming his judgment of the abandonment. See T. C. Keefer's "Canals of Canada" (1894); also Dr. Scadding's "Toronto of Old," p. 505, for the public sale of naval supplies at Penetanguishene, March 15, 1832, at the abandonment of the Establishment. (H.)

*Sir Francis Bond Head.

[13] Sir Francis Bond Head had utterly disregarded the numerous warnings that private drilling was in progress, if not disbelieved them. See for example, "A Veteran of 1812" (FitzGibbon), pp. 188-191. (H.)

acted in unison with him would be tired with his cajoleries. Whether this was a politic measure is not for me to determine, but it shows the forbearance of the Governor's policy, he being unwilling to do one single act that could be construed into harsh measures. He was determined to show by his lenity that there should be no ostensible cause of discontent.

I know that very many have censured this lenity as objectionable and have stated that steps should have been taken, either by proclamation or otherwise, to warn the people who were known to be drilling privately that such proceedings were unconstitutional and could not be sanctioned; that if persisted in, they would be put down by the authority of the law. Then, again, further agitation might arise and secret meetings might be extended, from which but little could be elicited. Mackenzie might also have been arrested and tried for overt acts of treason. But should any of his adherents be jurymen and he be acquitted, as he had been before, the affair would not be lessened by a trial. Under all these circumstances, therefore, the Governor's policy has worked for the best, as it now convinces the country how very few disaffected there have, in reality, been found to support so feeble a cause. All that Sir Francis considered necessary, knowing their movements as he did, was to swear in a number of special constables, in the event of any disturbance happening in the city, which he did not from the nature of things anticipate; and to order warrants to be prepared for Mackenzie's apprehension, which were out against him a short time preparatory to their movements taking place; and it is not a little extraordinary that he was not arrested, because on the 2nd of December, only two days previous to the assembling of the forces, he was seen in Toronto eyeing the public buildings in an unusual manner, which could only be particularly noticed by those in the secret.

From recent disclosures, it appears that his adherents were more numerous than they had been supposed to be. In bye districts, they were, as I observed to you before, principally confined to unlettered mechanics and farmers of no standing in society; consequently, although the Governor was informed of these committees in September, yet he did not think them of sufficient consequence to employ spies in order to watch their proceedings. It now turns out that there was a department in the City of Toronto, termed the executive, who regularly met for treasonable purposes and who carried on their proceedings with as much secrecy as the corresponding society in England. Some of these were men of reputed talent, and at one time respectable members of the community, but unhappily for them, their minds became tinctured with visionary projects, so deeply rooted as to carry them beyond the power of retracing the path of domestic quietude. They swore fealty to their unhallowed cause, and were thus hurried headlong into a vortex from which they never became extricated. I explained to you the nature of the Clergy Reserves which they bitterly complained of. Another grievance was the following:

You are doubtless aware that the form of government in this Province is a type of our own in England,¹⁴—a privilege that many colonies do not

---

¹⁴ It was such in form, but the Lieutenant-Governor believed it his duty to govern in fact; he thought government through a **ministry responsible to the people was Republicanism**. Responsible Government had been fairly well established in England, but it had not yet reached this Province. (See Note 15, *infra*.)

enjoy. The Governor is the chief magistrate, as representative of the King. The House of Assembly consists of delegates from various departments of the country, chosen by the people for the general transaction of public business. The Legislative Council is a House of Lords on a small scale, with the plain addition of Honourable to their names. They are appointed by the Crown and hold their tenure for life. It is as difficult to remove one of them as a nobleman in England. Therefore the greatest discrimination was necessary, in the first instance, to ascertain whether they were men of the strictest integrity and honour. Their power is very great, no laws or bills being carried into effect without their sanction. They are a check upon the House of Assembly precisely similar to the Lords at home. No form of government is better suited to a community if carried on and conducted by men of sound principles and discretion. Yet this was a source of contention with the radical party, not being framed to suit their revolutionary views. Roebuck, Hume, Mackenzie and others have misrepresented those gentlemen because they acted upon principle in accordance with their oaths. They endeavoured to alter the system by having the members elected by the people, to hold their tenure at the people's will and pleasure, but such an alteration would never answer. It would unhinge the whole government arrangements and create constant schism and contentions in the country.[15] Certain demagogues would be delighted with this, it being their ostensible object. Such political vagaries are happily now silenced; order is again restored, and both Houses feel a pride in co-operating together for the general weal of the Province by promptly sanctioning such measures most likely to promote the best interests of the people. But to proceed with our narrative.

What became of his executive and those in various districts who acted in unison with them I shall explain as we proceed, so will not detain you longer from a recital of facts, which I doubt not will interest you, although the subject is a rebellious one.

It was the evening of Monday, the 4th December last, that the public were first made acquainted with the fact that the plans of the rebels were brought to maturity. I was then in the vicinity of Chippawa, contiguous to the Falls, on a visit to my friends Captains John and Edgworth Ussher,[16]

---

[15] The main grievance is not included by Coventry in this category, and it is nowhere else stated by him. Sir F. B. Head insisted on his right to seek for persons suitable for the Executive Councils, and to ignore what the House of Assembly said about the fitness of men for executive responsibilities, and the Assembly's right to nominate them. The Demand for Responsible Government as to men as well as measures, which his six executive councillors thus made he repudiated and "politely bowed them out of (his) service" (Head, p. 66). This precipitated the stopping of the supplies, and raised the chief grievance about which the so-called Rebels complained. The subsequent general elections in Upper Canada, which commenced on June 20, 1836, and lasted for some weeks, changed the complexion of the House of Assembly in favour of the Governor, but this was chiefly accomplished by corrupt practices in which the Governor himself took a hand. The result only aggravated the situation, and increased the rancour of the defeated party, the more pessimistic of whom, losing patience, plotted the drastic measures that followed. (H.)

[16] Captain Edgworth Ussher was afterward assassinated at his home on the Niagara frontier by a citizen of the United States named Lotte, November, 1838. Their sister was the wife of George Mitchell, physician, at Penetanguishene, Ont. See A. C. Osborne's "Old Penetanguishene; Sketches of its Pioneer, Naval and Military Days," p. 55. (H.)

whose houses stand opposite to Navy Island, the scene of so much commotion afterwards. I was sometimes at one house, sometimes at the other, their estates lying contiguous. There we shortly became acquainted with the insurrection that had broken out in the vicinity of Toronto about 100 miles distant. In the general excitement of the moment, and the contradictory accounts that were brought us, it was difficult to get at the real truth of the affair, more especially as many in Chippawa and its vicinity were favourable to the rebels' cause, who circulated untruths and exaggerated statements to suit their own views. I never contemplated it possible that any attempt would be made to change the form of government, although I well knew that many idle and ill-designing people congregated nightly to discuss the question. Indeed, the hotel where I had been residing during the summer season became at last annoying to me every time I entered it, from the circumstance of so many discontented and disaffected individuals assembling there. They nevertheless always treated me very well, although it was evident that my principles, which I boldly divulged in favour of the existing Government, were often a source of disquietude to them. On my return of an evening to retire to rest, it became a sort of countersign among them, "Here comes the Tory." This I laughed off, not dreaming that matters were so nearly ripe for an insurrection. Latterly, I seldom troubled them with my presence, as I could plainly perceive they were too strongly tinctured with Mackenzie's principles for me to eradicate, or make any impression on. Whether they looked upon me, as I often thought, as a spy to their proceedings, or from whatever cause, it was evident some of the most abandoned would gladly have put an end to me, as I was privately warned to be careful in my wanderings to and from the Usshers', a solitary walk along the banks of the Niagara River for two miles. I was marked, and many supposed I certainly should be shot. This I but little heeded, being conscious that I had never done anything to injure a single individual in the neighbourhood. As a matter of prudence, however, my kind friends prevailed upon me to pay them a visit previous to my going to St. Catharines, where I had made arrangements to spend the winter. All these circumstances, combined, show how difficult it was, on the news arriving of the Toronto affair, to place any reliance in true matters of fact. Nor was it until I met with Captain Brooks afterward at Colonel Arnold's, that I knew to a certainty the real circumstances of the case.

I recollect one circumstance that happened a short time previous to the insurrection, which convinced me that very many were in the secret as to what was going forward and the time fixed upon for a general rising, which has since been corroborated by Mackenzie himself. This was the appearance of Dr. Chapin[17] from Buffalo, whom I casually met at my hotel where I was then staying. This was the commencement of December. It was late in the afternoon, after the usual dinner hour, so one was prepared for him. I had been out shooting and was also behind time. Mr. Coles accompanied me. We soon entered into conversation on sundry topics, one of which was relative to Mackenzie, whom the Doctor said he knew. At that time both Mr.

---

[17] Doctor Chapin of Buffalo. See Lindsey, Vol. II, p. 124. (H.) Also "Makers of Canada" Series, G. G. S. Lindsey's Edition, p. 411. Mackenzie calls him "the venerable Colonel Chapin."

9 H.P.

Coles and myself were ignorant with whom we were conversing. On enquiry afterwards we found he was one of Mackenzie's staunch adherents and without a doubt in the secret relative to his movements and the time fixed on for revolt, from the circumstance of Mackenzie proceeding directly to his house on his sudden flight to Buffalo. In the course of conversation, we spoke our minds very freely as to his general character and politics, and I distinctly recollect both of us stating that we believed him to be one of the greatest traitors and rascals that ever went unhung. He replied: " That may be your opinion, gentlemen, but many others differ from you." We nevertheless parted on very good terms, the Doctor giving us an invitation to call upon him, should business or pleasure lead us to Buffalo. The following morning he proceeded to the Short Hills,[18] a district known to be full of rebels. Where he went to from thence I never learnt or took the pains to enquire, but I conscientiously believe, as well as many others, that his ostensible object in coming over was to reconnoitre how the affair would terminate after the 7th of the month, the day agreed upon by the executive for the assembling of the rebel forces. For the organization of their plans I give them no credit. Never was a measure so weakly managed or carried into effect. It, however, tended to show, notwithstanding the belief to the contrary, how very few throughout the country could be found either ready or willing to carry things to extremities. One circumstance alone, throughout the whole train of events, certainly was well kept, namely the secret relative to the day appointed for a general muster, which Mackenzie himself stated was known three weeks beforehand. Out of the various characters implicated, many of whom were of the most abandoned and profligate, I never heard of but one who revealed the secret or was rash enough to betray them. This may be accounted for from the circumstance that had the delinquent been discovered he would inevitably have forfeited his life by assassination. But to proceed.

The rebel force assembled at Montgomery's Hotel,[19] about four miles distant from Toronto. Their plans, according to the declaration of their leader afterwards, were to proceed to the city, join the executive there, seize 4,000 stand of arms which had been placed in the City Hall, take the Governor into custody and hang him on his own flagstaff, place the garrison in the hands of the liberals, declare the Province free and call a convention together to frame a new constitution.

Unaccountable as this bold measure appears, numbers who joined the stan-

---

[18] The Short Hills. See Brig.-Gen. Cruikshank's "Insurrection in the Short Hills in 1838." (Ontario Historical Society's "Papers and Records," Vol. VIII, p. 5). (H.)

[19] "Montgomery's Tavern was a large wayside inn with a broad platform in front and with a lamp suspended over a central doorway. It stood within a few feet of the site now (1885) occupied by the brick hotel at Eglinton. It was owned by John Montgomery, a prominent Radical of those days." Dent, Vol. II, p. 43. The tavern was a well-known meeting-place of the discontented. Montgomery took part in the Rebellion, was tried for treason and convicted before Chief Justice Robinson: sentenced to death, his sentence was commuted to transportation for life: he with some others escaped from Fort Henry, Kingston, and went to the United States; he kept hotel at Rochester for some time. Pardoned in 1843, he returned to Canada and rebuilt his Tavern, which had been burned in December 1837: subsequently removing to Barrie, he lived there till his death, October 31, 1879, in his ninety-sixth year. For some further particulars of his early life (and portrait), see "Guide to the J. Ross Robertson Historical Collection in the Public Reference Library, Toronto," 891.

dard believed it was practicable, and actually left their homes with rifles, pikes and old muskets to put the plan into execution. Toronto, as I before observed, was at that time in a defenceless condition, no preparation having been made for any meditated attack further than the swearing in of a few special constables, such implicit reliance had the Governor in the general loyalty of the country. The whole of the troops had marched to the relief of Lower Canada, their assistance being required there in consequence of the known disaffection of the Papineau party, whose numbers were very numerous. At this juncture, so well had Mackenzie's adherents kept the secret that nothing whatever of their movements was known in Toronto, nor would even the Governor have been informed of it, had not the loyalty and courage of a few individuals, at the risk of their lives, overcome every obstacle. Those gentlemen were Captain Brooks, Captain Stewart and Alderman Powell.[20]

Part of the rebels' plans was to place guards at certain distances along the road on either side of Montgomery's Tavern, to stop any travellers and take them prisoners, until a reinforcement of men had arrived sufficiently numerous to march on to Toronto and execute their plans. Sheppard's Tavern,[21] on the Newmarket Road, was strongly guarded, and there they detained a gentleman whom Mr. Jebb was well acquainted with. He was on his way home to Newmarket from Toronto, but finding the road paraded by armed men, and the appearance of things very critical, he called at Captain Brooks'[22] house on the way, imploring him to join him with his assistance.

Although greatly fatigued, he ordered his horse, armed himself with a brace of pistols, and they proceeded together toward Sheppard's tavern, about eight miles from Toronto. They had not gone far before they discovered a vast concourse of men in the road, all well armed with rifles. One of the leaders, who was supposed to be Lount,[23] came forward and questioned them as to their place of destination. They replied, to Newmarket. Mr. Jebb, whom Lount knew, was allowed to pass. Captain Brooks was then examined. He, with great presence of mind, stated his name to be Brown, a neighbour of Mr. Jebb's, which satisfied Lount (or "Round Jacket," as he was nicknamed), and they both rode on together. They had the same ordeal to undergo with other guards, but finally reached Sheppard's, where they found Mr. Jebb's friend in custody. Shortly after Colonel Moodie,[24] Captain Stewart and

---

[20] Captain Hugh Stewart, Thomas Richard Brooks and Alderman John Powell (the eldest son of Chief Justice William Dummer Powell and afterwards Mayor of Toronto).

[21] Sheppard's Tavern was built on lot 16, Yonge Street, the place being now known as Lansing, and the crossroad leading westward as Sheppard Avenue. (H.)

[22] Captain Thomas Richard Brooks' house was on lot No. 8, a short way south of Hogg's Hollow, or York Mills. The locality is known now as Bedford Park, at the extreme northerly limit of the city. (H.)

[23] Samuel Lount, born in Pennsylvania in 1791 of an English father (from Bristol), while his mother was of English descent; he became a blacksmith and came to Upper Canada in 1811, settling at Holland Landing; he became a farmer and a surveyor, and acquired a modest competency. A sincere lover of constitutional government, he joined Mackenzie's ill-fated scheme; he was convicted of treason and hanged (with Matthews) at the Old Gaol, Toronto, in 1838.

[24] Colonel Robert Moodie, formerly of the 104th Regiment of Foot, was a veteran of the Napoleonic wars: he served in Canada during the War of 1812 and took part in the sanguinary battle of Queenston Heights. He had a large grant of land and retired on half-pay. In the Session of 1837-8, the Legislature granted a pension of

another gentleman rode up, not knowing the cause of the fracas. They consulted together as to the best course to be pursued, which they soon decided upon. Colonel Moodie, who was a determined, gallant old soldier, armed with a brace of pistols, instantly resolved that they should assist each other and proceed to Toronto, notwithstanding the apparent obstacles in the way. They rode three abreast, Captain Brooks, Colonel Moodie and Captain Stewart taking the lead, the other three following in the rear. On approaching Montgomery's Tavern they were stopped by the same individual, supposed to have been Lount, and questioned as to their destination. Moodie replied, "To Toronto." "You cannot go," said Lount, "you are our prisoners." Finding Moodie resolutely determined to work his way, notwithstanding so large an armed force, amounting then to about three hundred, he called upon the guards to do their duty and to fire. Although the distance was so short, yet, strange as it may appear, out of three rifle shots, only one took effect, which killed poor Moodie on the spot. He was caught by Captain Brooks and never spoke but once, merely repeating the word "Charge," as though engaged with an enemy himself on the field of battle. He was carried into Montgomery's Tavern and expired shortly after. In the confusion that took place it was difficult to remember the minutiæ, but Captain Brooks told me he thought Colonel Moodie never used his pistols on the occasion. It was of the greatest consequence to the rebels that no one should proceed to Toronto that night. They therefore proceeded to detain the rest of Moodie's party. Captain Brooks, perceiving this, went round the house, mounted his horse and prepared for escape. He was, however, fired at the second time, but fortunately escaped unhurt, galloping off, followed by Captain Stewart. They had not proceeded farther than the toll gate (it being a new macadamized road), than they were stopped again by two persons, one of whom presented a horse-pistol and fired upon them. This was none other than Mackenzie himself, whom Brooks well knew. The other, he asserts, was Dr. Morrison,[25] who had spectacles on. Brooks for the third time escaped unhurt. His pistol, which he presented at Mackenzie, unfortunately flashed in the pan, otherwise the world would have been well rid of a traitor who caused the loss of life to so many of his fellow creatures afterwards. The snapping of the pistol, however, caused Mackenzie to let go the reins of his horse, by which means he escaped. In the affray Stewart got to Toronto and first gave the alarm. Brooks reached the Government House about an hour afterward by a circuitous route, and there confirmed the melancholy intelligence of the death of Colonel Moodie.

Whilst these proceedings were carrying on, a few gentlemen had turned

£100 ($400) to his widow and children, (1837-8) 1 Vic., 3rd. Sess., Cap. 47 (U.C.). He is not to be confused with Colonel John Moodie (Sheriff of the County of Hastings), who was on the Provincial Establishment during the Rebellion. He was also a veteran, having served in the Low Countries and been wounded at Bergen-op-Zoom. He was the author of a few sketches, but had not the capacity of his wife, Mrs. Susanna Moodie, one of the Strickland family, whose works in Canada are well known.

[25] Dr. Thomas David Morrison, who received a licence to practise in 1824, one of the most prominent Radicals, member of the House of Assembly, Mayor of Toronto; afterwards arrested as a rebel and tried for treason, but acquitted. He afterwards went to Rochester, but returned in 1843 to Toronto, where he lived and practised until his death. He protested against many of Mackenzie's actions and assailed him in no measured terms. Captain Brooks was certainly mistaken.

out on a reconnoitring party along the Yonge Street road. This arose in consequence of some private information that had been given. There were present: Alderman Powell, Mr. Archibald Macdonnell, Colonel Fitzgibbon, Mr. Brock and Mr. Bellingham. It appears that Mr. Powell alone was armed with a brace of pistols. He rode alone as far as the Sheriff's Hill, about one mile from the city. The others had previously gone forward. Colonel Fitzgibbon,[26] after reconnoitring, returned home, thinking there was no danger to be apprehended. Mr. Powell and Mr. Macdonnell, not being quite satisfied, proceeded leisurely along until they reached the eminence called the Blue Hills. There they encountered four persons on horseback, riding abreast of each other. Mackenzie, who was one of the four, armed with a large horse-pistol, advanced forward and ordered these two gentlemen to halt. His companions, armed with rifles, instantly surrounded them and said they were their prisoners. Mr. Powell demanded by what authority. Anderson,[27] who was one of the party, cried out that their rifles were their authority. Mackenzie then asked many questions as to the force and preparations making in town, what guard was placed at the Government House, and whether an attack was expected that night; to all which questions Mr. Powell fearlessly replied that he, Mackenzie, might go and see. This answer enraged the rebels very much, and Mackenzie immediately ordered Anderson and Sheppard to march the prisoners into the rear and hasten on the men. Anderson took charge of Mr. Powell, and Sheppard undertook to secure Mr. Macdonnell. The former went first and the latter about ten yards behind. Anderson was excessively abusive toward the Governor, and said that he would let Bond Head know something before long. Mr. Powell asked him of what he had to complain, and reasoned with him on the impropriety and wickedness of his conduct. But it was of no avail; he replied that they had borne tyranny and oppression too long, and were now determined to have a government of their own.

Having reached Dr. Horne's gate, a person on horseback met them. Anderson ordered him to halt and enquired who he was. He replied— Thomson. Mr. Powell instantly said, "Mr. Thomson, I claim your protection; I am a prisoner." The gentleman whom they accosted turned out to be Captain Brooks, who recognized Mr. Powell by his voice and said, "Powell, the rebels have shot poor Colonel Moodie and are advancing on the city." On saying this Brooks put spurs to his horse and succeeded in escaping; for, although both Anderson and Sheppard turned round to fire at him, they could not effect their purpose. Upon this intelligence Mr. Powell (who was armed, although the rebel guard did not know it) made up his mind to effect an escape at all hazards, feeling assured that the salvation of the city depended upon prompt measures. He made several attempts to fall back, which being noticed by Anderson, he said if he persisted in attempting to escape he would drive a ball through him. They proceeded in this way as

---

[26] Colonel Fitzgibbon wrote various accounts of the outbreak of Mackenzie's rebellion, the most exhaustive account of his own share in the defence of Toronto being in "An Appeal to the People of Upper Canada," published in 1847. See Mary Agnes Fitzgibbon's "A Veteran of 1812—the Life of James Fitzgibbon," p. 186, et seq. (H.)

[27] Anthony Anderson, of Lloydtown, had been appointed to lead the Rebels with Samuel Lount; he was a man of great courage and some military experience. His death is thought to have been a great loss to the Revolutionary forces.

far as Mr. Heath's, when Mr. Powell suddenly drew out a pistol and fired at Anderson, who was riding close beside him; he fell instantly, and neither spoke nor moved afterward. Mr. Powell and Mr. Macdonnell, then rode off at full speed toward the city. Sheppard followed and fired at them, the ball whizzing between the two. Mr. Powell, finding his horse could not keep up, told Macdonnell to ride hard and give the alarm in the city.

At the Sheriff's Hill[28] they were again met by Mackenzie and the other guard. The former rode after Mr. Powell and, presenting his pistol at his head, ordered him to stop, on which Mr. Powell snapped his remaining pistol in Mackenzie's face, which he actually touched, but unfortunately it did not go off. Mackenzie's horse either took fright or he could not be stopped, for he ran on ahead of Mr. Powell, who suddenly drew up opposite Dr. Baldwin's[29] house at Spadina, up which avenue he galloped for about twenty yards, then jumped off his horse and ran into the woods.

Hearing himself pursued, he lay down for a short time behind a log, whilst a person on horseback passed by him within a few yards. At this crisis his feelings may be readily imagined as acute in the extreme, especially as some of the rebel guards had been stationed in the woods, and he did not know but they might be very numerous. There he lay and listened, and thinking his pursuer was far enough, he arose from his retreat behind the log and, running through the college fields, gained an avenue, down which he continued his course and reached the city. After informing the Governor, he went to the City Hall and performed duty for the night.

Doubtless you would like to know what became of Mr. Macdonnell.[30] He was recaptured at the Toll Gate and again made prisoner. I knew him well, a man of great coolness and courage, who afterward raised a company of volunteers, of whom he was Captain. Had he been armed as Mr. Powell was, in all probability Mackenzie would have been shot between the two fires.

We seldom read in history of so narrow an escape as that of Mr. Powell; for had it so happened that the latter's pistol, which he snapped in Mackenzie's

---

[28] Sheriff's Hill was better known as Gallows Hill. Sheriff W. B. Jarvis had his residence a short way above. The name Gallows Hill, however, did not have any connection with official proceedings by the Sheriff's hangman, although the term may have been applied in a facetious way. The circumstance of a fallen tree, underneath which teams had to pass when ascending through the notch, gave rise to the name "Gallows." See Scadding's "Toronto of Old," p. 425.

These operations of the insurrectionists on Gallows Hill, apart from the later conflict at Montgomery's Tavern, became the subject of some current doggerel verse at the time and for some years afterward:

"Mackenzie and his rebel band
Were beat on Gallows Hill, sir;
To Buffalo they did retreat
And said —' We use the mill, sir.'"

(the Prescott Windmill being evidently referred to in the last line). Sir F. B. Head erroneously applied the name of Gallows Hill in his Narrative to the gentle rise of ground at Montgomery's Tavern ("Head," p. 333), and the Misses Lizars ("Humours of '37," p. 161) and numerous other historical writers adopt the same error from him. (H.)

[29] Dr. William Warren Baldwin, Treasurer of the Law Society of Upper Canada, a moderate Radical, father of the better-known Robert Baldwin, the original "Baldwin Reformer."

[30] Mr. Archibald McDonald, wharfinger, 36 Front Street, Toronto.

face, had been first levelled at Anderson, in all probability both his own life and that of Mr. Macdonnell would have fallen a sacrifice. In the excitement of the moment, and so taken by surprise as they were, it is impossible to say how anyone would act. Prudence is out of the question; fortunately, however, the drama terminated in the preservation of both their lives, to be useful afterward in the service of their country.

Mr. Powell, Mr. Stewart and Captain Brooks having succeeded in reaching the city, contrary to the plans of the rebels, which were to prevent anyone from going there that evening, the schemes of Mackenzie and his party were totally frustrated. It appears that after the encounter with Mr. Powell, Mackenzie and his guards returned to Montgomery's Tavern, where he saw the murdered remains of poor Colonel Moodie, which, so far from exciting any pity in his savage breast, gave him infinite pleasure, for he afterwards in his narrative, applauded the act. Here he assembled as many men as he could, the numbers increasing to three hundred or four hundred, armed with pikes, Indian guns, old fowling pieces and rifles. So ill-managed were all their plans that they had not taken the precaution even to procure a single cannon from the States to defend their position in case of an attack. Never was so miserable a display of what he termed patriots in the cause of Freedom. Even those few, according to Mackenzie's own statement, on the first approach of danger turned out, like Sir John Falstaff's recruits, beggarly cowards. They took to their heels with affright and ran, unfortunately for the patriot cause, the wrong way, thus verifying the truth of Hudibras' assertion—

> "He that fights and runs away
> Will live to fight another day;
> But he that's in the battle slain
> Will never live to fight again."

Every opportunity was afforded them to collect their scattered forces and to arrange their plans, it being the decision of the Governor, knowing what a miserable set they were, to leave them in their encampment until the city was placed in a suitable posture of defence. Orders were immediately issued by proclamation for the militia of the country to assemble. Nobly was that call responded to, for never was an instance on record in the annals of history where a whole Province was so speedily up in arms for general defence, thus evincing to the world that so far from the inhabitants generally wishing for any change in the constitution, they were determined to fight for it to the last, in defence of their property, their wives, children and their country.

On Tuesday morning all was bustle and excitement. The Governor was armed in the Market Square with a musket like any private volunteer. He delivered an address to the people there assembled, calling upon them to co-operate with him in one common cause, and to defend the standard of their country against all who should dare to invade it. The enthusiasm of the citizens was unbounded; they rallied as if by magic, and by nine o'clock a sufficient number of armed volunteers had assembled to defend the garrison, banks and other public institutions, which the rebels had threatened to destroy. Steamboats were despatched to Hamilton and Niagara for volunteers, who promptly obeyed the call, and returned the following day laden with troops. Colonel MacNab, the Speaker of the House of Assembly, raised at Hamilton two hundred men in a few hours; Colonel Chisholm, of Oakville, a similar number; Sheriff Hamilton also returned with ninety-five from Queenston and Niagara. They all landed nearly at the same time amidst the cheers of the citizens, and marched up to the City Hall, were received, and received their arms and accoutrements, with ten rounds of ammunition each. Companies of men from all quarters kept pouring in, so that by Thursday morning upward of four thousand stand of arms had been given out for the service. Whilst these loyal fellows were on their way from different districts to the capital, the rebel party were scouring the country, setting fire to houses and committing depredations and plunder, the only course left them to pursue. They literally turned out a band of marauders, headed by Mackenzie himself, the puny hero of Patriotism, who revealed his real character by committing acts of incendiarism disgraceful to an English Turpin or the celebrated French robber whose head in wax you may recollect my mentioning having seen in Trinity College, Dublin. In these men some principle of honour was developed. Not so with Mackenzie, who stands conspicuous as the high priest of incendiarism and buccaneering. A party of about two hundred, headed by Mackenzie himself, came down to the Toll Gate, about one mile and a quarter from the city, and set fire to Dr. Horne's house within a short distance of it, which was totally consumed with all his furniture and outbuildings. It was a deliberate and premeditated act, performed by Mackenzie himself, whilst his reckless crew calmly looked on. He even broke up some of the furniture in the rooms and threw it, with the Doctor's papers, upon the flames which he had kindled. The reason he assigned afterward was that it was a rendezvous for his enemies. The Doctor was in the city at the time, and the family had fled on the approach of the banditti. On some of the neighbours expressing a desire to save the furniture, Mackenzie ordered his men to fire upon any one who should make the attempt. Had any of the family been present, he declared he would have served them as he had done an unfortunate dog which was left on the premises. The manservant begged to take away his clothes, but this even was refused by the "people's friend," as he styled himself, who, could he have played the violin, would have done it as calmly as Nero did when Rome was burning. Sheriff Jarvis's beautiful villa would have shared a similar fate, had it not been for the intercession of Lount, who stated that he had received some personal favours from the Sheriff and on that account would not accede to it. Mackenzie alleged it was spared because they had no proof that it was a rendezvous for their enemies, but the actual fact was Lount's expostulation (with whom Mackenzie did not wish to quarrel), and on this account there is one redeeming trait in his character, bad as it was. Acts of incendiarism were even sanctioned and encouraged by Dr. Rolph, the head of the executive, who advised the conflagration of the city itself as the best means to ensure success.[31] Yet this very (same) Doctor Rolph was one selected by the Governor to proceed with a flag of truce in company with Dr. Baldwin to ascertain what the rebels wanted. I apprehend, however, that there was policy even in this selection, as the Governor was well aware of Dr. Rolph's principles, although he did not anticipate he was so great a rebel as he afterward proved to be. The object the Governor had in view was to induce the rebels quietly to disperse, to spare the effusion of

---

[31] This seems to be unfounded; there is still doubt as to Dr. Rolph's part in the unfortunate outbreak.

human blood. They accordingly proceeded to headquarters and held a conference, which terminated, as might have been expected with two such representatives, in an insolent proposal of terms to which no Government could accede, not having the power to make the people more independent than they might be, if they chose, already. Startling as the assertion may appear, Dr. Rolph, during this mission, actually took one man prisoner, whom he handed over to Mackenzie's guard for custody, and this at a time when he was bearing a flag of truce from the conference to his Governor. Doubtless his duplicity was suspected and the Governor considered he might commit some overt act of treason whereby he might be apprehended, otherwise he would never have selected an individual whom he had publicly refused to admit into his councils. He absconded shortly after and took refuge in the neighbouring state. In the evening a piquet guard consisting of thirty-two men under the command of Sheriff Jarvis was posted on Yonge Street for general observation. They were attacked by Mackenzie's riflemen, but happily without the loss of any lives. The fire was promptly returned by the piquet guard, which drove the assailants back, leaving behind them one killed and several badly wounded. Some of the rebels had pikes made by Lount the blacksmith, then general in command, which they had no occasion to use, for after the firing of our men, according to Mackenzie's account, "they took to their heels with a speed and steadiness of purpose that would have baffled pursuit." I quote his words to show the mean opinion he had himself of his own forces. A few of these renegades reached headquarters, where they remained for the night, determining on the following morning, Wednesday, to act on the defensive. Patriotism, in the hour of danger, is a momentous word; at least it proved so in this instance, for they were given to understand that gentlemen of influence who had pledged to join them, wisely kept aloof. Even the executive who had commanded them to make the premature and unfortunate movement came not, neither did they correspond, and for a very good reason. They had, like their unfortunate brethren in arms, quietly decamped for fear of being taken prisoners. This disaffection Mackenzie considered inexplicable, yet two days afterward he pursued the same course himself, after he had tried his skill as a thief and a robber.

Not relishing the intelligence from the city, and fearing an attack, he thought the wisest plan would be to move off to some other neighbourhood. Accordingly, on Wednesday morning, the 6th, he accompanied a party to Dundas Street in search of plunder. Here they waylaid the great western mail, which they robbed with impunity, taking the driver and passengers prisoners to their camp—a great feat truly. So badly off, indeed, was Mackenzie himself, and having the idea of escape before his eyes, that he even stooped to the meanness of abstracting the passengers' money, which, although denied by him afterward at Buffalo, was proved by the testimony of respectable witnesses, and particularly by Thomas Cooper of Toronto, who was travelling that route on horseback. Mr. Cooper's affidavit was implicitly believed, he being known as a man of integrity and principle. He stated that he was taken prisoner and very roughly treated: his purse was handed to Mackenzie, who counted the money, amounting to forty-five dollars, three of which he generously returned, after seizing his horse, saddle and bridle. From Mr. Armstrong, his travelling companion, he also took a horse, saddle

10 H.P.

and bridle, as well as four dollars in money, one pound of tea and four pounds of coffee. At the house where he was staying, he even had the meanness to open the servant girl's trunk and take away fifteen dollars in money and her clothes,[32] which she entreated him to return, but in vain. In these clothes he doubtless escaped, as no other reason can be assigned for his keeping them. although the poor girl went on her knees and begged him to return them. He also stole half a dollar from a poor wretch who was travelling on foot. This was previous to the arrival of the mail. What his prize was then has never been ascertained, but supposed to be considerable, as a day seldom passes without the conveyance of money. After this deliberate act of robbery, he returned to headquarters and amused himself with reading the letters and papers, some of which he handed over to the prisoners for perusal. Some of the letters he carried with him to Buffalo, which he read aloud to a large audience who collected together to hear the ill-fated account of his unsuccessful project.

On Thursday morning, their energies were nearly exhausted, but as a last resource, a renegade Dutchman of the name of Van Egmond,[33] who had formerly been a plunderer in Napoleon's army, was despatched with forty riflemen to go and burn the Don Bridge, so as to cut off the communication with the Montreal Road. There being no guard there on his arrival, the work of incendiarism was commenced by burning the Widow Washburn's house contiguous, shooting a poor, defenceless woman, and robbing the mail. The burning of the bridge was not accomplished, in consequence of a reinforcement having arrived from Toronto, who speedily extinguished the flames. Mackenzie himself was also present, as Captain Brooks told me he had the impudence to hand over some letters to a gentleman of the party,[34] stating that the day was come when letters went through the country free of postage. How he escaped then from being shot has astonished many since. But he seemed like Mephistopheles,[35] who could disappear at the instant of danger.

At this juncture, a large reinforcement arrived at Toronto from Hamilton, Niagara, Cobourg, Oakville, Whitby, Scarborough, and other districts, of whose movements he doubtless obtained information, which induced his party to make good their retreat to headquarters. No time was lost in the city after the arrival of the volunteers, to prepare for a general dislodgement of the rebels, whose numbers, from exaggerated accounts, were greatly overrated. It was nevertheless an act of prudence to prepare for the worst. The arrangement for the attack devolved upon that gallant and experienced officer, Colonel Fitzgibbon. The men, being in excellent spirits, contributed not a little to the success of the undertaking, and when they found the Governor was to lead them on in person, their enthusiasm knew no bounds.

[32] The story of the servant girl's clothes was denied. It is an example of the numerous contradictory accounts in the current gossip of the time. Coventry complains that such contradictory accounts reached them at Chippawa. (H.)

[33] Van Egmond.—A full account of Colonel Anthony Van Egmond's career and of his participation in this rebellion, may be found in Miss Lizars' "In the Days of the Canada Company," p. 110, etc., and references also occur, in the same work, to his two sons, Edouard and Constant. See also Dent, Vol. II, p. 13 (footnote). (H.)

[34] There is a note on the margin in Coventry's handwriting—"Enquire of Brooks further about this." (H.)

[35] Mephistopheles.—The text in the MS. has Mephistocles, evidently a slip of the pen. (H.)

The advance guard consisted of three companies of young gentlemen of the city, with some discharged soldiers, commanded by Lieutenants Garrett, Coppinger and Nash.

The main body consisted of eight hundred men, composed of volunteer companies who had arrived that morning and the preceding day under the command of their respective captains.

Two companies of artillery, with two brass field-pieces, under the command of Captains Lackie and Stennett.

One troop of cavalry commanded by Captain Chalmers.

The right wing of two hundred men, commanded by Colonels Jarvis and McLean.

The left wing, composed of two hundred men commanded by Mr. Justice McLean,[36] formerly Colonel in Cornwall.

On arriving within sight of the rebels' headquarters, Montgomery's Tavern, they were seen in great numbers upon the hill occupying the main road. The principal ringleaders were present, consisting of Mackenzie, Silas Fletcher, Lount, Gibson and Van Egmond. Being informed by one of their guard that the Royalists were approaching, Mackenzie asked his men if they were ready to fight a greatly superior force, well armed and with artillery. They replied, yes; then said Mackenzie, " Go to the woods and do your best." About one hundred advanced at a quick pace down the hill, followed by the main body. Our troops in the meantime prepared for action, but before the cannon could be brought to bear, the rebels ran into the woods, from whence they opened a smart fire, but unsuccessfully. Justice McLean's company attacked them on the right and completely routed them. The artillery then moved toward Montgomery's Tavern, a very spacious frame building, with extensive stabling and outhouses adjoining. This place, as I observed to you before, was the rebels' headquarters. Here they had in custody fifty-four prisoners, whom they seized whilst travelling from the country to Toronto or *vice versa*. On the approach of our troops they were removed a short distance away, under the charge of Gibson, who was a member of the House of Assembly, but a notorious rebel, whose house Mackenzie generally made his headquarters for disseminating sedition around the country. Thinking it best to dislodge the residue of the rebels who remained in Montgomery's house, three rounds were fired through the building, which effectually discomfited them. Our troops then entered, where they obtained Mackenzie's papers and several flags, decorated with stripes and stars. One on a red ground bore the inscription, " Victoria the 1st and reform"; on the other side, " Bidwell and the glorious minority."[37] Mr. Bidwell was an eminent lawyer of considerable talent, and, having been disappointed at not obtaining the appointment of Attorney-General, was supposed to have co-operated in the furtherance of the present rebellion. No positive act of treason, however, being proved against

---

[36] Afterwards Chief Justice Archibald McLean.
[37] The complete form of the second legend, as given by Sir Francis Bond Head (" Narrative," pp. 322, 365, etc.), was: " Bidwell, and the glorious minority, 1837, and a good beginning." (H.)

him, he was allowed to banish himself to the States, which he did accordingly a few hours afterward.[38]

Gibson,[39] who had charge of the prisoners, was so closely pursued that he fled into the woods and made his escape to the States, where he now remains with the satisfaction of the loss of his property only, that having been confiscated. A party in advance, in pursuit of other rebels, having reached his house, in the moment of excitement against him, set fire to the building, which was totally destroyed. This was much against the Governor's wishes, but it was impossible to restrain the ardour and enthusiasm of our troops, who considered at the moment they were rendering a service to their country. Having a short time before passed the smoking ruins of Doctor Horne's house, and thinking he was accessory to that act of incendiarism, (which in all probability he was), our troops considered it no other than an act of retaliation, but it was ill-judged and imprudent to say the best of it. Our neighbours in the States have stigmatized the Governor as being implicated, but it was an act furthest from his wishes. Nor was he there at the time. Montgomery's Tavern, also, shared a similar fate,—a rash act done in the ardour of the moment, by an individual who swore it should never harbour traitors again. He raked the burning wood from the different fireplaces on to the floor, and in a short time the whole immense range of building was one mass of flame. The Governor, as well as hundreds of bystanders, were astonished at the sight, it bursting upon them so unexpectedly. The act, however, was done, and having no power to subdue the raging element, it was left to its fate. In the skirmish the insurgents had 8 killed and 13 wounded. On our side three men only, wounded. During the confusion Mackenzie, Silas Fletcher and Van Egmond pushed on to a valley called Hogg's Hollow, where they held a consultation which resulted in the impossibility of collecting their scattered forces. They therefore wisely resolved to adopt the motto " Sauve qui peut." Van Egmond, however, was taken prisoner and died in jail before his trial could come on.[40] Fletcher ran one

[38] Marshall Spring Bidwell, a lawyer of great eminence, had filled the chair in the House of Assembly and was acknowledged as a distinguished leader in public affairs. Had it not been for the wrong-headedness of Sir Francis Bond Head, Bidwell would have been elevated to the Bench; as it was he voluntarily retired to the United States. He practised law in New York for many years and achieved eminence at that Bar of very great men. He refused to return to Canada, although solicited to do so by Sir John A. Macdonald, and died in New York, October 24, 1872.

[39] David Gibson, a land surveyor, living near the present Willowdale; of Scottish descent, he was a man of high character and much respected by his neighbours. He became a Member of the House of Assembly and took a very prominent place in the counsels of his Party. His house was burned, it is said, by order of the Governor, but he escaped to the United States, settling at Rockport. Pardoned in 1843, he returned to his farm on Yonge Street, where he lived in peace and good repute; he died at Quebec, Christmas Day, 1864.

[40] Colonel Anthony G. W. G. Van Egmond, a native of Holland, had served under Napoleon; he resided in the " Huron Tract," in what is now the County of Waterloo, where he owned considerable land, and he was a rich and prosperous man. Being of advanced political opinions, he took part in Mackenzie's schemes. As he was born in 1771, at this time he was sixty-six years of age; in the Jail he was attacked with inflammatory rheumatism, and he was removed to the City Hospital on the block bounded by King, Adelaide, John and Peter Streets, where he died before he could be tried.

way[41] and Mackenzie, mounted on a very fleet horse, made his escape another. He was closely pursued by Messrs. Maitland and McLeod,[42] Captain Matthews, Colonel Halkett[43] and Colonel Fitzgibbon. The two former gentlemen, who were well mounted, rode like fox hunters in pursuit of the brush. At one time they were close at his heels, but he eluded their grasp and ultimately secreted himself in the woods at the back of Sheppard's Tavern, from whence he made his escape to Buffalo, where he arrived three days afterwards. Mr. McLeod told me nothing but the fleetness of Mackenzie's horse saved him, he being determined for one, to do his utmost toward bringing him to justice. Five or six shots were fired at the pursuers, but happily took no effect.[44] Thus ended that memorable day's proceedings, which for a time restored tranquility to the city and its vicinity.

A large number of the rebels who were taken prisoners were humanely released by the Governor and allowed to go to their homes, at the same time appealing to their feelings on the impropriety of their conduct, and his hope that a sense of gratitude for their liberation would prevent them acting in future, in opposition to a government which was at all times desirous to act upon principles of humanity and forbearance.

Our troops behaved with the greatest courage, numbers of whom shortly after returned to their homes, with the satisfaction of having faithfully discharged their duty in having so promptly crushed a rebellion in the bud, which, had it been allowed to get a head, would have crippled the energies of the country and deluged a fertile Province with blood.

[41] Silas Fletcher had hitherto been a farmer of lot No. 22, concession 3, East Gwillimbury township, a few miles north of Newmarket. He escaped at this time to New York State, as did likewise his kinsmen, William and Daniel Fletcher. Ultimately he settled at Laona, Chautauqua County, some ten miles south of Dunkirk, and did not return to Canada. £500 reward was offered for his apprehension. A letter from him in 1840 appears in Lindsey, vol. II, p. 72 (footnote). (H.)

[42] Deputy Sheriff McLeod had a few months before, in the fall of 1837, given the order to fire to the military guard which was conducting the escaped slave, Solomon Moseby, from the Niagara Gaol to the Ferry across the Niagara, to be delivered up to the U.S. authorities. The march had been blocked by some hundreds of negroes determined to prevent the delivery up of Moseby to certain torture and death. The guard killed two of the insurgents. See my paper, "The Slave in Upper Canada," read before the Royal Society of Canada, May, 1919, published in the Journal of Negro History, Washington, D.C., 1919.

McLeod afterwards, in 1841, was tried in Utica, New York State, on a charge of murder arising out of the *Caroline* episode; he was acquitted, as it was proved that he did not take part in the expedition. See my article, "An International Murder Trial," Journal of Am. Inst. Criminal Law and Criminology, Vol. X, No. 2 (August, 1919), pp. 176 seqq.

[43] Lieutenant F. Halkett, formerly of the Coldstream Guards, the person referred to here, was aide-de-camp to the Governor. After his first selection by Sir F. B. Head for this office (Head, p. 29), the appointment was cancelled (ib., p. 30), but Lieut. Halkett accompanied the Governor to Toronto as a guest, and the appointment was restored five months later (p. 419). (H.)

[44] At the time of the rebellion, the late Mrs. Archibald Jardine, of Beaverton, Ont., then a young unmarried woman, was employed as servant at Jacob Snider's house near the Montgomery Tavern. She informed the writer of this note (June 10, 1906) that on the day of the battle she gave Mackenzie and the other leaders their breakfast in the morning. "After the battle, Mackenzie," she said, "was the only one who returned to the stable of the Montgomry Tavern for a horse; the others fled on foot." This corroborates and somewhat elucidates Coventry's account of Mackenzie's escape. See Mackenzie's own account of his escape in Lindsey, Vol. II, pp. 102-122. (H.)

Every exertion was made to find the ringleaders, but in vain. So prompt were their movements in escaping, that justice was outwitted. Gibson moved north and succeeded in escaping on board a schooner from Presqu'Isle. Lount was concealed by one of the party for upward of three weeks, but was at length taken in a singular manner.[45] A boat was provided to carry him over to the States, manned by three men who were friendly to his cause. A violent storm coming on, they were driven from their course to the mouth of the Grand River. They landed about 12 o'clock at night, and knocked at the door of a small tavern, the landlord of which was known to one of the men, who worked in a foundry. He hospitably took them in shivering with cold, provided them with beds and a good breakfast in the morning, after which they again started, as the storm had abated. Previous to going, the landlord told this man whom he knew he was glad he had arrived as he wanted to see him relative to a plough he required cast. The man pretended he would attend to it as soon as they would return from the opposite shore, whither they were going for salt. Not knowing Lount or the rest of the men they proceeded, but had not gone far before they got entangled in the ice, vast quantities of which, during the winter season, collect at the mouth of the Grand River. Here they were observed by some gentlemen who have formed a new settlement along the lake shore, of whom my friend Mr. Cook is one, altho' he was not present on this occasion. Some planks were obtained and the men safely landed, leaving the boat to the mercy of the elements. They were not known, but (it) being a disturbed time and a rare occurrence at that season of the year to see an open boat on the lake, suspicions arose that they must be some of the rebel party making their escape. Accordingly they were taken before a magistrate, examined, and not giving a satisfactory account of themselves, were forwarded to Chippawa, where Lount was first recognized by a gentleman there who knew him. One very suspicious circumstance observed by the captors, was the witnessing Lount's anxiety to get rid of a bundle of papers which he pushed under the ice with one of the oars, and thus irrecoverably lost. He was removed to Toronto, examined, and fully committed for trial, the result of which I shall mention to you in due course.

Gilbert F. Morden, another individual, was taken prisoner at Grimsby and fully committed. On his examination he deposed to the course taken by several others who stole a boat on the lake shore, intending to proceed to Fort Niagara on the American shore. But a violent storm arising, they put into a creek about four miles from Niagara and ultimately succeeded in escaping through the woods, to reach the bank of the Niagara River, from whence they crossed over to Grand Island and finally escaped. This party was believed to consist of Mackenzie's son, Silas Fletcher, Goreham,[46] nephew to

---

[45] The capture of Samuel Lount and this party occurred at Hyde's Point, two miles and a half west from Port Maitland at the mouth of the Grand River, January 18, 1838, Messrs. Hyde and Imlack being the persons who overtook them with the boat. After exposure in an open boat for some days trying to cross Lake Erie, the party had become famished and stupefied. (II.)

[46] A sister of Samuel Lount was the first wife of Eli Gorham, proprietor of the early woollen factory in Newmarket, Ont., but she died early in the nineteenth century without issue. By a second wife, however, Eli Gorham's eldest son was Nelson Gorham, the person mentioned here. He was therefore not a nephew of Samuel Lount, unless by courtesy of language from his father's earlier marriage. Nelson Gorham, although not present in the conflict at Montgomery's, was indicted for high

Lount, and Jesse Lloyd. Mackenzie himself was to have joined them, but ultimately took another direction. He went more inland, proceeding to Smithville and the Short Hills, through the woods to MacAfee's, a farm house about eleven miles from Chippawa, opposite the upper end of Grand Island. Here he was paddled over in a canoe and ultimately reached Buffalo, as he says himself, after travelling three days, and one hundred and twenty-five miles. On his route, he was once stopped by a sturdy farmer, who challenged him as a horse stealer, from his being so well mounted and his own personal appearance so disguised and dirty. In all probability he had stolen it, having stolen two before, verified upon oath at the time he robbed the mail. Mackenzie, however, would not admit it but took out a pistol and threatened to shoot him if he did not let go his horse; at the same time bound him down by a dreadful oath not to say one word of the affair or create any alarm as he was Mackenzie himself. The oath he had taken preyed a good deal on the poor fellow's mind, who was relieved by one day meeting a magistrate to whom he mentioned the circumstance, without alluding to Mackenzie. The magistrate assured him that such an oath, taken under those circumstances with bodily fear, was not binding, and thus he revealed the route of the traitor. It was, however, then too late to intercept him. A reward of 4,000 dollars was out for his apprehension, altho' the party who had him in possession was then totally unaware of it. He travelled part of the way in waggons, and it was currently believed that on his arrival in the vicinity of Cook's Mills, (a radical district), that he was dressed in women's clothes, from the circumstance of a suspicious character calling at that time to ask for refreshments at a farm house, the inmates of which pressing the lady to stay, she declined and went on, altho' the night was extremely dark and gloomy. They since told a friend of mine they were certain it was a man, altho' they never could discover who the person was. But three days afterwards we heard of his arrival in Buffalo. In a short narrative that he published afterward, relative to the operations of the three days, he has studiously avoided saying anything relative to his escape, altho' he has mentioned the names of many with whom he was connected. As he could not tell whether they had all fled, it was an act of gross baseness to betray them. Entertaining, as I do, and always have done, so mean an opinion of his character, I think it highly probable he will some day divulge the particulars of his route, and implicate, as he before has done, the very individuals who fostered him on his journey. For having doffed the lion's mane, and hung a sheepskin on his recreant limbs, there is no further reliance to be placed on his conduct, even toward his ci-devant friends. This I firmly believe from the circumstance of his having told a friend of mine in Buffalo that there was only one man in Chippawa whom he could implicitly trust, whose name he mentioned. His duplicity also to Robert Gourlay, Esq'r, cannot easily be forgotten. Finding he could not make a rebel of him (although he entangled him so closely in the net of rebellion that he was banished the country),[47] he left him unheeded to his treason and left Canada at this time. (See Lindsey, Vol. II, p. 399, No. 26). He afterward settled in Chautauqua Co., N.Y., where he remained until after 1853, and subsequently returned to Canada. (II.)

[47] This is wholly untrue: Gourlay was banished in 1819; Mackenzie came to Canada in 1820 and began his public career in 1824. They were not congenial in any way, and Gourlay held Mackenzie in contempt. See my Life of Gourlay, published by the Ontario Historical Society, "Papers and Records," Vol. XIV. See also Note 48, *infra*.

fate. Not that Gourlay cared for the sympathy of Mackenzie one iota, but it never was his wish to carry his principles of independence further than the reform of what he considered a few abuses. I hope the day is not far distant when that gentleman, who has seen his errors, will be recalled from banishment, for he has now experienced, to use his own words, that—" During four years residence in the United States I have witnessed far worse than European domination—the domination of the worst of passions;—mobs, murders, sacrilege and profanity of every kind."[48]

In his last letter to Mackenzie, since his escape to Buffalo, he tells him that " Joseph Hume is a little man, but you less. You call yourself a patriot, yet you fly from home to enlist scoundrels for the conquest of your country. This is patriotism with a vengeance. You had no right to take up arms, and had you succeeded, so far from rejoicing, I would have turned my back upon America for ever."

I now leave Mackenzie to rest himself at Buffalo, and call your attention to our proceedings at home after his departure. The first act of the Governor after the dispersion of the rebels was to issue a proclamation to the Queen's faithful subjects.[49] He told them that although the country had been long suffering from the acts of concealed traitors, yet this was the first time that rebellion had openly avowed itself; that a concealed traitor was the most dangerous of all enemies: that they should be rooted out of the land, and he hoped that none who were loyal would rest until this was accomplished; that in furtherance of this object he offered rewards for the apprehension of the ringleaders, to wit;—

$4,000 for William Lyon Mackenzie, the principal.
$2,000 for David Gibson, Member of the House of Assembly.
$2,000 for Samuel Lount, blacksmith, who made the pikes.
$2,000 each for Jesse Lloyd[50] and Silas Fletcher, instigators of the proceedings, and present at the engagement on the 7th of December.
$2,000 for Dr. John Rolph, who recommended the burning of the city.
$2,000 for Dr. Charles Duncombe, Member of the House of Assembly, who corresponded with Joseph Hume.[51]

---

[48] This, together with the words quoted immediately below, is contained in a letter to Mackenzie from Cleveland, Ohio, January 14, 1838, in answer to a letter purporting to be from Mackenzie at Navy Island, January 8, 1838, but which Mackenzie afterward said that he neither wrote nor authorized. It will be found *in extenso* in the "Neptunian," Part 2, p. 17. See my Life of Gourlay, p. 88.

Gourlay's letter to Joseph Hume rebuking him for writing to Mackenzie the notorious letter containing the passage "baneful domination of the mother country," was written from New York in June, 1834.

Mackenzie and Gourlay had never met until 1833, although Gourlay countenanced him for more than three years, 1829-1832; he "sprung out of one," Gourlay said, but Gourlay had no respect for him. See The Neptunian, Part 2 and elsewhere.

[49] The Proclamation appears *verbatim* in a footnote in Lindsey, Vol. II, p. 96: it contains rewards for only the first five mentioned by Coventry. (II.)

One of the originals is in the possession of George G. S. Lindsey, Esq., K.C., grandson of Mackenzie.

[50] Jesse Lloyd, of Lloydtown, acted as messenger between the Rebels of Upper Canada and those of Lower Canada; he joined the rising in Upper Canada in December of 1837, and escaped to the United States.

[51] Dr. Charles Duncombe was a native of the United States. Born in New Jersey about 1796, he came with his parents to Upper Canada during the progress or immediately after the War of 1812, and settled in the London District.

$1,000 for Eliakim Malcolm, miller.
$1,000 for Finlay Malcolm, miller.
$1,000 for Robert Alway, Member of Parliament.[52]
$400 for James Anderson, shot by Mr. Powell.
$400 for Joshua Doan.

Alway and Malcolm were taken prisoners on their way to the west to join Dr. Duncombe, and sent off to Hamilton jail. Van Egmond, who owned a large tract of land near Lake Huron, was captured on the route of the rebels, and died in prison soon afterward from chagrin and vexation, a lesson to all restless individuals who, when they seek an asylum in a foreign country, should live contented under the existing laws, or return to the land that gave them birth.

Whilst these movements were going on in Toronto, Dr. Duncombe was concocting measures for revolt in the west, which, according to the time specified by Mackenzie, took place in that quarter. The poor deluded victims, who had nothing to gain by these operations, and who only acted through the instrumentality of an artful and designing few, had to bear the brunt of the contention, whilst their ignoble leaders cowardly took flight and left them to their fate. In consequence of this known disaffection, and idle fellows congregating around, it was considered advisable to send up a force to put a stop to their proceedings. Accordingly, Colonel MacNab, Speaker of the House of Assembly, was deputed to take the command.

Although the season of the year was very inclement, yet the volunteers joined his standard with alacrity. They displayed a courage and ardour rarely to be met with in cases of so sudden an irruption. But they well knew they had enlisted in a cause wherein the best interests of the country were at stake, as well as their future peace, quietude and happiness. Accordingly, no sooner was it known that the expedition was to march than hundreds flocked to the standard. From 300 to 400 proceeded west and reached Brantford on the Grand River in perfect order and good spirits. Here they were joined by 150 volunteers and 100 Indian warriors under their commander, Captain Kerr,[53] who married a daughter of the celebrated chief, Brant. The rebels, about 400 strong, hearing of their arrival, decamped during the night. A large collection of letters and papers, principally belonging to Dr. Duncombe and Eliakim Malcolm, were found in a field and safely secured by Colonel MacNab. The following morning our troops moved on, and regretted they had no opportunity of coming up with the enemy, who, it was greatly

---

Studying medicine, he was admitted to practice in 1819, and settled as a practitioner near Bishopsgate on the Town Line between Burford and Brantford. He soon acquired a large practice and great influence in the community. He was perhaps the most prominent rebel after Mackenzie himself. When Member of the House of Assembly for Oxford, he went to England on a mission for the Radicals; he joined in the rebellion and was a main leader in the western part of the Province. He escaped to the United States. When pardoned in 1843 he returned to Upper Canada for a very short time, and then returned to the United States, going to the Western States and ultimately to California, where he resided until his death.

[52] Robert Alway, Member for Oxford with Dr. Duncombe, was captured and imprisoned; he was afterwards released on finding security for good behaviour, as was Elias Moore, Member for Middlesex.

[53] Captain William Johnson Kerr was the son of Dr. Robert Kerr, of Niagara, who married a daughter of Mollie Brant, the sister of Joseph Brant, and the "Indian wife" of Sir William Johnson. He married Elizabeth, the youngest daughter of Joseph Brant.

feared, had dispersed and the leaders fled without giving an opportunity for action. This afterward proved to be the case. Our forces continued to move through the disturbed districts, and in two days they received an accession of 1,000 more volunteers, so anxious were the loyal and quiet settlers to rid the country of so great a scourge to its prosperity. Their arrival in the Township of Oakland, and the appearance of this large force parading the country, altered the general temperament of the disaffected, who sent in deputations to Colonel MacNab requesting permission to surrender their arms rather than risk their lives in a cause which they found was misrepresented to them. They stated that they had been greatly deceived and basely deserted by Dr. Duncombe, Malcolm and their colleagues.

In the Township of Norwich, upward of 200 of the rebels and disaffected assembled in a square formed by our volunteers, where they laid down their arms, promising faithfully to become good citizens and faithful subjects; that they had been deceived, and had no real grievances. By instructions from the Governor to Colonel MacNab, they were permitted to return to their homes and families, on the express condition that they should surrender if any further complaints appeared against them. The lenity shown them will, it is to be hoped, operate as a warning for the future, and teach them this lesson that industrious habits and peaceable lives tend more to true happiness than meddling with politics with which they are but little acquainted. It is no wonder that the people who had joined Dr. Duncombe's standard should become disgusted when they found he had united the character of robber with that of assumed patriotism. That faithless individual stooped at nothing in order to carry his measures. The farm houses of the loyalists were indiscriminately entered and plundered of blankets, caps, arms, ammunition, and provisions. When he found he was hotly pursued, instead of sharing the fate of his associates in robbery, and throwing himself, as they did, on the mercy of lenient conquerors, he treacherously fled from danger, leaving his deluded followers to bear the brunt of public ignominy and humiliation. There was too noble a spirit, however, in the pursuers to triumph over a fallen enemy, who rather shed a tear of pity for their misfortunes than trample upon them during that eventful moment of humiliation, when they sued for mercy, thus fulfilling the declaration of our inspired Bard of Avon, who says;—

> "The quality of mercy is not strained,
> It falleth like the precious dew from heaven,
> It blesseth him that gives, and him that takes."

So far from either Mackenzie's or Duncombe's assertions being true that nine-tenths of the Province were favourable to their measures, it turned out precisely the reverse, and proved by the foregoing pages that nine-tenths were favourable to the existing government. In some districts they were loyal to a man. The magistrates of Barrie, consisting of gentlemen of the highest respectability, publicly avowed that the whole population in their vicinity arose en masse to put down rebellion wherever it might be found, leaving the women and children to take care of their houses and farms. But their services were not long required, for order and tranquility were soon restored after the subjugation of Doctor Duncombe's adherents. It was also gratifying to reflect that all this was accomplished by the ardour and enthusiasm of the people themselves, without the assistance of hireling soldiers as they termed them, not one of whom was at that time to be found in the Province. After the insurrection in the west was quelled, and those who had not surrendered their arms had retired to their avocations, Colonel MacNab spent a few days in various districts, organizing companies of militia who had freely volunteered their services for public duty. Although the alarm had in a great measure subsided, yet it was impossible to tell how many concealed traitors might remain in the country. The organization, therefore, of volunteers was adjudged to be a salutary measure as a corps of observation until the arrival of troops from abroad. The disturbances in Lower Canada were not sufficiently quelled to allow any of the regulars to move at that period, so that the security of Upper Canada depended wholly on the loyalty of its inhabitants, to whom the greatest praise is due for their promptitude in coming forward so cheerfully and manfully to avenge the infraction of their laws, and to protect their property from the devastation that awaited them from a band of lawless miscreants. After making the necessary arrangements, the gallant Colonel returned to Hamilton with his troops, amidst the cheers and enthusiasm of the loyal citizens. Thus the men of Gore, who had been stigmatized by Mackenzie as a low, mean set, were among the very first to retaliate for so gross a libel on their bravery and courage, and to shew the insignificant traitor that they could accomplish what he did not much relish, for they dispersed his faction in the west altogether.

At Oakville, Toronto, Scarborough, Port Hope, Cobourg, Peterborough, Cornwall, Kingston, and all places along the lake shore, the greatest activity prevailed, accounts having reached many of those districts of a most exaggerated nature. This was the more readily believed, from the late disturbances in Lower Canada. So far, however, from damping their ardour, they manfully came forward in the general cause, and enrolled themselves under the banner of defence. Gentlemen and merchants of the first standing in society kept guard at night along the coast in unison with the poorest peasant in the land. All distinction was waived and absorbed in the one vital question of freedom under a lenient government, or tyranny under a democracy.

Nor was the Niagara district, in which I have been located since my residence in the country, behindhand in co-operation. Queenston, Niagara, Thorold, and St. Catharines responded to the call, and were soon equipped for service. Altho' the village of St. Catharines is small, yet it raised one company of foot under the command of Captain Adams, and two companies of horse under the respective commands of Messrs. Rykert and Macdonald, who were shortly after gazetted as captains. The boys even formed a company and organized a band of music, highly creditable to them. The ladies also shared in the general feeling, and evinced great presence of mind on the occasion. Being left so frequently at home by themselves, during the absence of their husbands, brothers and friends, they prepared for their defence in case of any attack from the rebels. They practised pistol and rifle shooting, and even mounted guard with muskets. One lady declared to me that she had no fire-arms in the house, but, that if any rebel came near her, she would knock his brains out with a poker. Those advanced in years participated also in the enthusiasm that prevailed. Sheriff Merritt, who had faithfully served his country during the former war with the States, when he heard of the base attempt to undermine the rising prosperity of the country by a band of lawless rebels, prepared to join the volunteers on their expedition to Toronto. He was with difficulty dissuaded by his relatives from going, on account of his age, but at length acceded to their request, though very reluctantly. It was, however, apparent that his heart was with them on their progress, which was fully evinced afterward when they returned victorious.

Never was a scene so full of enthusiasm, sufficient to convince any hostile country how difficult it would be to overrun the fertile soil of Canada, or destroy that feeling of loyalty for its Government, under whose protecting power the people have so implicitly relied and lived so happily. As this is a country with which you are but little acquainted except by books, which give but an indifferent account of it, I have deemed it necessary to enter more fully into particulars than may be considered requisite. Should I, however, begin to write prosy, you must pardon me on account of my feelings being actuated by the impulse of the moment.

I now return to my Chippawa friends, from whose residence I shall furnish you with a detail of our operations in that vicinity. Picture to yourself the magnificent River Niagara, near three miles broad, within sight of the Falls, and subdivided by two islands nearly opposite Mr. Ussher's; you have then an idea of my location. Navy Island opposite the house, half a mile distant, contains 300 acres of land. It is partially cleared and has been for several years inhabited only by one old woman and her daughter whose husband had the ill luck to drift over the Falls in a canoe about ten years ago. Her log house stands at the back of the Island, looking toward the American shore,—a retired spot, but extremely pleasant in spring, summer and autumn, but a dreary solitude in winter, being cut off from any communication with the mainland by reason of the ice. This was a favourite resort for all those fond of fishing and shooting, it being a famous place for whitefish, pickerel and maskinonge, as well as wild duck and teal, thousands of which in spring and fall frequent the spot, by reason of the sheltered swamps at the extremity of the Island. Here I have spent many pleasant hours, little dreaming that it would afterward become so renowned in history for one of the most singular events that ever happened. On this account I have been the more particular in my description of it, but you must wait awhile, having many other circumstances to communicate before I paddle you over in a canoe to that curious spot.

On hearing the intelligence from Toronto, the farmers and settlers around the country imagined that events were far worse than they turned out afterward. But such is the natural bias of mankind to mystify, that the imagination was most powerfully wrought upon. Every breeze that blew indicated that a lurking traitor was at hand, either to set fire to a house, or blow your brains out. It therefore became every man's business to look out, not only for himself, but for the welfare of his neighbours. Our neighbour, Mr. Dobie, an intelligent farmer, Captain Ussher and ourselves were the only efficient hands in this retired spot, to mount guard and patrol the shore. The weather was extremely cold, and the frontier being bleak and dreary, particularly at night, rendered the service to be performed no sinecure. Our armory consisted of a brace of pistols, a rifle, a double-barrelled gun, and a single, with plenty of balls and ammunition. So that in case of an attack, the enemy would have found a warm reception, particularly as Harry, the black servant had heard, that in the event of the rebels succeeding, he would be immediately sent out of the country and sold in slavery again. We had frequent visitors from Chippawa and Fort Erie, so that in the day time we were never dull, and one great source of amusement we had was conversation relative to wars in former times, both civil and uncivil, a topic we had not broached for a considerable time. As night approached the wind must evidently have whistled louder than usual, from the number of times we went to the door and paced the room, indicative at any rate of squally times. I made up my mind at the outset to take the affair very coolly, not believing it possible, as I observed to you before, that there could be many disaffected throughout the country generally; though I was well aware that Chippawa itself, only two miles distant, was so disloyal a place that, like the city formerly for which Abraham interceded, scarce ten men could be found in it who were true to the existing Government. This I imagined arose from its proximity to the States and intercourse with the Buffalonians. A contiguity therefore to so radical a neighbourhood might make us the more watchful, which indeed we were, not taking off our clothes for many nights together. Every hour did we pace up and down the river's bank, but heard nothing for the first few nights save now and then the hooting of an owl or the whistling of loons from their quarters in a creek on Grand Island. The dogs also partook of the general unsettlement, apparently conscious that some dire event was stirring, for they would go away for days together and at a time when they were most wanted at home. When any derangement takes place in the common order of events, such trifles weigh but little in the general scale; altho' the Romans paid as much attention to the cackling of geese as that of an army, their movements being frequently regulated by these simple omens.

Captain Ussher, an active officer, brother to the one at whose villa I was located, resided, as I informed you, on the adjoining farm. They were both men of undaunted courage, but being known to be thorough Tories like their father and the rest of the family, rendered their situation more likely to be marked by ill-designing men. The former was quickly on the alert to call out his company of militia. He had the greatest difficulty in collecting them together, partly from the circumstance of many being from home to reconnoitre the aspect of affairs, and others who being tinged with Mackenzieism waited in the back ground to join the strongest side. This circumstance would have weighed but little even on the present occasion, as the rebellion, as far as Mackenzie and his adherents were concerned, was crushed at the outset throughout the country, but his having escaped to Buffalo ultimately altered the face of things *in toto*. It produced a reaction in our internal movements that disturbed the whole Province from one end to the other.

Whilst his operations were concocting there, we were all quiescent, with the exception of keeping guard, listening from time to time to the silly and ridiculous reports that mischievous individuals invented to frighten old women, and those among the men who were half inclined to radicalism, but ashamed to own it. Men who halt between two opinions are seldom at ease in their minds, and this was the characteristic of the Chippawayans. It nevertheless had a bad effect. All business was suspended, and the people's time was therefore principally spent in rummaging up old guns, pistols, firearms of every description, and cleaning them up for action on either side as circumstances might require. Never was so sudden a transition from peace to war, a subject that superseded every other topic and was well exemplified by a song sung at our quarters by Mr. Watkins, formerly in the Navy.—" Twas in the merry month of May."

When it was ascertained that Mackenzie had arrived at Buffalo, great curiosity was excited to find out his movements. Numbers crossed the River to see him, and to ascertain what plans he would adopt for the future. This was soon elicited, for in a few days after he had rested from his fatigue and the fright that generally attends cowardly minds, he divulged his operations to Dr. Chapin at whose house he had sought an asylum. That gentleman protected him from the insults of those who had, like himself, run away for their lives, disgusted with his movements. Others on the contrary, from a spirit of revenge at the reflection of having their property confiscated, still clung to his standard, hailing him as the Jack Cade of Upper Canada, thirsting still to carry fire and sword amongst his enemies. Their numbers, however, were few and principally confined to men of low origin and desperate habits, suited at all times for buccaneering expeditions, whereby they thought they could not only enrich themselves, but harass the Government. As soon as it was found that public curiosity was excited in Buffalo and its vicinity, it was publicly announced that Mackenzie would hold a meeting and explain his views. This plan of publicity doubtless originated with himself, who had assurance enough for anything, and (was) sanctioned by a set of broken down characters who had eluded both law and justice by absconding from their creditors. Consequently, having no character like their chief juggler behind the curtain to lose, they lent a ready ear to any scheme, however absurd, that might be broached on the occasion. The season of the year was also auspicious, for inland navigation had long since closed, and most of the steamboats laid up for the winter, leaving hundreds of boatmen, canallers, sailors, firestokers and workmen of various grades out of employ, whose time hung heavy on their hands. These worthies having no other amusement but playing bowls, sitting in groceries and low taverns, smoking, tossing, gambling and drinking, were on the *qui vive* for any encounter, however hazardous. Amidst such a medley, it will readily be imagined that a pretty large meeting might be collected together, which was in reality the case. From 1500 to 2000 is a fair estimate of those who congregated and whom Mackenzie addressed as gentlemen and intelligent fellow mortals. I saw a shrewd Scotch engineer the following day who, being gifted with a very retentive memory, gave me nearly verbatim the sum and substance of his oration. This I took down in writing; (it) was read over, signed by the individual, witnessed by Captain Barlé, formerly of Brussels, and myself, sent off by express to headquarters with recommendations to keep a sharp lookout as mischief was evidently brewing.

The tenor of this discourse was, as you may imagine, to create in the minds of his hearers sympathy for his alleged misfortunes in not having succeeded in his plans. All his assertions were distorted, but being wrapt up in the cloak of probability struck the gaping audience with astonishment, and so wrought upon them that men, who went there merely as idle spectators, came away ready at a minute's warning to grasp a rifle and shoot the first Canadian Tory that came in their way. This, I say, was the issue, and, to give the Devil his due, he played his cards on that occasion, well suited to his restless, ambitious views. He told the pretended sons of liberty that the hour was come when it became the duty of all within the audience of his voice and elsewhere to come forward manfully in aid of so glorious a cause, to render Canada as independent as themselves; that nine-tenths of the inhabitants were groaning with oppression and sighing for that happy state of independence which they enjoyed; that the scheme was still practicable, altho' he unluckily did not succeed in consequence of a mistake in the day named for their general rising. He also stated that for ten years he had devoted his time, his talent and his purse to consummate this glorious event, and that he was still as much devoted to the cause as at any period of his life; that there never was a finer opportunity than the present, when the resources of the country were so weak, having no troops within the Province or any means of defence; and that those who called themselves loyal were merely a few hirelings who were paid by the Government. As to England sending out troops, it was folly for a moment to entertain the thought, as they were all wanted at home to keep down the Irish, who were on the eve of rebellion likewise. There was an abundance of fine land in the country, and those who chose to join the standard would be rewarded with 300 acres each as soon as the expedition was accomplished. At this liberal offer every eye glistened. "'Tis true, gentlemen," said he, "we shall want blankets at this inclement season of the year, some other clothing, some arms and a good supply of ammunition, but above all, on the hazard of the die, some of the ready rhind called specie. Nothing," he observed, "could be accomplished without this. It was the sovereign panacea." Many stared at this assertion, as a poser; but considered they could get along tolerably well with plunder. In fact, he summoned recruits from a nation with whom we had been for years on terms of peace and friendship, to form a regular buccaneering expedition, as it afterward commenced. He read a number of confidential letters that he had plundered from the mails, the contents of which he thought would tickle the ears of his audience, and wound up his harangue by assuring them that the long disputed Boundary Question would then be settled.[54] This was considered a prodigious feat, and drew forth bursts of applause, after which he took his departure with Doctor Chapin, under escort of twelve armed men, so alarmed, even then, was he of his personal safety, fearing he might be assassinated before he could carry his plans into effect, so as to share in the universal plunder and take up his residence at Burlington Castle, near Hamilton, the spot he had fixed upon for his councils. I think I see you smile, and well you may. Howbeit, the intellient audience separated, many of them a full inch higher, with their consequence, in anticipation of reaping this golden harvest, 300 acres of the fertile soil of Canada. Their dreams were like those of Abdallah, on this all-absorbing conquest, but which unhappily the beams of the morning dispelled. Others on the contrary began to think that a bird in the hand was worth two in the bush, and therefore lost no time in disposing of their rights at the best market they could find. Strange as the infatuation may appear, I have been credibly informed that considerable speculation was entered into, not only in the land department but "patriotic scrip," which was paid away for provisions and clothing. This was to become payable when all rogues and plunderers became honest men. I need scarcely remind you that a heavy discount soon ensued, as the grand desideratum was never accomplished, consequently the coffers of the deluded victims were ultimately minus to the amount of the outgoings. Patriotism, however, was the order of the day for a long time. They wore a strip of white ribbon round the arm, as an emblem

---

[54] This account of Mackenzie's address in Buffalo is the most complete available; it is only briefly mentioned in Lindsey, Vol. II, p. 125. (H.)

of the purity of their intentions, and ate more pork and molasses at the public expense than had been consumed for many winters.

Whatever novel scheme is offered to delude weak-minded people, there are sure to be numbers found silly enough to enlist in the cause, no matter whether religion or politics. Recall to mind the Crusades to the Holy Land, when thousands perished with hunger and the sword; also the scheme of Dick Brothers [55] to rebuild the walls of Jerusalem, who had a vast army enlisted in the cause, altho' the king of France absolutely refused to furnish his quota of ten thousand wheelbarrows. Nevertheless the subject is not entirely forgotten, for within a few years the spot fixed upon for the New Jerusalem was Grand Island, within sight of us here, a survey of which was actually made for carrying the project into execution. A sawmill is now in operation there which can furnish a good supply of lumber when the scheme is complete.

Such chimeras have their day and will continue to do so as long as people are found silly enough to countenance Owen's visionary scheme for Harmony Settlements, [56] or Mackenzie sly enough to dupe a nation proverbially cautious in what is commonly termed—being taken in. Perhaps among the recorded events of history there never was so audacious a piece of effrontery as at present. Yet I shall hereafter shew you that not only were the half-starved enrolled in the patriotic cause, but men of substance and fortune actually found weak enough to contribute hundreds and thousands of dollars to carry this visionary scheme into operation. So true it is, as Pope justly observes, that amidst the human family there are found men of various grades ever grasping at phantoms never within their reach. Such men are only to be pitied for their folly,—and even this is thrown away upon them, as they view even realities with a jaundiced eye—

"You think this cruel? Take it for a rule,
No creature smarts so little as a fool."

---

[55] Richard Brothers, an extraordinary enthusiast, was born, December, 1757, at Placentia, Newfoundland; partly educated at Woolwich, he entered the Royal Navy as midshipman in 1771 and saw some active service. He became Lieutenant in 1783, and was discharged on half-pay in the same year, which he continued to draw until 1789, when he ceased further to draw it as he refused to take the oath required. He gradually grew into the belief that he had a divine mission, that he was the Prince of the Jews, a descendant of David, and the nephew of God. In 1794 he published a book of interpretation of prophecy, "A Revealed Knowledge of the Prophecies and Times" (My copy is a Philadelphia reprint of 1795). He was suspected of treasonable practices, but after examination by the Privy Council he was committed as a criminal lunatic, thus antedating Robert Gourlay by a quarter of a century. He had many followers, some of them of great intelligence and high station.

After a very singular and interesting life he died in 1824. He was perhaps the first advocate of Anglo-Israelism, at least in our language.

Several of the works of Brothers and his followers are in the Riddell Canadian Library, Osgoode Hall.

[56] Robert Owen, born at Newtown, Montgomeryshire, 1771, who after a successful career as cotton-mill proprietor, adopted a crude and heterodox political economy; he bought from the "Rappites," the colony of Harmony on the Wabash River, and established a new colony on his own principles as "New Harmony," Indiana. He took an active part in the Co-operative movement in Britain, and was the leading Socialist for many years before his death in 1858. His son, Robert Dale Owen, is better known than Owen himself, but Owen was a self-sacrificing, devoted servant of humanity; his theories were not successful, but his life deserved the "Well done" of the Great Master.

But to proceed. A committee was formed to frame the outline of a new Constitution, which was to be carried into effect as soon as a sufficient force was collected to take possession of the land of promise. In the meantime, they framed what is termed a provisional government, of which Mackenzie was constituted chairman, but not cashier,—this was managed by a committee: nevertheless he contrived to get his share of the booty so generously bestowed by the Buffalonian sympathizers.

The result of the subscription entered into furnished a variety of supplies for the new recruited Jack Cade brigands, who sadly wanted blankets to keep out the cutting blast of a northwest wind which blew keenly on this memorable occasion. Those who had no promises to pay, commonly called dollar notes, contributed something to the common stock in the shape of barrelled pork, flour, molasses, tobacco, potatoes and whiskey, it being considered stingy not to shew patriotism by a small contribution into the general treasury.

Those who enlisted belonging to the temperance society drank water, the only store that ultimately never became exhausted. Another class, by far the most numerous, took their bitters in the morning and drank whiskey or brandy when they could get it. But the officers, who were appointed to marshal the ranks, being men of energy and strong minds, fared sumptuously on fowls, turkeys and venison; drank wine with their almonds and raisins after dinner, and now and then a glass of champagne to elevate their spirits afterwards, so liberally did some of the merchants come forward in aid of the cause. This sketch may appear to you exaggerated, but is a positive fact and a remarkable one too in the annals of excitement, showing how delusion may carry men beyond the limits of prudence and common sense.

Business, however, was to be entered upon, the main point of which consisted in arms and ammunition. Altho' many were willing to feed the hungry and clothe the naked, yet the same individuals clung most tenaciously to their rifles, preferring the use of these weapons themselves rather than their acting by proxy. No resource was therefore left but going to the fountain head, the Government, whom the brigands conceived better able to provide so necessary a portion of their outfit than private individuals. Accordingly the arsenals were promptly thought of, it being considered superfluous to keep a quantity of muskets idle and liable to corrode at a period when there could be no earthly use for them in a time of profound peace. A few loose cannon, too, might with safety be abstracted, more especially as the people had absolutely paid for them. Therefore no great harm could accrue by the people also having a share in the use, it being philosophically argued that it was a joint stock concern. This is the great advantage of free institutions. Preparations being completed, the command of these ragamuffins, amounting to no more than 300 men, at the first devolved upon an individual of the name of Van Ranselaer,[57] son of the postmaster of Albany. A man of aspiring notions, who firmly believed the Canadians could be as easily subdued as the Spaniards in South America, he panted with ambition to become a

---

[57] Ranselaer Van Ranselaer was the son of the General Van Ranselaer who commanded the American troops at the Battle of Queenston Heights in 1812; the son had no merits but a fine manner suitable to his name and descent; he was a drunken braggart with little military knowledge and less common sense, and showed a proper contempt for his Canadian associates and subordinates.

second Bolivar. Gifted with idle, extravagant habits, which his father prudently would not indulge him in to his own ruin, he thought this a fine opportunity to repair his shattered finances, which ultimately plunged him in jail to meditate on his follies. He was appointed General, or Gineral as Major Downing calls it, on full pay—a title with us in England betokening a man of some rank. Not so, however, on the other side, there being more generals there than men to command. It has, however, one advantage, that those who want common sense involuntarily feel elevated by it. This preliminary fixed, the drums beat and the wry-necked fifer became nearly broken-winded with his exertions to induce the bystanders to enlist in the glorious cause; but it was of no avail with the calculating ones, although the tempting offer of 300 acres of land stared them full in the face. Many were more than half inclined to join the standard, especially when they saw the flag, worked by the pretty Buffalonian ladies, so remarkably handsome, but on second thought they cautiously kept aloof just to see how the game would commence, and what chance there would be of any opposition, an event apparently never contemplated by the ringleaders.

In a movement of so much consequence it was thought advisable to get along by degrees, and to keep on the safe side as long as they possibly could. Accordingly, the advance guard reached an old Indian settlement called Tonawonta, half way between Buffalo and the Falls, and opposite to the heart of Grand Island. Here they made a halt. All was safety so far as the enemy was concerned, but at home they had to look out for their own government officers, having violated the laws by pilfering the cannon and muskets, to say nothing of food and clothing which they occasionally picked up on the way. You may be sure that, between two fires, they did not halt long. Accordingly on the following morning, they ferried over to Grand Island amounting in numbers to 220 men, a wonderful force truly to take possession of Upper Canada. But nothing is accomplished without confidence. The Tonawonta natives gladly supplied them with boats to get rid of so desperate a crew from their quiet village, and even supplied them with salt for their porridge. The rear rank, consisting of the commissariat department and about 100 others, were still behind in charge of the eatables and drinkables. These soon followed, forming altogether as rough a picnic expedition as was ever beheld.

I believe I told you that Grand Island belongs to our neighbours. Therefore, to secure themselves from molestation, they agreed to make the conquest of Navy Island belonging to the British Government, and inhabited only by one old woman and her daughter, whom they sent over to Grand Island in snug quarters there at a log hut within sight of their previous location. This was wanted for the head officers of the New Convention,—a dwelling compared with which, Jack Straw's castle on Hampstead Heath is a palace. Having safely landed with a couple of six pounders, they commenced operations for fortifying themselves, being determined to act on the defensive until a further reinforcement arrived from Kentucky and elsewhere. They imagined that the novelty of the expedition would spread like wildfire, and that thousands would join them in their winter quarters preparatory to opening the spring campaign.

That no opposition should be made to their landing, they kept the place of their destination a profound secret, and marched through a wild forest for four or five miles, frequented by nothing whatever but deer and wildcats. It so happened, however, that early intelligence reached us, and had it been acted upon promptly, the whole trouble, confusion, expense and inconvenience might have been easily avoided. It was early in the morning of the 11th of December, I was at Captain Ussher's, when a respectable farmer called to give his deposition relative to their movements. He stated he wished to do so from a fear that his cattle and property would be plundered by these brigands on their march. He owned a large farm on Grand Island, as well as three hundred acres of land in Upper Canada, and therefore claimed our protection by dispersing the pirates as quickly as possible. He happened to be at Tonawonta at the very time when they embarked. Suspecting their place of destination, which on enquiry was confirmed, he hastened through the Island to the shore, took his canoe, came over and gave us the information. This was the first intelligence that reached us. We took down his deposition in writing, witnessed it, and after breakfast Captain Ussher mounted one of his horses and rode off to the commanding officer,[58] then at Fort Erie, to give him intelligence. It was considered an event so highly improbable that no further notice was taken of it further than passing the communication on to another quarter. We were displeased, being firmly convinced that the farmer's testimony was implicitly to be relied on, but having no authority to act, nothing could be done, although Mr. Ussher volunteered for one to go over and keep guard. There were also numbers in readiness to join him. The remainder of the day we kept a sharp lookout, allowing no boats to pass without permission of a magistrate, yet notwithstanding our vigilance some spies had been known to cross higher up the river. One of these, however, corroborated the farmer's testimony by mentioning the circumstance at a small tavern about half a mile distant, where I called every hour to ascertain if there were any suspicious characters. At four o'clock in the morning we went down to Chippawa and stated this fact also, but the Colonel was as little inclined to belief as the other; he promised, however, that a conference should be held in the course of the day, which was accordingly done, but the golden opportunity was lost by reason of the time that elapsed in passing, repassing and conferring together. A handful of men at that crisis would have prevented the direful disasters that afterward occurred. I wished for the spirit of Lord Peterborough's movements at that juncture to act promptly, in order to prevent the annoyance which must inevitably arise frome those marauders taking quiet possession of an Island from which, if they intrenched themselves well, they could with difficulty be removed. The militia are all very well as secondaries, but from the circumstance of being so little engaged in warlike operations, they make but poor primaries in a case of emergency of this kind. This does not arise from any defect in personal courage, because the late events have proved this fact to the contrary. It arises from a want of organized plans and extension of service, to teach them the importance of every position and advantage to be taken of the movements of an enemy, which can only be acquired by tact and experience.

I nevertheless agree with my friends that common foresight and prudence should have induced the Colonel of the District, in the absence of any regu-

---

[58] Probably Colonel Kenneth Cameron, formerly of the 79th Highlanders, and at that time Assistant Adjutant-General.

lars, to send over a guard to the Island, knowing as he must have done that Mackenzie was in Buffalo inflaming the minds of the people to revolt against us.

From ocular demonstration, it was proved on the following day[59] that our information was correct, for we could plainly see the pirates walking around the Island and preparing their fortifications. All night long the axe was heard, felling trees for breastwork and the construction of shanties as temporary huts to shelter them from the cold until they could convey lumber over for building, which was soon effected, necessity being with them the rallying point to raise quarters as speedily as possible, not only for themselves but for the anticipated Kentucky boys. We could see them cutting down and carrying away fern and brushwood for beds to repose on. They kept up large fires, most of them being apparently accustomed to night campaigning in the open air.

Dreary as our midnight patrolling was, before the arrival of the *Gineral* and his advanced guard, you may readily suppose we were no better off after the arrival of our piratical neighbours, whose plans we were totally ignorant of. They might come over in boats, burn the houses and pillage the country, then return with the greatest alacrity without being caught, for we had, as I before stated, no other guard along the frontier. Fortunately, however, they were too closely engaged in their military tactics and shanty building to trouble us, although the circumstance of their being armed and not knowing precisely their numbers was a source of great alarm all round the country.

The very taking possession of our soil, small as the Island is, aroused the indignation of the loyalists, and prompted them to greater exertion than they had hitherto manifested. The news which had gone forward to Toronto as doubtful was no sooner confirmed, than volunteers marched from all quarters, and despatches were forwarded to the Lower Province to recall all the regulars they could spare. Order being partially restored in that quarter since the destruction of Saint Charles, and the flight of the prominent leaders, the troops promptly obeyed the call and prepared for departure.

In common seasons their transportation by water would have been impracticable, such an occurrence being rarely remembered of steamboats plying toward the end of December. This season, however, as if aided by a superintending power in favour of our cause, was mild, enabling the boats to run without interruption from the ice. Detachments of the 24th and 32nd regiments quickly arrived at Toronto, from whence they rapidly pushed on without the harass and fatigue of travelling by land. Whilst these brave fellows were on their route, volunteers from various districts had arrived from as far north as Port Hope, Cobourg, Prescott and other settlements along the lake shore. Colonel MacNab[60] also had returned from the west and pushed on with three hundred men, joined by Captain Kerr and his two hundred Indians who had painted their faces red, a custom among them on warlike expeditions. We were not a little pleased at their arrival, having some chance of being relieved on our midnight guard.

---

[59] Possession was taken by the "Patriots" of Navy Island, December 13th, 1837.

[60] Colonel (afterwards Sir) Allan Napier MacNab arrived at Chippawa, December 20th. His name is found spelled in many ways—McNab, McNabb, M'Nab, M'Nabb, Macnab, Macnabb. He was placed in command on this frontier and was afterwards knighted for his services.

The quiet village of Chippawa suddenly assumed quite an animated appearance from the influx of so many strangers. So rapid had been the movements of the troops that in a very short time upward of four thousand had arrived to our protection. Bands of music, bugles, marching, counter-marching, drilling, firing, cannon exercising, the bustle and stir of the commissariat department, waggon loads of bread, beef, pork and potatoes moving along the road from the surrounding farms, presented a spectacle quite novel to me, who for the first time was located in the very heart of the contending parties. Private houses were all turned into barracks and the Methodist Chapel into a hospital. Our worthy clergyman turned the sword of the Spirit into an instrument of war, nothing in fine being thought of but preparations for defence in the event of an invasion. This all-engrossing topic superseded every other consideration.

I should tell you that, in conformity with the Colonel's assurance, preparations were made for going over to the Island, to make remonstrance against American citizens taking possession of our territory.[61] Accordingly, some of the magistrates, accompanied by volunteer rowers, proceeded on their way thither. This was an ill-judged experiment,[62] as they must have been aware that the brigands were too numerous, and too well armed, to allow them to land, although it was their policy to have done so, which would have secured the party prisoners, and secured the boat. Willing, however, to show us that they, in reality, had commenced their fortifications, and possessed cannon, so soon as the boat neared the northern extremity of the Island, they opened their battery and fired a six-pounder upon the adventurers. This was too warm a reception, so they deemed it most prudent to return, which they quickly did, without accomplishing the end in view. Two or three more shots were fired, but without effect, their artillerymen not being in sufficient practice to level a good aim, or make that allowance in the art of gunnery with a moving object, so as to do any injury.

So incredulous were the authorities in power as to their numerical force, considering that merely a few lawless fellows had gone there on a freak, that they determined on another experiment, which took place shortly after, and would doubtless have succeeded had they manned a sufficient number of boats. Unluckily, however, as I hinted at the outset, we had no boats of any consequence, but they were very quickly supplied from Queenston and elsewhere. The sleighing being good, a grand movement took place, and it was really curious to see the rapid arrival of so many boats. In a few days near one hundred were collected together. I saw one immense boat that would hold fifty men, drawn all the way from Hamilton, a distance of forty-four miles.

---

[61] Lieutenant-Governor Sir Francis Bond Head, as early as December 13th, 1837, had sent a remonstrance to Governor Marcy, of the State of New York, concerning the agitation at Buffalo to procure countenance and support for the disaffected in Upper Canada. Head. 332, Leg. Ass. 97; the Governor, December 19, issued a Proclamation against attempts to set on foot military expeditions or enterprises in violation of the laws of the land and the relations of amity between the United States and the United Kingdom, Leg. Ass. 98; this was almost a dead letter, and practically nothing was done for weeks to check the movement. On Navy Island being occupied, Head, December 23, sent Archibald McLean, Speaker of the House, to Washington with a full account for the British Ambassador, Henry S. Fox, Head 335; Leg. Ass. 98.

[62] I have not seen this "experiment" of the Magistrates noted by any other writer.

by thirty-six oxen—a sight I shall, in all probability, never witness again. Schooners also were ordered from the shores of Lake Erie, and every other kind of craft that the country possessed. The two first boats were soon brought into service without waiting for a general attack, which, at one time, was determined on. These were manned by a reconnoitring party,[63] consisting of intrepid young fellows who had freely volunteered their services. The current being strong, they were towed up the river a little beyond Mr. Ussher's. The party, consisting of six in one boat and eight in the other, proceeded toward the Island, intending to row down the stream between Navy and Grand Islands. The object in view was to ascertain what force was stationed at the back part, where the old lady's cottage stood, then taken possession of by Van Ranselaer and Mackenzie, with their aide-de-camps. No sooner, however, had they reached the line opposite the extremity of the Island, than a brisk cannonading, with six-pounders, opened upon them. It was an interesting and novel sight, though an alarming one, lest our brave countrymen should be swamped by a cannon ball. At the first fire we distinctly saw where the ball struck the water, well directed as to the line, but too much elevated, so that the ball passed over their heads and struck some distance off. The second shot was better directed and fell very near the bow of the boat. Finding it would be impracticable to get round, they rowed back and returned to Chippawa, about midway in the current on this side, but sufficiently near to the Island for any experienced riflemen to have done great execution. By this time a vast number had assembled with their rifles, who kept up one incessant firing, but all to no effect. I should think, at the least, there were two hundred balls fired, still no harm done, which satisfied us there was less to fear from the brigands than had by many been anticipated, although it had been given out that their aim was as unerring as the Indians'. Whilst the boats kept gliding along, our fine fellows only laughed at them, twirling at the same time a hat on the end of a boarding sword, with which they were all well armed, as well as pistols. Before they cleared the Island, another cannonading commenced, with similar ill-success. The ruffians discharged seven six-pounders, but none near enough to either boat even to splash them. One ball, I noticed, dropped in the water midway between the two boats. This was the second best shot that was made. On reaching Chippawa they gave three cheers, and landed amid the applause of the bystanders. After Mr. Ussher had played "God Save the Queen" on his bugle.

---

[63] Richard Arnold's account is as follows (Dent, Vol. II, p. 215):

"The next day (i.e., December 26, 1837) I and several other volunteers accompanied Captain Drew on a reconnoitring expedition. We set out from Chippawa Creek in a small boat and proceeded to circumnavigate Navy Island, where we could see the rebels in full force. As we approached the island they fired round after round at us, and the bullets whistled thick and fast over our heads. Our position was one of extreme peril. 'What a fool I am!' exclaimed Captain Drew, 'to be here without a pick-up boat. Should we be disabled we shall find ourselves in a tight place.' One of the rowers in our boat was completely overcome by fear, and funked. 'I can't help it, boys,' said he—and threw himself at full length along the bottom of the boat. We made the trip, however, without any accident. The next day we made another expedition in a large twelve-oared gig, with a picked crew, chiefly composed of lake sailors. Again the shots whistled over our heads, and struck the water on both sides of us, but in the course of a few hours we found ourselves back again in Chippawa Creek without having sustained any injury. We had by this time become used to being under fire, and didn't seem to mind the sound of the whistling bullets."

we walked down to see the results. I examined the boats carefully, but no symptoms of a single bullet mark out of the two hundred fired on the occasion, convincing us that the recruits must be better practised in the art of gunnery before they attempted to cross over and pay us a visit.

These reconnoitring parties ceased soon afterwards, and a Council of War was held as to the best course to pursue to dislodge the marauders. It was desirable, if possible, to spare the effusion of human blood, and on this account it was considered advisable to act on the defensive, particularly as our reinforcements were numerous, and detachments arriving daily from distant districts. The Jewish Monarch declared formerly that in the multitude of councillors there is safety. Unfortunately, however, from there being too many, the court was harassed much longer with apprehensions of alarm than was consistent with the general character of the British nation. This indecision was afterward a source of reproach by the American authorities, who considered that it was our duty to remove a lawless band who had taken possession of our soil contrary to the existing treaty between the two countries. Colonel MacNab was of opinion that the first shedding of blood by forcibly removing them would weigh but trifling in the scale of contention and prevent numbers afterward falling a sacrifice by the sword, an idea which was looked upon by the most intelligent men as a moral certainty. Indeed, it was on the eve of being accomplished, but afterward countermanded. A plan of the Island was drawn by my friend Captain Ussher and myself, where every spit was marked, so intimately acquainted were we with its location, from having gone over so frequently on shooting expeditions. This was forwarded to the Governor, preparatory to his taking a circuit along the frontier.

Whilst the subject of attack was under consideration, various magistrates assembled at Fort Erie in council, who drew up a remonstrance, signed by Mr. Merritt, chairman, requesting the Mayor and authorities at Buffalo to inform them whether the aggressions complained of were noticed by them, or in any way sanctioned, or whether in reality any preparations were making for hostilities—an event wherein there appeared some probability, from the circumstance of drummers parading the streets of Buffalo on recruiting service.

Dr. Trowbridge, the Mayor, an intelligent and highly reputable man, finding the enthusiasm of the people had gone beyond the power of the law to restrain their proceedings, resigned his situation in favour of Mr. Barker. Previous to this, however, he wrote a reply to the magistrates assembled at Fort Erie, assuring them that everything practicable would be done to restore order, and that, so far from the Government wishing to sanction the proceedings of the rabble, every precaution would be taken to allay the excitement.

Doubtless many speculative men were at work behind the scenes with a view of aggrandizement in the event of the marauders succeeding. But the most influential and respectable classes used their utmost endeavours to put the law in force and prevent a violation of neutrality. They issued the following proclamation and held a meeting which resulted in ordering Mackenzie and his gang to quit the city within six hours, which they accordingly did, and made the best of their way to Navy Island as a place of security:

Address to the Citizens of Erie County from the Mayor and 140 *of the leading men of Buffalo.*

The undersigned inhabitants of Buffalo and Black Rock, have witnessed for a few days past, with deep regret and mortification, large bodies of men thronging our streets and public houses employed in enlisting volunteers, collecting arms and other munitions of war, and organizing themselves into military corps for the open and undisguised purpose of crossing into Canada to aid with their arms in the civil contest now waging between a portion of the people and the government of that province.

However much we may sympathize with our neighbours of Canada, or desire to see them emancipated from foreign domination, we should recollect that we live under laws of our own making, which it is not less our pride than our duty to obey and enforce, and in the strict execution of which, consists our real liberty and the superiority of our political institutions.

Many of our citizens, judging doubtless by the unrestrained freedom with which we are permitted to canvass and express our opinions of other governments, are not aware of the fact that the arming of men or fitting out military expeditions to act against a country with which we are on terms of amity, is forbidden, as well by our own municipal laws, as by the law of nations, and subjects the offenders to severe penalties.

The object of this notice is to apprise those who are acting under such delusion, that they are violating the laws of their country, and to beseech them to abandon at once an enterprise which, while it exposes them to punishment, promises but little advantage to those whose cause they wish to serve.

Should this advice be disregarded, we call upon the Civil Officers of the City and County to interfere and put a stop to these illegal proceedings, and we severally pledge our personal aid in causing the laws to be executed.

Buffalo, December 14, 1837.

Had these resolutions been promptly followed up by the marshal and others in authority, quiet would soon have been restored and the rebellious faction disbanded. But a strong party of speculators arose in their favour and winked at their proceedings, allowing boats to convey arms, ammunitions and provisions to them, which might easily have been prevented. Certain authorities even saw cannon with the United States mark upon them, and yet took no measures to secure them or to detain the parties who were known to be the pilferers. A steamboat[64] was also hired for the conveyance of recruits, arms, ammunition, etc., to the Island, which had arrived from Rochester and other districts in sleighs, where the jurisdiction of the marshal extended. A guard also, in time of peace, being allowed to watch the boat at night, without any warning that it was an infringement of neutrality, was truly unaccountable. Strange as this conduct may appear to you, I have it from the best information—gentlemen who were over there when the marshal conversed with Van Ranselaer and who saw a cannon in his boat belonging to the American Government. Conduct so reprehensible could not escape

---

[64] This was the *Caroline*, a steamboat about 75 feet long and of 46 tons burden, the property of William Wells, of Buffalo, which was cut out of her berth in the ice at Buffalo and brought down to Schlosser, December 28th, plying across to Navy Island.

the censure of our authorities, who, finding that so much listlessness and apathy prevailed, considered it high time to look out for themselves, having previously ascertained that the American militia refused to act.

All these circumstances being taken into consideration, a Council of War, which was held at Chippawa, determined upon some vigorous measures to prevent further aggressions upon our territory, and to open the eyes of the deluded Buffalonians as to the impolitic course they were pursuing, They would have rejoiced had the authorities on the other side done their duty by putting a stop to innovations so hourly notorious. After allowing the American authorities a fortnight, and finding all their remonstrances unavailing, they determined to act decisively and to perform that service which it was the bounden duty of the American Government to have done themselves. No alternative remaining,[65] six boats were manned under the command of an intrepid officer, Captain Drew, with instructions from Colonel MacNab to proceed at night and take possession of the piratical steamboat, the *Caroline*, which was known to be illegally conveying cannon, arms, ammunitions, recruits and provisions over to the marauders and rebels on Navy Island. She was seen plying on the afternoon of the 28th,[66] and not returning, it was supposed she would moor there for the night. In whichever case, however, they were to take possession of her at all hazards. Accordingly, about ten o'clock at night, the preparations were completed and the boats manned and well armed for the expedition. A more hardy or intrepid set of fellows could nowhere be found, all in good spirits, and ready to achieve any event however hazardous. On nearing the Island, they found that the said steamer had left in the evening for Schlosser on the American shore, thinking to be protected, and beyond our control, but the result proved the contrary. The first two boats kept ahead of the rest, having more experienced rowers, and, on arriving alongside, were hailed by the sentry for the countersign. No satisfactory answer being given, the party on guard fired, but without effect; the boat was soon boarded and taken possession of, but not without the loss of several lives in the confusion that ensued. This is a brief outline of the proceeding, columns of which have been written on the subject containing more untruths than I need trouble you with. As the current was too strong toward the Rapids and Falls, to tow her over, which was the original intention, she was set fire to in three or four different places, un-

---

[65] Captain Drew, R.N., who was in command of the expedition, in his report, December 30th, says: "I directed five boats to be armed and manned with forty-five volunteers," Leg. Ass., 90. G. T. D. says: "Five boats were prepared, well manned, well armed and with muffled oars," Can. Monthly, Vol. III, p. 290. Richard Arnold says: "The expedition consisted, as far as I can remember, of seven boats, each containing seven men, *i.e.*, four rowers and three sitters," Dent, Vol. II, p. 216. The number of boats is given as seven by most authors, and is probably correct. Sir Allan MacNab, under oath in the McLeod Trial, says "they were seven in number . . . seven or eight men in each boat . . . about forty persons." Trial, 124. "The boats did not all return at the same time. Five arrived at about the same time, two at a different time." Trial, 125. John Harris gave the same evidence. Trial, 129. "Seven boats left Chippawa, five only reached the *Caroline*, five returned in company." With this Edward Zealand agrees word for word, Trial, 135. Robert Armour says. "Seven started, five crossed the river," Trial, 147; so do Christopher Bier, Trial, 157, 159; Hamilton Robert O'Reilly, Trial, 162, 165; Sheppard McCormick, Trial, 169; Frederick Claverly, Trial, 170, 175, and several others. The fact seems to be that seven boats started, but two lost the way and did not cross the river.

[66] This should be "29th."

moored, and allowed to drift her course over the Falls, a species of navigation
that was certain to consign her to oblivion forever. The night was very dark;
consequently, as you may suppose, it was a very grand sight to see her gliding
with the current towards the whirlpool of her destination, whither she in due
time approached, and no vestige of her remains were ever seen afterward.[67]

The boats quietly rowed back into the Chippawa, having two prisoners[68]
and three of the party wounded, one of whom, Mr. McCormack,[69] suffered
severely, and afterward received a pension for his bravery; the other two
soon recovered. After eliciting all the information they could obtain from
the prisoners, they were allowed to return home the following day, it appearing
that they were strangers who had taken shelter there for the night, the small
tavern at Schlosser being quite full. Many others similarly situated took
to their heels as fast as they could on escaping from the vessel.

The American papers, as you may suppose, published the most exag-

[67] It seems quite certain that the *Caroline* did not go over the Canadian Falls,
nor as a whole (at least) over the Falls at all. Her engines seem to have sunk and
portions of her charred woodwork went down the river and over the Falls on the
American side.

[68] Both British subjects; one was Sylvanus Fearns Wrigley, of the Township
of Dumfries, who had enlisted with Dr. Duncombe; after Duncombe's men were dispersed, he crossed the Niagara River to join the "Patriots." He was on his way to
Navy Island where he was captured. He was detained in jail for three months and
then discharged on giving bail for good behaviour. The other was Alfred Luce, a
native of Lower Canada, who had also joined Dr. Duncombe; he shared in Wrigley's
adventures until his capture. He was released the following day and sent across the
ferry to the United States, as there seemed to be no doubt whether he was not a citizen
of that country. Dent, Vol. II, 213; Leg. Ass., 91.

[69] Lieutenant Shepherd McCormack (so named by Drew in his official Report,
December 30, 1837, Leg. Ass., 90; but both names are spelt in different ways, e.g.,
the pensioning Statute, 1838, 1 Vic., c. 46, calls him Sheppard McCormick) was shot
in several parts of his body and also received two cuts from a cutlass. He was permanently injured: he received a pension from Upper Canada of £100 ($400) per
annum, counting from December 29, 1837.

The Preamble of the Act is worth copying:
"Whereas Sheppard McCormick, Esquire, a retired Lieutenant in the Royal Navy,
received several severe wounds in action at the capture and destruction of the Piratical
steamer *Caroline* in an attempt to invade this Province by a lawless banditti, by which
he is disabled, and it is just and right that he should receive a Pension during such
period as he may be so disabled by said wounds."

He received the pension until his death, when it was continued to his widow.

It was the conventional thing for all loyal Canadians, from the Lieutenant-Governor down, to call the Canadian Rebels and their U. S. "Sympathizers," "*Pirates*";
they were "Pirates" to precisely the same extent and in the same way as William
of Orange and his English and Dutch followers. "Pirates," however, offset "Patriots,"
with "apt alliteration's artful aid." "Banditti" ("we call them plain thieves in
England") is another term of opprobrium equally well deserved; "a Banditti" is
not quite without precedent in our literature; but then I recall a student of mine,
Consule Planco, speaking of "the distance between one foci of an ellipse and the other."
And Parliament is like Rex, *super grammaticam*.

The second reported wounded was Captain John Warren, formerly an officer in
the 66th Regiment; his wounds were trifling and he resumed duty the following day,
Dent, Vol. II, 212; Leg. Ass., 89, 90. The third was Richard Arnold (wrongly called
John Arnold in the official Report, Leg. Ass., 90). His story is given in Dent, Vol. II,
214—he was "struck by a cutlass on the arm and got a pretty deep gash just above the
elbow;" he was "invalided and sent home to Toronto in a sleigh next day;" there his
"wound healed rapidly, leaving me none the worse." He died in Toronto, June 18,
1884; he always was properly proud of being the last man to leave the *Caroline*.

gerated statements, alleging that forty or fifty individuals were on board when the steamer was unmoored, who had no time to escape; but this, from the nature of things, was totally impracticable, as some time elapsed in setting fire to the vessel. She was also moored so tight with a chain that the party had considerable difficulty in unloosing her. During these preparations, therefore, ample time was afforded for any one to escape. I saw several of the gentlemen who went on the expedition, the following morning, but in the confusion that ensued and the darkness of the night, it was difficult to elicit the loss of the enemy. Mr. Chandler thought only one,[70] and three or four wounded; Lieut. Elmsley told me he believed five or six, which I believe to be the sum total of their loss. One only was actually found, who had acted in the capacity of sentry; he was interred in Buffalo amidst a large concourse of sympathizing spectators. But however many might deplore his fate, others considered he had voluntarily placed himself in danger, when he ought to have been industriously employed elsewhere.

You may be sure that so unlooked-for an event created no small sensation; it had, however, a most beneficial effect—that of stirring up the citizens to do their duty by endeavouring to preserve neutrality. Meetings were held; militia and volunteers were enrolled, and they then began to look after their own property instead of foolishly furnishing a gang of marauders with food, from whom they could not possibly derive any return or even thanks. Many, however, still thought differently, being violently excited and threatening vengeance. A more trifling circumstance than this, you may recollect, involved the Greeks and Romans in a ten years' war. But in the present instance it terminated in declamation and idle words, which were much cheaper than troops and gunpowder.

The rebels on the Island were also very indignant at losing so great an augmentation to their resources; they vented their spleen by opening a brisk cannonading the following morning on our houses opposite, as well as the military waggons and passengers who were passing and repassing along the frontier. This they had occasionally done for a week, without doing much damage. I am sorry, however, to inform you that three lives[71] were unhappily lost. One individual, who had taken shelter in Mr. Ussher's barn, was so seriously wounded in the abdomen that he died soon afterwards; another had his legs shot off; the third, on undergoing amputation, sank with exhaustion.

The houses which contained companies of guards were battered severely; a ball went through the upper part of a room where twenty or thirty men were stationed. In the adjoining house, a tavern, two balls went through, which induced the parties to decamp. A red-hot ball fell near Captain Ussher, which was afterward preserved. In the house beyond, where I had been located for a month, a ball entered the front door through the parlour

---

[70] Captain Drew in his official report said, "I regret to add that five or six of the enemy were killed, Leg. Ass., 90; but it is reasonably certain that there was only one killed; this was Amos Durfee, of Buffalo, for the murder of whom Alexander McLeod was tried at Utica, N.Y., in 1841. There were several wounded more or less severely.

[71] MacNab, writing to Lt.-Col. Strachan from Chippawa, January 19, 1838, says: "Three of our brave and loyal Militia have unfortunately lost their lives in the service of their country against the Rebels and their piratical allies upon Navy Island. They were all killed by gunshot wounds." Leg. Ass., 264.

and just took the corner of the dining table, forming a line on the surface as if ruled, went through Mrs. Ussher's bedroom and did considerable damage. Six others passed the house in different places, which ultimately rendered it untenable. It was high time, therefore, to shift apartments below stairs into a kitchen, which was built behind an embankment; here we were safe, but it was beyond a joke the whizzing of the balls, which at times came very near us. You would have imagined that the people here were disciples of Charles the 12th of Sweden, had you seen the number of people congregated on the frontier, not only in waggons looking over to the Island, but on foot. They were even imprudent enough to stand in groups as a mark for the rebels to fire at. I was one morning walking with Mr. Meredith and Dr. Hamilton in front of Mr. Ussher's house, when a warm firing commenced. A ball passed behind us within sixty yards and tore up the ground; the whizzing noise induced us to put our hands to our ears, and I for one involuntarily lowered my head, upon which Dr. Hamilton coolly replied, it was better to walk on quietly upright: he, however, was used to such matters in the last war. Strange as it may appear, I believe now that it is possible even to be fond of the excitement, for Mr. Merritt's son, who was up there one day, went away quite disappointed that he could not see them fire. And on those days when the cannonading did take place, I have heard the bystanders exclaim: "Go it, ye devils, and take better aim." There were many hairbreadth escapes, and considering the immense number of times they fired, it is extraordinary so few fell a sacrifice. A short time before the breaking out of the affray, we had built a foot-bridge across the creek at the back of Mr. Ussher's house. Captain Adams told me he was marching his men across when a ball struck in the bank close beside them. I also saw one strike the water under the bank where three officers were passing on horseback.

Doubtless you will ask where the balls were procured in so short a time for the use of the ruffians, for I can call them no better. Some they stole from the arsenals, but the greater part were cast at a foundry in Buffalo, the proprietor of which, I apprehend, entered into a bad speculation. But he was weak to think that the scrip would ultimately be paid, and that he should some day have a rich Canadian farm at the termination of the conquest, and there sit down with an "otium cum dignitate" like the Romans at the end of a Punic War. Whilst these outrages were perpetrated in front of Mr. Ussher's house, Mackenzie and the *Gineral* were at the back part of the Island concocting mischief. The former framed a most imprudent proclamation which was published in the *Buffalo Journal*, and intended for general distribution here when their forces were strong enough to effect a landing. I do not intend to trouble you with many documents of this kind, as it would swell my pages larger than I wish. This, however, is a curiosity in the annals of history, so read it just to be convinced of the consummate impudence of a man who fled his own country as a mere adventurer, and who ultimately effected his escape here from a punishment he so richly merited.[72]

The deluded people who perused this precious document began to think seriously that there would be a chance for plunder and a prospect before them of obtaining good farms with but little trouble. Under this false impression, meetings were held in various districts, where inflammatory speeches were

---

[72] Mackenzie's long Navy Island proclamation of six pages appears in Lindsey, Appendix G, and a lengthy discussion of it in Dent, Vol. II, Appendix. (H.)

made by lawyers, clerks and others, which resulted in many hot-headed individuals taking their rifles and proceeding to the general rendezvous on Navy Island. During the excitement, sleighs laden with arms and provisions, provided at the expense of private individuals, were passing and repassing continually. That the names of those might not be made public who were active in the proceedings, money was forwarded by ladies who entered their names in the patriot cause. Well, with all the exertions made, and the immense advantages held out, to the praise of the respectable portion of American citizens be it said that not more than about eight hundred men could be collected together, and those, as I before observed, consisted of the most reprobate and abandoned classes of society, who were fit for little else than marauders and buccaneers, many of them doubtless glad of the opportunity to escape their own prisons.

The insurrection being quelled at Toronto and in the West, the Governor crossed the Lake to take a survey of the frontier. Landing at Niagara, he proceeded to Queenston and from thence to Chippawa, along the shore to Fort Erie, opposite Buffalo, the termination at that time of the guarded coasts. On his return he was accompanied by Mr. Merritt and two other gentlemen, who pointed out as they rode along everything worthy of notice on our own frontier, as well as the opposite shore and the Island where the rebels were encamped. I was standing opposite Mr. Ussher's, unconscious of their approach, when the Governor politely withdrew from his Company, shook hands and expressed his satisfaction at finding all along the line so vigilant and at their posts. I asked him when the marauders would be dislodged, as they were a source of great annoyance to us by their frequent firing. He replied that, in a few days, on the arrival of the artillery then on its way, it would be effected. At this intelligence from the fountain head we were satisfied. I have no doubt at the time this was fully contemplated, but on a Council of War being held, it was considered advisable, if possible, to spare the effusion of human blood. On leaving Chippawa, however, he left orders with the Colonels in command to use their own discretion.

The artillery at length arrived, and a number of men were despatched up the River to raise embankments and breastwork, preparatory to a general bombardment. This was done at night, the first set of men being obliged to retire from their work in consequence of cannon having been fired to dislodge them, which was soon effected. None of the workmen received any injury, but the works having first commenced in front of my friend's house, sad dilapidation ensued; the front wall fell in soon afterward, which rendered the building quite unsafe and uninhabitable. At length the works were completed, and our mortars and cannon being in readiness, a regular attack was contemplated, but so many schemes and plans were devised that nothing effectual took place after all. Three schooners were manned and stationed up the River under the command of Captain Graham, Lieutenant Drew and Lieutenant Elmsley, three gentlemen of confirmed bravery. They were to cut off all communication, by water, with Buffalo; then there were near one hundred boats of various sizes in readiness, which, when manned, were to effect a landing at one end of the Island, whilst the artillery were playing upon the centre and northern end; these, however, were quiescent, to try the effect, first of all, of the bombardment. When this commenced, the bravadoes were alarmed not a little. The 24-pounders and mortars raked the trees and the shanties, tore up the ground and killed some of the rebels;

but the main body still clung to the Island. Had the boats been ready manned, a landing might with ease have been effected during their panic; this scheme was, however, overruled; so much for a multiplicity of councillors, in which we are told safety consists. The prolongation of storming the Island had a bad effect, inasmuch as the alarm was unabated; it also drove many peaceable families from their homes and domestic firesides at an inclement season of the year. I never could comprehend the policy of their operations, further than what I stated before—the desire to prevent the dreadful massacre that must have ensued, for very few I apprehend would have escaped, so indignant were the people on this memorable occasion.

That you may judge the situation of the contending parties, I hand you a small map of our positions, sufficient to guide your ideas to the spot remarkable in history. There lay entrenched a handful of desperate fellows who kept a whole country in agitation for upwards of a month, and we residing within cannon shot, liable at a moment's impulse to have a ball sent through the house, or perhaps a leg shot off whilst perambulating the bank of the River.

From the time of their arrival there, on the 13th December, to the period of their evacuation on the 15th January, you may be sure such restless adventurers were not idle in concocting mischief. Fortunately, however, through the fickleness of their plans and their constant differences and quarrels, no measures were effected for our annoyance further than what I mentioned relative to their occasional cannon exercise and rifle shooting. It was imagined, however, that one night they were ripe for some expedition, and in order to give signals and divert us from their movements, they lighted up a machine which was moved to and fro on the Island. From it issued a most dazzling and brilliant light, which could be seen for many miles around. It was supposed to consist of tar barrels and other inflammable materials, which burnt for several hours. No movement however took place. They had schemes to divert our attention in various ways, which were afterward acknowledged.

Van Ranselaer had full powers vested in him to conduct all the military operations, and that there should be no obstruction toward carrying his plans into effect, he had also the power to arrest any member of the executive, as recommended by Dr. John Rolph, who was their president in Toronto whilst their plans were maturing. All appeared to unite in their General's plans with the exception of Mackenzie, who, being gifted with such fickle, arbitrary and impatient views, ultimately thwarted every measure contemplated. He would suggest fifty schemes and in as many minutes abandon them for new ones, a pretty character to carry into effect the revolutionizing a colony so powerful as Canada.[73] At heart, he proved to be an innate coward, being the very first to be frightened at the cannonading and bombardment of our artillery, so that the only step left for Van Ranselaer to pursue was to keep him employed in their general correspondence, which was freely carried on by spies, notwithstanding our vigilance. They knew all our movements, although we could gather nothing of their's from their peculiar locality

---

[73] Coventry's delineation of Mackenzie's hypochondriac condition here is not essentially different from that in Dent, Vol. II, p. 15, etc. Curative methods had not then attained the development they have since done, and allowance must be made for this fact. (H.)

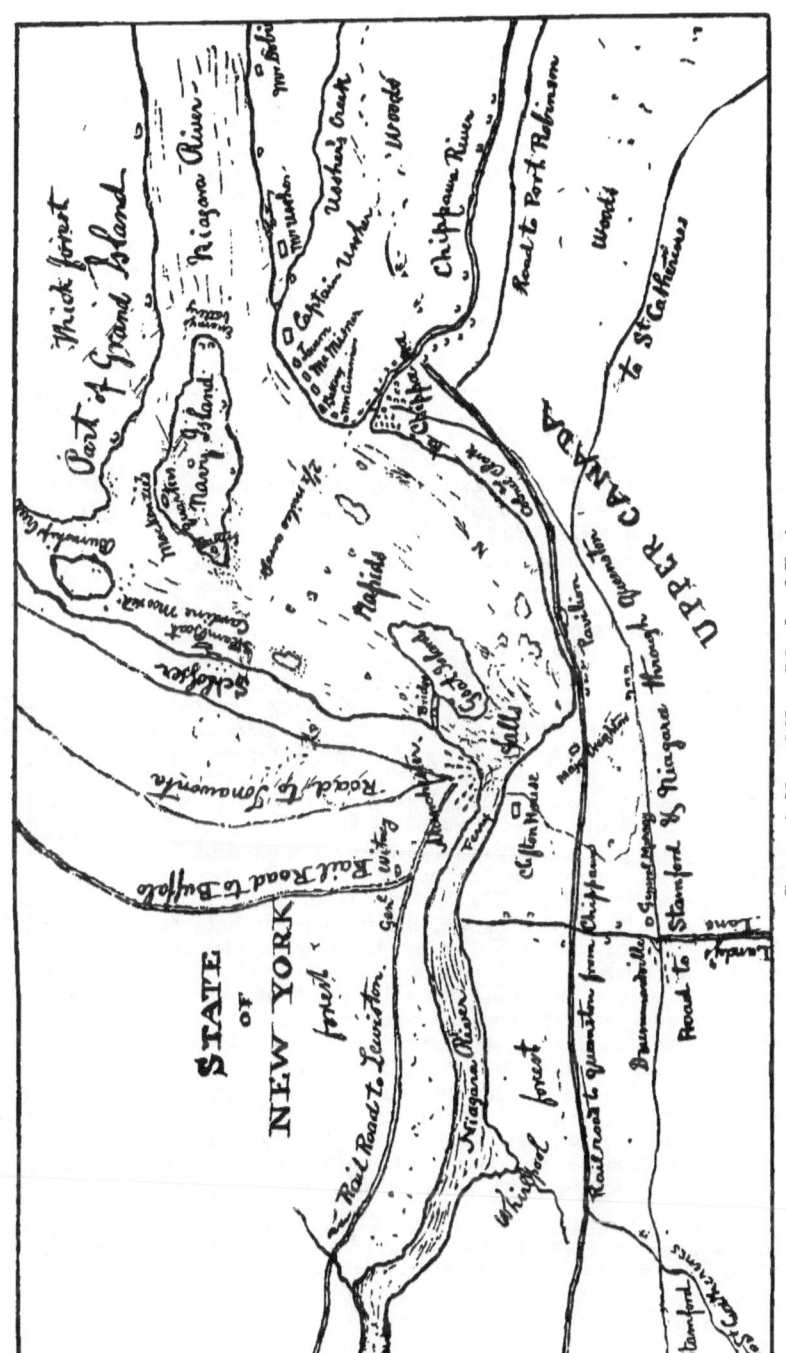

Coventry's Map of Navy Island and Environs.

on an island. At one time they contemplated crossing over, a few miles up
the River, secreting themselves in the woods, and obtaining from 200 to 300
rebels still at hide and seek, marching on through the woods and bye-places
to Niagara, seize upon the steamboats lying there, and crossing over direct
to Toronto. Such a visionary plan could never have succeeded, as we had
strong reinforcements all along the frontier, and dragoons patrolling in every
direction to convey the earliest information. Although Mackenzie himself
approved of the scheme, and volunteered to be foremost in coming over, yet
his coward heart failed him. Our 24-pounders and bombshells aroused all
the horrors of a guilty soul; he made his escape from the Island at a time
when everything was planned and a steamboat ordered to bring them over.
He secreted himself in the house of a friend at Buffalo, and soon afterward
levelled as great abuse against the American journals as he had formerly done
against our own. He even proposed that the men who had been fools enough
to join his standard, should charge the American troops stationed to watch
their movements. Afterward they were to seize the boats and embark from
the city. This produced an altercation between the head of the executive
and the military. This fracas induced Mackenzie to leave abruptly for
Rochester, where he hoped to gain sufficient confidence to establish a printing
press at their expense, but they knew better.

Van Ranselaer, being now left to his own management, and placing no
reliance upon any assistance to be obtained so near our headquarters, turned
his attention westward, hastened by the arrival of General Scott[74] from
Washington with 600 regulars to put a stop to their proceedings. During
this time, their forces kept increasing, many placing more confidence in the
firm decision of Van Ranselaer than in the pusillanimity of Mackenzie, who
never had any regular organized plans. Knowing Scott was too brave a
general to tamper with them, they had recourse to every subterfuge to evade
his scrutinizing eye. A large party armed with rifles set out from Buffalo,
as they stated, to have a regular fox hunt in Cattaraugus, a district away
from the scene of action. Toward night, however, they veered round and
contrived to reach the Navy Islanders, so badly was the coast guarded, and
so little precaution taken, notwithstanding the profession of the American
government to enforce a strict neutrality. The fact is, they had not sufficient
force to guard the lines. Their regular troops were in Florida, and the
militia were determined not to act, so that the handful of men that General
Scott brought with him was of no use unless concentrated at one particular
point, to which they ought to have repaired at first and cut off all communication. As a proof of this assertion, Mr. Garrow, the marshal, met a party
with a United States field piece proceeding to the rebels and was allowed
to pass, from his inability to detain the parties. Governor Marcy, also,
although a long time in the service, was equally unfortunate in his movements.
It was a novel contest that required a man of energy and promptness, without
any tampering to preserve popularity; but it is not my province to censure
our neighbours further than the statement of matters of fact. My object
is to shew you our proceedings against the machinations of an artful, designing,
lawless set of villains, whose ostensible object was plunder, could they find

---

[74] This was General Winfield Scott; taken prisoner in the War of 1812, he lived
to take an active part in the Mexican War, and to be Commander-in-Chief of the Army
of the United States at the outbreak of the Rebellion of the Southern States.

a leader to carry their plans into execution. Thus things went on from day to day for near a month, with no prompt measures on either side to dislodge the marauders. This supineness I equally condemn in our own commanders as with those on the opposite shore. They however, took a different view of the question, preferring to act on the defensive, and to await the result of their landing. They objected to storming the Island on account of losing so many lives. But where is the difference, I would ask, in accomplishing an object, whether the sanguinary affray takes place on an island or the main shore? As things ultimately turned out, their quiescence, however, succeeded, but nine cases out of ten in the annals of history, a speedy operation at the onset is a great saving of human life. One of their expectations was that the marauders would be starved out, it being considered impossible that 800 men could be fed long together upon private subscription. As it was, they frequently ran short, and on one occasion actually stole 20 barrels of our pork, to say nothing of flour.

After an ineffectual attempt of General Arcularius to bring Van Ranselaer to any terms, it was left to General Scott, on his arrival, to compel him to surrender the cannon and arms which had been stolen from the American arsenals. Accordingly, on his arrival at Manchester, contiguous to the Falls, he despatched a messenger over to the Island for Van Ranselaer to wait upon him relative to the cannon, &c., assuring him on his word of honour that he should not be molested. Accordingly, our hero arrived in his boat, mounted with an American swivel cannon, and proceeded direct to the hotel at Manchester where the General and several of the Buffalo authorities were in waiting. Some friends of mine were over there at the time, anxious to see a man whom they considered a second Bolivar. They described him as remarkably tall, well dressed in black, with a military cloak; about 35 years of age and endued with a countenance that never appeared gifted with a smile. On landing, a messenger handed him a large bundle of letters which he hastily read and thrust into his pocket, taking but little notice of any of the bystanders. In fine, he seemed wrapped up with his own ideas as a hero or some individual who was engaged in an expedition. His eye was keen and penetrating as Warwick's a few months ere he requested the loan of six feet of earth to be buried in.

On reaching the hotel, he took his seat amidst the assembled conclave and said but little, listened attentively to the lecture of the General on the illegality of his conduct, the anxiety of his father to quit so disreputable a life, the danger he stood in from the anger of his own government, who would assuredly prosecute him for retaining the stolen cannon and arms, independently of the utter hopelessness of so futile an attempt to subvert a nation whose internal government had been misconstrued and misrepresented by an unprincipled individual. He called upon him therefore, immediately to deliver up the stolen property or he would certainly be compelled to do so by the force of arms. This reasonable request was also seconded by several gentlemen of high respectability in attendance, who implored him to consider the folly of any attempt to persevere in a course so derogatory to the character of a family so inimical to his proceedings, as well as the government to which he owed allegiance. In reply, he said but few words, was not aware he held any property belonging to the state: considered it belonged to private individuals, but on his return would consult with his associates and furnish a reply within the term of six hours specified. He wished them good morning, went quietly to his boat and proceeded to his quarters on the Island unmolested according to the agreement entered into.

Things had now arrived at a crisis, and although possessed of nerve, and a determination, if possible, not to be thwarted in his reckless plans, yet like all other General Bobadils, a safe retreat was no mean subject of consideration, especially as he was now placed, as it were, between two fires. Accordingly, a short period prompted them the course to pursue, especially as their supplies were nearly gone, with the exception of water, a beverage at all times excellent to allay thirst. either in peace or war. They therefore speedily determined to collect the stolen cannon as a matter of necessity, place it in a boat and send it over, which was accordingly done, rowed across the river and landed clandestinely on the American shore to the care of no one. At 2 o'clock the following morning the posse comitatus prepared for departure, which they effected as quietly and as little known to us as on the day of their first arrival.

They marched through the dreary woods on Grand Island, on a bitter cold morning, and reached Tonawonta, where numbers who had not secreted their arms were disbanded. Many took a circuitous route and kept the quiet possession of their rifles and muskets. They were in a most beggarly and miserable plight as you may suppose, many of them nearly famished, who had to feed like hogs on peas and potatoes, and as full of vermin as a skunk or a polecat. Well for them their encampment was broken up that they might escape dying with hunger, as we had stationed three schooners to cut off any supplies from Buffalo, which were expected by the steamboat *Barcelona* which was to take the place of the *Caroline*.

Doubtless General Scott's arrival materially hastened their departure, although in all probability they would have pursued a similar course after prolonging their encampment, as the 24-pounders and bombshells were unwelcome messengers about their ears.

Nearly a day elapsed before we knew of their departure and great conjecture arose as to their point of destination. In the course of the day one solitary individual was seen waving a flag but this was looked upon with suspicion. In the afternoon authentic intelligence arrived of the event, yet, very many even then were incredulous, altho' from the circumstances of seeing none on guard as usual, it was apparent some movement had taken place. To settle the question, a party volunteered to go over; it was considered a hazardous undertaking, more especially as many surmised that they had excavated subterraneous caverns to enter, and knowing the schemes they planned to deceive us it was no wonder we were anxious to learn the result. At the time, the information of very few could be relied on, as so many strange rumours were afloat, and so many spies over here awaiting our movements and spreading reports to mislead us. A great number assembled on the shore as you may imagine, to know the result, and many anxious hearts were relieved when a general huzza proclaimed that the island was once more in our possession and the British flag flying.

Their movements had been so rapid to clear out, as they termed it, that one poor wretch was left behind,[75] who was glad enough to hail his rescuers from the thraldom he had so long been entrammelled in. He stated that he was asleep, and knew nothing of their movements; on his examination but

---

[75] He was arrested as a spy, but soon released.

little could be elicited from him, further than that he had been a hewer of wood and drawer of water and was heartily glad that the expedition was abandoned. He was soon released from captivity, having been taught a lesson for his folly that he will not easily forget.

Had it been Brobdignag Island, greater curiosity could not have been evinced to see it. An old shoe or a slip of cloth were as great curiosities as some of the relics they show you in France: grape shot, pieces of punched iron from steam boilers, furnished from Black Rock foundry, were as precious as current coin; and as to pikes, they were trophies of too intrinsic value to fall to the lot of many; they decorated halls and curious cupboards, whilst half a bombshell or a cannon ball embellished a lady's work table. The few of the rebels who wore shirts carried them away, filthy as they were, on their backs, as scarce a vestige of linen was found with the exception of part of the tail of a shirt that had bound up a wounded leg. Nothing can exceed the miserable condition of a buccaneer's life, far worse than that of savages, for they know no better.

The number who were killed or wounded by our bombardment was never ascertained,[76] as their burying place was on Grand Island, where they occupied a log-hut as hospital. One newly made grave was found, which, on digging the earth away, was found to contain the body of a poor wretch who was supposed to have been shot by their own party, as he was lying with his arms pinioned; who this individual was has never been ascertained.[77]

The miserable state of existence they must have endured baffles all description. It is almost impossible to convey to you the disgusting scene which was exhibited. The shanties wherein the miserable wretches bivouacked were scarce fit receptacles for pigs, being strewed with beans, peas, pork rind, vermin and dirt. Their beds were composed of brushwood, and nothing to shelter them from the inclemency of the weather but pine branches. Here they congregated at night, eating, drinking, smoking, swearing and sleeping. For an occasional bivouac on a deer hunting expedition, such a lodgement would pass current, but for fifty or sixty human beings to assemble nightly for one month together, betokens a race of desperadoes worse than savages.

Mrs. Mackenzie[78] was over there part of the time living in a dirty house at the back of the Island, which I before described to you. The only accommodation for her at night was on a shelf covered with straw, where she could hear all the swearing and contention that was going forward between her husband and the General,—a forlorn fate for a woman who once moved in a respectable sphere of life, now united to a degraded being possessed of every ignoble propensity. She has a large family,—an outcast upon the wide world

---

[76] Existing accounts mention that the casualties on the Island were one killed by a round shot and one slightly wounded by a splinter. Dent, Vol. II, 224, note.

[77] I have not seen any reference to this circumstance in any of the other accounts.

[78] Mrs. Mackenzie, née Isabel Baxter, a native of Dundee, was married to William Lyon Mackenzie at Montreal, 1822, when Mackenzie was living in Dundas. She was a woman of sterling character, a devoted wife and mother. She was the only woman who spent any time on Navy Island. "She arrived there only a few hours before the destruction of the Caroline, and remained nearly a fortnight with her husband, making flannel cartridge bags and inspiring with courage by her entire freedom from fear all with whom she conversed. At the end of about a fortnight, ill-health obliged her to leave." Lindsey, Vol. I, 38; Vol. II, 163.

Navy Island was abandoned by the "Patriots," January 14, 1838. Dent, Vol. II. 223.

which execrates the very name of her worthless partner, who having left the
path of honest industry had hurried headlong into a vortex from which he
can never be extricated. Altho' punishment is withheld from him further than
a guilty conscience, bad enough at all times, yet the retributive hour must
arrive when he will have to suffer for the horrid calamities he has inflicted
upon so many of his deluded and unfortunate fellow creatures.

It seems almost incredible that one poor halfbred[79] Scotchman should
have been the cause of all this turmoil, but such is the weakness and folly
of mankind generally, especially where any novelty occurs, that a visionary
brain, however reckless, always aspires to obtain converts, until the fatal bubble
bursts. It was so in the present instance. Landed once more on their own
shores, you would imagine they would slink away to their homes and betake
themselves to some honest employment. Not so; the delusion still continued
and many imagined that the thorny road they had passed was merely one of
the routes to the Garden of Eden, in the shape of 300 acres of land, which
they were ultimately to enjoy when their labours were terminated.

When Mackenzie ran away from justice and was known to be secreted
in Buffalo, it would have been a politic measure had the authorities complied
with the Governor's request and given him up. No one can be more averse
to this proceeding than myself in a general way, because many flee their
country from persecution and untoward events over which they have no
control. But when an abandoned character,—notorious as an adventurer,
a robber, an incendiary, a murderer,—flees from justice, it is the bounden
duty of every government, as a protection to themselves, and in accordance
with the treaties, to deliver up such an individual to the law as a dangerous
member of society at large. This was the case with Mackenzie. Mr. Bethune
was sent by the Governor to Buffalo to claim the rebel fugitive, but Governor
Marcy, on the part of the United States, declined complying with the
application,[80] alleging that the offences charged against him, being incidents
of the revolt, merged in the higher crime of treason, which was a public
offence only. Governor Marcy was doubtless glad to get rid of the application,
which he had a favourable opportunity of doing in consequence of Mackenzie
suddenly quitting Buffalo with Van Ranselaer and going over to Navy Island,
over which he said he had no jurisdiction. So the viper was harboured, by
an underhand movement, to sting the very parties afterward whose fostering
hand had protected him. This is not the first time that designing men have
been taken in their own craftiness, and fallen into the pit which they had
dug incautiously for others. We were the more astonished at the supineness
evinced on this occasion, on account of the President's proclamation issued
on the 5th, wherein Martin Van Buren states that he is fully determined
rigidly to enforce the laws of Congress in regard to the observance of a
strict neutrality. Now as our Governor did not apply for Mackenzie to be
given up on account of his political opinions, I apprehend there was some
partiality shown in favour of Republicanism, by retaining him, when they

---

[79] A more vituperative adjective; Mackenzie was a pure Scot.
[80] This account of the course followed by Governor Marcy agrees with that given
by Lindsey, Vol. II, p. 129, both writers having evidently derived it from public prints
of the time. (II.)

There can be no doubt now that Governor Marcy was right in International law;
Mackenzie was no more guilty than the St. Albans Raiders whom Canada refused to
deliver up to the United States.

had him in their power so frequently, as he passed and repassed to Buffalo on his way from Navy Island.

The same Government which professes to act justly has at different times demanded their subjects from us for theft and misdemeanours, and which applications have been strictly attended to. Yet, in a case of so heinous a nature as robbery of the mails and private individuals, incendiarism and attempts at assassination as in the cases of Powell, Brooks and others, that professed friendly, equitable Government, for which the marshal was responsible, refuses to comply with the Governor's request to do one single act toward furthering the ends of justice advantageous to the quietude and harmony of both countries. Surely after this no individual, however depraved, can with propriety be given up on our side. You cannot be surprised then, from this inference, that tranquility would be soon restored, when the delinquent in question was allowed to roam about their country, holding meetings, publishing seditious papers and enlisting men after the evacuation of their stronghold.

The intentions of the American Government at the fountain head, were doubtless sincere; for Mr. Forsyth distinctly says, in his despatch to the district attorney, that every individual without distinction is to be immediately prosecuted who violates the laws of the United States, whose declared determination was to preserve peace and amity with foreign powers. He even mentions the names of Mackenzie[81] and Doctor John Rolph, the two leaders who had fled their country, yet no proceedings were instituted against them; they were allowed to roam at large and not only stir up sedition but even to be accessory to robbing the arsenals. At any rate as far as Mackenzie was concerned, he then was taken up, examined and liberated upon bail, an act of great injustice to the peace and welfare of both countries. This subject, however, I leave in the hands of the two respective governments and proceed with our narrative.

The ground was covered with snow, no road through the forest but their own making, no light but the stars to guide them, and the thermometer 10° below zero, yet withal the ardour of the fugitives was not damped, altho' many were wounded and half starved. Economists of the present day talk of many being degenerated in physical strength, but it appears to me that when upheld by energy and the desire of aggrandizement, exploring or conquest, he has the same power of undergoing fatigue and privation as ever, exemplified in the case before us, in polar discoveries, in journeys across the Rocky Mountains or various other parts of the globe. Instances have come under my own observation of men travelling from 150 to 200 miles over the snow with snowshoes, not a hut on the way for shelter and reposing at night amidst a temperature of from 18deg. to 20deg. below zero, surrounded with snow only, yet these sons of the Universe were healthy and capable of performing similar exploits. I saw them contiguous to the shores of Lake Huron and found it was no uncommon feat to perform. Your sympathy therefore for the marauders before us who had so short a distance to travel, need not start one tear from your eye, nor induce you to heave a sigh for their apparent forlorn condition.

---

[81] Mackenzie was afterwards prosecuted and confined in the common jail at Rochester for nearly eleven months. Dr. Rolph took no part in the military operations of the Rebels and "Sympathizers."

Well, they continued their desolate march and finally landed, some at one place, some at another, anxious to preserve their muskets and rifles from the searching eye of General Scott, who, to convince the Government he had done something, managed to get hold of some of the ill-gotten booty; but so little precaution was taken to place them in a safe asylum that even some of these were afterward purloined when occasion required them to join Sutherland, who had gone forward to Cleveland, a port on Lake Erie at the junction of the Ohio Canal. Here I leave them to reconnoitre.

Our forces on the frontier now turned their thoughts homewards, having performed an arduous duty in watching and guarding the frontier. They would nevertheless have gladly exchanged their inactive life for bustle and conflict. I frequently heard them say they longed for the General and his forces to come across, that they might show them the contempt they were held in. So great was their enthusiasm for the protection of their property and families, that they daily panted to go over and dislodge them. Perhaps after all, things turned out for the best, for altho' glory is a word of powerful meaning, yet there is but little satisfaction for those who fall in the conflict, when the end may be finally accomplished without the loss of many valuable lives.

When it was ascertained the route the rebels had taken, the artillery was removed. The schooners moored in the Chippawa, and the greater part of the troops who had performed the most arduous duty, were ordered home. A general move took place, preparatory to which the Colonel thanked them on behalf of the Governor for their loyalty and services, not doubting but when required they would be ready and willing to buckle on the shield of defence and rally round the standard of their Constitution in behalf of their country's cause. To this appeal there was no dissent, and " God Save the Queen " resounded midst universal applause.

www.ingramcontent.com/pod-product-compliance
Lightning Source LLC
Chambersburg PA
CBHW032106220426
43664CB00008B/1150